Constitution of Townships in Quebec.

144. The Lieutenant Governor of Quebec may from Time of Time, by Proclamation under the Great Seal of the Province, to take effect from a Day to be appointed therein, constitute Townships in those Parts of the Province of Quebec in which Townships are not then already constituted, and fix the Metes and Bounds thereof.

145. Repealed. (65)

XI.—ADMISSION OF OTHER COLONIES

Power to admit Newfoundland, etc., into the Union.

146. It shall be lawful for the Queen, by and with the Advice of Her Majesty's Most Honourable Privy Council, on Addresses from the Houses of the Parliament of Canada, and from the Houses of the respective Legislatures of the Colonies or Provinces of Newfoundland, Prince Edward Island, and British Columbia, to admit those Colonies or Provinces, or any of them, into the Union, and on Address from the Houses of the Parliament of Canada to admit Rupert's Land and the North-western Territory, or either of them, into the Union, on such Terms and Conditions in each Case as are in the Addresses expressed and as the Queen thinks fit to approve, subject to the Provisions of this Act; and the Provisions of any Order in Council in that Behalf shall have effect as if they had been enacted by the Parliament of the United Kingdom of Great Britain and Ireland. (66)

As to Representation of Newfoundland and Prince Edward Island in Senate.

147. In case of the Admission of Newfoundland and Prince Edward Island, or either of them, each shall be entitled to a Representation in the Senate of Canada of Four Members, and (notwithstanding anything in this Act) in case of the Admission of Newfoundland the normal Number of Senators shall be Seventy-six and their maximum Number shall be Eighty-two; but Prince Edward Island when admitted

---

(65) Repealed by the *Statute Law Revision Act, 1893*, 56-57 Vict., c. 14, (U.K.). The section reads as follows:

X.—INTERCOLONIAL RAILWAY.

145. Inasmuch as the Provinces of Canada, Nova Scotia, and New Brunswick have joined in a Declaration that the Construction of the Intercolonial Railway is essential to the Consolidation of the Union of British North America, and to the Assent thereto of Nova Scotia and New Brunswick, and have consequently agreed that Provision should be made for its immediate Construction by the Government of Canada: Therefore, in order to give effect to that Agreement, it shall be the Duty of the Government and Parliament of Canada to provide for the Commencement, within Six Months after the Union, of a Railway connecting the River St. Lawrence with the City of Halifax in Nova Scotia, and for the Construction thereof without Intermission, and the Completion thereof with all practicable Speed.

(66) All territories mentioned in this section are now part of Canada. See the notes to section 5, *supra*.

shall be deemed to be comprised in the Third of Three Divisions into which Canada is, in relation to the Constitution of the Senate, divided by this Act, and accordingly, after the Admission of Prince Edward Island, whether Newfoundland is admitted or not, the Representation of Nova Scotia and New Brunswick in the Senate shall, as Vacancies occur, be reduced from Twelve to Ten Members respectively, and the Representation of each of those Provinces shall not be increased at any Time beyond Ten, except under the Provisions of this Act for the Appointment of Three or Six additional Senators under the Direction of the Queen. (67)

---

(67) Spent. See the notes to sections 21, 22, 26, 27 and 28, *supra*.

APPENDIX II PART B: The Constitution Act, 1982

The text that follows reproduces the statute as published by Supply and Services Canada, *The Constitution Act, 1982* (Ottawa: Canadian Government Publishing Centre, 1982) omitting only the French translation.

CONSTITUTION ACT, 1982

PART I

CANADIAN CHARTER OF RIGHTS AND FREEDOMS

Whereas Canada is founded upon principles that recognize the supremacy of God and the rule of law:

Guarantee of Rights and Freedoms

Rights and freedoms in Canada

1. The *Canadian Charter of Rights and Freedoms* guarantees the rights and freedoms set out in it subject only to such reasonable limits prescribed by law as can be demonstrably justified in a free and democratic society.

Fundamental Freedoms

Fundamental freedoms

2. Everyone has the following fundamental freedoms:

(*a*) freedom of conscience and religion;

(*b*) freedom of thought, belief, opinion and expression, including freedom of the press and other media of communication;

(*c*) freedom of peaceful assembly; and

(*d*) freedom of association.

Democratic Rights

Democratic rights of citizens

3. Every citizen of Canada has the right to vote in an election of members of the House of Commons or of a legislative assembly and to be qualified for membership therein.

Maximum duration of legislative bodies

4. (1) No House of Commons and no legislative assembly shall continue for longer than five years from the date fixed for the return of the writs at a general election of its members.

Continuation in special circumstances

(2) In time of real or apprehended war, invasion or insurrection, a House of Commons may be continued by Parliament and a legislative assembly may be continued by the legislature beyond five years if such continuation is not opposed by the votes of more than one-third of the members of the House of Commons or the legislative assembly, as the case may be.

Annual sitting of legislative bodies

5. There shall be a sitting of Parliament and of each legislature at least once every twelve months.

Mobility Rights

Mobility of citizens

6. (1) Every citizen of Canada has the right to enter, remain in and leave Canada.

Rights to move and gain livelihood

(2) Every citizen of Canada and every person who has the status of a permanent resident of Canada has the right

(*a*) to move to and take up residence in any province; and

(*b*) to pursue the gaining of a livelihood in any province.

Limitation

(3) The rights specified in subsection (2) are subject to

(*a*) any laws or practices of general application in force in a province other than those that discriminate among persons primarily on the basis of province of present or previous residence; and

(*b*) any laws providing for reasonable residency requirements as a qualification for the receipt of publicly provided social services.

Affirmative action programs

(4) Subsections (2) and (3) do not preclude any law, program or activity that has as its object the amelioration in a province of conditions of individuals in that province who are socially or economically disadvantaged if the rate of employment in that province is below the rate of employment in Canada.

Legal Rights

Life, liberty and security of person

7. Everyone has the right to life, liberty and security of the person and the right not to be deprived thereof except in accordance with the principles of fundamental justice.

Search or seizure

8. Everyone has the right to be secure against unreasonable search or seizure.

Detention or imprisonment

9. Everyone has the right not to be arbitrarily detained or imprisoned.

Arrest or detention

10. Everyone has the right on arrest or detention

(*a*) to be informed promptly of the reasons therefor;

(*b*) to retain and instruct counsel without delay and to be informed of that right; and

(*c*) to have the validity of the detention determined by way of *habeas corpus* and to be released if the detention is not lawful.

Proceedings in criminal and penal matters

11. Any person charged with an offence has the right

(*a*) to be informed without unreasonable delay of the specific offence;

(*b*) to be tried within a reasonable time;

(*c*) not to be compelled to be a witness in proceedings against that person in respect of the offence;

(*d*) to be presumed innocent until proven guilty according to law in a fair and public hearing by an independent and impartial tribunal;

(*e*) not to be denied reasonable bail without just cause;

(*f*) except in the case of an offence under military law tried before a military tribunal, to the benefit of trial by jury where the maximum punishment for the offence is imprisonment for five years or a more severe punishment;

(*g*) not to be found guilty on account of any act or omission unless, at the time of the act or omission, it constituted an offence under Canadian or international law or was criminal according to the general principles of law recognized by the community of nations;

(*h*) if finally acquitted of the offence, not to be tried for it again and, if finally found guilty and punished for the offence, not to be tried or punished for it again; and

(*i*) if found guilty of the offence and if the punishment for the offence has been varied between the time of commission and the time of sentencing, to the benefit of the lesser punishment.

Treatment or punishment

12. Everyone has the right not to be subjected to any cruel and unusual treatment or punishment.

Self-crimination

13. A witness who testifies in any proceedings has the right not to have any incriminating evidence so given used to incriminate that witness in any other proceedings, except in a prosecution for perjury or for the giving of contradictory evidence.

Interpreter

14. A party or witness in any proceedings who does not understand or speak the language in which the proceedings are conducted or who is deaf has the right to the assistance of an interpreter.

Equality Rights

Equality before and under law and equal protection and benefit of law

15. (1) Every individual is equal before and under the law and has the right to the equal protection and equal benefit of the law without discrimination and, in particular, without discrimination based on race, national or ethnic origin, colour, religion, sex, age or mental or physical disability.

Affirmative action programs

(2) Subsection (1) does not preclude any law, program or activity that has as its object the amelioration of conditions of disadvantaged individuals or groups including those that are disadvantaged because of

race, national or ethnic origin, colour, religion, sex, age or mental or physical disability.

Official Languages of Canada

Official languages of Canada

16. (1) English and French are the official languages of Canada and have equality of status and equal rights and privileges as to their use in all institutions of the Parliament and government of Canada.

Official languages of New Brunswick

(2) English and French are the official languages of New Brunswick and have equality of status and equal rights and privileges as to their use in all institutions of the legislature and government of New Brunswick.

Advancement of status and use

(3) Nothing in this Charter limits the authority of Parliament or a legislature to advance the equality of status or use of English and French.

Proceedings of Parliament

17. (1) Everyone has the right to use English or French in any debates and other proceedings of Parliament.

Proceedings of New Brunswick legislature

(2) Everyone has the right to use English or French in any debates and other proceedings of the legislature of New Brunswick.

Parliamentary statutes and records

18. (1) The statutes, records and journals of Parliament shall be printed and published in English and French and both language versions are equally authoritative.

New Brunswick statutes and records

(2) The statutes, records and journals of the legislature of New Brunswick shall be printed and published in English and French and both language versions are equally authoritative.

Proceedings in courts established by Parliament

19. (1) Either English or French may be used by any person in, or in any pleading in or process issuing from, any court established by Parliament.

(2) Either English or French may be used by any person in, or in any pleading in or process issuing from, any court of New Brunswick.

Proceedings in New Brunswick courts

20. (1) Any member of the public in Canada has the right to communicate with, and to receive available services from, any head or central office of an institution of the Parliament or government of Canada in English or French, and has the same right with respect to any other office of any such institution where

(*a*) there is a significant demand for communications with and services from that office in such language; or

(*b*) due to the nature of the office, it is reasonable that communications with and services from that office be available in both English and French.

Communications by public with federal institutions

(2) Any member of the public in New Brunswick has the right to communicate with, and to receive available services from, any office of an institution of the legislature or government of New Brunswick in English or French.

Communications by public with New Brunswick institutions

21. Nothing in sections 16 to 20 abrogates or derogates from any right, privilege or obligation with respect to the English and French languages, or either of them, that exists or is continued by virtue of any other provision of the Constitution of Canada.

Continuation of existing constitutional provisions

22. Nothing in sections 16 to 20 abrogates or derogates from any legal or customary right or privilege acquired or enjoyed either before or after the coming into force of this Charter with respect to any language that is not English or French.

Rights and privileges preserved

Minority Language Educational Rights

23. (1) Citizens of Canada

(*a*) whose first language learned and still understood is that of the English or French linguistic

Language of instruction

minority population of the province in which they reside, or

(*b*) who have received their primary school instruction in Canada in English or French and reside in a province where the language in which they received that instruction is the language of the English or French linguistic minority population of the province,

have the right to have their children receive primary and secondary school instruction in that language in that province.

Continuity of language instruction

(2) Citizens of Canada of whom any child has received or is receiving primary or secondary school instruction in English or French in Canada, have the right to have all their children receive primary and secondary school instruction in the same language.

Application where numbers warrant

(3) The right of citizens of Canada under subsections (1) and (2) to have their children receive primary and secondary school instruction in the language of the English or French linguistic minority population of a province

(*a*) applies wherever in the province the number of children of citizens who have such a right is sufficient to warrant the provision to them out of public funds of minority language instruction; and

(*b*) includes, where the number of those children so warrants, the right to have them receive that instruction in minority language educational facilities provided out of public funds.

Enforcement

Enforcement of guaranteed rights and freedoms

24. (1) Anyone whose rights or freedoms, as guaranteed by this Charter, have been infringed or denied may apply to a court of competent jurisdiction to obtain such remedy as the court considers appropriate and just in the circumstances.

Exclusion of evidence bringing administration of justice into disrepute

(2) Where, in proceedings under subsection (1), a court concludes that evidence was obtained in a manner that infringed or denied any rights or freedoms guaranteed by this Charter, the evidence shall be excluded if it is established that, having regard to all the circumstances, the admission of it in the proceedings would bring the administration of justice into disrepute.

General

25. The guarantee in this Charter of certain rights and freedoms shall not be construed so as to abrogate or derogate from any aboriginal, treaty or other rights or freedoms that pertain to the aboriginal peoples of Canada including

Aboriginal rights and freedoms not affected by Charter

(*a*) any rights or freedoms that have been recognized by the Royal Proclamation of October 7, 1763; and

(*b*) any rights or freedoms that may be acquired by the aboriginal peoples of Canada by way of land claims settlement.

26. The guarantee in this Charter of certain rights and freedoms shall not be construed as denying the existence of any other rights or freedoms that exist in Canada.

Other rights and freedoms not affected by Charter

27. This Charter shall be interpreted in a manner consistent with the preservation and enhancement of the multicultural heritage of Canadians.

Multicultural heritage

28. Notwithstanding anything in this Charter, the rights and freedoms referred to in it are guaranteed equally to male and female persons.

Rights guaranteed equally to both sexes

29. Nothing in this Charter abrogates or derogates from any rights or privileges guaranteed by or under the Constitution of Canada in respect of denominational, separate or dissentient schools.

Rights respecting certain schools preserved

30. A reference in this Charter to a province or to the legislative assembly or legislature of a province shall be deemed to include a reference to the Yukon Territory and the Northwest Territories, or to the appropriate legislative authority thereof, as the case may be.

Application to territories and territorial authorities

Legislative powers not extended

31. Nothing in this Charter extends the legislative powers of any body or authority.

Application of Charter

Application of Charter

32. (1) This Charter applies

(*a*) to the Parliament and government of Canada in respect of all matters within the authority of Parliament including all matters relating to the Yukon Territory and Northwest Territories; and

(*b*) to the legislature and government of each province in respect of all matters within the authority of the legislature of each province.

Exception

(2) Notwithstanding subsection (1), section 15 shall not have effect until three years after this section comes into force.

Exception where express declaration

33. (1) Parliament or the legislature of a province may expressly declare in an Act of Parliament or of the legislature, as the case may be, that the Act or a provision thereof shall operate notwithstanding a provision included in section 2 or sections 7 to 15 of this Charter.

Operation of exception

(2) An Act or a provision of an Act in respect of which a declaration made under this section is in effect shall have such operation as it would have but for the provision of this Charter referred to in the declaration.

Five year limitation

(3) A declaration made under subsection (1) shall ceáse to have effect five years after it comes into force or on such earlier date as may be specified in the declaration.

Re-enactment

(4) Parliament or the legislature of a province may re-enact a declaration made under subsection (1).

Five year limitation

(5) Subsection (3) applies in respect of a re-enactment made under subsection (4).

Citation

34. This Part may be cited as the *Canadian Charter of Rights and Freedoms*. **Citation**

PART II

RIGHTS OF THE ABORIGINAL PEOPLES OF CANADA

35. (1) The existing aboriginal and treaty rights of the aboriginal peoples of Canada are hereby recognized and affirmed. **Recognition of existing aboriginal and treaty rights**

(2) In this Act, "aboriginal peoples of Canada" includes the Indian, Inuit and Métis peoples of Canada. **Definition of "aboriginal peoples of Canada"**

PART III

EQUALIZATION AND REGIONAL DISPARITIES

36. (1) Without altering the legislative authority of Parliament or of the provincial legislatures, or the rights of any of them with respect to the exercise of their legislative authority, Parliament and the legislatures, together with the government of Canada and the provincial governments, are committed to **Commitment to promote equal opportunities**

(*a*) promoting equal opportunities for the well-being of Canadians;

(*b*) furthering economic development to reduce disparity in opportunities; and

(*c*) providing essential public services of reasonable quality to all Canadians.

(2) Parliament and the government of Canada are committed to the principle of making equalization payments to ensure that provincial governments have sufficient revenues to provide reasonably comparable levels of public services at reasonably comparable levels of taxation. **Commitment respecting public services**

PART IV

CONSTITUTIONAL CONFERENCE

Constitutional conference

37. (1) A constitutional ·conference composed of the Prime Minister of Canada and the first ministers of the provinces shall be convened by the Prime Minister of Canada within one year after this Part comes into force.

Participation of aboriginal peoples

(2) The conference convened under subsection (1) shall have included in its agenda an item respecting constitutional matters that directly affect the aboriginal peoples of Canada, including the identification and definition of the rights of those peoples to be included in the Constitution of Canada, and the Prime Minister of Canada shall invite representatives of those peoples to participate in the discussions on that item.

Participation of territories

(3) The Prime Minister of Canada shall invite elected representatives of the governments of the Yukon Territory and the Northwest Territories to participate in the discussions on any item on the agenda of the conference convened under subsection (1) that, in the opinion of the Prime Minister, directly affects the Yukon Territory and the Northwest Territories.

PART V

PROCEDURE FOR AMENDING CONSTITUTION OF CANADA

General procedure for amending Constitution of Canada

38. (1) An amendment to the Constitution of Canada may be made by proclamation issued by the Governor General under the Great Seal of Canada where so authorized by

(*a*) resolutions of the Senate and House of Commons; and

(*b*) resolutions of the legislative assemblies of at least two-thirds of the provinces that have, in the aggregate, according to the then latest general census, at least fifty per cent of the population of all the provinces.

Majority of members

(2) An amendment made under subsection (1) that derogates from the legislative powers, the proprietary rights or any other rights or privileges of the legislature or government of a province shall require a resolution supported by a majority of the members of each of the Senate, the House of Commons and the legislative assemblies required under subsection (1).

Expression of dissent

(3) An amendment referred to in subsection (2) shall not have effect in a province the legislative assembly of which has expressed its dissent thereto by resolution supported by a majority of its members prior to the issue of the proclamation to which the amendment relates unless that legislative assembly, subsequently, by resolution supported by a majority of its members, revokes its dissent and authorizes the amendment.

Revocation of dissent

(4) A resolution of dissent made for the purposes of subsection (3) may be revoked at any time before or after the issue of the proclamation to which it relates.

Restriction on proclamation

39. (1) A proclamation shall not be issued under subsection 38(1) before the expiration of one year from the adoption of the resolution initiating the amendment procedure thereunder, unless the legislative assembly of each province has previously adopted a resolution of assent or dissent.

Idem

(2) A proclamation shall not be issued under subsection 38(1) after the expiration of three years from the adoption of the resolution initiating the amendment procedure thereunder.

Compensation

40. Where an amendment is made under subsection 38(1) that transfers provincial legislative powers relating to education or other cultural matters from provincial legislatures to Parliament, Canada shall provide reasonable compensation to any province to which the amendment does not apply.

Amendment by unanimous consent

41. An amendment to the Constitution of Canada in relation to the following matters may be made by proclamation issued by the Governor General under the Great Seal of

Canada only where authorized by resolutions of the Senate and House of Commons and of the legislative assembly of each province:

(*a*) the office of the Queen, the Governor General and the Lieutenant Governor of a province;

(*b*) the right of a province to a number of members in the House of Commons not less than the number of Senators by which the province is entitled to be represented at the time this Part comes into force;

(*c*) subject to section 43, the use of the English or the French language;

(*d*) the composition of the Supreme Court of Canada; and

(*e*) an amendment to this Part.

Amendment by general procedure

42. (1) An amendment to the Constitution of Canada in relation to the following matters may be made only in accordance with subsection 38(1):

(*a*) the principle of proportionate representation of the provinces in the House of Commons prescribed by the Constitution of Canada;

(*b*) the powers of the Senate and the method of selecting Senators;

(*c*) the number of members by which a province is entitled to be represented in the Senate and the residence qualifications of Senators;

(*d*) subject to paragraph 41(*d*), the Supreme Court of Canada;

(*e*) the extension of existing provinces into the territories; and

(*f*) notwithstanding any other law or practice, the establishment of new provinces.

Exception

(2) Subsections 38(2) to (4) do not apply in respect of amendments in relation to matters referred to in subsection (1).

Amendment of provisions relating to some but not all provinces

43. An amendment to the Constitution of Canada in relation to any provision that applies to one or more, but not all, provinces, including

(*a*) any alteration to boundaries between provinces, and

(*b*) any amendment to any provision that relates to the use of the English or the French language within a province,

may be made by proclamation issued by the Governor General under the Great Seal of Canada only where so authorized by resolutions of the Senate and House of Commons and of the legislative assembly of each province to which the amendment applies.

Amendments by Parliament

44. Subject to sections 41 and 42, Parliament may exclusively make laws amending the Constitution of Canada in relation to the executive government of Canada or the Senate and House of Commons.

Amendments by provincial legislatures

45. Subject to section 41, the legislature of each province may exclusively make laws amending the constitution of the province.

Initiation of amendment procedures

46. (1) The procedures for amendment under sections 38, 41, 42 and 43 may be initiated either by the Senate or the House of Commons or by the legislative assembly of a province.

Revocation of authorization

(2) A resolution of assent made for the purposes of this Part may be revoked at any time before the issue of a proclamation authorized by it.

Amendments without Senate resolution

47. (1) An amendment to the Constitution of Canada made by proclamation under section 38, 41, 42 or 43 may be made without a resolution of the Senate authorizing the issue of the proclamation if, within one hundred and eighty days after the adoption by the House of Commons of a resolution authorizing its issue, the Senate has not adopted such a resolution and if, at any time after the expiration of that period, the House of Commons again adopts the resolution.

Computation of period

(2) Any period when Parliament is prorogued or dissolved shall not be counted in computing the one hundred and eighty day period referred to in subsection (1).

Advice to issue proclamation

48. The Queen's Privy Council for Canada shall advise the Governor General to issue a proclamation under this Part forthwith on the adoption of the resolutions required for an amendment made by proclamation under this Part.

Constitutional conference

49. A constitutional conference composed of the Prime Minister of Canada and the first ministers of the provinces shall be convened by the Prime Minister of Canada within fifteen years after this Part comes into force to review the provisions of this Part.

PART VI

AMENDMENT TO THE
CONSTITUTION ACT, 1867

Amendment to *Constitution Act, 1867*

50. The *Constitution Act, 1867* (formerly named the *British North America Act, 1867*) is amended by adding thereto, immediately after section 92 thereof, the following heading and section:

"Non-Renewable Natural Resources, Forestry Resources and Electrical Energy

Laws respecting non-renewable natural resources, forestry resources and electrical energy

92A. (1) In each province, the legislature may exclusively make laws in relation to

(*a*) exploration for non-renewable natural resources in the province;

(*b*) development, conservation and management of non-renewable natural resources and forestry resources in the province, including laws in relation to the rate of primary production therefrom; and

(*c*) development, conservation and management of sites and facilities in the province for the generation and production of electrical energy.

Export from provinces of resources

(2) In each province, the legislature may make laws in relation to the export from the province to another part of Canada of the primary production from non-renewable natural resources and forestry resources in the province and the production from facilities in the province for the generation of electrical energy, but such laws may not authorize or provide for discrimination in prices or in supplies exported to another part of Canada.

Authority of Parliament

(3) Nothing in subsection (2) derogates from the authority of Parliament to enact laws in relation to the matters referred to in that subsection and, where such a law of Parliament and a law of a province conflict, the law of Parliament prevails to the extent of the conflict.

Taxation of resources

(4) In each province, the legislature may make laws in relation to the raising of money by any mode or system of taxation in respect of

(*a*) non-renewable natural resources and forestry resources in the province and the primary production therefrom, and

(*b*) sites and facilities in the province for the generation of electrical energy and the production therefrom,

whether or not such production is exported in whole or in part from the province, but such laws may not authorize or provide for taxation that differentiates between production exported to another part of Canada and production not exported from the province.

"Primary production"

(5) The expression "primary production" has the meaning assigned by the Sixth Schedule.

Existing powers or rights

(6) Nothing in subsections (1) to (5) derogates from any powers or rights that a legislature or government of a province had immediately before the coming into force of this section."

Idem

51. The said Act is further amended by adding thereto the following Schedule:

"THE SIXTH SCHEDULE

Primary Production from Non-Renewable Natural Resources and Forestry Resources

1. For the purposes of section 92A of this Act,

(*a*) production from a non-renewable natural resource is primary production therefrom if

(i) it is in the form in which it exists upon its recovery or severance from its natural state, or

(ii) it is a product resulting from processing or refining the resource, and is not a manufactured product or a product resulting from refining crude oil, refining upgraded heavy crude oil, refining gases or liquids derived from coal or refining a synthetic equivalent of crude oil; and

(*b*) production from a forestry resource is primary production therefrom if it consists of sawlogs, poles, lumber, wood chips, sawdust or any other primary wood product, or wood pulp, and is not a product manufactured from wood."

PART VII

GENERAL

Primacy of Constitution of Canada

52. (1) The Constitution of Canada is the supreme law of Canada, and any law that is inconsistent with the provisions of the Constitution is, to the extent of the inconsistency, of no force or effect.

Constitution of Canada

(2) The Constitution of Canada includes

(*a*) the *Canada Act 1982*, including this Act;

(*b*) the Acts and orders referred to in the schedule; and

(*c*) any amendment to any Act or order referred to in paragraph (*a*) or (*b*).

Amendments to Constitution of Canada

(3) Amendments to the Constitution of Canada shall be made only in accordance with the authority contained in the Constitution of Canada.

Repeals and new names

53. (1) The enactments referred to in Column I of the schedule are hereby repealed or amended to the extent indicated in Column II thereof and, unless repealed, shall continue as law in Canada under the names set out in Column III thereof.

Consequential amendments

(2) Every enactment, except the *Canada Act 1982*, that refers to an enactment referred to in the schedule by the name thereof in Column I thereof is hereby amended by substituting for that name the corresponding name in Column III thereof, and any British North America Act not referred to in the schedule may be cited as the *Constitution Act* followed by the year and number, if any, of its enactment.

Repeal and consequential amendments

54. Part IV is repealed on the day that is one year after this Part comes into force and this section may be repealed and this Act renumbered, consequentially upon the repeal of Part IV and this section, by proclamation issued by the Governor General under the Great Seal of Canada.

French version of Constitution of Canada

55. A French version of the portions of the Constitution of Canada referred to in the schedule shall be prepared by the Minister of Justice of Canada as expeditiously as possible and, when any portion thereof sufficient to warrant action being taken has been so prepared, it shall be put forward for enactment by proclamation issued by the Governor General under the Great Seal of Canada pursuant to the procedure then applicable to an amendment of the same provisions of the Constitution of Canada.

English and French versions of certain constitutional texts

56. Where any portion of the Constitution of Canada has been or is enacted in English and French or where a French version of any portion of the Constitution is enacted pursuant to section 55, the English and French versions of that portion of the Constitution are equally authoritative.

English and French versions of this Act

57. The English and French versions of this Act are equally authoritative.

Commencement

58. Subject to section 59, this Act shall come into force on a day to be fixed by proclamation issued by the Queen or the Governor General under the Great Seal of Canada.

Commencement of paragraph 23(1)(*a*) in respect of Quebec

59. (1) Paragraph 23(1)(*a*) shall come into force in respect of Quebec on a day to be fixed by proclamation issued by the Queen or the Governor General under the Great Seal of Canada.

Authorization of Quebec

(2) A proclamation under subsection (1) shall be issued only where authorized by the legislative assembly or government of Quebec.

Repeal of this section

(3) This section may be repealed on the day paragraph 23(1)(*a*) comes into force in respect of Quebec and this Act amended and renumbered, consequentially upon the repeal of this section, by proclamation issued by the Queen or the Governor General under the Great Seal of Canada.

Short title and citations

60. This Act may be cited as the *Constitution Act, 1982*, and the Constitution Acts 1867 to 1975 (No. 2) and this Act may be cited together as the *Constitution Acts, 1867 to 1982*.

SCHEDULE

to the

CONSTITUTION ACT, 1982

MODERNIZATION OF THE CONSTITUTION

Item	Column I Act Affected	Column II Amendment	Column III New Name
1.	British North America Act, 1867, 30-31 Vict., c. 3 (U.K.)	(1) Section 1 is repealed and the following substituted therefor: "1. This Act may be cited as the *Constitution Act, 1867.*" (2) Section 20 is repealed. (3) Class 1 of section 91 is repealed. (4) Class 1 of section 92 is repealed.	Constitution Act, 1867
2.	An Act to amend and continue the Act 32-33 Victoria chapter 3; and to establish and provide for the Government of the Province of Manitoba, 1870, 33 Vict., c. 3 (Can.)	(1) The long title is repealed and the following substituted therefor: "*Manitoba Act, 1870.*" (2) Section 20 is repealed.	Manitoba Act, 1870
3.	Order of Her Majesty in Council admitting Rupert's Land and the North-Western Territory into the union, dated the 23rd day of June, 1870		Rupert's Land and North-Western Territory Order
4.	Order of Her Majesty in Council admitting British Columbia into the Union, dated the 16th day of May, 1871		British Columbia Terms of Union
5.	British North America Act, 1871, 34-35 Vict., c. 28 (U.K.)	Section 1 is repealed and the following substituted therefor: "1. This Act may be cited as the *Constitution Act, 1871.*"	Constitution Act, 1871
6.	Order of Her Majesty in Council admitting Prince Edward Island into the Union, dated the 26th day of June, 1873		Prince Edward Island Terms of Union
7.	Parliament of Canada Act, 1875, 38-39 Vict., c. 38 (U.K.)		Parliament of Canada Act, 1875
8.	Order of Her Majesty in Council admitting all British possessions and Territories in North America and islands adjacent thereto into the Union, dated the 31st day of July, 1880		Adjacent Territories Order

SCHEDULE

to the

CONSTITUTION ACT, 1982—*Continued*

Item	Column I Act Affected	Column II Amendment	Column III New Name
9.	British North America Act, 1886, 49-50 Vict., c. 35 (U.K.)	Section 3 is repealed and the following substituted therefor: "3. This Act may be cited as the *Constitution Act, 1886.*"	Constitution Act, 1886
10.	Canada (Ontario Boundary) Act, 1889, 52-53 Vict., c. 28 (U.K.)		Canada (Ontario Boundary) Act, 1889
11.	Canadian Speaker (Appointment of Deputy) Act, 1895, 2nd Sess., 59 Vict., c. 3 (U.K.)	The Act is repealed.	
12.	The Alberta Act, 1905, 4-5 Edw. VII, c. 3 (Can.)		Alberta Act
13.	The Saskatchewan Act, 1905, 4-5 Edw. VII, c. 42 (Can.)		Saskatchewan Act
14.	British North America Act, 1907, 7 Edw. VII, c. 11 (U.K.)	Section 2 is repealed and the following substituted therefor: "2. This Act may be cited as the *Constitution Act, 1907.*"	Constitution Act, 1907
15.	British North America Act, 1915, 5-6 Geo. V, c. 45 (U.K.)	Section 3 is repealed and the following substituted therefor: "3. This Act may be cited as the *Constitution Act, 1915.*"	Constitution Act, 1915
16.	British North America Act, 1930, 20-21 Geo. V, c. 26 (U.K.)	Section 3 is repealed and the following substituted therefor: "3. This Act may be cited as the *Constitution Act, 1930.*"	Constitution Act, 1930
17.	Statute of Westminster, 1931, 22 Geo. V, c. 4 (U.K.)	In so far as they apply to Canada, (*a*) section 4 is repealed; and (*b*) subsection 7(1) is repealed.	Statute of Westminster, 1931

SCHEDULE

to the

CONSTITUTION ACT, 1982—*Continued*

Item	Column I Act Affected	Column II Amendment	Column III New Name
18.	British North America Act, 1940, 3-4 Geo. VI, c. 36 (U.K.)	Section 2 is repealed and the following substituted therefor: "2. This Act may be cited as the *Constitution Act, 1940*."	Constitution Act, 1940
19.	British North America Act, 1943, 6-7 Geo. VI, c. 30 (U.K.)	The Act is repealed.	
20.	British North America Act, 1946, 9-10 Geo. VI, c. 63 (U.K.)	The Act is repealed.	
21.	British North America Act, 1949, 12-13 Geo. VI, c. 22 (U.K.)	Section 3 is repealed and the following substituted therefor: "3. This Act may be cited as the *Newfoundland Act*."	Newfoundland Act
22.	British North America (No. 2) Act, 1949, 13 Geo. VI, c. 81 (U.K.)	The Act is repealed.	
23.	British North America Act, 1951, 14-15 Geo. VI, c. 32 (U.K.)	The Act is repealed.	
24.	British North America Act, 1952, 1 Eliz. II, c. 15 (Can.)	The Act is repealed.	
25.	British North America Act, 1960, 9 Eliz. II, c. 2 (U.K.)	Section 2 is repealed and the following substituted therefor: "2. This Act may be cited as the *Constitution Act, 1960*."	Constitution Act, 1960
26.	British North America Act, 1964, 12-13 Eliz. II, c. 73 (U.K.)	Section 2 is repealed and the following substituted therefor: "2. This Act may be cited as the *Constitution Act, 1964*."	Constitution Act, 1964

SCHEDULE

to the

CONSTITUTION ACT, 1982—*Concluded*

Item	Column I Act Affected	Column II Amendment	Column III New Name
27.	British North America Act, 1965, 14 Eliz. II, c. 4, Part I (Can.)	Section 2 is repealed and the following substituted therefor: "2. This Part may be cited as the *Constitution Act, 1965*."	Constitution Act, 1965
28.	British North America Act, 1974, 23 Eliz. II, c. 13, Part I (Can.)	Section 3, as amended by 25-26 Eliz. II, c. 28, s. 38(1) (Can.), is repealed and the following substituted therefor: "3. This Part may be cited as the *Constitution Act, 1974*."	Constitution Act, 1974
29.	British North America Act, 1975, 23-24 Eliz. II, c. 28, Part I (Can.)	Section 3, as amended by 25-26 Eliz. II, c. 28, s. 31 (Can.), is repealed and the following substituted therefor: "3. This Part may be cited as the *Constitution Act (No. 1), 1975*."	Constitution Act (No. 1), 1975
30.	British North America Act (No. 2), 1975, 23-24 Eliz. II, c. 53 (Can.)	Section 3 is repealed and the following substituted therefor: "3. This Act may be cited as the *Constitution Act (No. 2), 1975*."	Constitution Act (No. 2), 1975

Index

Reader Response Questionnaire
(see over)

Fold here

To the User of this Book

We would like to know what you think of D.N. Sprague's *Post-Confederation Canada: The Structure of Canadian History Since 1867*. Your comments will help us improve the book for future editions.

1. What type of course did you use this book for?
   _____ college
   _____ university
   _____ continuing education
   _____ other (please specify)

2. What is your major area of study?

Fold here

_____

3. Which chapters, if any, were not used in your course?

4. What single change would most improve the book?

with all the information they needed to begin the destruction of Macdonald's government.

In the disclosures that unfolded from April through October 1873, two major issues emerged. One was nationalism, in the sense that Sir John A. Macdonald, "the founder and father of Canada," had been caught accepting campaign contributions apparently from American as well as Canadian favourites. The other was the question of corruption: the morality of soliciting large cash contributions from expectant recipients of government patronage. Parliament and the country had become unusually sensitive to both matters in 1873. That summer, Macdonald tried to divert Canadians' attention by charming Prince Edward Island into Confederation (with the promise of a railway, of course). But the "Pacific Scandal" kept resurfacing. By November, the Prime Minister had lost control of his majority.

Heightened sensitivity on matters of national integrity brought about Macdonald's downfall. Ironically, the unravelling of his control was a fitting confirmation of his success over the previous decade. In 1867, there had been no national integrity to violate. At best, the country was four provinces agreeing to disagree on the somewhat neutral ground of Ottawa. Six years later, there was at least some semblance of national purpose, and therefore a basis on which to assert that the present government had behaved scandalously. Virtue triumphed, and the ministry led by Sir John A. Macdonald resigned on November 5. Not surprisingly, Hugh Allan subsequently surrendered the charter for the railway he had bought with $350 000 in campaign contributions.

— 2. Government True to "Sound Principles" —

Soon after John A. Macdonald resigned in disgrace over the Pacific Scandal, a government headed by the leader of the opposition attempted to take control of Parliament with minority standing in the House of Commons. The new Prime Minister, Alexander McKenzie, was understandably anxious to solidify a majority. Consequently, he sought a dissolution of the second parliament soon after taking Macdonald's place; and the third general election was set for January 1874. At last contestants stood for something resembling national political organizations. Macdonald's group had been well organized from the start, but the other factions—Repealers, Anti-Ministerialists, Reformers, etc.—were simply the opposition. It was not until the Pacific Scandal that Mackenzie became their leader and spokesman for dramatizing the differences between those on their side of the House and the group opposite.

When he addressed his own electors in Lambton County, Ontario, the new Prime Minister suggested that the main difference between his party and the other was morality, not ideology. Both professed similar truths, he said, but the previous government was distinctive for its deviation from decency. Its "members were elected by the corrupt use of Sir Hugh Allan's money," while Mackenzie's "Reformer-Liberals" were true to "sound principles." They could be counted upon to "elevate the standard of public morality . . . and . . . conduct public affairs upon principles of which honest men can approve, and by practices which will bear the light of day." Macdonald's "corruptionists" gave bribes to placate provinces, and took bribes from expectant private contractors. Not surprisingly, the new Prime Minister promised to dismantle the main bribe: he would renegotiate the "impossible" gift of the railway to British Columbia. Instead of proceeding with such lavish projects, Mackenzie would institute "reforms." They would cost the public almost nothing, yet benefit the country enormously. In this sense, his main purpose was to demonstrate an alternative to the "mercenary" approach of the rival coalition.

Three kinds of reform were promised. One was electoral innovation. The second was constitutional change. The third was fiscal stringency. With regard to the first, cleaner elections were pledged by changing the Elections Act to bring in simultaneous voting. The proposal was based on the assumption that if everyone voted on the same day, an incumbent government would be less able to win key constituencies, one by one, as was the established practice. Other proposed reforms included abandoning open voting in favour of the secret ballot, trial of controverted elections by a judge rather than a House of Commons committee, and extension of the franchise beyond property owners.

Mackenzie promised two constitutional reforms. One was a revision of the militia system, intended to make it more Canadian and less vulnerable to domination by patronage appointees. He proposed a national military college to supply the militia with real officers rather than political favourites. The creation of a Canadian officer corps implied a fairly robust nationalism. So too did Mackenzie's other proposed reform: creating a supreme court, apparently eliminating the British Privy Council as Canada's last court of appeal.

The promised fiscal reforms pertained to public and private spending. Mackenzie indicated a need for an "insolvency law" to facilitate the declaration of personal bankruptcy without subsequent imprisonment for debt. Yet at the same time, as an example of the way to avoid bankruptcy in the first place, Mackenzie promised to scale down the level of government spending. He denounced Macdonald's railway plans as particularly extravagant. These would be scaled down to an affordable level. Overall, honest and frugal government were supposed to inspire a sense of Canadian confidence and pride. Invigorated pride would raise Canada in spirit and the constitutional reforms would lessen dependency upon Britain, advancing the country among the community of nations. Here was Alexander Mackenzie's promise to his own electors. Although his method was a slower way to build a country, in the new Prime Minister's opinion, it was the only proper approach.

The electorate seemed to agree. Mackenzie triumphed in Lambton, and Reformer-Liberals triumphed elsewhere as well. Mackenzie's group returned with a two-to-one majority of 138 seats over the opposition. Since the victory occurred everywhere except British Columbia ("the spoiled child of Confederation"), Alexander Mackenzie felt justified in voicing strong words of satisfaction with the conquest, saying the country had "pronounced its condemnation of the Pacific Scandal . . . .the old corruptionists are fairly stupefied." With such a great victory for the party that promised to remain true to "sound principles," everything Mackenzie had promised in Lambton could be enacted with ease. What Mackenzie failed to appreciate fully was the richness of the variety of the many denominations of Canadian "virtue."

The Reformer-Liberals consisted of no fewer than four different strains of reform-minded politicians, each pulling at the unity of one nominal party. One such group originated in Ontario: old moralists such as the leader himself and George Brown, out of Parliament but still active in politics through his ownership of the most formidable newspaper in Canada, the Toronto *Globe*. The distinguishing characteristic of such long-time "gritty" opponents of Macdonald's coalition was their essentially oppositional turn of mind. The "Grits" were almost republican in their assumption that society was little more than an agglomeration of individuals asking nothing more than an impartial referee in disputes arising between individuals in pursuit of their private interests. The power of the state that they envisioned was essentially negative, designed to prevent combinations of wage-earners, for instance, from forcing their will upon their employers. Nor was the state to favour combinations of capitalists in their projects, for example, railways. Government was to play a limited, self-denying, frugal role; it was not to be an independent, active, and ambitious power in its own sphere. As Mackenzie expressed his philosophy on a visit to his Scottish homeland in 1875: "I have believed . . . and I now believe, in the extinction of all class legislation, and of all legislation that tends to promote any body of men or any class of men from the mere fact of their belonging to a class of higher position . . . in the community." In Canada, he continued, "we take the ground simply and completely that every man stands equal in the eye of the law, and every man has the same opportunity by exercise of the talent with which God has blessed him to rise in the world, in the confidence of his fellow-citizens, the one quite as much as the other."

A contrasting variant of such liberalism was the Quebec variety championed by A.A. Dorion. His was the old *Rouge* position, more temperate in its *independantisme*, but otherwise still quite incompatible with the pro-British, ultra-Protestant tradition promoted by Brown and the *Globe*. The *Rouges* were ardently anti-Protestant, and hypersensitive to insults from Protestant nationalists. At home in Quebec, their chief enmity was with the Roman Catholic clergy; the *Rouges* were demanding that the Church learn a neutral role in the secular politics of the day. To the clerical hierarchy, such a stance seemed totally irresponsible. The Holy Father himself, Pope Pius IX, had issued an encyclical as recently as 1864, in which clergy were ordered to commit themselves to fighting a host of 80 errors, including the notion of the separation of church and state, pantheism, naturalism, absolute rationalism, moderate rationalism, indifferentism, latitudinarianism, socialism, communism, and secret societies. To make all the foregoing more emphatic, in July 1870, the Church proclaimed the Dogma of Papal Infallibility. The freshly reasserted position of spiritual authority made certain bishops in Quebec even more militant than they had been, and even more committed to what they perceived as their special mission for the future.

Clerical ascendancy and ultramontanism (an orientation more to Rome than to local secular or clerical leaders) led to open conflict between the Church and the anticlericals. The most outspoken young anticlericals were associated in a literary society called the Institut Canadien. The Bishop of Montreal, Ignace Bourget, denounced them for propagating errors the Pope was condemning; when the Institut reciprocated by denouncing the bishop as a meddler, Bourget brandished threats of excommunication. The animosity reached ferocious proportions in 1874 when an excommunicated liberal, five-year-dead, was awarded Roman Catholic burial by court order. Backed by the law and English units of the militia, Joseph Guibord was placed according to his relatives' wishes in a Roman Catholic cemetery. But Bourget ruled that Guibord's new-found resting place in reinforced concrete was profane, and thus seemed to have the last word in the dispute. The alliance between the Church and Quebec Conservatives, the *Bleus,* emerged the stronger.

The central problem for Quebec Liberals was to draw a distinction between liberal Roman Catholicism (condemned by the Pope), and Roman Catholic Liberalism (theoretically not inimical to the ultramontane doctrines of the Quebec Church). The first evident steps in this direction were not to be taken by Dorion, but years later by the young Wilfrid Laurier who proclaimed that his liberalism was nothing more than being "one of those who think that everywhere, in human things, there are abuses to be remedied, new horizons to be opened up, and new forces to be developed" by the power of government and its projects. Such pronouncements placed Laurier more in the tradition of Macdonald's brand of liberalism than the unfettered individualism of the *Rouges*, Mackenzie, and Brown; but Laurier still did not immediately win many friends in Quebec. In 1874, Mackenzie was partnered with three *Rouges* like Dorion—individuals who were even less popular than Laurier with the Quebec Church, and who were traditionally despised by the Grit reformers of Ontario.

Two other kinds of partisans in Mackenzie's Reformer-Liberal party were even more evidently on his side by reason of circumstance. The first were those independent nationalists espousing Canada First, who called themselves a "movement" in 1874. They allied with Mackenzie because of their revulsion with Macdonald's "sordid and mercenary" means of national consolidation. Still, they admitted that the first Prime Minister had been an active builder between 1867 and 1873. As soon as it became evident that Mackenzie intended little more than the few reforms he promised at Lambton, they would oppose him just as they had criticized Macdonald on other grounds. Thus, Edward Blake—perhaps the most delicately temperamental politician in Canada—emerged as the leader of such criticism as early as October 1874, when he hinted that Mackenzie was far too cautious in the reforms he was willing to pursue. "How long is this talk . . . of the desirability, aye, of the necessity of fostering a national spirit among the people of Canada, to be mere talk?" he asked his audience in Aurora, Ontario on October 3. "It is impossible to foster a national spirit," Blake continued, "unless you have national interests to attend to . . . ." He concluded with the prophesy that "The time will come . . . when we shall realize that we are four millions of Britons who are not free . . . ." Only then would Canada move from collaboration to independent action.

George Brown was inclined to dismiss such talk as empty, "juvenile" rhetoric. In response to the demand for Canada First, Brown snorted, "God save the grand old British race first." His attitude was echoed by the last of the remaining groups in the Reformer-Liberal party, amounting to about half of the membership of Mackenzie's cabinet. They were the turncoat ministerialists, individuals formerly associated with Macdonald's party. They accepted few, if any, of the doctrines of "Canada First" or of dogmatic Grit liberalism; and coming from Nova Scotia, New Brunswick, or Ontario, they had nothing to do with *Rouge* liberalism. But they were with Mackenzie in 1874 because, along with much of the rest of the country, they could not condone what Macdonald had done with his majority. The "loose fish," as Macdonald called them or "shaky fellows" in George Brown's description, waited to see what Mackenzie would do with his majority.

— 3. A Railway in Principle —

The attempt to adhere rigidly to principle in the midst of contradictory liberalisms meant that Mackenzie was never able to develop a strong team of ministers and enjoy the luxury of distributing responsibility among a competent crew of trusted lieutenants. To a remarkable degree, Alexander Mackenzie looked after the important affairs of government on his own. Ostensibly, he was the Minister of Public Works, a crushing job in itself given the work of superintending the railway projects. But he also retained the initiative in preparing most of nearly 100 pieces of legislation touching on the affairs of many other departments in the first session of Parliament. Remarkably, by November 1875, he had launched all the reforms he believed necessary. Not everything had been completed as promised in his Lambton address, but "not one [promise] . . . has been left to rust or die out," he said at the end of the year. The election reforms, a new military college, reform of the militia, bankruptcy legislation, the Supreme Court, and the railway had all been pursued more or less as promised. Mackenzie continued to believe that the need for reform would "never cease as long as this world is peopled by sinners," but he did feel that the most flagrantly wicked of his own generation were in retreat at the end of the first session of his government, and he settled into what Canada Firsters denounced as a cautious, unimaginative, penny-pinching administration.

Mackenzie's railway policy was the prime illustration for the alleged inaction and penury. The Prime Minister abandoned his predecessor's promise of building a through-line from British Columbia to eastern Canada over a period of ten years. Such a railway was ahead of demand, he said, and beyond the means of a small country such as Canada, then sliding into the worst trade depression since 1857.

Declining orders for Canadian exports meant diminished imports and (without tax increases) reduced government revenue from taxes on trade. The potential shortfall of income was significant: the volume of exports—increasing each year since Confederation—declined ten percent between 1874 and 1975, and diminished each year thereafter through 1879. Under the circumstances, Mackenzie pursued a cheaper alternative railway policy. His scheme, in principle, was piecemeal construction to follow rather than to promote settlement, and to supplement rather than to supersede navigable "water stretches." In Mackenzie's approach to the problem of western transportation, freight and passengers would move by steamer over the Great Lakes as far as Port Arthur. There a railway would take them to the chain of lakes 80 kilometres west. Than it was back to boats for the 435 kilometres over Shebandowan Lake, Lac des Milles Lacs, Rainy Lake, Rainy River, and Lake of the Woods (see map 2.1). At the northeast corner of the last lake, the railway would resume; by this means cargo would be transported the remaining 185 kilometres to Red River. For the foreseeable future, that terminus, roughly the site of present-day Winnipeg, would be the western limit of the Pacific Railway as well. As soon as possible, there would be a through-line built from Port Arthur to Winnipeg, and also from Winnipeg south along the east side of the Red River to the United States border. Mackenzie did not believe, however, that the country could afford, in his lifetime, to build the expensive line over the mountains to British Columbia, and the astronomically expensive section traversing the north shore of Lake Superior. His biographer, Dale Thomson, has argued that Mackenzie's was the only feasible alternative given the reduced government revenue in the depressed years between 1873 and 1878; he points out that roughly one quarter of the entire federal expenditure was allocated for public works, even with the truncated system supported by Mackenzie. The implication is that the railway was still the government's first priority. With increased revenue to spend, more of the railway would have been built. But Pierre Berton, and most other

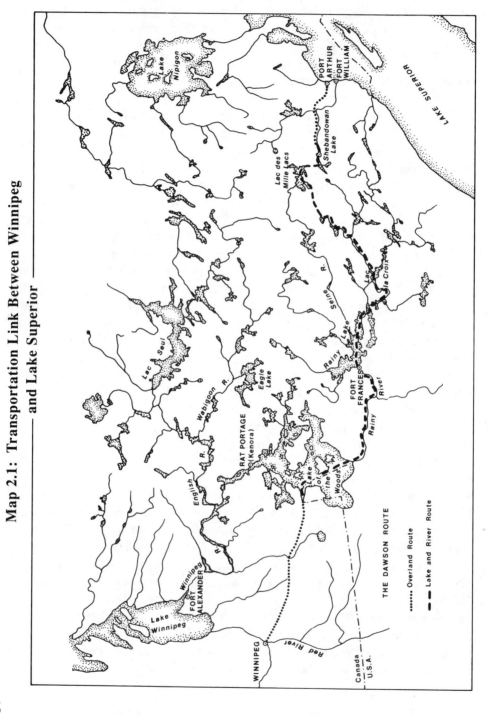

Map 2.1: Transportation Link Between Winnipeg and Lake Superior

THE DAWSON ROUTE

•••••• Overland Route

▬ ▬ Lake and River Route

historians, are convinced that "it is doubtful that, given prosperity, he would have accomplished any more than he did." Mackenzie was opposed in principle to building the railway from wilderness to wilderness.

Despite the apparent disagreement on what Mackenzie might have accomplished with the railway given better financial conditions, historians do seem to share the assumption that the railway had to be built—and as quickly as possible. Research in the United States, however, has shown that the settlement of that country's west (much drier than Canada's) was quite feasible using improved water routes and wagon roads in much the same fashion advocated by the Canadian Prime Minister in 1874. Had Mackenzie developed his "water stretches" alternative more fully, he might have been able to point out that as late as 1870, in the already settled part of Canada, the existing railways carried less freight than the water-borne carriers. Then he might have asserted that the North West possessed a system of natural waterways almost as attractive as the St. Lawrence-Great Lakes system, and pointed the accusing finger at the other side of the House to argue that the "members elected by the corrupt use of Sir Hugh Allan's money" were railway promoters first, Fathers of Confederation second, and opportunists always. His Reformer-Liberals, he might have continued, would pursue Canada's western destiny through her northern waters. Mackenzie's party would make the St. Lawrence navigable from tidewater to the Rocky Mountains. The big project would be a canal from Port Arthur to Lake Shebandowan, and improvements around the more than 70 portages to Lake of the Woods. Then, rather than moving overland, the route of the fur-traders over the Winnipeg River to Lake Winnipeg would be followed. From there, north was the Nelson, south the Red, and west the Saskatchewan and the Assiniboine. Later, as settlement advanced and as capital accumulated in enterprising private hands, there would be railway connections as well, but not with the extravagant government subsidies that were required to build them ahead of demand.

The one flaw in such an imaginary scenario was the reality that Mackenzie was no more interested in Liberal seaways than Conservative railways. Nor were many in his party any less infected with the railway mania than the Conservatives. What concerned Mackenzie, and mightily, was expenditure. That was the basis for his "water stretches" railway policy in the first place. Since his alternative could not succeed without significant improvements to the waterways in their natural state, and since dredging and lock-construction were only relatively less expensive than the railways (not cheap in absolute terms), in the end, Mackenzie's government had to admit that its water stretches policy was not to be pursued as a real alternative to railways.

To establish *some* transportation link with Manitoba, Mackenzie decided in the last year of his administration to accelerate construction of a railway link between Port Arthur and Winnipeg, and to finish the line along the Red River south to the United States. Since the Pembina Branch, as the second line was called, was far shorter and ran over loamy, level ground all the way to the American border, the north-south link became more or less operational first. When it linked up with the St. Paul and Pacific Railroad at the end of 1878, the Pembina Branch functioned as the main link between Manitoba and the rest of the world until the other line to Port Arthur came into service in 1882, four years after Mackenzie had been turned out of office.

In the meantime, intending settlers and their freight travelled west from Ontario by ship as far as Duluth, Minnesota, then by train through the United States to the Pembina Branch. That was a transportation system assisted by water stretches, but not the one that might have been, nor the scheme Mackenzie espoused in principle.

— 4. Extinguishment of "Indian Title" —

Mackenzie's government was more successful in clearing Canadian title to the West than in promoting transportation improvements for its settlement. Earlier, Macdonald's government had purchased title to Rupert's Land from the Hudson's Bay Company, rather than the people actually in possession of the land. In 1869, the Indians and Métis had no intention of relinquishing their claims.

In the previous chapter, it was shown that the Métis settlers around Red River had effectively dissuaded the government from annexing their region as a colony of the Dominion. In that success, they appeared to have won effective guarantees that their land, religion, and language would be secure under the new regime. It is unclear whether Macdonald and his associates had made promises they intended to honour once Rupert's Land was securely in their grasp, but it is apparent that the opposition despised the major provisions of the Manitoba Act from the time of its introduction to the House of Commons in May 1870. Not surprisingly, once in power, Mackenzie took important steps to vitiate what were regarded as the most objectionable features of the Manitoba Act—the land promises. The assurance of continuity in the occupancy of riverfront lots, an unqualified guarantee in Section 32 of the law, was changed in 1874 into a less definite opportunity. In the new act, "persons satisfactorily establishing undisturbed occupancy . . . and peaceable possession" of their riverfront homes were assured confirmation of ownership by the Dominion. In practice, the proof that was demanded was documentation of ownership by deed from the Hudson's Bay Company or improvements of the land in the sense of fenced and cultivated acreage, the construction of houses and outbuildings. But the HBC had given very few deeds to its settlers in the years between 1835 and 1869; and since the Métis tended to "ranch" the buffalo more than they "farmed" the land, less than 20 percent of the original population passed the homestead test. The "Old Settlement Belt" of Manitoba was thus cleared of its original population at almost no cost to the Government of Canada. The other benefit of this policy (from the standpoint of officialdom in Ottawa) was that it freed the reserve of the one-half million hectares promised to the children of the "half-breed heads of families" in Section 31 of the Manitoba Act. Having lost their riverfront homes, the Métis tended to leave Manitoba with their children. Enterprising "land agents" tracked them to their new locations and obtained assignments of the children's allotments of land, or, having failed to find such persons in preliminary searching, they devised fraudulent transfers. The irregularities in such practices were so complicated that the Legislative Assembly of Manitoba (predominantly Ontario-born by 1878) enacted a special code of property law concerning the "estates" of "half-breed infants." Not surprisingly, the Dominion government allowed such legislation even though there were good grounds for not doing so in Section 91 (24) of the BNA Act.

Government policy was to clear the land of Métis and Indians to make way for "actual settlers"—and to do so as economically as possible. At first, the Indians seemed even less movable than had been the Métis in 1869. At Fort Frances in 1870, for instance, Colonel Wolseley offered gaudy presents to one chief who rejected them on the spot, saying: "Am I a pike to be caught with such bait as that? Shall I sell my land for a bit of red cloth? We will let the palefaces pass through our country, but we will sell them none of our land, nor have any of them to live amongst us." Another chief further west rejected comparable offerings on the same premise: "We want none of the Queen's presents; when we set a fox-trap we scatter pieces of meat all round, but when the fox gets into the trap, we knock him on the head."

Still, between 1874 and 1877, most of the Indian lands between Manitoba and the Rocky Mountains (south of 60° N. latitude) were

Map 2.2: Areas Ceded by Treaty to Canada by Indians, 1871-77

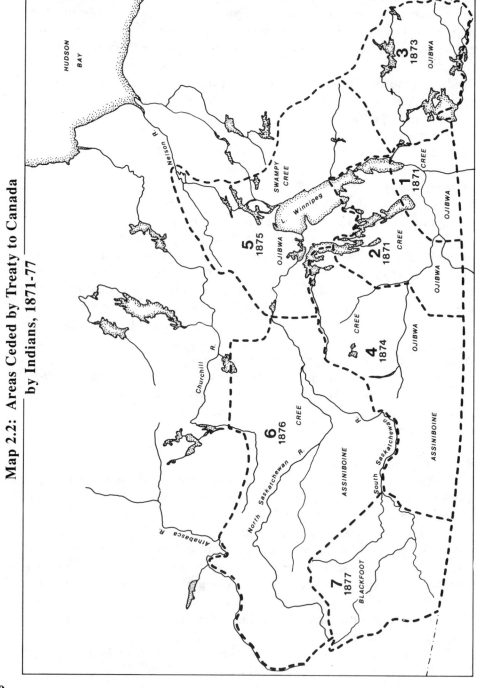

transferred from the native people to the Government of Canada at almost no immediate cost to the Dominion (see map 2.2). Military force was not the reason. In fact, the few soldiers Canada sent West were paramilitary constables, the North West Mounted Police, whom the Indian chiefs tended to welcome because they were a force to discipline the predatory whiskey traders and wolf hunters—interlopers mainly from the United States. A large force was not needed for such police work. As originally constituted in 1873, the NWMP consisted of 150 constables. When Mackenzie's government sent them west from Manitoba in 1874, the force was still only 300 because the Prime Minister was no more inclined to extravagance in budgeting for the national police than for national transportation.

Nor was encroaching settlement the reason behind the Indian capitulation between 1874 and 1877. In the entire decade between 1870 and 1880, there were no more than a few thousand settlers west of Manitoba. Most newcomers went no further than the rich lands in the vicinity of the Red River, which began to prove its potential for wheat production as early as 1876, the year the first surplus of Red Fife was shipped from Manitoba by way of Minnesota for milling in Ontario.

The few pioneers who moved further west tended to locate in compact settlements on the very shore of the great river system that was the main artery of the territory fit for farming. Similarly, a number of Métis villages appeared along the Saskatchewan River and in the Qu'Appelle Valley from the migration of people displaced from their home province (see map 2.3). The Métis had been hunting buffalo in the region for generations. Having lost their place in Manitoba, the North West was a logical place to which they might retreat.

In the late 1870s, however, the buffalo began to disappear from the North West, with disastrous consequences for the Indians as well as the Métis. The threat of starvation and the decimation of their people by smallpox propelled the Native Peoples into the treaty-making process between 1874 and 1877. Pestilence came to the Indians first. At least half of the population of the bands in what are now Saskatchewan and Alberta died of smallpox in the early 1870s. Those who survived the epidemic then had to face the crisis of a dwindling food supply. Systematic extermination of the beasts that had provided the Plains Indians with their sustenance, shelter, and even their fuel, was begun in the United States to clear the land of obstacles to railways and agriculture. There were perhaps 60 million buffalo milling back and forth over the invisible border when the slaughtering began. By 1875, the herds had diminished enough to threaten

Map 2.3: Dispersal of the Métis from Manitoba, 1870-85

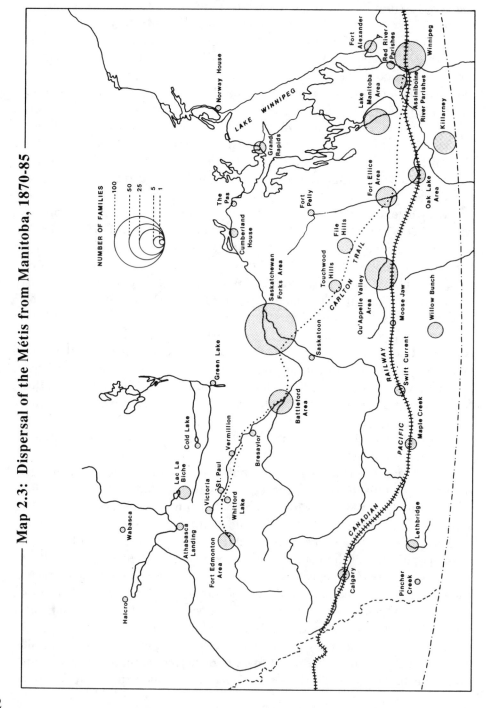

famine. As the spectre of famine followed the experience of epidemic, the Indians' will to resist was broken.

Canada did not finish what nature had begun. The police did not exterminate the weakened survivors of disease and starvation. In fact, in all Canadian history such a policy was pursued in only one locality, on Newfoundland, where the Beothuk people situated on the coastal bays and inlets were first driven inland then hunted and slaughtered like seals "with just as little remorse." The last died in 1829; but by the early 1840s, Newfoundlanders were beginning to feel profound guilt for the crime of genocide committed by their fathers. They regretted not having pursued the more humane route to expropriation that was followed elsewhere. In the other Atlantic provinces and British Columbia, small parcels of land were set aside by the local governments as Indian reserves after most acreage had been allocated for settlement or other development.

Where agricultural settlement expanded more rapidly, as in the United Province of Canada, negotiation preceded settlement; and the resulting reserves granted by Imperial authorities were usually more adequate to the Native Peoples' needs. The subject of native-white relations in the United Province of Canada was a more equitably-administered Imperial responsibility because the British dreaded the occurrence of the costly wars that were such a conspicuous feature of the American experience with Native Peoples. After Confederation, the Government of Canada intended to carry on the same appearance of orderly justice. Since the government sought to negotiate "extinguishment of Indian title" on the Prairies in advance of settlement, the hard times of the early 1870s prepared the way for vast, cheap settlements.

The British had needed more than 30 treaties to clear the territory north of Lake Ontario and Lake Erie; Canada extinguished Indian title to almost the entire Prairie West with just four treaties concluded between 1874 and 1877 (see map 2.2). To be sure, the Native Peoples did bargain for more than Canada was at first willing to offer. In addition to the promise of reserves and token annuities, Canada finally agreed to protect the Native Peoples from hunger and disease, and to provide education as well as necessary implements for easing the transition from reliance on the buffalo to new independence oriented towards ranching and farming. At least, that was how the Indians understood the treaties. Canada regarded them more cynically, as ceremonial exercises, not agreements with sovereign nations, or even binding contracts with a Canadian sub-population. The one unreality led to others—the price paid for the land, for example, hardly reflected value received. The latent guilt over such inherent fraud

43

was assuaged by pretensions of benevolent paternalism embodied in Canada's Indian Act of 1876. By one statute, every aspect of reserve life came under the control and regulation of the white officials charged with the responsibility of promoting the Native Peoples' recovery from "savagery." Of course, the vast program of forced assimilation was supposed to be self-sustaining, from the proceeds of Native Peoples lands and labour. Of that Mackenzie was reassured. He needed such reassurance in 1876 because Macdonald's party was beginning to recover its full voice of opposition. Non-confidence motions, normally "a somewhat solemn or grand matter," according to Mackenzie, were starting to be served up "for breakfast, dinner, and supper."

— 5. Mackenzie's Opposition —

In his first two years in opposition, Sir John A. Macdonald languished like an old warrior expiring from mortal wounds. Since he was nearly 60 years old, suffered ill health, and was fully disgraced by the Pacific Scandal, Macdonald had good reason to think that his political career was finished in 1874. Not surprisingly, he attended Parliament infrequently; when he did so, his participation was not as a leader who seemed anxious to court popularity, as when he opposed Mackenzie's introduction of the secret ballot. The Prime Minister defended the innovation on the grounds that employees risked losing their jobs if they voted contrary to the demands of employers. Macdonald insisted that when a person voted, he ought to be manly enough to assume responsibility for his actions.

While the leader of the opposition lacked lustre or popularity prior to 1876, the more effective opponent of the government was Lord Dufferin, the Governor General. The Queen's representative refused to accept the proposition that Confederation, or earlier constitutional developments, had made the Crown a mere symbol of power in Canada. If Mackenzie pursued a policy that ran contrary to Dufferin's vice-regal instincts, the interventionist Lord Dufferin insisted that the Prime Minister convince him that he was wrong. After one of their many disputes, he informed Mackenzie that "You said last night you are not a Crown Colony, which is true, but neither are you a Republic." To Dufferin, Canada's in-between status meant that "within the walls of the Privy Council I have as much right to contend for my opinion as any of My Ministers, and in matters of moment they must not expect me to accept their advice merely because they give it, but they must approve it to my understanding and conscience . . . ."

When Mackenzie aimed to negotiate a reciprocity agreement with the United States in 1874 using George Brown as Canada's ambassador, Dufferin objected, suggesting that a British dependency should work through a commission named by the Colonial Office. When Mackenzie sought legislation creating a Supreme Court in 1875, Dufferin recommended disallowance in London on the grounds that Canadian legal independence conflicted with every British subject's right to appeal to the Crown (meaning the Judicial Committee of the Privy Council) as the final arbiter of disputes. And when Mackenzie pursued the railway policy that brought British Columbia to the brink of separation in 1876, Dufferin insisted that the Government of Canada had no choice but to live with the bargain that had been struck in 1870. In each dispute, the nationalist Prime Minister and the interventionist Governor General eventually compromised: George Brown did indeed negotiate (but every near-agreement had to be referred to London for Colonial Office approval until the talks finally resulted in a treaty the American Senate rejected); a Canadian Supreme Court was created (but only in principle, since appeals to the British Privy Council were allowed to continue); and Mackenzie did agree to abide by the spirit, if not the letter, of the Pacific Railway promise. Thus, the two strong-minded leaders had been able to moderate their differences. Perhaps the telephone installed between their offices in September 1877 (the first in Canada), was the important link that facilitated such communication. As the advertisement for the new instrument explained, "When conversation is carried on in the ordinary tone and the words are clearly enunciated, intercourse can be kept up with as much ease as if the two individuals were in the same room."

Macdonald resented Mackenzie's nationalist stance vis-à-vis Great Britain. He considered such measures as the Supreme Court "veiled treason," but avoided opposing him on slippery constitutional ground. For two years, Macdonald lacked an appropriate alternative on which to focus his limited energy. Then in 1876, the tariff appeared to be the question on which Macdonald might seem to out-distance Mackenzie's own nationalism without ruffling Canadians' British patriotism.

Until the introduction of the personal income tax, the tariff was the most important source of revenue, accounting for about three quarters of the government's income. In the context of the previously mentioned recession, however, imports diminished and government revenue declined proportionately. Expansion of local manufacturing was little help. For example, a number of manufacturers had taken advantage of designs not protected by the Canadian Patent Act. Since 70 percent of consumer durable goods were imported, almost anything was fair game for import-replacing manufacturing, and some manufacturers did prosper by copying American designs for which there were already markets in the Dominion. One agricultural implement-maker reported that "wherever" he expanded, "the American manufacturers have retired from the field for the reason that we can undersell them. They make a very nice machine; it is the same machine . . . that we sell." But where Americans charged $100 for their product, the Canadian sold his for $75; and the treasury of Canada lost $15 every time a farmer bought an implement from the Canadian rather than the American supplier.

There were two conventional ways for Mackenzie's government to deal with the problem of declining revenue. One was to increase the excise tax on domestic manufacturing. The other was to increase the rate of taxation on the dwindling volume of imports. But Richard Cartwright, the Minister of Finance, believed in free trade as a matter of principle; he was supported in that position by most of his fellow cabinet ministers. They had already compromised their free-trade scruples more than they had intended by raising the 15 percent tariff of the previous government to 17.5 percent, and Cartwright would not stand for any other tax on trade, given the generally weak state of the economy. But how was the government to cope with the $134-million national debt inherited from Macdonald? The interest charges alone were $6 million, roughly one-third of all receipts projected for 1876. In Cartwright's view, the problem was essentially a moral issue. The evil was the "past extravagance and folly" of Macdonald's party. The cure was "prudence and economy until this present trial is passed."

Cartwright's moralism posed a multi-faceted opportunity for the opposition. Macdonald's party could appear to resist government policy for national rather than partisan—principled rather than mercenary—reasons. Cartwright had asserted that a tariff increase would be detrimental in social as well as revenue-generating effects. To the extent that import duties discouraged foreign trade and jeopardized customs returns, they might also encourage domestic manufacturing, urban growth, and threaten the essentially rural character of the Dominion. In Cartwright's view, urbanization had to emerge gradually from the prosperity of the farms and forests. Lumber and cheese (the principal exports of the day) were shipped to world markets. In prosperity, such trade enabled rural producers to increase their consumption of domestic as well as imported goods; this nurtured the appropriate growth of cities, Cartwright felt. The imposition of a high tariff during a period of stagnation would stimulate "unhealthy growth of towns." Such intervention would cause growth "at the expense of the rural districts." Of course, Cartwright's argument could be easily inverted by pointing out that rural districts produced people as well as cheese—four children per family, on average. Most young people had to find employment in town or migrate. The Prairie West had more than 100 million acres suitable for farming, almost one million new farms. Why not pursue a policy of westward expansion using eastern-made tools of development? In the catch-phrases of Cartwright's opponents, a "judicious readjustment of the tariff" would enable Canada to pursue a "National Policy" for industrialization and settlement.

The less lofty but equally compelling attraction from a partisan standpoint was the vast new area of patronage indicated by tariff policy. Any manufacturer intending to launch an enterprise with costs in excess of world prices could find real encouragement and gratitude for the party awarding the tariff subsidy, just as labour might be persuaded to support a fiscal policy that promised to protect them from the unfair competition of workers who were supposed to be employed at starvation wages in Europe. Even farmers could develop an interest in a scheme that would tend to encourage greater consumption of their own produce. One group after another would be heard and accommodated exactly as Macdonald had learned to "obtain touch" with seekers of other favours.

The convenient vehicle for selling the high tariff in its loftier aspect was the political picnic, where voters and their families would gather on sunny summer afternoons to feast on sandwiches and politics. Macdonald's colleagues would eventually denounce the custom as "nothing but a lot of people walking about a field and some nasty provisions spoiling on a long table in the sun," but for the "Old Chieftain," the picnic device was a convivial way to build support, much preferred to angry harangues from mountains of newsprint. Macdonald, "a happy soul whom everybody likes," seemed to enjoy his political picnicking. Mackenzie lamely responded with picnics of his own; but his colleagues grumbled that their leader was incapable of learning "these little arts . . . . There was no gin and talk about Mac."

Mackenzie preferred to remain true to his promises of delivering reform and more reform. Consequently, in the last session before dissolution, he delivered a final purifying gesture by introducing a local-option prohibition law permitting local authorities to impose complete abstinence on the picnickers, drunks, and tipplers of an entire district.

Then in September 1878, after the third summer of the campaign, the electorate defeated the party whose politics were mainly its principles.

Sir John A. Macdonald and his party were clear on a program. Moreover, unlike the old matter-of-fact, even crass, consolidation of national boundaries by cash promises and railway schemes, the new recipe for action, no less tangible, was calculated to arouse a "national sentiment." Macdonald called his group the "CANADIAN PARTY which declares we must have Canada for the Canadians." This was not the racial nationalism of Canada First, nor the anticolonial nationalism of Alexander Mackenzie. Macdonald's brand was advertised as economic nationalism, distancing the country from the United States rather than from Britain. "You cannot get anything by kissing the feet of the people of the United States," he said. In Macdonald's view, the way to the bright future was where Great Britain had pioneered. "England, gentlemen, was the greatest Protectionist country in the world until she got possession of the markets of the world . . . . " The tariff would work the same magic for Canada, he promised. Like Britain before, Canada would "give a sprat to catch a mackerel."

The Reformer-Liberals denounced Macdonald's "National Policy" as so much "humbug" and "bunkum." Cartwright ridiculed the proposition, saying that it would only benefit the rich, "the poor and needy manufacturers who occupy those squalid hovels which adorn the suburbs of Montreal, Hamilton, and every city of the Dominion." It was a tax upon 95 percent of the people chiefly to benefit the top five percent. But the electorate was tired of recession and pious inactivity. In September 1878, the Reformer-Liberals were routed. "Nothing has happened in my time so astonishing," Mackenzie complained. There was also bitterness in his complaint that "Canada does not care for rigid adherence to principle in government."

Suggested Reading

General histories that cover the Mackenzie years include P.B. Waite, *Canada 1874-1896: Arduous Destiny* (1971). Equally useful is Dale Thomson's biography of the Prime Minister, *Alexander Mackenzie: Clear Grit* (1960). Other important Grits have also received full biographical treatment. George Brown's attempts to negotiate reciprocity are found in J.M.S. Careless, *Brown of the Globe: Statesman of Confederation, 1860-1880* (1963). Joseph Schull gives an account of Edward Blake's unwillingness to lead or be led in *Edward Blake: The Man of the Other*

Way (1975). Generally, however, the Mackenzie "interlude" has been rather undeservedly neglected by historians. Only certain aspects of the period have received serious attention.

The make-up of Mackenzie's group as a party has been described by Escott Reid in "The Rise of National Parties in Canada," *Papers and Proceedings of the Canadian Political Science Association* (1932), and F.H. Underhill, "The Development of National Parties in Canada," *CHR* (1935). Here, however, the Liberals' *Rouges* component has received the greatest attention, especially in more recent work. English readers have M. Ayearst, "The *Parti Rouge* and the Clergy," *CHR* (1937), and Lovell Clark, *The Guibord Affair* (1971). Two book-length works on the subject in French are Jean-Paul Bernard, *Les rouges: libéralisme, nationalisme et anticléricalisme au milieu du XIXe siècle* (1971), and Pierre Savard, *Aspects du catholicisme canadien-français au XIXe siècle* (1980).

Mackenzie's railway policy has received more attention—especially criticism. Harold Innis, *A History of the Canadian Pacific Railway* (1923), and Pierre Berton, *The National Dream: The Great Railway, 1871-1881* (1970), have described Mackenzie's approach primarily to condemn it. But Peter George's 20-page Foreword to a 1971 reprint of Innis raises a minority opinion on the matter by focusing on the issues of construction ahead of demand and the axiom of indispensability, as both have arisen in the scholarship of Albert Fishlow, *American Railroads and the Transformation of the Ante-Bellum Economy* (1965), and Robert W. Fogel, *Railroads and American Economic Growth: Essays in Econometric History* (1964).

Another aspect of the Mackenzie years to which historians have paid recent attention concerns Canada and native people. D.N. Sprague has criticized the administration of the land promises to the Métis in *Canada and the Métis, 1869-1885* (1988). The traditional account of the essential justice of the Canadian Indian policy found in G.F.G. Stanley, *The Birth of Western Canada* (1936), has been challenged by John Tobias in "The Subjugation of the Plains Cree," *CHR* (1983), and more recently, as well, by Jean Friesen in "Magnificent Gifts: The Treaties of Canada with the Indians of the Northwest, 1869-76," Royal Society of Canada, *Transactions* (1986), and E. Brian Titley in *A Narrow Vision: Duncan Campbell Scott and the Administration of Indian Affairs in Canada* (1986).

Several other questions concerning the Mackenzie years remain relatively untouched. For example, it is clear from Thomson's biography of the Prime Minister that the period between 1874 and 1878 was an important one in Canadian constitutional history for defining the place of

Canada in the British Empire, and for clarifying the role of the Governor General in Canadian domestic politics. But fuller studies of both issues remain to be done. Similarly, it is clear from Waite's account of national politics and general economic themes that the depression that began in 1873 had important consequences for reductions in both workers' wages and national revenue; but in other respects (particularly concerning banking and manufacturing), the economy continued to grow. Here as well, more research is needed to enlarge understanding of the anomalies of growth in recession. Studies by James Gilmour, *Spatial Evolution of Manufacturing: Southern Ontario, 1851-1891* (1972), R.T. Naylor, *The History of Canadian Business, 1867-1914* (1975), and Ben Forster, *A Conjunction of Interests: Business, Politics, and Tariff, 1825-1879* (1986), hardly touch on either subject for the period in question.

**Delegates to the
second Quebec conference, 1887.**

*"Macdonald denounced the resolutions of
the . . . conference as the emanations of a
mere party gathering . . . . Still, a truly
remarkable protest against centralism had
been made."*

CHAPTER 3
YEARS OF CRISIS,
1879-1896

— 1. A Tariff and a Railway —

Although the National Policy had been popularized in rhetorical flourishes that Mackenzie's party called "humbug," the Conservatives' program was not merely an electoral image. For good or ill, the tariff Macdonald promised in 1878 was the most conspicuous and controversial feature of the budget submitted to Parliament on March 14, 1879.

It had taken the Minister of Finance, Leonard Tilley, nearly three months to make all of the adjustments for the new schedule of duties. Some items, such as raw cotton and the machinery for manufacturing processes such as textile production, were exempted completely. Other commodities, without particular pattern, were taxed to the sky. Such chaos was the result of every manufacturer seeking his own order; and the process of endless lobbying made Tilley's work a nightmare since protection seekers were said to have "waylaid him" by night and by day. Ultimately, the government called in a statistician skilled in the art of tariff scheduling. Depending upon the article, the final rates ranged from 0 to 35 percent, most falling around the 25 percent level.

The new tariff was debated in the House of Commons from mid-March until the end of April 1879. Throughout that time, Macdonald's Conservatives repeatedly stated their commitment to a policy of permanent indirect subsidies to industry on the premise that it was impossible for manufacturing to flourish in the Canadian state under conditions of free trade. It was indeed true that some manufacturers had asserted that the tariff would have to be permanent. If such a need were valid and general, then Macdonald's innovation was truly a National Policy. But in 1879, the issues had not been examined in national development terms. At the time of its introduction, the tariff was simply good politics. Protectionism was popular with the electorate, and a "conjunction of interests" was found with manufacturers. Ben Forster has shown that wherever producers had a field entirely to themselves, they could obtain practically any duty they wanted. Where one manufacturer's output was another's input, compromise was necessary. Even so, such compromise was not infinitely elastic. No consideration was given to the use of the tariff or outright bans of certain imports to encourage cross-regional industrialization. There was no provision for discouraging Ontario manufacturers from importing cheap Pennsylvania steel, for example, to encourage the coal and iron industry of the Atlantic provinces. The tariff identified the interest of Canada as a whole with those of the already dominant industries in Ontario and Quebec. To a large extent, Macdonald was striving to consolidate his party by working a new field of patronage in the industrial sector. The tariff was "balanced and calculated" (in Forster's characterization). But this was more the result of the government's attempt to accommodate the conflicting interests of industrialists whose support it wished to elicit, than a rational strategy aimed at cross-regional industrial growth. As Forster admits, "The government did not perform a predictive function; it only responded to existing demands . . . ."

The same patronage theme became even clearer in Macdonald's resurrection of the Pacific Railway project. Mackenzie's approach had been piecemeal construction on the basis of public works. Contractors bid to build sections Canada owned. Macdonald's alternative was rapid construction by a subsidized private corporation. When investors did not rush to take advantage of what would appear in retrospect to have been more than generous support from the government, one syndicate particularly close to Macdonald personally, a group led by the president of the Bank of Montreal, George Stephen, came forward with demands for even greater support, which the cabinet secretly accepted in the autumn of 1880.

The new terms were so extraordinary that the government had to persuade the country that Canada faced a do-or-die challenge. Macdonald's political problem was to make rapid construction regardless of cost seem like a reasonable response to a genuine emergency. The syndicate had been promised a cash subsidy roughly equivalent to the annual national revenue, i.e. $25 million; arable land approximately equal to one fifth of all such territory on the Canadian Prairies, ten million hectares; title to the three sections of railway already completed or under contract at public expense (in all, 1 200 kilometres valued at $38 million); a traffic monopoly for the rest of the century; and a perpetual exemption from taxation. In return, Stephen's syndicate agreed to build 1 000 kilometres from Port Arthur to Callender, and about 2 000 kilometres from Winnipeg to Kamloops, by May 1, 1891.

In December 1880, Macdonald brought the railway contract before Parliament thinking that he could secure ratification before the New Year. But opposition members attacked the railway scheme even more vehemently than they had opposed the tariff, using every argument and strategy they could imagine to persuade the government to revise the terms. The debate raged without end until the Christmas recess, resumed in January, and ran non-stop to the end of the month.

The opposition's arguments—including Edward Blake's five-hour speech—elaborated two basic propositions. One was that the contract was extravagant; the other was that the arrangement was sinister. Both objections would be assuaged if Macdonald would abandon his obsession with rapid construction, the opposition said. Critics advocated building the "prairie section as fast as settlement demands," and indefinite "postponement" of the Rocky Mountain and Lake Superior sections. The opposition argued that the slower pace would permit greater economy and obviate the need to offer the reckless inducements that Blake predicted would "ruin the public credit."

The aspects of the arrangement denounced as sinister were the size of the land grant and the implications of the monopoly. The opposition argued that the government was making the North West a fief of the recipients of its patronage, having liberated it so recently from the HBC. The new corporate master of so much of the land was also to be the exclusive carrier of the region's freight. The role of transportation monopolist was denounced the more heatedly, since Stephen and Smith were already proprietors of the rail connection between Winnipeg and the lakehead by way of Minnesota. In 1880, wheat sold in Toronto for $1.10 per bushel; transportation charges consumed about half of the price. The first third of the trip, over Stephen's already completed railway, accounted for most of the cost. Manitobans were understandably anxious to see the rail-line over Lake Superior in other hands. To their horror, the government proposed to give it to the same syndicate that owned the only alternative route east.

Western hopes that the debate in Parliament might make a difference were dashed in February 1881. None of the proposed amendments was adopted. The most important act of incorporation in the history of Canada was thus presented and debated in Parliament much like a controversial treaty negotiated with a foreign power. The measure was criticized, alternative wordings were proposed; but in the end, the contract was accepted whole. How would the electorate react? Would the resurrected railway and the new departure in tariff policy meet with the approval of the voting public?

Macdonald could not be certain; he therefore attempted to hedge his uncertainties by taking advantage of the opportunity for redistribution of electoral boundaries presented by the results of the 1881 census. Most of the provinces of Canada had shown a 17 percent increase over their 1871 population. The two exceptions were Ontario and Manitoba, which had both grown faster than the national average. Manitoba's population had grown to 62 000 in 1881 from 12 000 in 1870. Ontario's population grew from 1.6 million to just under 2 million during the same period. According to the BNA Act, Quebec was always to have 65 members of the House of Commons; the other provinces would have entitlement to Members of Parliament proportionate to their populations. If all provinces grew at the same rate, the House of Commons would always have the same number of members, and legislative reapportionment would never be necessary. But since the populations of Manitoba and Ontario had grown significantly faster than that of Quebec or of the rest of the country, both were entitled to increased representation. Ontario was now to be represented by 92, increased from 88, members, and Manitoba could expect one additional member, bringing its total to five. Its fifth riding was added to the electoral map without creating great protest. The four new constituencies of Ontario were another matter. The controversy focused on how many of the old electoral boundaries would have to be redrawn to accommodate the new. In 1882, all 88 of the old constituencies ceased to exist, and 92 new electoral districts were created to accommodate Ontario's right to four additional seats in the House of Commons. In Parliament, Macdonald said this was to assure that each constituency was approximately equal in population. In private, he did not hesitate to admit that the purpose of redistribution was to "hive the Grits," since electoral boundaries were run to make each Conservative vote count for more, every expected Liberal vote a bit less.

Where the tariff had generated a debate, and the railway contract nearly a filibuster, Macdonald's Redistribution Act precipitated what P.B. Waite has described as a "sustained howl." Although the measure affected Ontario most particularly, other provinces joined in the protest with nearly equal indignation. In the end, Macdonald was perhaps outdone by his own cleverness because once the ballots were counted (and there were ballots, thanks to Mackenzie's reforms of electoral practices), it was discovered that Macdonald's party had done less well in 1882 than in 1878. Even so, the Conservatives did win an overall majority—even from Ontario. Macdonald had spent his last mandate translating the image of a National Policy into the two realities of tariff protection and intended railway construction. Public opinion seemed to approve. The electorate must have known by 1882 that the tariff would mean higher prices, and that the CPR would require a mounting national debt. But both inflationary policies had given a boost to the economy when slow growth and deflation were the twin woes of politicians. In the apparent prosperity that followed tariff protection and national mobilization for the construction of the CPR, Canadians may have glimpsed a vision of the nation Macdonald and his supporters claimed they were building; but they also doubtless perceived a tangible benefit in the form of higher profits, steadier employment, and a faster pace of economic and population growth than would have been the case with lower government spending and freer trade.

— 2. Mobilization for the CPR —

If the CPR's launching resembled a mobilization for national emergency, the frenzied construction that followed was the appropriate continuation. Four-hundred-and-forty kilometres of track were laid in 1881. William Cornelius Van Horne, an American railway builder, was recruited from his superintendency of an American railroad to fill the position of engineer-in-chief, to make the distance covered in 1882 an even 800 kilometres. He succeeded. By the end of the 1882 construction season, the crews were pushed to within 120 kilometres of Medicine Hat. They had crossed the Prairies. The other sections, one over the Rocky Mountains and the other over the north shore of Lake Superior, took several more years to complete, but not from inattention. All sections were pursued at the same frantic pace, as if in mobilization for modern war.

While noting that the Canadian railway was a national priority, it is still appropriate to remember that the CPR was the instrument of a commercial company's path to private profit. In the commercial sense, the syndicate that received the public's money looked after themselves very well indeed. Thus, the directors decided to change the common-sense choice of a route through the fertile, rolling agricultural land in the Saskatchewan River Valley in favour of a more southerly route close to the American border, through the near desert of Palliser's Triangle (see map 3.1). Since settlement was bound to follow where the railway led, the decision had dire consequences for the future of Canadian agriculture. Why, then, was the southerly route preferred? There are two reasons— both related to profits. First, they wanted their mainline close to the border in anticipation of the future competition with the Northern Pacific Railroad also under construction in the United States (through Montana bound for Seattle). The monopoly clause would run for just 20 years. After that time, the NP might have branch lines running north across the border like pickets in a fence. The greater the distance between the two mainlines, the more threatening the branches.

The other reason pertained to the CPR's status as landowner. Settlements had already begun to appear in the Saskatchewan Valley. Taking an alternative route that was uninhabited, the CPR had possession of future town sites as well as farm land where the territory was suitable for agriculture. Where the land was not "fairly fit for settlement" the railway could still take its acreage from the best agricultural land north of the main line, and serve settlers there with branches to be constructed later. That would mean longer hauls; but insofar as revenue was a function of the distance freight traveled before reaching the mainline, more profits were assured by the same stroke.

Such factors as the choice of route indicate that the CPR's directors were careful to assure future maximum income for themselves. In this sense, they were far-sighted, cautious managers. But for the construction phase, they were almost reckless: building without estimates and buying ready-made railways in the East to connect with Atlantic ports. Stephen knew that Macdonald's government could ill afford to see the railway languish should it fail in its attempt to recruit short-term private capital to maintain the frantic pace. Thus, Van Horne would boast one day that he "never estimated the cost of any work," and Stephen would return unblushing for more government subsidies, loans, or dividend guarantees the

Map 3.1: Route of the CPR

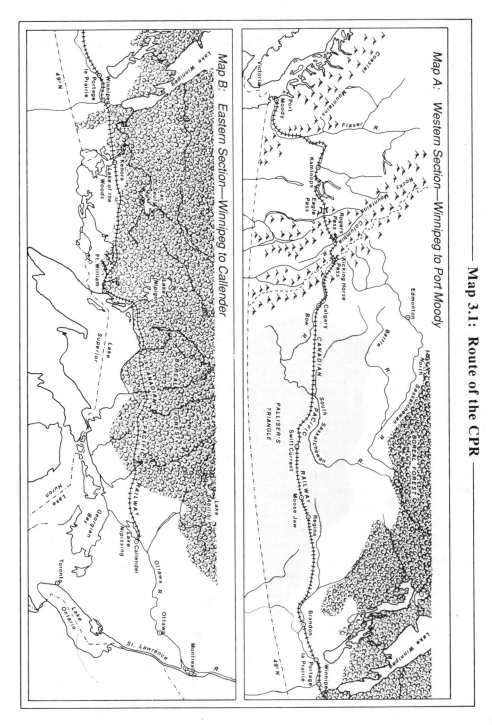

Map A: Western Section—Winnipeg to Port Moody

Map B: Eastern Section—Winnipeg to Callender

next. By 1884, the CPR was demanding $30 million over contract. Rather than declare the railway forfeit, Macdonald somehow found $23 million. But a year later, Stephen was back demanding yet another aid package. Private capital simply would not come forward to keep pace with the frenzied construction. This time Macdonald balked.

— 3. Victory in Defeat —

Ironically, the railway and the government were saved by a crisis that ought to have been even more disturbing than the CPR's passing into receivership. On March 26, 1885, just as the railway was becoming technically bankrupt, rebellion erupted in the North West.

Over the course of the previous seven years, neglect and injury had brought three distinct populations in the West to the brink of a war of secession. The first consisted of settlers affected by the railway's change of direction far to the south. In many cases, they were angry and disappointed by frustrated land speculation. Their violence was entirely rhetorical. The actual fighting in the uprising was launched by Métis and Indians of the same vicinity.

In the early 1880s, the Native Peoples of the North West faced a period of crisis nearly as awful as the smallpox epidemics and the disappearance of the buffalo in the 1870s. The new scourge was famine, resulting from Canada's failure to keep its treaty promises. Instead of the promised assistance, the Government of Canada had responded with a policy Gerald Friesen has described as "submit or starve." Native Peoples refusing to move on to reserves received no assistance. Those who submitted to the wardship of the reserve system were starved one day and fed the next on the assumption that such prodding was the appropriate incentive to transform them into self-supporting farmers. Moreover, Canada insisted that the kind of farmer the Native Peoples must become were the individualistic, independent producers that survived in memory as the heroic pioneer-settler of eastern Canada. The Native Peoples, however, preferred to pool their resources and pursue the same mechanized agriculture of their neighbours—but on a larger scale. Sarah Carter has shown that by prohibiting the more collectivist model, Canada discouraged Native Peoples from agriculture in general.

Of course, the disappearance of the buffalo and the need for economic adjustments was felt by the Métis, as well. But they also suffered from competition with the railway because the Red River cart or York boat was no contest against box cars on rails, or even steamboats on the Saskatchewan. Moreover, about 80 percent of the Métis population of Manitoba had lost legal ground for claiming riverfront lots in their home province when the Mackenzie government amended the terms of Section 32 of the Manitoba Act. Having lost their homes in the old Red River colony, many attempted to start afresh along various rivers further west and north (see map 2.3, previous chapter). The issue that drove the Métis to war was their difficulty in obtaining assurances that they would be able to confirm title to the land to which they had retreated after leaving Manitoba.

According to Canada's homestead law, the Dominion Lands Act of 1872, a grid of 36-section townships starting at 95° W. longitude and 49° N. latitude (near the southeast border of Manitoba) was to be extended westward through the Prairies (see map 3.2). Theoretically, all even-numbered sections (except 8 and 26, the HBC reserve) were open to homestead for a $10 registration fee. Closed to settlement as free grants were odd-numbered sections of every township. Sections 11 and 19 were held back to support future schools; the rest of the odd-numbered sections were reserved for the purpose of funding railways. Such a system was complicated enough; but in practice, the situation was even more confusing to potential settlers because in most areas, during much of the 1870s and 1880s, those sections deemed open for homestead were actually unavailable. The government was constantly withdrawing huge blocks of even-numbered sections for one patronage scheme or another. The most bizarre example of this was the withdrawal of some four million hectares in 1882 for division among more than 100 Conservative Party favourites posing as "colonization" promotors. Where actual settlers did find land open for homesteads, they had to survive three years on their quarter-sections performing settlement duties that included cultivation and house construction before passing the inspection of the Department of the Interior and receiving title to the land.

From the standpoint of bureaucratic control, such a pattern of orderly survey and multiple access assured rational development and steady revenue. But from the Métis point of view, the checkerboard of imaginary townships with restricted free access was unrealistic and unjust; such a grid pattern did not take into account the course of the rivers on whose banks people traditionally took root. The Métis wanted free land in the form of the familiar riverfront lots. When they petitioned Ottawa to permit the irregularity, they were met at first with a long and indifferent silence. Thomas Flanagan has shown that the most the Government of Canada

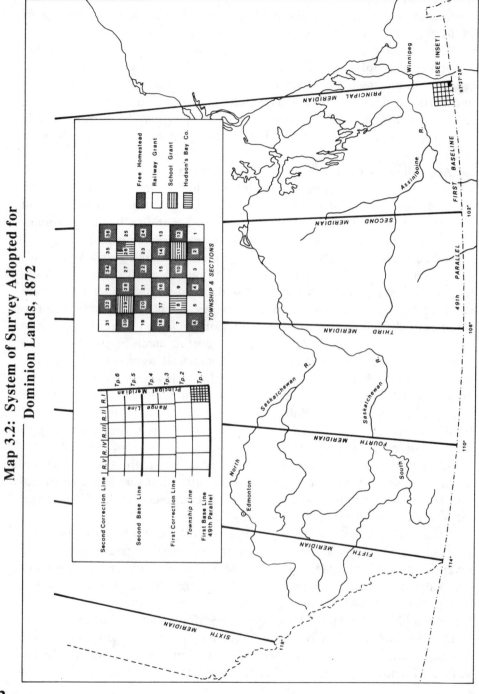

Map 3.2: System of Survey Adopted for
Dominion Lands, 1872

would concede was regular homesteads. Having suffered land-loss on such terms before in Manitoba, the Métis decided to mount another resistance. Naturally, Louis Riel seemed the appropriate choice as leader.

Since 1870, Riel had been living as a hunted villain and a haunted visionary. First, there had been no amnesty (promised during negotiations for the Manitoba Act). Instead, there was a price on his head offered by the province of Ontario. Then, after being elected on three occasions to the Canadian House of Commons by a Manitoba constituency between 1872 and 1874, Riel was refused his place in Parliament. Instead, he was offered an amnesty conditional upon his acceptance of five years' banishment. By 1884, the exile period was well passed and Riel was comfortably settled among his people in Montana. There he had married, found employment as a school teacher, and had become a citizen of the United States. In June 1884, a delegation appeared in Riel's settlement and persuaded him to return with them to lead the resistance in Saskatchewan.

With claims of his own that he hoped to advance, Riel returned and did well the work that needed doing. By March 1885, however, the Métis settlers learned that their claims for land patents were not to be recognized; Riel's claim for a personal indemnity was denied at the same time. The appropriate next step (from the standpoint of all disappointed claimants) was to proclaim independence. Louis Riel was declared president and pope on March 19. Had there been a purpose to Sir John A. Macdonald's studied neglect of the North West, it was about to be realized because the great railway soon fulfilled its first and most dramatic popular mission.

On March 23, the general officer commanding the Canadian militia, Frederick Middleton, was ordered to alert the militia from Winnipeg to Nova Scotia. Four days later, the same day Macdonald temporarily refused George Stephen's latest loan demand, skirmishing broke out between the Métis cavalry and the North West Mounted Police near Fort Carlton (see map 3.3). Then the Indians near Frog Lake rose in rebellion and troops were ordered west—by train.

In 1870, Wolseley and his men had had a terrible time getting as far as Red River. A short 15 years later, a more serious threat much further west was dealt with promptly and easily, thanks to the railway. To be sure, there were still four gaps in the line over Lake Superior, distances that had to be crossed on foot or by sleigh in the numbing cold of late winter. But in comparison with the trek led by Wolseley, Middleton's several thousand troops were whisked to the vicinity of the new disturbance. By May 15, Louis Riel had surrendered. By May 26, the last Indian resistance was

63

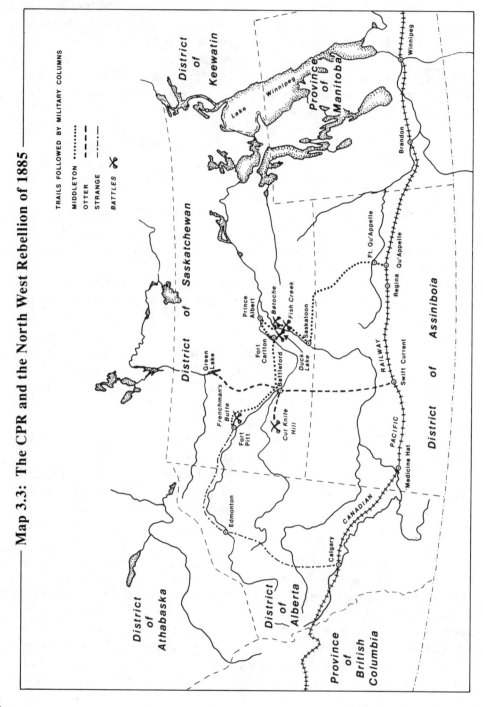

Map 3.3: The CPR and the North West Rebellion of 1885

silenced. About 100 combatants (50 on each side) had died in the fighting. The fallen Canadians were sewn in their blankets and buried at places with quaintly Western names such as Fish Creek and Batoche. The other troops went home to heroes' welcomes in Winnipeg, Toronto, Montreal, and Halifax in time to help with the 1885 harvest. In the euphoria of such speedy victory, there was no difficulty persuading Parliament and the nation that the railway was worth an additional $5 million to rush on to completion.

— 4. Reaping the Whirlwind —

With fresh government support, the CPR moved quickly to close all of the gaps in the mainline by the end of the 1885 construction season, and the two long lines of steel met in British Columbia in a last spike ceremony on November 7. To many Canadians, the completion of the railway was a momentous occasion, a great symbol of the country having been "stitched down." But while the completed railway did bring the provinces into closer physical proximity, a unity that was symbolized by the adoption of standard time zones in the same year, all of the regional diversities of the country were still painfully apparent. Indeed, they were reinvigorated by events that developed in the aftermath of the North West Rebellion as the glory of having driven the last spike for the railway was darkened by the long shadow cast by the Regina scaffold where the execution of Louis Riel occurred on November 16.

The minister responsible for Indian affairs, John A. Macdonald, had no intention of assuming responsibility for the rebellion, even though seven years of crass mismanagement (perhaps studied neglect) had magnified simple questions over land titles and treaty obligations into monumental frustrations that ultimately drove the people to armed resistance. The Government of Canada intended to put the burden of villainy entirely upon the shoulders of the rebels, and on one rebel in particular, Louis Riel.

A number of leaders were captured, but Riel was the only one charged with high treason as defined by the fourteenth-century English "Statute of Treasons." His life hung on the question of whether he did "most wickedly, maliciously, and traitorously . . . levy and make war against our said Lady the Queen." Since Riel's participation—indeed his leadership—was beyond doubt, the matter appeared settled even before the court began to hear the case. But the issue at the trial was Riel's sanity. If he was found to be insane, then the government was morally bound to pity rather than to punish him. Riel denied to the end that he was mad. He declared "humbly through the grace of God I believe I am the prophet of the new world." It delighted him that the Crown prosecutors found such declarations reasonable. His jury of six white Protestant males was not so easily persuaded. After finding Riel guilty, it recommended mercy on account of his mental state. However, the instructions from the Minister of Justice to the stipendiary magistrate trying the case were that he was bound to ignore the recommendation for clemency. Riel must hang. There were appeals, of course, and when they all failed—as they had to fail—the man who was held responsible for the rebellion paid the full price of his life on November 16.

To Ontario Protestants, Riel's execution was just punishment for two rebellions. Even if he had not been quite right in 1885, he was lucid enough in 1870 and Protestant Ontario still considered the Red River Resistance no less a rebellion than the later episode. Consequently, there were few regrets in Protestant Canada over the execution of the troublemaker who kept returning. All rebels had to be equal before the law. The Toronto *Mail*, a Conservative newspaper, asserted that the majesty of the law was even more important than the survival of Confederation.

Quebec spokesmen were quick to reply that the real motive for insisting upon the hanging was Ontario's desire to punish a Roman Catholic implicated in the murder of the Orangeman, Thomas Scott. Protestant bigotry blinded the seekers of revenge to Riel's "madness" and the jury's recommendation for clemency. Quebeckers said the man deserved pity more than punishment.

A storm of controversy divided Roman Catholics and Protestants for nearly six months in the public press, then found a new platform for debate when Parliament resumed in the spring of 1886. In the latter arena for controversy, the Prime Minister remained silent. A.G.P.R. Landry, president of the Quebec Conservative Association, moved a resolution expressing regret that Louis Riel had been executed. Macdonald did not speak against the motion. Nor did Edward Blake (leader of the Liberal party since 1880). He would not "construct a political platform out of the Regina Scaffold." Blake's default enabled another member of his party, Wilfrid Laurier, to become the rising star of the Liberals, with a speech that was poignant but not maudlin, scathing but not unseemly in its criticism. Laurier offered an indictment that hinted that the government had been playing a political game all along. "Had they taken as much pains to do right, as they have taken to punish wrong," Laurier suggested, "they never would have had an occasion to convince those people that the law cannot be violated with impunity, because the law would never have been violated at all." Laurier's thinly-veiled accusation that Macdonald had manipulated the people of the North West into an action that would give him an opportunity to dramatize the usefulness of Stephen's railway was met with silence from the Prime Minister. Macdonald said nothing, not one word to confirm or deny the charge.

Ultimately, the Landry motion was defeated. Only 52 Members of Parliament affirmed regret; 146 voted acceptance of the execution. The division was free, did not follow party lines, and therefore stood as an indication of the politicians' sentiments on the question. About one third of the Liberals voted with the Conservatives in approval of the hanging. Nearly half of the Quebec Conservatives either abstained or voted with the regretters to censure the government.

In Quebec itself, opinion was divided in similar proportions, half-approving and half-regretting. Consequently, the controversy offered an ideal opportunity for the rising politician, Honoré Mercier, to complete the work of diverting attention from hated Liberal Roman Catholicism to the more benign Roman Catholic Liberalism of Laurier, by taking Laurier's attack on Macdonald one step further and contending that French-Canadians' safety in Confederation was threatened. Mercier called for a new centrist coalition, neither Liberal nor Conservative, drawn together into a Parti national, and hammered away at his theme of the insult paid to Quebec by the judicial murder of *"notre frère"* until he and the *nationalistes* had won control of the provincial legislature early in 1887.

— 5. Disunity —

The revitalization of Quebec nationalism was consistent with a general drive towards strong provincial governments, a trend that led most people in Canada to elect provincial administrations dedicated to opposing the central government. In New Brunswick and Nova Scotia, the basis for the revolt against Ottawa was almost entirely economic. The economies of both provinces, oriented so prosperously towards shipbuilding, the fisheries, and transoceanic commerce in the 1860s, had begun to show signs of deep decline in the 20 years following Confederation. During the period of the golden age of wooden shipbuilding, 1865-69, 662 000 tonnes of shipping had been launched in British North America (compared to 626 000 in the United States or 470 000 in Great Britain during the same period). But later, between 1885 and 1890, a mere 134 000 tonnes of wooden ships were constructed in Canada. Elsewhere, shipbuilding flourished, with iron as the new material of construction. But in the Maritimes, shipbuilding simply went into decline. At Yarmouth, Nova Scotia, formerly one of the most important maritime centres of Canada, the builders and owners of wooden ships gradually shifted their capital from active promotion of shipbuilding and shipping to passive investment, mere stockholding in other lines of enterprise, frequently in other countries or other regions of Canada. Investors who did support local enterprise focused on land-based industry such as coal mining and sugar refining. In a sense, such growth was dramatic, but thousands of "saw and hatchet men" preferred to continue working in wood and moved south to become housebuilders in such places as Boston's "streetcar suburbs." By the 1880s and 1890s, one fifth of all carpenters in Boston were Nova Scotia-born. In other words, people were being displaced from their old occupations faster than new employment was developing. As a result, populations that had grown between 15 and 20 percent per decade in Nova Scotia and New Brunswick in the 1850s and 1860s, shrank to nil or minus rates in the 1880s. Unable to aim enough alternative industry at the Canadian market, the once prospering Maritimes appeared to be economic backwaters and demographic railway stations, the most valuable export becoming the population itself.

W.S. Fielding, the Premier of Nova Scotia, blamed Confederation for the disturbing trend, and argued that free-trade with the United States was preferable to the kind of protection provided by Canada. In 1886, he moved his legislature to agree "that the financial and commercial interests of the people of Nova Scotia, New Brunswick, and Prince Edward Island would be advanced by these Provinces withdrawing from the Canadian Federation and uniting under one Government . . . ." He then went to the people for support in an election, and they gave him 29 of the 39 seats in the Assembly. Subsequently, the idea of Maritime Union for free trade died away; however much his critics legitimately complained that the manoeuvre was simply a cynical ploy in the first place, the fact remained that an anti-Canadian sentiment did have great appeal in Atlantic Canada in 1886, just as in 1867.

Ironically, the central government that was criticized for serving "Empire Ontario" at the expense of the others was only slightly less criticized by Ontario's provincial administration, led by Oliver Mowat since 1872. Indeed, Mowat is generally considered the "father of the provincial rights movement in Canada" since he had been quarreling with Macdonald long before Fielding or Mercier. In Mowat's case, however, the primary object was consolidation of an already strong economic position by confirming coordinate power with Ottawa. Mowat had no quarrel with the National Policy as long as it continued to work to his province's advantage. What Mowat did oppose—and mightily—was Macdonald's wish to whittle down the provinces in the course of building "Empire Canada." To defend Ontario's predominance, Mowat went to court repeatedly, seeking judicial support for his own understanding of the division of powers. The turning point in the process involved an apparently trivial point of law arising from the licensing of taverns.

According to John A. Macdonald's theory of Confederation, the powers of the provinces and the central government fell into two neat compartments. Section 91 of the BNA Act gave the government in Ottawa authority "to make Laws for the Peace, Order and Good Government of Canada." For "greater Certainty, but not so as to restrict the Generality" of this overarching power, 28 illustrations of such areas of activity were enumerated. What remained for the provinces was a far less impressive list of "subjects" of a "merely local or private nature," such as "shop, Tavern . . . and other Licences in order to the raising of a revenue" enumerated in Section 92. In Macdonald's theory, Mowat could seek the enactment of a provincial statute, a kind of municipal by-law, requiring tavern owners to pay a fee to operate in his province. The power Mowat could not exercise, in Macdonald's view, was the regulation of commerce under the guise of raising a revenue.

The theory of Oliver Mowat and other proponents of provincial power was that the words of Sections 91 and 92 actually placed legislative powers in three compartments. The first consisted of 28 powers belonging exclusively to the government in Ottawa, the enumerated powers in Section 91. The second compartment was the list of 16 classes of legislation assigned exclusively to the provinces in Section 92. The third compartment was the "Peace, Order and Good Government" preamble to Section 91, words that Macdonald took as his sanction for unrestricted generality. But for Mowat, the general power was simply a 29th subject—national emergencies.

Tavern licensing became a prime point of conflict because Ontario set regulations for such premises at the same time that a fee was collected and the license awarded. John A. Macdonald and a hotel keeper named Archibald Hodge perceived the legislation as a dangerous encroachment on federal jurisdiction. Hodge paid his license fee, but insisted upon waiting for a statute from Ottawa before he would see himself in any way restricted with respect to his hours of operation. In May 1881, because he allowed his billiard-playing patrons to continue at their pool tables after the 7 p.m. Saturday closing hour set by the Ontario statute, Hodge was prosecuted for a breach of the Ontario Liquor License Act. Subsequently, he appealed his conviction all the way to the Judicial Committee of the Privy Council of Great Britain, and there the British Law Lords ruled in favour of Ontario in 1883. In their view, the legislation was "entirely local in its character and operation," and they agreed that it was intended primarily to raise a revenue through the licensing function. The Law Lords might have severed the regulatory aspect of the licensing act from the rest of the statute, and struck down the one part leaving the other, but they did not. Instead, they accepted the whole and confirmed Oliver Mowat's favourite doctrine of co-ordinate power:

> When the British North America Act enacted that there should be a legislature for Ontario and that its Legislative Assembly should have exclusive authority to make laws for the province, and for provincial purposes in relation to the matters enumerated in S. 92, it conferred powers not in any sense to be exercised by delegation, [according to Lord Fitzgerald,] but authority as plenary and as ample within the limits prescribed by S. 92, as the Imperial Parliament, in the plenitude of its power, possessed and could bestow. Within these limits of subjects and areas the local legislature is supreme, and has the same authority as the Imperial Parliament of the Dominion . . . . (Quoted in G.F.G. Stanley, *Short History of the Canadian Constitution* [1969], pp. 119-120.)

Later, after the Government of Canada argued in another case that the regulation of liquor traffic had to be considered a matter relating to the "Peace, Order and Good Government of Canada," the Law Lords once again ruled in favour of Ontario in 1896. This time, Lord Watson extended the doctrine of coordinate power even further than Lord Fitzgerald had done in 1883, saying "the Dominion Parliament has no authority to encroach upon any class of subjects which is exclusively assigned to provincial legislatures by section 92 . . . . " Placing the peace, order, and good government clause in a third compartment, Watson asserted that

> If it were conceded that the Parliament of Canada has authority to make laws applicable to the whole Dominion in relation to matters which, in each province, are substantially of local or private interest, upon the

assumption that these matters also concern peace, order and good government of the Dominion, there is hardly a subject enumerated in section 92
upon which it might not legislate, to the exclusion of the provincial leglisla-
tures. (Quoted in G.F.G. Stanley, *Short History of the Canadian Constitution*
[1969], pp. 120-121.)

In this way, Macdonald's original theory of Confederation, indeed his
hope of what the union might become, had been defeated by the country's
most powerful local premier. Since the tide of centralization had obvious-
ly begun to turn in the constitutional sense as early as 1883, and politically after 1885, the dissenting premiers thought that they might join forces
in 1887 to establish the principle of coordinate power even more broadly
than the Law Lords had recently allowed. They and their fellow dissenters gathered on the 20th anniversary of Confederation for a second
Quebec conference (in October 1887) to formulate resolutions affirming
an even more robust array of provincial powers. Most notably, they
demanded a greater share of the national revenue and abandonment of
Ottawa's free use of the disallowance power in Section 90 of the BNA
Act. Predictably, Macdonald denounced the resolutions of the first
premiers' conference as the emanations of a mere party gathering. After
all, only one of the attending premiers was from Macdonald's own party.
Still, the fact remained that with only Prince Edward Island and British
Columbia prepared to stand by Macdonald's conception of Confederation, and with five of the most populous provinces having declared
against him, a truly remarkable protest against centralism had been made.
    What did the electorate prefer? In Nova Scotia (the province that
approved Fielding's separatist resolution overwhelmingly in June 1886),
the voters cast their ballots overwhelmingly in support of Macdonald's
party in the federal election of February 1887. Nova Scotia was not
unusual in its apparently divided loyalties. All other provinces that had
sent a dissenting premier to the Quebec conference had exhibited the
same tendency to prefer Macdonald's centralizing Conservatives to
govern Canada, even though they were just as clear in their preference for
retaining outspoken provincial power advocates locally. It was contradictory and from the politicians' perspectives even perverse, but the pattern
was rational when interpreted as the proof that Canadians wanted a clear
national as well as a salient regional identification. They wanted a strong
country; but at the same time, they were determined to prolong the
vitality of each provincial jurisdiction.

— 6. The End of an Era —

The issue of the kind of country Canadians wanted was placed in a different context in 1891 when the general election of that year developed as a plebiscite on economic nationalism versus continentalism. The Liberals, led by Wilfrid Laurier (since 1887), advocated abandonment of the protective tariff in favour of unrestricted reciprocity with the United States, a retreat not inconsistent with the provincial autonomy position advocated by most premiers. But Macdonald asserted that reciprocity would threaten the provinces by jeopardizing the overall economy. Some Ontario Liberals agreed that free trade with the Americans was essentially economic union, a first step towards political annexation, as did Laurier's predecessor in the Liberal leadership, Edward Blake, who observed with a certain philosophical detachment that "political union with the United States, though becoming more probable, is by no means our ideal, or as yet our inevitable future," and refused to support his party's policy accordingly. Others asserted that free trade had nothing to do with political independence, but they were confounded by the Conservatives who stressed that, at the minimum, reciprocity with the United States was at least a reduction of the tie to Great Britain. Appealing to the old flag and the old allegiance, they argued that the continuation of the tariff was indispensable for the survival of Canada as a "British" country. The election was close, but Macdonald's Conservatives were once more victorious.

Even so, the last battle of the old champion of national consolidation was a Pyrrhic victory since the 76-year-old Prime Minister began to suffer a series of paralytic strokes within weeks of the 1891 election. On the evening of Saturday, June 6, Sir John A. Macdonald died with no Conservative ready to replace him. Macdonald's death was thus a crisis for his party, but also for the country. More than any other single person or project, it was the force of Macdonald's amiable personality and his brilliant use of patronage that had secured the union of diverse provinces in the first instance, and subsequently promoted their consolidation. The man who in a sense made Canada was mortal; so also perhaps was his creation.

The first to suffer the predictable effects of Macdonald's demise were the leaderless Conservatives who subsequently drifted towards a dangerously militant Ontario Protestantism that Macdonald had struggled to dampen to keep the Roman Catholic vote. Two years before his death, in March 1889, an Ontario MP moved that the power of the Dominion should be used to disallow a recent provincial statute of Quebec, inimical because it set a precedent for intervention by an authority unknown to the British Crown. The law in question was the Jesuits' Estates Act which called for a papal division of $400 000 among various religious orders in consideration of Jesuit property lost at the time of the cession of New France to Britain. To ultra-Protestants, the measure appeared to be a kind of repeal of the Conquest itself. But after several days of debate, the motion to disallow the Jesuits' Estates Act was defeated 188 votes to 13, 12 of which represented Ontario constituencies.

Here the matter might have remained, but the Toronto Mail editorialized that "the abandonment of Quebec to the Ultramontane and the Jesuit will be the death of Canadian nationality . . . ." Having struck a sensitive nerve in Ontario, a nerve that the "Noble Thirteen" Members of Parliament had failed to arouse in the House, their most eloquent spokesman, D'Alton McCarthy, then found himself leading an appeal to the people. An Equal Rights Association was formed in Toronto in June 1889 demanding parity for all religious denominations and special privileges for none: an old slogan in Ontario, and a liberal-democratic doctrine that sounded lofty in principle. In this case, however, democracy meant repression of minorities on a national scale. First, it involved withdrawal of the long-established public support to Roman Catholic schools in most provinces and the Territories, then withdrawal of the customary toleration that was sometimes accorded the French language outside Quebec in New Brunswick, Ottawa, and most recently, by statute, in the West. Ultimately, equal rights would have to mean utilization of Dominion power to coerce the provinces because, eventually, French-speaking Canadians would seek refuge in a militantly defensive Quebec. There, at the last ditch, they would outnumber English-speaking Protestants, and by the same doctrine of majority rule, the French-Canadians would tell the English to attend schools and speak the language that accorded with the majority in Quebec. But since Ottawa could claim that the French-speaking people of Quebec were part of the wider Canadian minority, in this sense not a majority at all, they might say, in McCarthy's words: "No. This is a nation, the provinces have great powers for local government, but all these must be subject to unwritten laws which must regulate the whole Dominion." What McCarthy meant was that Canada had to become one centralized British state. Except for his dogmatic position on the Jesuits' Estates question, it should be clear why McCarthy was in other respects a thoroughly orthodox Conservative, why he was at one time thought to be a likely successor to Macdonald.

Since McCarthy had made himself obnoxious to Quebec by his position on minority rights, the person to whom the Tory leadership passed, after an interregnum presided over by J.J.C. Abbott (who admitted that "I am here because I am not particularly obnoxious to anybody"), was Sir John Thompson, a lapsed Methodist and convert to Roman Catholicism. Acutely aware that he was the first Roman Catholic Prime Minister in Canada, and that every Protestant in the country (especially those in the Orange Lodge) would be watching for signs that he was favouring his co-religionists, Thompson was careful to avoid the appearance of doing so.

Thompson's timidity led to rigidity in adherence to convenient principles. Where McCarthy had favoured disallowance of the Jesuits' Estates Act because it was "offensive" to the character of the rest of Canada and threatened national unity by its exceptionalism, Thompson supported tolerance because matters of religion and education, indeed, language, were all local and within provincial jurisdiction. Consequently, when Manitoba acted more boldly than Quebec to resolve its own inheritance of tangled linguistic and educational concerns, Thompson and McCarthy found themselves on the same side of non-interference with the provincial legislation. The problem was complicated, however, by the differences between the Manitoba and Quebec initiatives. The Jesuits' Estates Act of 1888 was positive and clearly within Quebec's constitutional power: no one's rights were diminished, and the act could still come into effect even without the papal arbitration aspect (if that novelty were somehow beyond the provincial constitution). In the Manitoba case, however, rights were emphatically denied, and to institute its language and schools legislation, the province of Manitoba had to amend a statute of Great Britain to make its denials. In 1890, the government of Manitoba made English the sole language of record and debate (denying status to French), and declared that henceforth all public schools would be non-denominational institutions using English as the sole language of instruction (here denying status to French as well as the various church bodies administering the public schools sanctioned by the Manitoba Act of 1870, confirmed by Imperial statute in 1871).

Since Thompson's position was that it was not for Canada to interfere, the aggrieved minority was forced to seek relief from the courts. Ultimately, in 1979, the Supreme Court did overturn the language law. But in the 1890s, the first case heard concerned schools, and turned on the question of their character at the time of the union with Canada: the court ruled that there were no "public" schools in 1870 because they were supported by private donations entirely, and therefore not protected by Section 93 (1) of the British North America Act and Section 22 (1) of the Manitoba Act (see Appendix IIA).

After the question was decided in 1892, the only remedy short of parliamentary coercion was the right of appeals to the "Governor General in Council" for relief in cases "affecting any right or privilege of the Protestant or Roman Catholic minority." The plaintiffs made their appeal. But Thompson still refused to act. Then he died suddenly in 1894, and was succeeded by Mackenzie Bowell, former Grand Master of the Orange Order. After two years of his failure to persuade Manitoba to change the law, the leadership passed to Charles Tupper. By 1896, however, the situation was so far out of hand that even the most pragmatic approach was bound to be almost hopeless. By this time, the only resort for the embattled minority was to appeal to Canada to act on the unused provision of Section 93 (4) which permitted Parliament to enact "remedial laws" to preserve "any right or privilege of the Protestant or Roman Catholic minority in relation to education." The courts had established that much: the Manitoba School Act of 1890 had affected denominational schools, and the central government did have the right to overturn such provincial legislation by overriding federal legislation. But intervention was sure to antagonize the Protestant majority across Canada and arouse a fresh crisis in Dominion-provincial relations. Even so, continuing to withhold the remedial bill would confirm Quebec's worst fear that they had no future beyond their own province.

It was against the background of the Manitoba Schools question that the next general election occurred. After nearly 20 years in power, the Conservatives were vulnerable to defeat.

Suggested Reading

General histories that cover the politics of the period from Macdonald's return to power to his death and the subsequent disarray of the Conservative Party are P.B. Waite, *Canada, 1874-1896: Arduous Destiny* (1971), and, from the perspective of the development of the West, *The Canadian Prairies: A History* (1984), by Gerald Friesen. A general business history addressing the leading policy initiatives of the period is Michael Bliss, *Northern Enterprise: Five Centuries of Canadian Business* (1987). More detailed treatment of the implementation of the tariff is found in Ben Forster, *A Conjunction of Interests: Business Politics and Tariffs* (1986).

For specialized studies of the railway, readers might enjoy Pierre Berton's second volume on the CPR, *The Last Spike* (1971). The other railway citations in the bibliography to the previous chapter are also appropriate, but additional works are recommended to readers interested in criticism of the implications of the CPR's contract approved by Parliament in 1881, the route choice in the same period, and the company's enormous power then and later. One is the harshly critical book by Robert Chodos, *The CPR: A Century of Corporate Welfare* (1973); another is Chester Martin's critique of the impact of the railway on settlement in *"Dominion Lands" Policy* (1973); a third is the balanced general work, *The History of the Canadian Pacific Railway* (1977), by W. Kaye Lamb.

The building of the railway is closely associated with the dislocation of native people and the North West Rebellion in 1885. Berton's book offers a colourful overview of that crisis. More analytical accounts are found in Thomas Flanagan, *Riel and the Rebellion 1885 Reconsidered* (1983), and D.N. Sprague, *Canada and the Métis, 1869-1885* (1988). Where Flanagan offers a vindication of government policy, Sprague makes an indictment. Readers interested in the military aspects of the rebellion should read Desmond Morton, *The Last War Drum: The North West Campaign of 1885* (1972), Bob Beal and Rod Macleod, *Prairie Fire: The 1885 North West Rebellion* (1984), and Walter Hildebrandt, *The Battle of Batoche: British Small Warfare and the Entrenched Métis* (1985).

Another body of literature concerning the native people of the North West is new material that focuses on individuals besides Riel and events other than the military action. For example, George Woodcock has published a biography of *Gabriel Dumont* (1975). The book's subtitle, *The Métis Chief and His Lost World*, reveals Woodcock's belief that Dumont was in many respects a more important leader than Riel. Other works tending to shift the focus from the rebellion theme are D.J. Hall, "The Half Breed Claims Commission," *Alberta History* (1977), and Doug Owram, *Promise of Eden* (1980), particularly the chapter entitled "Disillusionment: Regional Discontent in the 1880s." Sarah Carter's work on Indian agriculture appears in "Two Acres and a Cow: 'Peasant' Farming for the Indians of the Northwest, 1889-97," *CHR* (1989).

A number of recent works shed light on the revolt of the eastern provinces in the 1880s. Quebec's position is covered briefly but clearly in A.I. Silver, *The French Canadian Idea of Confederation, 1867-1900*

(1982), and by Susan Mann Trofimenkoff in *The Dream of Nation: A Social and Intellectual History of Quebec* (1982).

The economic background to the revolt of the Maritime provinces is found in C.K. Harley, "On the Persistence of Old Techniques: The Case of North American Wooden Shipbuilding," *Journal of Economic History* (1973), and in David Alexander and Gerry Panting, "The Mercantile Fleet and its Owners: Yarmouth, Nova Scotia, 1840-1889," *Acadiensis* (1978). The struggle to develop a different economy has been analysed by T.W. Acheson, "The Maritimes and 'Empire Canada'" in D.J. Bercuson, ed., *Canada and the Burden of Unity* (1977), and also in Acheson's "The National Policy and the Industrialization of the Maritimes, 1880-1900," *Acadiensis* (1972). The demographic response to the decline in shipbuilding is outlined by Alan A. Brookes, "Outmigration from the Maritime Provinces, 1860-1900," *Acadiensis* (1976). For Fielding's political response, see C. Bruce Fergusson, *The Mantle of Howe* (1970).

Oliver Mowat's revolt against Macdonald's centralist aims is described by Christopher Armstrong, "The Mowat Heritage in Federal-Provincial Relations," in Donald Swainson, ed., *Oliver Mowat's Ontario* (1972), and Armstrong's book-length study, *The Politics of Federalism: Ontario's Relations with the Federal Government, 1867-1942* (1981). The more technical legal aspects of the conflicting interpretations of the BNA Act are summarized for the general reader in G.F.G. Stanley, *A Short History of the Canadian Constitution* (1969). Readers interested in more detail, particularly concerning the opinions of the British Law Lords on specific cases, should consult G.P. Browne, *The Judicial Committee and the British North America Act* (1967).

The special case of the Manitoba Schools question is introduced by Lovell Clark, ed., in *The Manitoba Schools Question* (1969), and rebutted by J.R. Miller, "D'Alton McCarthy, Equal Rights, and the Origins of the Manitoba Schools Question," *CHR* (1973).

**La Tuque Pulp Company,
La Tuque, Quebec, ca. 1916.**

SOURCE: LEONARD DAVIS COLLECTION/NATIONAL ARCHIVES OF CANADA/PA-110909

*"Almost overnight, Canada emerged as the
world's leading exporter of wood pulp."*

CHAPTER 4
VISIONS OF CONTINUITY AND FULFILLMENT, 1897-1911

— 1. Laurier—A Politician Like Macdonald —

The election of 1896 might have marked a decisive turning point in Canadian politics; after an eternity in the wilderness (only five years in office since Confederation), the Liberals defeated the Tories and stayed in power for the next 15 years. But the succession was primarily a change in names, rather than of policies or even of styles of leadership. Both themes were first evident in the election that marked the shift in dynasties.

The primary issue in the contest of 1896 was the Manitoba Schools Question, in the handling of which both parties seemed clear imitations of the Macdonald tradition in politics. At the last minute, the Conservatives backed a Remedial Bill purporting to restore minority educational rights in Manitoba, forced Parliament to debate the measure in day and night sittings, then withdrew the proposal and went to the people. Consequently, during the campaign, they were able to treat the unpassed Remedial Bill as a possibility rather than as an accomplished fact. Individual Conservative candidates could tailor the party's intentions to local preferences.

The Liberals' handling of the awkward problem was to refer to one of Aesop's fables in which the warming sun is more effective than the blustering cold in compelling a traveler to shed his defence of a heavy overcoat. With reference to the possibility of the Tories' coercion of the Manitoba premier, Laurier said the Conservatives were "very windy. They have blown and raged and threatened, but the more they have threatened and raged and blown, the more that man Greenway has stuck to his coat." Naturally, Laurier's glib affability did not please everyone. The Roman Catholic hierarchy and the ultramontanes in Quebec were especially antagonistic to his apparent weakness on the principle of confessional schools. They preferred Tupper's belated but strongly worded Remedial Bill. Of course, public endorsement by the ultramontanes jeopardized Conservatives in Protestant Canada, but many voters in Ontario and most of the Manitoba electorate were certain that the Tories would drop coercion as soon as they were returned safely to power. A majority of Manitobans voted Tory. Elsewhere, Canadians tended to prefer the more straightforward solution of Laurier.

Shortly after the election, the new Prime Minister did persuade the Manitoba premier to compromise. An urban school with a linguistic or religious minority of 40, and a rural school with a minority of 25, could have bilingual instruction and one-half hour of daily catechism. Moreover, the Laurier-Greenway compromise did not reopen the antagonism of the issue locally. In the next general election, that of 1900, Manitobans joined the rest of the country in the renewal of the Liberals' mandate, so pleased were they with the wily arts of Macdonald pragmatism reaffirmed and continued by Wilfrid Laurier.

— 2. Continuing Macdonald's National Policy —

Essential continuity rather than abrupt change was to be seen in matters of policy as well as political style. With respect to the tariff, for example, such continuity was doubly remarkable because Laurier had been a convinced free-trader until 1891. In 1896, the Liberals were conspicuously silent on the matter; but once in power, the issue had to become a matter of declared intention. Expediency dictated retention of the tariff. The high tariff was retained. The first budget treated the country to a schedule of duties essentially the same as Macdonald's. As a gesture towards farmers there were some token reductions on their machinery. And as a nod in the direction of the free-trade past, a second column of reduced duties applied to countries willing to reciprocate. Basically, however, the structure was to remain as Macdonald's government had left it—as a 35 percent sales tax on consumer imports.

Although the tariff was the central feature of Macdonald's advertised strategy for national development, more broadly construed, the National Policy involved federal subsidies to create an east-west transportation network as well as federal control of Prairie lands to insure unimpeded settlement of the West. Both additional policies were elaborated by Laurier's government along lines that were consistent with long-established Tory policy. In the promotion of railways, an arrangement was struck with the CPR in 1897 whereby the Government of Canada agreed to pay one third of the cost of constructing a more southerly route through the Rocky Mountains by way of Crow's Nest Pass, giving the company access to its rich mineral lands in the Kootenay range, developed in the new century by the CPR mining subsidiary, COMINCO. In return, the railway agreed to cheaper rates for moving certain freight to and from the Prairies. The CPR promised a 19 percent discount on the cost of moving cereal crops east and lower rates on building materials or agricultural machinery shipped west.

In land settlement, the new Minister of the Interior, Clifford Sifton, worked more aggressively than any of his predecessors to develop the West in accordance with a policy that put speed of development ahead of any other considerations. Millions of hectares reserved for railways and Indians were taken back and opened for homestead, and newcomers were actively recruited through paid agents, attractive "colonization rates" for traveling expenses, and reduced administrative complications in the procedures for entering homestead entries and patents.

Almost immediately, the old policies pursued with renewed vigour seemed to pay large benefits long withheld. The great depression that had begun in 1873 (abating only briefly between 1879 and 1883), showed unmistakable signs of lifting completely in the late 1890s. Naturally, the development was a prosperity for which the new Prime Minister and his newly oriented party were only too happy to take full credit.

Several other factors explain the surge of growth. First, an infusion of gold from newly opened mines in South Africa, in large enough volume to cause inflation on a global scale, made the price of Canadian staples rise. Between 1896 and 1914, the index of staple-commodity prices rose 32 percent. Food stuffs—particularly grains—nearly doubled in price, in the latter case because of the increasingly urban setting of Europe's population and a relative decline in European food production.

Another factor contributing to the boom was technological change that invited Canadians to exploit completely new staples. There were innovations in hard-rock mining, for instance, that reoriented Canadians to "the land God gave Cain." Previously, the Shield had been exploited as a source of fur or was simply by-passed as an obstacle to agriculture. In the new century, Canada's mantle of Pre-Cambrian rock became a treasure-trove of minerals such as nickel and silver. Other technological changes led to new uses of the same previously valueless territory. There were beginnings in hydroelectricity generation, for example; but more immediately important was the development of a technique for making paper from ground wood fibre.

Prior to the introduction of the new technology for making paper, nearly all of the world's supply was manufactured from cotton and linen rags. The old product was satisfactory in every respect but price. The new paper made from wood pulp was infinitely less durable, but proportionately cheaper. Any country with trees unsuitable for lumbering could lead in its production. For this reason, the jack-pine of the Shield and the stands of spruce replacing the white pine cut from Quebec and New Brunswick began to fall before the pulpmaker's cutters at the end of the nineteenth century, as the larger white pines had fallen to the British timber buyers in the first half of the 1800s. An industry that had not existed at the time of Confederation emerged suddenly as one of the leading sources of economic growth by 1914. In fact, no other country turned to the new staple with the same emphasis. Almost overnight, Canada emerged as the world's leading exporter of wood pulp.

As the typical use of eastern forests became timber-cutting for paper-making, the relative decline in lumbering for sawlogs in the East was more than offset by a spectacular rise in logging for that purpose in British Columbia. Great stands of douglas fir and western red cedar on the slopes of mountains rising immediately from navigable coastal water meant that capital intensive economies of scale were practicable in BC almost as soon as the railway was completed to the West Coast. A lumber industry that barely existed in 1880 expanded dramatically between 1890 and 1910. British Columbia production tripled every decade and continued that pace of development until 1920. By then, more than half of all the large sawmills in Canada were located in the country's westernmost province.

All Canadian staples, new as well as old, were bulky cargoes sold thousands of kilometres from their points of origin, and were therefore highly responsive to even slight changes in shipping charges. Another factor fueling the boom was a dramatic fall in transoceanic freight rates that accompanied the completion of the world's shift from wooden-hulled sailing vessels (leaky and requiring large crews) to the new norm in commerce, the steel-hulled "tramp steamers" (watertight and less heavily manned).

Together, all such factors created and sustained a new trade and prosperity. That, in turn, stimulated both immigration and settlement. Between 1878 and 1891, immigrants had moved into Canada at the rate of about 50 000 per year. After 1896, the rate of immigration was four times that of the earlier period, bringing almost two million people to Canada between 1897 and 1911. About half settled in cities; the others migrated to the mines and bush camps in the Shield, or to the free land on the Prairies where new farms emerged at the rate of about 30 000 per year.

The vast transfer of population west, coupled with the other factors mentioned above, resulted in spectacular growth in the output of agricultural staples, particularly wheat, and the value of the production of grain increased even more rapidly than the output of BC lumbering. In 1896, production stood at eight million bushels; over the next few years the annual yield of wheat doubled and kept expanding until it reached 232 million in the 1912 crop year. Given the new volume of freight, the CPR groaned under the burden of the annual harvest.

In the early 1880s, critics had complained that a transcontinental railway through empty territory would not generate enough revenue to pay for its axle grease. By 1899, many Canadians were saying that no number of railways was sufficient: "We want all the railways we can get," Manitobans asserted.

The more-lines-the-better meant increased convenience and cheaper rates—especially the latter. Since 1895, William Mackenzie and Donald Mann (ex-CPR contractors) had been working to improve service at reduced cost by creating a system of branch lines in Manitoba, and extending them west towards Edmonton, and east to Thunder Bay. By 1901, they had created a regional rival to the CPR, a railway they called the Canadian Northern. Moreover, since they did not have to carry the burden of an unprofitable section north of Lake Superior, they were able to cut rates significantly below the CPR's low Crow Rate and still make a profit shipping grain from the Prairies to Thunder Bay.

The success of Mackenzie and Mann's regional rival to the CPR in the west convinced the directors of the national railway's eastern competitor, the Grand Trunk, that they might spawn a second successful line in the west as well. The Grand Trunk's proposal was to build a Grand Trunk Pacific starting at Winnipeg and terminating at Prince Rupert, BC. Fearing jeopardy by the newcomer's eastern connections, Mackenzie and Mann believed that they had no choice but to seek government support to extend their Canadian Northern to Montreal.

With two regional railways aspiring for transcontinental status to rival the Canadian Pacific, Laurier paled at the thought of attempting to disappoint either. But he was just as reluctant to turn down the two firms and confront the public with a no-growth option. As a result, Laurier said yes to everyone but his closest advisors, including the Minister of Railways, A.G. Blair, who resigned over what followed: the Grand Trunk was authorized to strike out across the Prairies as the Grand Trunk Pacific, and Mackenzie and Mann won bond guarantees to build the Canadian Northern towards the Atlantic. There was more. Since the existing and proposed railways were all relatively southern, a third line, the National Transcontinental, was to be built from Moncton to Winnipeg through the northern frontier of expected mining and pulp-wood development (see map 4.1). Since Laurier disliked the idea of government ownership, once completed, the National Transcontinental was to be leased to the Grand Trunk. In this way, two firms had competed for the honour of building the one additional transcontinental that was probably needed, both received the consent they sought, and Laurier threw in one more 3 000 kilometre railway for good measure. Another interesting feature of the arrangement was that any government-subsidized construction would utilize Canadian rails to encourage the newly emerging domestic steel industry. The entire package was "National Policy" in the grand manner, a sure winner for the election coming up in 1904. Laurier's policy would be popular because it disappointed the least number of speculators, contractors, and local politicians, and was the most consistent with Laurier's own optimistic boast that Canada was "the star towards which all men who love progress and freedom shall come for the next hundred years." He proclaimed his optimism with such convincing amiability that one Toronto newspaper recognized just how completely he had "that strange and mysterious gift, which Sir John Macdonald possessed in almost equal degree." Like his predecessor, Laurier appreciated that economic nationalism was the one issue on which Canadians could almost always be expected to rally. Under Macdonald, the National Policy was partisan. Under Laurier, it became a hallowed tradition.

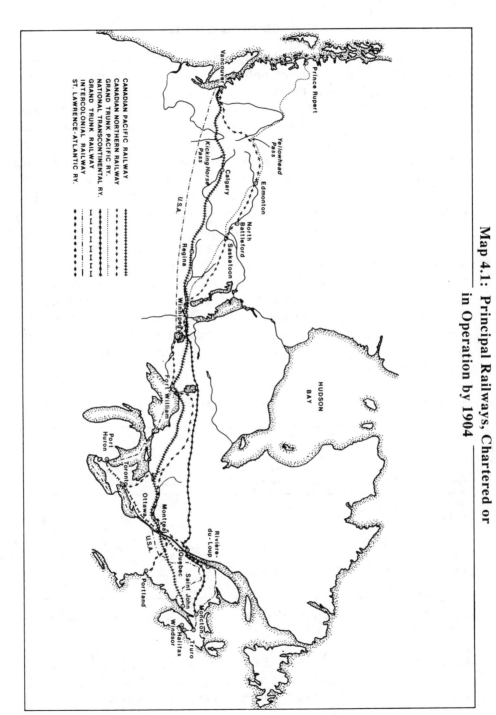

Map 4.1: Principal Railways, Chartered or in Operation by 1904

— 3. Economic Change —

Although there was more continuity than change in the transition from Tory to Liberal development policies, few persons complained. The policies were believed to be producing novel results; the economic changes between 1890 and 1910 seemed to mark a clear break from the past. The country was becoming more urban, and the development of the Prairies proceeded at a dizzy pace. Here as well, though, both phenomena masked striking continuities. Perhaps the most important was that Canada continued to be dangerously dependent upon the sale of a few staple commodities on the world market in raw or semifinished form. The wheat of the West, accounting for one third of the value of Canadian exports by 1911, was only the most dramatic illustration of such dependency. Less well publicized was the continuing dependence of the "industrial" East upon agriculture exports of its own. Wood pulp, minerals, and hydroelectricity became glamour staples for central Canada in the new century; but eastern dairy products and livestock were more valuable to the overall economy in the Laurier years. Indeed, table 4.1 shows that livestock, meat, and dairy products (produced mainly in Ontario and Quebec) were actually more important in national exports than western wheat until after 1905.

Table 4.1 Value of Exports, Selected Years ($ millions, 1900 prices)

Years	Fish	Livestock Meat and Dairy Products	Forest Products	Grain	Iron Ware	Other Exports	TOTAL
1885	10.8	23.7	24.4	14.3	.5	14.2	87.9
1890	8.4	22.5	29.1	.2	.6	30.3	91.1
1895	11.8	31.0	27.3	15.9	1.1	26.2	113.3
1900	11.2	53.3	33.2	32.7	3.7	49.1	183.2
1905	9.9	55.3	35.5	23.3	5.8	61.5	191.3
1910	13.2	43.9	39.7	63.6	7.8	71.2	239.4

SOURCE: K.W. Taylor, "Statistics of Foreign Trade" in *Statistical Contributions to Canadian Economic History*, vol. 2 (1931), pp. 38-44.

Only in the last several years of the 15-year "wheat boom" did the value of the western staples surpass eastern animal and dairy products. The inescapable conclusion is that new staples and new regions emerged as sources of supply, but overall, the East continued to be the dominant agricultural region, and staples continued to dominate exports. In fact, a higher percentage of workers found employment in manufacturing and related work in 1881 than in 1901.

Why had Canada such a truncated manufacturing sector, oriented overwhelmingly to the domestic market? One explanation is that there was a fatal flaw in the values and expectations of Canadian entrepreneurship. According to R.T. Naylor, Canada suffered from a deeply entrenched tradition of merchant capitalism (an orientation to trade, activities such as merchandising, land speculation, or simple banking). Naylor thinks such a tradition biased investors against industrial capitalism (relatively higher risk, capital intensive ventures such as secondary industry). L.R. Macdonald has replied to Naylor's argument with evidence that merchant ventures demanded equal or higher fixed costs than the early forms of manufacturing: "Entry into and exit from manufacturing was not difficult," says Macdonald. But Macdonald and Naylor's other more recent critics (such as William K. Carroll) have not explained why the manufacturing sector continued to lag behind the primary or staple sector of the economy.

An altered version of the "merchants against industry" hypothesis could shift the emphasis from Naylor's point about "weak entrepreneurship" to his corollary argument concerning "industrialization by invitation." In this view, the manufacturing sector remained stunted because too many Canadians waited for foreigners to develop the economy for them; and when foreigners did invest, they did not usually develop secondary manufacturing for the world market. They tended to put their capital into one of several categories: enclave industry linked forward to manufacturing elsewhere, resource-extraction tied to the vertical integration of foreign industry, or tariff-induced branch-plant manufacturing intended only to replace imports.

The first category of foreign investment exploited cheap Canadian labour and energy in a form of industrialization that was more closely associated with manufacturing abroad. In the case of aluminum, for example, Americans began to exploit cheap labour and hydroelectricity in Quebec in 1902 with the Northern Aluminum Company, a subsidiary of ALCOA. The output of the plant constructed at Shawinigan Falls was ingots produced from bauxite mined in the Caribbean. Such material might have been used as inputs in Canadian manufacturing and did have something of this effect. By 1910, nonferrous metal products had risen to tenth position among secondary industries in Canada. But as late as the

1980s, three quarters of the Canadian primary aluminum industry was still exported to the world in raw ingot form.

In a second kind of direct foreign investment, the product was not linked forward to Canadian secondary manufacturing at all. In the case of foreign investment in newsprint production, for example, mills were built in Canada for the sole purpose of supplying paper to the investing newspapers of the United States. Canadians enjoyed the benefit of exporting trees in the value-added form of newsprint, but the paper from such mills did not contribute to Canadian manufacturing in other respects.

In the third type of direct foreign investment, foreigners built Canadian branch plants, for one reason: to avoid the tariff. A Singer sewing machine assembled in the United States was foreign; the same machine assembled in Canada was Canadian. By 1913, according to Michael Bliss, there were more than 400 American branch-plant assembly operations located in Canada. In a sense, they produced articles that were "Made in Canada," but each sold for about 30 percent more than the United States or world price, and therefore all such products were not exportable.

In all three patterns of direct investment from abroad, the resulting manufacturing did not connect with local organic development or produce articles of secondary manufacturing for export. But none of the patterns addresses the issue of export opportunities for indigenous entrepreneurs. Where such existed they did not go unnoticed for long. According to Ian Drummond, it is "simply not true that all, or most, of the new firms in industry and mining were foreign promotions." Nor is it accurate to portray Canadian bankers as timid in their support of local entrepreneurs. It seems to follow that the industrial sector unfolded in its truncated form mainly because Canadians and foreigners found staples and branch plants the easiest route to assured profit. There were no government policies to encourage a more national or more industrial development strategy. As a result, the economy expanded—with tremendous Canadian participation— but not away from the traditional staple orientation.

— 4. Population Growth and Change —

If continuity characterized Canadian economic growth between 1890 and 1910, it would appear that change was the keynote of population patterns in the same period. In 1891, 44 percent of Canada's population lived in Ontario and 31 percent resided in Quebec. About 20 percent of the country's population lived in the Maritimes and only five percent were counted in the West. Just 20 years later, the number of Canadians living in the Atlantic region had fallen below 13 percent of the national total. Quebec's share had fallen to 27 percent, and Ontario had declined to 25 percent overall. The reason for the relative decline in the East was the rapid settlement of the West: in 1911, almost one fourth of the entire population of Canada lived west of the Ontario border, and the increase would have been even greater were it not for the effect of a fine or "head tax" imposed on each intending immigrant to British Columbia from China and Japan after Asian newcomers completed their contribution to the building of the CPR in the mid-1880s. Since a few thousand such persons still landed each year, Canada increased the discriminatory landing fee to $100 in 1990 and finally to $500 per head in 1903. The number of Asiatic immigrants arriving in 1904 became nearly negligible; but the immigration welcomed from Europe still increased British Columbia's population by more than 100 000 persons by 1911. In the same period, Ontario and the Prairies each received roughly one million newcomers, but Ontario lost almost as many persons to the West and to the United States as arrived from abroad. As a result, Ontario grew only slightly from 2.1 million to 2.5 million between 1891 and 1911. Neither Quebec nor the Maritimes attracted much of the immigrant population. Both saw a large percentage of their native-born move to the United States rather than to other provinces. Since Quebec had a higher birth rate than the Maritimes, Quebec's population increased from 1.5 to two million; the Atlantic region's remained at about one million.

The spectacular increase in the population of the West meant that the territory between Manitoba and British Columbia had to be accorded some kind of provincial status in the new century. In 1905, that promotion was granted in the form of Autonomy Bills that created Alberta and Saskatchewan with nearly the same powers as the other "partners" in Confederation. Both new provinces gained more local political autonomy and additional representation in the House of Commons and Senate. But neither Alberta nor Saskatchewan was granted control of the natural resources within the new provincial boundaries. The Crown lands in both were retained for "Dominion purposes." Retention of the public domain by the central government was one controversial aspect of the Autonomy Bills.

Another and more hotly-debated point concerned the issue of language and schools. The statute that first made provision for schools in Alberta and Saskatchewan, the North West Territories Act of 1875, required

89

denominational institutions, and the majority and minority languages of central Canada. Like early Manitoba, the Territories were to be French-speaking and Roman Catholic, as well as English-speaking and Protestant. But in the period from 1875 to 1905, emigration from Quebec (or the repatriation of French-speaking Canadians from the United States) had not proceeded as expected. Migration from Ontario, the United States, Great Britain, and from Europe (after 1896) were the central tendencies.

In part, the pattern was the result of government recruitment practices. The most actively recruited newcomers were English-speaking settlers from the United States and the British Isles. It was believed that these sources offered the highest class of immigrants because the British were British and the Americans had money. On average, American immigrants brought $500 cash and $350 worth of settlers' effects, compared with the Europeans who arrived almost penniless—only $15 cash and personal property combined. Balancing their poverty was the Europeans' willing-ness to settle on empty prairie or work for low wages. They also did not grumble about the necessity of learning English to fit into the emerging society of the West. It was for this reason (and also in order to avoid charges of seeking to depopulate French-Canada), that Clifford Sifton's Department of the Interior did little to stimulate a flow of population from Quebec to the Prairies. The principal promoter of French-speaking migra-tion to the West was the Church, but its effort to promote repatriation of compatriots from the United States was not as strong as its attempt to keep Quebeckers in their home province. As a result, the West filled rapidly with newcomers who spoke English, or who were eager to learn the language. Ironically, the factory towns of New England became less alien to migrating French-Canadians than was the Canadian West. In Manchester, New Hampshire, for example, at the largest textile mill in the world in 1900 (the Amoskeag Manufacturing Company), about one third of the labour force was French-Canadian. Ironically, there was more French spoken in New Hampshire than in the Canadian West. The largest French-speaking community west of Ontario was St. Boniface, Manitoba, with less than 4 000 people. By 1905, with the exception of small pockets of rural French-Canadians or desperately poor Métis communities, the West was effectively "British."

Predictably (given the Manitoba precedent), many Westerners ex-pected that the Autonomy Bills would erase the dualism of language and education that had been imposed originally by Dominion statute in 1875, and diluted by stages through territorial ordinances. But French-Canadians and Roman Catholics hoped to maintain at least the principle that the schools would be confessional ones and that the French language would have equality with English. When the Minister of Justice presented Autonomy Bills in accord with both principles, Clifford Sifton resigned from the government in disgust. In the resulting fury over religion and language, Laurier defended the principle of confessional schools, but ultimately had to retreat closer to Sifton's position, without getting him back in the cabinet. Thus, French lost status as an official language, and the West lost its strongest voice in the government.

— 5. Long-term Impact of the National Policy —

The larger question raised by the Autonomy Bills was the issue of the kind of country Canada was becoming. Without a moment's hesitation, the Siftons of the Dominion were prepared to affirm that Canada was British, even though the data on population migration seemed to suggest that Canada's ultimate destiny was inundation by European immigration and absorption by the United States—especially the latter. In every period between 1861 and 1900, more people left Canada than arrived. Even as the balance of net-migration shifted to positive figures, emigration still increased, and the country to which Canadians tended to go was most frequently the USA.

There are two theories that explain why so many Canadians moved south. One focuses on a phenomenon called "demand pull." In this view, Canadians were attracted to the United States because there were higher rewards offered to skilled workers in that country. They left their homeland because there was more demand for carpenters, for example, in the Boston area than in Lunenburg. The evidence that tends to support the demand-pull thesis is the predominance of skilled workers in the stream of emigrants. At the same time, however, there was a large emigration of unskilled workers from Quebec. They arrived in New England only to tend machines in textile mills or shoe factories.

The theory that accounts for the emigration trend in general is a displacement thesis which argues that the tariff insured that goods manufactured in Canada could be sold at higher prices without ensuring commensurate wage increases. By J.H. Dale's estimate, the 30-percent tariff had driven real wages in Canada about 20 percent below those offered for all types of employment in the United States. Assuming that native-born Canadians were less willing to tolerate such lower wages, it follows that the unskilled as well as the skilled moved to the United States

91

in order to take up the higher pay for equivalent work. In the fairly prosperous two decades before 1873 (and before the higher tariff, enacted in 1879 as an inducement to manufacturing to keep "our work people" from leaving), American officials recorded the entry of 345 000 immigrants from Canada. If they had not emigrated (all other factors being equal), the population of Canada in 1874 would have been about nine percent higher. In the years of rapid growth in the economy and decline in the standard of living relative to the United States, 1896-1926, more than 1.5 million Canadians became landed immigrants in that country. Had that group remained in the land of their birth, the 1926 population of Canada would have been 16 percent greater. From such a crude measure, it would appear that the tariff was not very effective as a means of keeping the population at home. According to Dales, it was a powerful inducement for Europeans to enter Canada, even though the Dominion did not attract as many immigrants as might have been the case were the standard of living comparable to the United States. Even so, the two million immigrants who arrived from Europe during the Laurier boom expected opportunities that were significantly better than what they had left behind. The displacement aspect of their arrival from Europe, according to Dales, is that far from being a "national" policy, the tariff actually operated as a kind of foreign aid program: it encouraged the native-born to leave, and the vacancies created by their departure were rapidly filled by newcomers from abroad.

The long-term effects of the tariff, according to Dales, were ironic indeed. When the accumulating consequences of national railway and Dominion Lands policies are subjected to the same closer, critical scrutiny, other ironies emerge to contradict the visions of fulfillment nurtured by surface appearances. In the case of the railways, the continuing subsidies meant that the network doubled in mileage in the decade after 1904. By 1914, 14 railway lines crossed Saskatchewan; 21 radiated from the single city of Winnipeg. By the railway criterion, Canada had become the greatest country in the world: 56 000 kilometres. But such an expanded system was more, at least 30 to 50 percent more, than the country needed.

Building, and overbuilding was a tremendous accomplishment (and boost to everyone directly involved in the construction process), but there were negative consequences that became apparent even during the boom. One was the sheer size of the liability in the commitment of so many millions of dollars to sure losers. Banks and other institutions would not have ventured such sums without government guarantees to the security of the railway bonds. By 1911, that level was nearly equivalent to the entire annual revenue of the Government of Canada: $133 million. The government guarantee meant that a significant portion of investment capital from every region went into the sure-thing of railway development, rather than risky, but ultimately more worthwhile ventures.

The region that suffered most from the capital drain was that of the Atlantic provinces. Branch banks recruited increasing levels of savings, but dramatically reduced Maritime-region loans as a percentage of Maritime-origin deposits. According to James Frost, "an enormous sum of capital was being drained away." Railways whose loans were guaranteed by the government were one of the prime attractions. Conversely, national freight-rate policy made investment locally even less attractive. T.W. Acheson has shown that the Atlantic provinces needed something like the West's Crow rate for Atlantic produce being transported by the Intercolonial Railway to central Canada. Equally important, the region needed a tariff that would deprive Ontario and Quebec manufacturers of their cheap Pennsylvania coal and steel in order to encourage these industries in Atlantic Canada. But the railway and tariff policies that prevailed discouraged the economic development of the one region most in need of government assistance for growth.

The ironic aspect of Dominion Lands development, according to contemporary critics of the Department of the Interior and Immigration Branch under the Liberals, was to be found in the homestead policy. Almost 20 million hectares of reserved lands, especially the lands handed the railways in the 1880s, were taken back and opened for settlement; the spectrum of acceptable homesteaders was broadened. Certain Tories (such as the Premier of Manitoba, Rodmond Roblin), complained that in the "frenzy" to promote western settlement as rapidly as possible, the government had flooded the country with "foreign trash." The policy was self-defeating, he said, because the West, though settled, was increasingly non-British in a "British country." Others tended to ignore the cultural dilemma and measured success of Dominion Lands policy by the simpler bushels-harvested criterion. Here fulfillment seemed unqualifiable.

Both perspectives ignored the real danger of Dominion Lands policy: its impact on timber resources. By 1896, the magnificent stands of white pine in Quebec and New Brunswick were completely cutover and the end of "merchantable" white pine was foreseeable in Ontario. Lumbermen avoided the obvious implications for the future by telling themselves that if the government reserved stump land from other exploitation and protected it from fire, the pine would regenerate naturally. Thus the first Dominion forest reserves were created early in the new century, without any limitation on logging practices and no provision for reforestation. The first surveys of old cutovers showed that without reforestation, the rate of natural regeneration was no greater than ten percent. In the old pineries of eastern Canada, spruce and balsam fir grew up instead. Pulpwood resulted.

The history of forestry in the West should have taken a different turn since the new field of scientific forestry came into existence while the vast timber resources of the Prairie provinces, the Territories, and the railway belt of BC were still Dominion Lands, held back from local control for the supposedly loftier fate of "Dominion purposes." Regrettably, there were none. The national government had learned nothing about forest management from the experience of the eastern provinces—nothing except the tradition of rewarding political friends with lucrative "timber limits." An enormous opportunity was lost. Instead of creating a model of sustained yield forestry on Dominion Lands for the older provinces to emulate, a land the size of Europe was thrown away to be shorn of its assets with absolutely no limit to exploitation or provision for future production. Dominion forest reserves reserved nothing. As with railway and tariff policy, truly far-sighted programs were not even attempted in the interest of maintaining the continuities that nurtured the illusory visions of fulfillment.

Suggested Reading

General histories that cover the subject of late nineteenth- and early twentieth-century political and economic development include *Canada, 1896-1921: A Nation Transformed* (1974), by R.C. Brown and R. Cook. A more recent general work, and one that follows a more coherent chronological principle of organization, is the first 100 pages of *Canada, 1900-1945* (1987), by Robert Bothwell, Ian Drummond, and John English. More detailed examination of the economic developments of the period are found in several of the relevant chapters of *Canada: An Economic History* (1980), by W.L. Marr and D.G. Paterson, and Michael Bliss, *Northern Enterprise: Five Centuries of Canadian Business* (1987).

The monographic literature that pertains to the emergence of particular staples is old but still worth reading. V.C. Fowke's *National Policy and the Wheat Economy* (1957), is a classic of the genre. Also useful, especially to correct the tendency to overemphasize the importance of western agriculture, is H.A. Innis, ed., *The Dairy Industry in Canada* (1937), and H.A. Innis, *Settlement and the Mining Frontier* (1936). For the rise of the pulp and paper industry to the position of dominant product of the forests, see J.A. Guthrie, *The Newsprint Paper Industry* (1941). The work that documents Canada's failure to implement a policy for sustained yield forest development in any chronological period or level of jurisdiction is R. Peter Gillis and Thomas R. Roach, *Lost Initiatives: Canada's Forest Industries, Forest Policy and Forest Conservation* (1986).

Other historians have addressed the issues of staple development and politics in particular provinces. The book by H.V. Nelles, *The Politics of Development: Forests, Mines and Hydro-Electric Power in Ontario, 1849-1941* (1974), is perhaps the best example of such work. A more controversial but similar study is Martin Robin's survey of British Columbia's resource development, *The Rush for Spoils: The Company Province, 1871-1933* (1972).

The transportation improvements that attended the boom in new staples are covered by the work on particular railways: G.R. Stevens, *Canadian National Railways*, 2 vols. (1973), and T.D. Regehr, *The Canadian Northern Railway: Pioneer Road of the Northern Prairies, 1895-1918* (1976). Provocative accounts of national railway policy appear in R. Chodos, *The CPR: A Century of Corporate Welfare* (1973), and T.D. Regehr, "Western Canada and the Burden of National Transportation Policies," in D.J. Bercuson, Ed., *Canada and the Burden of Unity* (1977).

The problem of manufacturing development, like that of unlimited railway construction, is very much tied to national policy, particularly policies that encouraged foreign ownership, immigration, and de-industrialization of the Atlantic provinces. The Maritime critique appears in T.W. Acheson, "The National Policy and the Industrialization of the Maritimes, 1880-1910," and James D. Frost, "The Nationalization of the Bank of Nova Scotia, 1880-1910," both in David Frank, ed., *Industrialization and Underdevelopment in the Maritimes, 1880-1930* (1985). R.T. Naylor's "Rise and Fall of the Third Commercial Empire of the St. Lawrence," in Gary Teeple, ed., *Capitalism and the National Question in Canada* (1972), advances the merchants against industry hypothesis; L.R. Macdonald criticizes Naylor's thesis in "Merchants against Industry: An Idea and its Origins," *CHR* (1975). More recently, William K. Carroll has joined in the same debate with *Corporate Power and Canadian Capitalism* (1986).

A work that aruges that the tariff had an early and deliberate impact on encouraging foreign manufacturing is an article by Michael Bliss, "Canadianizing American Business: The Roots of the Branch Plant," in Ian Lumsden, ed., *Close the 49th Parallel, etc.: The Americanization of*

Canada (1970). The book that focuses on the tariff and immigration is J.H. Dales, *The Protective Tariff in Canada's Development* (1966). A less technical version of Dales' thesis is found in "Protection, Immigration and Canadian Nationalism" in Peter Russell, ed., *Nationalism in Canada* (1966), or "Some Historical and Theoretical Comments on Canada's National Policies" in B. Hodgins and R. Page, *Canadian History Since Confederation: Essays and Interpretations* (1972).

**Interior of urban working-
class housing, ca. 1900-1910.**

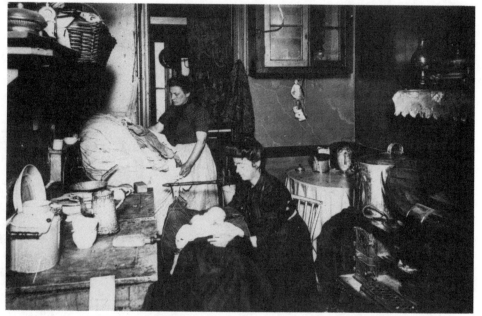

*"Middle-class, Protestant support for
temperance reform reflected the popular
assumption that poverty was largely a
self-inflicted condition."*

CHAPTER 5

SOCIAL COSTS OF URBANIZATION, 1870-1914

— 1. The Rural Ethic in an Urban Setting —

About one third of the newcomers from Europe who migrated to Canada between 1891 and 1911 settled in the cities. Here they were joined by an even larger stream of native-born Canadians on the move from rural parts of their homeland. In 1891, only 1.5 million people (or 30 percent of the population) lived in towns of even 1 000 or more persons. The rest of the population was designated rural. By 1911, 46 percent of Canada's population was counted as urban. Of course, much of the "urban" population resided in towns that were barely more than country villages. At the time, only four cities held 100 000 or more persons. The largest was Montreal with a population of 491 000. The next largest was Toronto with 382 000, then came Winnipeg with 136 000, and Vancouver in fourth place with just over 100 000. Canada's two western cities had grown phenomenally, but even the eastern metropolitan areas had doubled in size betwen 1891 and 1911. Most of the increase was by migration, especially internal migration. In the four largest cities of Canada, the foreign-born outnumbered the native-born only in Winnipeg. Montreal continued to be 80 percent native-born in the new century and although Toronto was far more attractive to immigrants, it remained overwhelmingly "British."

Since most of Canada's metropolitan residents had rural Canadian origins, what can be said about the culture or values they brought to the cities? What impact did the urban environment have on their old orientation? In simplest terms, rural life had conditioned Canadians to believe in "honest toil" and the efficacy of individual initiative for gaining a "modest competence" and social advancement. Time spent at leisure was somewhat suspect, indebtedness was considered foolish, and poverty was regarded as divine retribution for slothfulness or folly. There was a social category known as the "deserving poor" consisting mainly of widows, orphans, or other exceptional "unfortunates." But even they did not receive much sympathy, and the others were excluded from any "coddling" or inducement to comfortable idleness. In the world of rural Canada—Roman Catholic as well as Protestant—the "rough" hired man was supposed to apply his talent, budget his time, live a sober, Christian life, and accumulate a surplus to become a "respectable" farmer in his own right. The fisherman toiled and saved for his own schooner, and the apprentice was supposed to strive to gain possession of his own shop. In the pre-industrial world of independent producers, poverty was considered temporary and success was never definitive.

The metropolitan environment that emerged in places such as Montreal and Toronto by 1911 severely challenged the basic premise of the rural ethic of success through industry. Most workers were anything but independent producers. They laboured for wages in large, highly mechanized establishments, at simple tasks, dictated by the pace of the machinery. Employers were increasingly free of skilled craftsmen, and the traditional distinction between "rough" and "respectable" labour was all but obliterated. Moreover, the unskilled or barely skilled wage earners newly arrived from the farms of Canada or the fields of Europe accounted for nearly half of the overall population of Canada's largest cities. Were they, the emergent urban working class, rewarded well enough to accumulate a surplus? or was their bottom-rung position necessarily permanent for themselves and their families? That was the central question for the survival of the rural ethic in the new urban context.

— 2. Urban Poverty —

The average low-skilled worker earned about $10 per week in turn-of-the-century Montreal or Toronto. Prices were low. Food, shelter, and fuel—a bare subsistence for a family of five—cost $9.64 per week in Montreal, $9.68 in Toronto. Assuming a man worked every day of his six-day work-week (he did not suffer illness, or unemployment from seasonal or cyclical shut-down of his workplace), he was able to support a family of typical size with more than 30 cents surplus each week for extras such as clothing, entertainment, or savings.

The reality, however, was that the average worker did suffer constant interruption of his expected employment. Most firms reduced hours of operation or closed shop completely during the months of most severe winter, and every firm suffered from periodic down-turns in the business cycle. Poor sanitation, along with contaminated food, meant that one's health was equally uncertain, a fact that gave Montreal one of the highest infant mortality rates in the world: one in four of all newborn infants was not likely to survive its first year of childhood in the slums of Canada's largest city.

The central problem for the average working-class family was that the "bread winner's" earnings were not proportional to his hard work and earnest hopes for improvement. The result was that women imposed new limits on their fertility and devised ingenious supplementary income strategies. The effect of fertility limitation was a nearly 50 percent drop in the Ontario birthrate of 1911 in comparison with 1871, and a 20 percent decrease in the Quebec birthrate during the same period. Neither government nor the medical profession approved of the decline. Women exercised control of their fertility despite official discouragement. New technology provided new methods of birth control, but the condoms that became available for the first time in Canada in the early 1890s were considered unnatural paraphenalia suitable only for prostitutes and libertines. Parliament decided that the advertisement or sale of "sheaths" or any other devices "intended or represented as a means of preventing conception or causing abortion" was "obscene" and made either action an indictable offence under Section 179c of the 1892 criminal code. Consequently, women resorted to other methods of birth control such as coitus interruptus, various spermicidal kitchen concoctions, or self-induced abortion. According to Angus and Arlene McLaren, "abortion was to be of special importance" because unwelcomed pregnancy occurred so frequently. The popular solution was to regard interruption of menstruation as a symptom of potential rather than actual pregnancy. Until a mother felt definite foetal movement within her womb, she was free to regard the upset of prior menstrual regularity as something to be "put right." Various patent medicines and home remedies were used by women wishing to be "made regular." If abortion potions proved ineffective, mechanical—illegal—intervention was the last resort. More and more physicians responded by calling for the criminalization of all forms of abortion at any stage of pregnancy. They campaigned especially stridently against the idea that a woman was not truly pregnant until she felt the foetus "quickening" after the third month of pregnancy. But according to the McLarens, doctors and the clergy were "never to be totally successful in convincing women of the immorality of abortion. For many it was an essential method of fertility control." The birthrate continued to fall.

Other evidence of women's struggle to balance family resources pertains to their strategies for generating cash income to supplement the portion of wages provided by a male head of household. Taking in boarders was one common practice, so common that the census of 1911 reported that the average occupancy in single-family dwellings was six persons, while the normal family consisted of just five people. Five dollars per month was a typical charge for a boarder. That could make a real difference in reaching barest subsistence. But for a working-class family to prosper in turn-of-the-century Montreal or Toronto, more than boarder revenue was needed. Other members of the family had to enter the ranks of paid labour.

Women and children could work in domestic service and factories, at about half the wages paid to men. Still, by 1911, 20 percent of the paid labour force were women and the child component had risen to 10 percent. Not included in these figures were the number of women and children who turned the family's five-room, cold-water flat into a home workshop by day to perform the many tasks needed, for example, in the finishing of garments in the needle trades. So many, and so varied, were such attempts to enhance a family's income that one must reconsider the $10-per-week figure that was the average working man's earnings, because another $10 or $15 might be contributed by the work of other family members and boarders. On that account, it was possible for working class families to prosper by ruthless underconsumption and utilization of a whole family's labour. In effect, parents shortened their children's childhood (the years of play and preparation for adult careers), and denied the youngest family members some of the warmth and comfort of a mother working in the home. The entry of women and children into the paid labour force was not optional. According to Terry Copp, "One income was not sufficient to relieve a family from the most abject poverty" in Montreal; Michael Piva has arrived at substantially the same conclusion on the "condition of the working-class" in turn-of-the-century Toronto.

— 3. Working-Class Rebellion —

The threat of inescapable poverty created by low wages and uncertain employment meant that a significant number of workers rebelled against the rural ethic of individualism and sought security in collective action. Since the early 1880s, two different kinds of labour organizations had been attracting members in Canada—both were continent-wide developments. One, the Knights of Labor, had been organizing "all producing classes" of the United States since the late 1860s. Its principle of organization was to bring the entire working public of a particular geographical area into one united "local" rather than to organize by separate firm or job classification. Briefly, the movement showed signs of success. A spectacular victory of Knights affiliates against an American railway company in 1885 encouraged massive recruitment in Canada, especially in Ontario where 250 locals formed almost immediately. Later, more than 100 appeared in Quebec and a few others emerged on the Prairies and in the Atlantic provinces. But the successful membership drive in central Canada (embracing roughly 40 percent of Ontario's working class) did not lead to spectacular success against the "non-producers." Employers in every Knights locality continued to set wages as elsewhere. Even so, Bryan Palmer has argued that the Knights of Labor was not a failure. He thinks that the immiseration of unskilled workers was at least retarded because, in Palmer's opinion, employers had to think more carefully and act more cautiously before adopting measures likely to provoke strike action. Palmer seems to ignore that workers learned the more obvious lesson: a union was only as good as its strike results. Since their strikes almost invariably failed, one by one, the Knights of Labor locals folded. By 1900, they were virtually extinct.

The labour movement that survived the 1890s was the second form of organization, that of the "trade unions," associations of workers organized by craft such as "typographers" (one of the oldest, active since the 1850s). Normally craft unions were affiliated internationally with their counterparts in the United States. In 1883, representatives of various craft unions in Canada associated into a Trades and Labour Congress cutting across craft boundaries. But the principle of organization—and action—remained the same: skilled workers organized by trade, acting more or less independently of the national or international organization. That principle was pursued all the more emphatically after the all-encompassing-union concept seemed disproven by the failure of the Knights of Labor. The result was spectacular growth of trade unions after the turn of the century, from 400 locals in 1897 to 1 000 in 1902; 1 775 by 1914.

More and better organized unions meant more strikes— nearly 800 in Ontario and the Atlantic provinces between 1901 and 1914. Consequently, in the same period, 60 different employers' associations emerged to ensure that the odds of success would continue in their favour. In the face of a strike, the owners of industry could still rely on the traditional expedient of replacement workers protected by the power of the militia. But the increasing reliance on troops as an "aid to the civil power" (more than 20 occasions between 1900 and 1914, compared to about ten instances in the 30 years before), led business to seek more subtle control strategies.

A favourite novelty was "arbitration." The Government of Canada's Department of Labour mediated disputes on a voluntary, non-binding manner under the auspices of a Conciliation Act that had spawned the new department in 1900. Such state intervention became mandatory in certain disputes indicated by the title of the Railway Labour Disputes Act of 1903. Four years later, during an enormous strike involving Bell Telephone, the Minister of Labour gained the power to intervene in almost any other dispute as business pleased. The Industrial Disputes Investigation Act of 1907 empowered him to interrupt a strike with a "cooling off" period until a tripartite board of investigators collected the facts and made a non-binding recommendation for settlement. Paul Craven has shown that in the more than 100 cases that came under the act between 1907 and 1912, government was anything but an "impartial umpire." Indeed, the very act of interrupting the strike with arbitration proceedings was a form of strikebreaking in the sense that workers lost the power to time their withdrawal of service to maximum advantage. Moreover, there was no protection for a union from later retaliatory action by an employer—nothing to prevent companies from using the period during which striking was illegal to displace militant workers with more docile replacement employees.

To prevent strikes from arising in the first place, another control strategy of employers was a new form of paternalism: adjusting the factory environment to provide pleasant dining and toilet facilities, athletic associations, literary societies, and even complaint departments. Since the fundamental problem of low wages remained, the new paternalism, in fact, was a form of manipulative coercion, specifically intended to head off profit squeezing without resort to overt repression. Not surprisingly, *Industrial Canada*, the publication of the Canadian Manufacturers Association, urged its readers to go as far as providing their workers with improved housing, arguing that "Workmen who have comfortable homes are more efficient, contented and reliable . . . . Out of the slums stalk the Socialist with his red flag, the Union agitator with the auctioneer's voice, and the Anarchist with his torch." In advocating such amelioration of living conditions, the manufacturers' journal stressed that no humanitarian sentimentality was involved. The idea was "a cold business proposition." Employers invested vast sums to increase the efficiency of their steam-driven machines. *Industrial Canada* asked, "Why not spend a little on better housing or factory amenities to increase the efficiency of your human machines?"

— 4. Middle-Class Civic Mindedness —

Other urban Canadians posed a similar but broader question: "why not spend a little to improve the city environment as a whole?" Initially, in the 1880s, such civic-minded reformers sought merely to *purify* city life in the sense of getting rid of its most glaring aspect—poor sanitation. The logical twin of the purity crusade was a City Beautiful or Garden City movement (promoting green space, zoned development, and suburban residential expansion).

A more political reaction of the rural ethic to the urban setting was the view which seemed to recognize that the industrial city was a new kind of society demanding new forms of administration. A large number of the middle-class reformers believed that most of the evils of the new industrialism would disappear if cities were governed as model business corporations. Such transformation meant "nonpartisan" administration of municipal affairs by a Board of Control, a Commission, or a City Manager. Running a city like a business also entailed raising a revenue from the sale of a product, and expenditures of derived profits on essential social services.

The product of a "progressive city" would be the utility base. Civic reformers across the country founded the Union of Canadian Municipalities in 1901 under the leadership of O.A. Howland of Toronto with the specific mission of taking over urban transportation, water, and gas. Where utilities had an interurban aspect, such as telephone communications or hydroelectrical generation, a province might also become involved in the process of the "municipalization" of utilities. Opponents denounced such measures as "gas and water socialism" and effectively defeated the movement, for example, in Montreal. But in most Canadian cities, reformers persuaded their communities that cheap and reliable basic utilities were so essential "to induce manufacturing establishments to locate in the city" that such services could not be left in private hands. To do so would hinder the "Board of Control" from offering attractive rates to industrial newcomers. The pitch was, "Municipal ownership and industrial progress go hand in hand." Moreover, since small-scale users of the utilities were charged higher rates, a well managed municipal corporation was expected to make a "handsome profit." Incidentally, public ownership also served the public health by guaranteeing pure water, for example, as a special side benefit. Normally, however, even public health measures tended to be justified on "sound business" rather than humanitarian grounds. In Toronto, it was argued that the loss of each infant in the mortality statistics somehow cost the city $1 000, but a comprehensive public health program (including free innoculation against diptheria, etc.) cost a mere $5 per child.

— 5. Social Regeneration through Child Saving —

Cost-effective social services included more than a public health program, of course. In addition, a progressive city was expected to provide a professional uniformed police force, fire protection, and, especially, a new kind of school system. From the standpoint of typical middle-class reformers, there was nothing wrong with paying workers $10 per week. They assumed that no employer could recruit a man to work 60 hours per week if the reward were less than a "decent subsistence." It followed that such a market-determined "minimum wage for an unskilled labourer . . . might be taken as the point below which comfort ends." If there was evident hardship in the lives of the working poor, it was because they were the ones who drank too much, who frittered away precious earnings on cheap frills or course pleasures such as gambling or hiring the services of prostitutes. Consequently, one of the reformers' favourite remedies for poverty was banning the bar, because saloons were the prime meeting places for wastrels, whores, and hardened criminals. In fact, the prohibition panacea was so popular by the end of the nineteenth century that Canada held its first-ever national plebiscite on the question in 1898; and the "dry" side won by a slim majority in every province except Quebec. Consequently, the government hesitated to move on the question.

Still, the widespread middle-class, Protestant support for temperance reform reflected the popular assumption that poverty was largely a self-inflicted condition. The same suspicion was evident in the middle-class concern that the urban poor were untrustworthy parents. The main abuse was removal of children from school to exploit their labour for supplemental income. By focusing on the children, the "civic reform" movement was able to find a central purpose that promised "social regeneration" without challenging the basic premises of capitalism.

At the end of the civic reform era, W.J. Hanna outlined a formula to "launch a generation" for the Civic Improvement League of Canada. His ideal included regulation of the conditions of the employment of women to guarantee that each child had a healthy mother; regulation of the distribution of milk and water to ensure a pure supply of both of those essential commodities; town planning to guarantee access to fresh air and recreational open spaces; and the provision of compulsory graded instruction to assure each child a proper education. Since Hanna's recipe was touted as the minimum to "launch a generation," it was expected that there would be no excuse for continuing poverty after the plan's enactment except sloth or "feeblemindedness."

Much of Hanna's formula had been enacted by provincial and municipal governments in Canada between 1900 and 1910, a trend that was reflected in the rising cost of municipal government and the growth of a "tertiary" sector of the labour force. By 1907, the annual budgets of Winnipeg and Toronto were as large as that of the province in which each city was located. By 1910, the tertiary sector of the workforce, meaning the white collar and service components (admittedly, still based largely in private industry), had nevertheless grown faster than employment in manufacturing or resource development. The tertiary sector was one third of the entire labour force and reflected the rise to importance of a new middle class, perhaps the most important transformation of Canada and a shift that explains two other phenomena: first, the trust of civic reformers in managerial talent to deal with social problems; and second, the rather naive faith that there were no fundamental evils inherent in capitalism itself. The middle-class reformers did not question the notion that people were paid roughly what they were worth and that every person's employment or unemployment was an individual and private responsibility. They did promote schemes for workers' compensation covering disability by industrial accident. What they did not entertain was the idea that wages themselves should be insured against seasonal or cyclical misfortune, or that wages could be held by the state above some socially determined minimum. The rural ethic had moved to town and discovered bureaucracy, but in other respects it had remained unaltered. So also had English-speaking Canadians continued to nurture their old loyalty to Britain and the Empire, as Prime Minister Laurier discovered to his surprise and disappointment early in the new century.

Suggested Reading

General works touching on the issues of the social implications of large-scale urbanization are *Canada, 1896-1921: A Nation Transformed* (1971), by Ramsay Cook and R. Craig Brown; and, the more recent survey of *Canada, 1900-1945* (1987), by Robert Bothwell, *et al*. But the most detailed overview appears in Bryan D. Palmer's, *Working Class Experience: The Rise and Reconstitution of Canadian Labour, 1800-1980* (1983).

The condition of the urban working class is described in Terry Copp, *The Anatomy of Poverty: The Condition of the Working Class in Montreal, 1897-1929* (1974), Michael J. Piva, *The Condition of the Working Class in Toronto, 1900-1921* (1979), Eleanor Bartlett, "Real Wages and the Standard of Living in Vancouver, 1901-1929," *BC Studies* (1981), and Angus McLaren and Arlene Tigar McLaren, *The Bedroom and the State: The*

Changing Practices and Politics of Contraception and Abortion in Canada, 1880-1980 (1986). Works that analyse the Canadian working-class in contexts other than Canada's metropolitan centres are Edmund Bradwin, *The Bunkhouse Man* (1972), a reprint of his pioneering study of labour in the bush camps; Cole Harris, "Industry and the Good Life around Idaho Peak," *CHR* (1985), is a thorough study of one British Columbia mining district; and T.K. Hareven and R. Langenback, *Amoskeag: Life and Work in an American Factory City* (1978), views a large French-Canadian community in New Hampshire.

Specialized studies of the early organized rebellion of the working class include Gregory S. Kealey and Bryan Palmer, *Dreaming of What Might Be* (1982), on the Knights of Labor; and Craig Heron and Bryan Palmer, "Through the Prism of the Strike: Industrial Conflict in Southern Ontario, 1901-14," *CHR* (1977), on strikes by the craft unions in the industrial heartland of Canada.

The employers' reactions to worker organization are treated sympathetically by Michael Bliss in *A Living Profit: Studies in the Social History of Canadian Business, 1883-1911* (1974), and in his biography of *A Canadian Millionaire: The Life and Business Times of Sir Joseph Flavelle, Bart., 1858-1939* (1978). Less sympathetic is the latter half of the article by Heron and Palmer, cited above, or the book by Paul Craven, *"An Impartial Umpire": Industrial Relations and the Canadian State* (1980), which explores the partnership of the state and business to neutralize organized labour.

Two articles provide good overviews of the civic reform movement in Canada. Paul Rutherford, "'Tomorrow's Metropolis: The Urban Reform Movement in Canada, 1880-1920," is a clear account of the bureaucratic orientation of the new middle class, and John C. Weaver, "'Tomorrow's Metropolis' Revisited: A Critical Assessment of Urban Reform in Canada, 1890-1920," is useful for its characterization of the significance of municipal ownership of the urban utility base. Both articles appear in A.F.J. Artibise and G.A. Stelter, eds., *The Canadian City: Essays in Urban History* (1977). A book-length account of the civic reformers that shows how the civic purity crusade came to a focus in "child saving" is Neil Sutherland, *Children in English Canadian Society: Framing the Twentieth-Century Consensus* (1976). Other book-length accounts of urban reformers' quest for "social regeneration" include Christopher Armstrong and H.V. Nelles, *Monopoly's Moment: The Organization and Regulation of Canadian Utilities, 1830-1930* (1986); and Ramsay Cook, *The*

Regenerators: Social Criticism in Late Victorian English Canada (1985). Both emphasize ironic consequences: the regulators created structures the corporations easily "captured" for their own purposes, and the "regenerators" who sought a more relevant Protestantism fostered deeper irrelevance through greater secularization of organized religion.

**Meeting of the Alaskan
Boundary Tribunal, London, 1903.**

*"If Canada assisted Great Britain . . . it
seemed to follow that the British would be
even more helpful in assisting Canada . . . ."*

CHAPTER 6

IMPERIALISM AND THE NATIONAL POLICY, 1897-1911

— 1. The Beginning of External Affairs —

Throughout most of the nineteenth century, Canadians enjoyed a splendid exemption from the crises of the world beyond their own borders. They had little to fear outside their own continent since Canada enjoyed the security and even some of the prestige of an imperial power. Britain might have withdrawn her garrisons, but the Canadians were not totally abandoned. The late-nineteenth century was a time of British naval supremacy, and as long as the mother country maintained the fleet's ascendency, Canada would be protected by it.

Such a state of affairs was particularly attractive to Canadians because British seapower was provided entirely by the British taxpayer; Canada had no tribute to pay, only allegiance. Unfortunately, as the century drew to a close, costs escalated and the British renewed their interest in an expanding empire. The colonies, denounced as "deadweights" in the 1860s, came to be celebrated as the jewels in the imperial crown in the

1880s. Within Europe, however, Germany simultaneously began to realize industrial and imperial ambitions of its own. A particularly ambitious German naval program in the 1890s led to a countervailing expansion on the part of Britain. In the face of the costs involved, British politicians began to wonder, as in 1763, if the time had not come for colonials to contribute their mite for the defence of empire.

The issue surfaced in 1897 when colonial leaders were gathered in London to help celebrate the Diamond Jubilee of Queen Victoria. Laurier attended with other representatives of the "self-governing colonies." Together, they heard the British Colonial Secretary, Joseph Chamberlain, make three discrete suggestions. One was the creation of some "machinery of consultation" in order to discuss the "objects which we shall have in common." And, since with management there must also come responsibility, Chamberlain thought it proper to consider how the colonies might wish to apportion responsibility for such common purposes. Naturally, the second point led Chamberlain to a third "personal suggestion"—the idea that the colonies might wish to make regular cash contributions towards expansion of the British navy. On the last point, Chamberlain pointed out the benefits of British seapower for Canada in particular. He said "if Canada had not behind her today . . . the great military and naval power of Great Britain, she would have to make concessions to her neighbours . . . ." In his view, the imperial link had enabled Canada "to control all the details of her own destiny." Without imperialism, Chamberlain asserted that Canada "would still be, to a great extent, a dependent country."

Laurier politely replied that Canadians did indeed have reason to cherish and maintain their loyalty to Great Britain. However, the vastness of Canada's public works projects, for instance railways, meant that the Dominion had no surplus for military expenditure; also, the idea of an imperial federation appeared premature. "I am quite satisfied with the condition of things as they are," he said. For the moment, the British initiative was thus stalled. Since Chamberlain's suggestions had been packaged as nothing more than personal hints, and since Britain was for the moment securely at peace, the conference proceeded to a pleasant conclusion without resentment on either side.

Circumstances soon changed. In 1899, the pace of inter-imperial rivalry in Africa brought the tensions of colonial war to Canada and the other Dominions as Britain mounted an effort to defeat an uprising of the descendants of Dutch settlers in South Africa, a territory claimed by Britain and jealously regarded by Germany. Canada and the self-governing colonies were invited to participate in the defence of British interests. At first, the Canadian Prime Minister responded by pointing out that the conflict posed "no menace to Canada." He said it was a "secondary war," typical of those in which "England is always engaged." A large number of English-speaking Canadians subsequently denounced their leader's refusal as timidity and hypocrisy. What had he meant in 1897 at the imperial conference when he asserted that "We all feel pride in the British empire?" Like Chamberlain, a large number of Canadians had recently found new value in the empire, believing that Canada was developing into a strong country precisely because it was part of a larger imperial system. They perceived no contradiction between "imperialism" and "nationalism," nor were they in any sense bashful on the subject. A popular turn-of-the-century history of Canada by Sir Charles G.D. Roberts had claimed that "a good Canadian Nationalist must be a good Imperialist." He and other such nationalists protested so loudly against Laurier's aloofness that the Prime Minister stated a week after his first announcement that he had recently become aware of a "desire of a great many Canadians who are ready to take service." Within days of arguing that the South African war was none of Canada's business, Laurier announced, in mid-October, that 1 000 volunteers were to be recruited to serve in the war simply because it was British.

Canada's enthusiasm for the Boer War then proved keener than the opportunity the Prime Minister offered. Before the conflict was over, 8 372 Canadians were accepted into service to do their duty for imperial solidarity. Such jingoism was enough to provoke loud rumblings of protest from anti-imperialists, other Canadian nationalists who suspected that Canada's first official adventure was setting a dangerous precedent for later, larger, and more foolish military action. Laurier attempted to counter such criticism by stating flatly that the South African episode "cannot be regarded as a departure . . . nor construed as a precedent for future action." But Henri Bourassa, the major spokesman for the group known as *autonomistes*, replied that "the precedent is the accomplished fact." In Bourassa's opinion, the event marked "a constitutional revolution, the consequences of which no man can calculate." At the very least, it did mark the end of what O.D. Skelton, Laurier's friend and official biographer, was to call "passive loyalty." In Skelton's view, however, Canada's participation in the South African war was a step forward, a move towards "responsible partnership" with Britain. If Canada assisted Great Britain more actively abroad, it seemed to follow that the British would be even more helpful in assisting Canada in North America.

— 2. Conflict of Empires —

The first assistance required of Britain after the South African war concerned the boundary between Alaska and the Northwest Territories. When
the United States purchased Alaska from Russia in 1867, it was understood that the boundary between the Russian and British possessions had
been settled by treaty in 1825, and that the acquisition included a "panhandle" that ran south to Portland Inlet (see map 6.1). However, the treaty
did not seem to specify a clear width for the coastal zone, nor did the
Anglo-Russian agreement clarify the division of Portland Inlet. British
Columbians wanted the matter settled almost as soon as they entered
Confederation; but there was no pressing reason for Great Britain or the
United States to be concerned with such a trivial matter until July 1897,
when ships returned to Seattle and San Francisco from spring supply trips
with literally tons of gold washed from the gravel of creeks draining into
the Klondike River. An American adventurer, George Washington Carmack, had made the discovery the previous August; the first haul was the
yield of just a few hundred people who rushed to the scene as news of
Carmack's luck spread through the North. Instantly the importance of the
region of the upper reaches of the Yukon River was transformed from that
of a fur reserve to a lucrative mining frontier—but of what country?

The Klondike itself was indisputably Canadian. The troublesome question concerned access to the gold. By the American reading of the old
treaty, the Alaskan panhandle extended eastward as far as the summit of
the coast range. Canada and the British contended that the boundary did
indeed run parallel to the height of land but at no point did the American
zone extend further inland than "ten marine leagues" from the ocean. In
the Americans' interpretation, the Yukon territory was land-locked. In the
Canadian view, it had an outlet to the sea at Skagway.

Naturally, gold-seekers did not wait for a boundary settlement. They
followed the most direct routes despite the interruption of disputed boundaries. Most landed at Skagway, where they saw the American flag snap-
ping in the coastal breeze. Later, they saw Union Jacks flying over the first
point of undeniable Canadian jurisdiction—the summits of the mountain
passes leading inland. One route led to the headwaters of the Yukon River
by way of Chilcoot Pass. The other was a steeper climb over White Pass,
then a different descent to the same headwaters of the Yukon.

The police at their mountaintop stations did more than show the flag.
Every intending prospector was required to have "at least 1 150 pounds of
solid food" and the necessary "tents, cooking utensils, prospectors' and

Map 6.1: Alaska Boundary Dispute

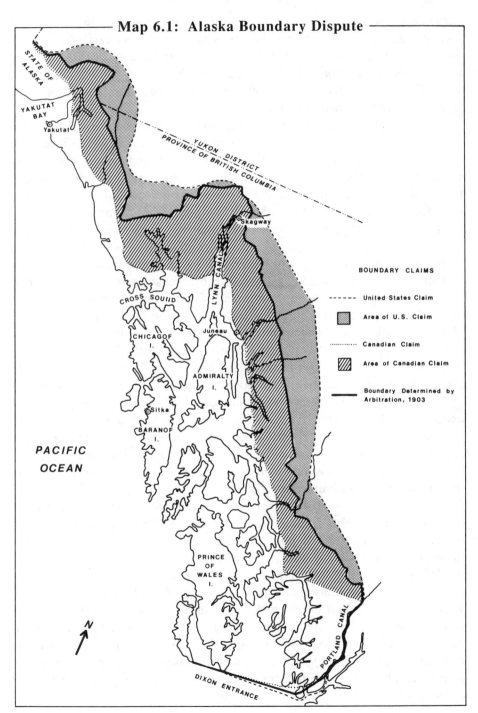

STATE OF ALASKA

YAKUTAT BAY

Yakutat

YUKON DISTRICT
PROVINCE OF BRITISH COLUMBIA

Skagway

CROSS SOUND

LYNN CANAL

CHICAGOF I.

Juneau

ADMIRALTY I.

Sitka

BARANOF I.

PACIFIC OCEAN

PRINCE OF WALES I.

N

PORTLAND CANAL

DIXON ENTRANCE

BOUNDARY CLAIMS

------ United States Claim

Area of U.S. Claim

.... Canadian Claim

Area of Canadian Claim

Boundary Determined by Arbitration, 1903

carpenters' tools." Moreover, all newcomers were required to pay various fees and duties on their effects before admission to the territory. In 1898 and 1899, the North West Mounted Police admitted more than 30 000 newcomers, from whom they collected more than $150 000 in taxes. At the same time, the police turned back everyone whose equipment or other resources were deemed inadequate.

After clearing customs, the gold-seekers made their descent to the Yukon and followed the river downstream to the point at which it met the Klondike. In 1896, the site of the confluence of the two rivers was an uninhabited swampy plain. Soon the area was the busiest riverine intersection in the North; it developed the appearance of a town almost overnight. By 1899, the place had been named Dawson City and accommodated a population of 20 000. Dawson was indeed a city. Such phenomenal growth was fairly common in similar circumstances elsewhere. What distinguished Dawson City was the degree to which order was maintained. Dawson City saloons closed every weekday from 2 to 6 a.m. and every weekend from midnight Saturday to 6:00 a.m. Monday. There were 13 reported murders on the Klondike during the gold rush period; all but one led to a conviction and an execution. On this account, Dawson City was probably more orderly than Winnipeg. Certainly there were more police on the Klondike—almost 300 constables—and they had broader discretionary powers than in any other area of North America. To a large extent, they made up their own laws as they went along. "These were not cases of flexible interpretation," according to William Morrison. "These were matters of actual invention of non-existent law to fit a specific situation . . . ." Such improvisation extended far beyond issues of social decorum, and included issues of admission or expulsion of newcomers, expropriation of stores from retailers, and the regulation of Indian affairs. The Yukon was recognized as a special district in 1898, but it still did not have normal institutions of respresentative government. The "police state" aspect, in Morris Zaslow's characterization, or unrestrained police "paternialism," in Morrison's analysis, meant that Dawson City residents were compelled to behave even more decorously than those of a typical, medium-sized Canadian town, despite the fact that the population consisted mainly of American newcomers who were on the move and on the make. The miners objected to the denial of self-government. Two of Dawson's three newspapers considered themselves voices of opposition whose mission it was to complain about every aspect of administration, but they never denounced the police force *per se*. Above all else, they had to admit that the NWMP did guarantee orderly exploitation and transportation of the gold.

With the completion of a railway between Skagway and Whitehorse in 1901, and with the elaboration of steam navigation on the Yukon River between Whitehorse and Dawson, the resource was accessible to capital-intensive exploitation. Mechanization did follow the railway, but the peak of placer mining was reached in 1903. Geologists continued to search for the mother lode, the supposed source of the alluvial gold washed down into the creek beds. Even though they never found it, expectations for great prospects were high at the turn of the century.

In 1903, the parties to the boundary dispute agreed to submit the treaty of 1825 to a judicial opinion from a panel of six judges: three American, one British, and two Canadian. Unfortunately, Canadians were naive in thinking that the Americans would allow the matter to be decided on strictly legal grounds, or to believe that the British would ally with them against the United States. Britain had in the past sacrificed Canadian interests to placate American ambition; such compromise was all the more likely in 1903 because the American President was unusually belligerent in asserting his country's interests. Regarding Alaska, Theodore Roosevelt instructed State Department officials in Britain to convey the message to the British government that only one decision would be acceptable from the arbitration panel. If the tribunal did not uphold the American claim, Roosevelt said, "I am going to send a brigade of American regulars up to Skagway and take possession of the disputed territory and hold it by all the power and force of the United States." The result was that the British judge, Lord Alverstone, sided with the Americans, the award went to the United States, and the two Canadians not only refused to sign the document, they issued a public statement condemning the decision.

Across Canada, newspapers joined in a general condemnation of the affair as another instance of the British having sacrificed the interests of a "loyal colony" for the sake of pleasing the appetites of a greedy, upstart republic. Laurier himself criticized the Americans for their "grasping" behaviour, and wondered aloud in Parliament whether the time had not come for Canada to behave less like "a small colony, a growing colony, but still a colony . . . ." In Laurier's view, "The difficulty is that so long as Canada remains a dependency of the British Crown the present powers that we have are not sufficient for the maintenance of our rights." This was certainly true. Laurier continued, however, to utter a statement that most historians have come to regard as recklessly naive. "It is important," he added, "that we should ask the British Parliament for more extensive power, so that if ever we have to deal with matters of a similar nature again, we shall deal with them in our own way, in our own fashion, according to the best light that we have." What Laurier seemed to ignore in the temper of the moment was that the Alaskan Boundary Dispute—in its ultimate resolution in 1903—was not a matter of who had the better "light," but of which country had the greater might.

— 3. National Defence —

No loosening of ties with Britain immediately followed the souring of Anglo-Canadian relations by Lord Alverstone's behaviour, even though Laurier did take a small step towards greater independence in 1904 by nationalizing the militia. Prior to the change, the General Officer Commanding was required to be a British soldier of command rank, colonel or better. Henceforth, he was to be a native of the Dominion. To some, even such a small, symbolic step was provocative and repugnant, a sentiment that was appealed to by the retiring GOC, D.D. Dundonald, the Earl of Cochrane, who said: "Men of Canada, keep both hands on the Union Jack."

Another influence that gave Laurier pause regarding pursuing independence further was the Governor General, Lord Minto, who pointed out shortly after the Alaska boundary arbitration that "if Canada wishes to possess complete treaty making powers she must be prepared to back her claims with her own forces." But how could the population of six million expect victory against 81 million Americans in an all-out confrontation of force? For that matter, how could Britain? The reality was that Theodore Roosevelt wielded a "big stick." Sometimes the best option was to join Britain in sensibly ducking when it was swung in Canada's direction. Consequently, national support for imperialism and the inability of Canada to oppose the Americans effectively on their own combined to check Laurier in making Canada more independent of Britain; but neither factor settled the issue of how much Canada should pay to maintain British friendship.

In 1909, the issue of the dollar value of imperialism surfaced more urgently than ever. The First Lord of the Admiralty announced that naval supremacy was being lost to Germany. He advocated an immediate crash program for building more of the latest ultimate weapon—specially-armored, big-gun battleships such as the dreadnought. The cheerleaders in the arms race chanted "We want eight and we won't wait." Were the Canadians ready to contribute?

It was moved in the Canadian Parliament by George Foster that the country "should no longer delay in assuming her proper share of responsibility and financial burden incidental to the suitable protection of her exposed coast line and sea ports." Foster advocated an immediate cash contribution such as was recently granted to Britain by New Zealand.

Laurier responded with a substitute motion to embrace the response of Australia which was to provide for its own coastal defence. He disliked any gesture resembling the payment of cash tribute and proposed, instead, the launching of a Canadian navy to relieve the British of North American responsibilities. After consulting later with the leader of the opposition, Robert Borden (leader of the Conservatives since Tupper's retirement in 1901), Laurier hinted that cash support of the Royal Navy might be possible in exceptional circumstances. But for the present, the emphasis fell on the creation of a small Canadian navy for coastal defence. The compromise united the House of Commons and the Laurier-Borden motion received unanimous support late in 1909.

Canadians at large were deeply divided, however, on the question of creating a national coast guard. On one side, nationalists whose concept of the nation placed them squarely within the British Empire could not imagine any navy but *the* navy, the naval service of Britain

> Whose flag had braved a thousand years
> The battle and the breeze.

By comparison, any naval service in Canada would be a "tin pot navy." Imperialists preferred to make a direct cash contribution to Britain to the extent of a dreadnought or two, as the Admiralty saw fit.

On the other side, centred largely in Quebec, were the nationalists whose hopes for a more autonomous Canada remained undaunted. For them autonomy dictated neither tribute nor armament, since they believed that even a limited Canadian navy would invite future jumps on the imperial bandwagon in an endless succession of secondary wars like the South African affair.

Given that Laurier's strength in Parliament was largely dependent upon support from Quebec (54 of Quebec's 65 seats had gone Liberal in the most recent election), the government was extremely cautious in framing the Naval Service Bill, presented to the House of Commons in mid-January 1910. The proposed legislation authorized a naval service and a college for the training of officers. But the force that was described to the House was clearly just a coast guard that would eventually consist of five light cruisers and six destroyers. Moreover, like the militia, the 11-ship navy was to be commanded by personnel answerable to Canada. Laurier emphasized that in times of "emergency" they would not automatically come to the assistance of the Royal Navy. "The position which we take," Laurier explained, "is that it is for the Parliament of Canada, which created the navy, to say when and where it shall go to war."

For Robert Borden, Laurier's proposal showed but half-hearted support of the empire. In his opinion, the British were already "confronted with an emergency which may rend this empire assunder before the proposed service is worthy of the name." Consequently, Borden chose to disregard the previous unanimity, and advocated a "free and loyal contribution" to the mother country instead.

In the end, Laurier's compromise prevailed, and pleased no one. Imperialists ridiculed the idea of a "tin pot navy" and *autonomistes* warned that its creation was the greatest "backward step" to have been taken in 50 years. Since the split between imperialism and autonomy was also one of English versus French, the country showed signs of beginning to break along lines of its primary antithesis, a division that was particularly dangerous because both sides were equally patriotic. What divided the imperialists from the *autonomistes* was not concern for Canada, but the method of acquiring a more powerful national existence and the purposes for which the new powers would be used.

— 4. A New Direction in Tariff Policy —

After the navy controversy, Laurier was ready for relaxation and excape. The aging Prime Minister went west in the hope of gaining some approval, if not unqualified recognition, for the fruits of his other policies. The Prairies had gained prominence since Laurier had come to power, and the recent award of provincial status was well received in Alberta and Saskatchewan. The West was, therefore, the one region outside Quebec in which Laurier was still likely to receive something of a hero's welcome. The crowds did cheer Sir Wilfrid from June to September as he paraded from Winnipeg to Vancouver and back. It was just the tonic the old politician needed.

But all was not approval and recognition. At nearly every stop along his regal progression, there were angry petitioners, especially farmers. Their principal complaints pertained to the apparatus for storing and marketing grain, and to alleged discrimination in the Canadian economy as a whole. On the marketing side, they hated the spread between the per-bushel price a producer received from grain companies for a wagon-load of grain (the "street" price), versus the price of a load of grain sufficient to fill an entire railway box car (the "track" price), or a ship-load at a point of export (the "spot" price). Increasing numbers of farmers were deciding that "pooling" the output of their separate farms was the solution; such a collective process would occur voluntarily among themselves or by compulsion under a Crown corporation. Given that Canadian farmers were producing almost one third of the wheat on the entire world export market by 1910, it followed that either form of pool would have enormous leverage on the world price to the benefit of prairie producers.

Even so, the optimum price for wheat was only one of the major issues. The farmers' other complaint was discrimination under the tariff. Quite simply, they demanded exemption because they produced for a world market of unprotected prices, but everything they consumed was purchased at prices inflated domestically by the tariff. At Saskatoon, one farmer asked Laurier what had happened to the Grit in the old Liberal party. He reminded the Prime Minister that it was Laurier who had once promised "to skin the Tory bear of protection." This Liberal wanted to know "what you have done with the hide." Such a question put Laurier completely off balance. He could only say that his blood was "a little cooler now." But such a disclaimer only vindicated what the Westerners had suspected, and they were not pleased with the confirmation that there was little to choose in the difference between Liberals and Conservatives.

Having returned to Ottawa in September with angry protests and cheering still ringing in his ears, the Prime Minister then had to face evidence of faltering popularity in his home province. Quebec had cast the majority of its vote for Liberals for the first time in 1896, and had given him steadily more of the total in each election since. But in November 1910, the voters had their first opportunity to express displeasure with imperialism, in a by-election where Liberals normally won with ease. This time the Liberal candidate was defeated by an autonomiste critic of Laurier's navy, an unknown politician supported only by the powerful pen of Henri Bourassa and his newspaper, *Le Devoir.*

Soon after the defeat in Drummond-Arthabaska, the farm protest resumed. This time 1 000 protestors representing the newly-formed Canadian Council of Agriculture, a group purportedly representing the farmers of every region of the country, descended upon Ottawa and reiterated the demands made during the prime ministerial tour of the past summer.

Laurier's response was cordial, yet evasive. He found demands for such action as government encouragement of farmers' cooperatives and public ownership of grain elevators "too radical," but there was one concession he might make. Although Laurier announced nothing definite at the time, negotiations were underway and at an advanced stage by December 1910 for a general relaxing of the tariff, particularly as it related to the interests of agriculture.

Earlier, the Americans had proposed full-scale discussion of the question of reciprocal free trade; Laurier had initially been hesitant. He became progressively more interested as such a bold new policy seemed likely to divert public attention from the imperialism controversy, and to bolster support for Laurier's Liberals in regions where they were faltering and most dependent—the West, Quebec, and the Maritimes.

By mid-January, face-to-face negotiations resulted in an agreement to be implemented by concurrent legislation from Congress and the Canadian Parliament. W.S. Fielding, the long-time Finance Minister and erstwhile advocate of free trade, was positively giddy when he reported the proposal to Parliament on January 26. As soon as the legislatures of the United States and Canada enacted it into law, there would be free trade in a wide range of natural products (particularly agricultural produce) and certain manufactured goods useful in farming (barbed wire and cream separators, for example). In addition, reciprocal reductions were also to be allowed on a few other trade goods in the future.

At first, the opposition was stunned. Anticipating an election in the near future, Borden observed that there was "the deepest dejection" among Conservatives because they feared that "the government's proposals . . . would give it another term in office"—Laurier's fifth. It was true that Liberals and Conservatives alike had welcomed the idea of a restoration of that reciprocity which was supposed to have made the decade after 1854 so prosperous. Renewal of reciprocal free trade had been a shared goal of every political leader at one time or another since the lapse of the original agreement in 1866. Even Sir John A. Macdonald, the father and guardian of the National Policy, had explored the possibility of freer trade with the United States as late as 1891 in order to blunt the Liberals' battle cry that year. But when Macdonald found the Americans unresponsive, he decided protectionism was still patriotic. The cry of patriotism in 1891 foreshadowed what was to follow in 1911, and later.

Still, the Conservatives' initial reaction was to share enthusiasm for the agreement for its economic implications. Their only lament on the day of its announcement was that reciprocity was a Liberal rather than a Conservative coup.

5. "Borden and King George, or Laurier and Taft?"

The initiative taken by Toronto business proved decisive in showing Robert Borden good ground on which to oppose reciprocity. Sir Edmund Walker, the president of the Canadian Bank of Commerce, led the way on February 16 when he addressed the Toronto Board of Trade, criticizing the tariff agreement because it seemed to place continentalism ahead of the British connection. Four days later, 18 prominent businessmen (identifying themselves as Liberals) echoed the same theme when they issued an open letter to the public denouncing the agreement because it would tend "to weaken the ties which bind Canada to the Empire." Ontario business, which had little to fear from a relaxation of trade restrictions on commodities covered by the proposed change, opposed the policy anyway, possibly due to a fear that the relaxation of the tariff was a precedent that would ultimately lead to the repudiation of the principle of protection in general. Others, such as Walker, were deeply involved in the financing of the new railways. If traffic ran increasingly North-South, instead of East-West, their investments were in jeopardy. For those who opposed the change on grounds of self-interest, it was more convenient to place such opposition on the higher level of principle (imperialism), and then, after drawing attention to the Naval Service Bill, to suggest that the two issues combined pointed to a sinister "inner meaning" (dissolution of empire). In this way, reciprocity became entangled inextricably with imperial relations, and the stage was well set for opposition politicians to follow.

Clifford Sifton, the maverick Liberal who had left the ministry in 1905 to oppose minority rights, now left the party to fight reciprocity. Other Liberals—ready to make the same move over the militia act of 1904, or the naval service legislation of 1910, or the host of petty personal grudges that are bound to accumulate around a government 15 years in power—took the occasion of the controversy that developed around reciprocity to disassociate themselves from Laurier and contribute, if possible, to his downfall.

Robert Borden's mood of defeat steadily shifted to one of quiet confidence. The Conservatives decided to filibuster the passage of the trade bill, and force the government into an election that Borden thought he was bound to win. The debate dragged through March and April, then adjourned for two months so that Laurier could attend another of the increasingly regular conferences on imperial defence in Britain. Upon his return, the debate resumed and intensified after the passage of the measure through Congress near the end of July. Since there seemed no end to the Canadian filibuster, the Prime Minister decided to challenge the opposition to a September election, and Parliament was dissolved on July 29.

Laurier did not fear the outcome. From an economic standpoint, the case for free trade in natural products was strong. No abrupt repudiation of protected industry was contemplated, therefore, the branch-plant factories would not shut down. More importantly, there appeared to be substantial benefits for fishermen, miners, forest workers, and most cash-crop farmers. The benefits, however, were entirely hypothetical and looked to the long-term. It is perhaps a truism that the short-run always determines an election result. In that of 1911, voters were told that fruit growers would face immediate and stiff competition from American producers; railway workers were warned that there would be instant and massive layoffs from the East-West transcontinentals because so much trade would suddenly start running North-South; and Roblin of Manitoba told the grain producers of his province that Minneapolis would surpass Port Arthur as a buyer's market if Canadian and American farmers suddenly marketed their produce in the new place. One way or another, all critical points seemed to suggest that the country was tolerably prosperous in 1911; why disturb the *status quo*?

If the short-term argument against modifying the tariff was more persuasive than the long-term hypothetical benefit, appeals to patriotism were probably even more telling. Ironically, the Americans themselves did the most to assist Canadian imperialists via some remarkably stupid speeches in support of the proposal. The most quoted man in Canada became "Champ" Clark, the new Speaker of the House of Representatives, when he said that he was "for it" because of his "hope to see the day when the American flag will float over every square foot of the British North American possessions, clear to the North Pole."

Such was precisely the point that the Conservatives and former Liberals, including Clifford Sifton, were making. They said that closer trade with the Americans would not only weaken the empire; reciprocity would probably mean the end of Canada as well. Premier Walter Scott of

Saskatchewan attempted to answer that free trade was simply good economics and ridiculed the appeal to economic nationalism, saying: "We may remain loyal while sending our flax crop over a high tariff wall into the United States but if the wall be removed and we obtain consequent higher prices for our flax we become disloyal." George Foster thought "yes." He appealed to a vision of a country strengthened by independence in North America and unity with Britain, saying: "Canadian natural resources for the purposes of Canadian development, Canadian markets for Canadian producers, Canadian traffic for Canadian carriers, and a Canadian nation with complete freedom of self-government and the closest possible union and cooperation with the British empire."

On the basis of the optimistic projection of the *status quo*, the rising tide of British imperialism, and a deeply-rooted distrust of the United States, the country outside Quebec repudiated Laurier. If Borden was to win a majority in the House of Commons that represented Canada as a whole, he needed some representation from Quebec. But what made the Conservatives so popular in Ontario (their stand on imperialism) should have made them all the more odious to French Canada. While Laurier's naval policy was mildly imperialist, Borden's was brazenly so. Assuming that the *autonomistes* were more interested in defeating imperialism than was Laurier, they should have united behind the Liberal leader as the lesser of two evils once it became apparent how strong the Conservatives were outside of Quebec. They did not; and that fact gave the election of 1911 an especially interesting, as well as an important, twist.

Henri Bourassa, probably the most influential individual in Quebec, thought that he might defeat Laurier's naval policy without furthering Borden's. His plan was to work for the election of a block of *autonomiste* canadidates who would be independent of the Conservatives as well as of the Liberals, yet a force large enough to deny either party a majority. With the balance of power in the House of Commons, they might then force revisions of the hated Naval Service Bill.

Bourassa's strategy was plausible early in the campaign. The evidence for its success was Borden's willingness to cooperate in the scheme by refusing to run candidates in opposition to Bourassa's. The Conservatives ran only in the eastern townships and the few English-speaking ridings of Montreal. The rest of the province was left as a clear field for *autonomistes* and Liberals.

By mid-September, however, it had become evident that Laurier's strength outside Quebec was even less than Bourassa originally expected. By that time, it should have been clear to the powerful editor of *Le Devoir* that votes for the third party were simply, in the words of *La Presse*, "a vote for imperialism with a vengeance." But Bourassa stubbornly refused to throw his support behind his one-time friend. Two days before the election, Laurier knew that he was beaten. And so was Bourassa. It was a Borden *majority* government that took the seals of office. The 16 *autonomistes* elected were well short of commanding the balance of power—even if they threatened to side solidly with the 87 Liberals. Borden's party had a free rein, coming to power with 118 seats and owing no favours to Quebec. What followed was government for the "progressive" imperialist majority, and majority rule with a vengeance.

Suggested Reading

General works that cover the subject of external affairs and nationalism during the Laurier years include R.C. Brown and R. Cook, *Canada: A Nation Transformed* (1974), and Robert Bothwell, *et al., Canada, 1900-1945* (1987). A fuller account, however, of relations between Canada, the United States, and Great Britain appears in C.P. Stacey, *Canada and the Age of Conflict: A History of Canadian External Policies*, vol. one, *1867-1921* (1977).

A number of specialized works examine the imperialist thrust of English-speaking Canadian nationalists. Carl Berger's *Imperialism and Nationalism, 1884-1914: A Conflict in Canadian Thought* (1969), and his *Sense of Power: Studies in the Ideas of Canadian Imperialism, 1867-1914* (1970), are the two most important works on the theme. A narrower but similar subject with a longer history, the idea of imperial federation, is covered by John Kendle, *The Round Table Movement* (1975). Robert J.D. Page examines what he considers the high-point of imperialist sentiment in "Canada and the Imperial Idea in the Boer War years," *JCS* (1970).

The *autonomistes'* reaction to imperialism is described in Berger's work. But more detailed studies of Henri Bourassa are also available. See Joseph Levitt, *Henri Bourassa on Imperialism and Bi-culturalism, 1900-1918* (1970). For the domestic purposes for which Bourassa hoped to see greater autonomy applied, see Levitt's "Henri Bourassa and Modern Industrial Society, 1900-1914," *CHR* (1969), or his book-length treatment of the same subject, *Henri Bourassa and the Golden Calf: The Social Program of the Nationalists, 1900-1914* (1969).

North American disputes that were not well served by imperialism are illustrated best, perhaps, by the Alaska boundary dispute. Morris Zaslow, *The Opening of the Canadian North, 1870-1914* (1971), contains some excellent chapters on the Klondike gold rush. Pierre Berton's popular account, *Klondike: The Last Great Gold Rush, 1896-1899*, rev. edition (1972), is a detailed rendition of the more colourful aspects of the subject and should be read in combination with the more scholarly William R. Morrison, *Showing the Flag: The Mounted Police and Canadian Sovereignty in the North, 1894-1925* (1985). Norman Penlington, *The Alaska Boundary Dispute: A Critical Reappraisal* (1972), concludes that the British position was the only reasonable course. Desmond Morton, *Ministers and Generals: Politics and the Canadian Militia, 1868-1904* (1970), provides another perspective, not on the boundary dispute simply, but of the blend of British imperial interests and Canadian domestic political concerns as they came into conflict over control of the militia.

For Laurier's defeat in 1911, see W.M. Baker, "A Case Study of Anti-Americanism in English-speaking Canada: The Election Campaign of 1911," *CHR* (1970), or the volume by Paul Stevens, *The 1911 General Election: A Study in Canadian Politics* (1970).

**Canadians on the crest
of Vimy Ridge, April, 1917.**

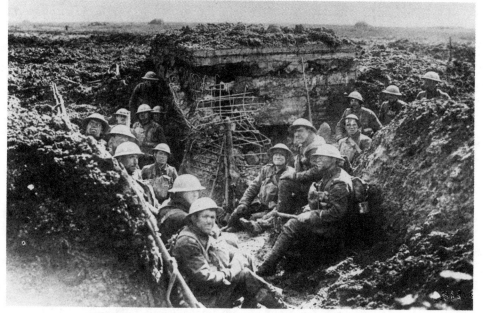

SOURCE: NATIONAL ARCHIVES OF CANADA/PA-1101

*". . . the Canadian achievement was a source
of enormous pride for everyone who believed
that the athletic accomplishments of war can
have deep meaning."*

CHAPTER 7
THE IMPERIAL TRAGEDY, 1912-1921

— 1. Attempted Reform at the National Level —

In 1911, as in 1874, a new government came to power on a wave of popular moral indignation. In Borden's case, however, there were broader intentions at stake than the simple vindication of Canadian virtue. Unlike Mackenzie, who professed to be little more than an honest version of Sir John A. Macdonald, Borden claimed he was a new leader for a new era. Laurier's reluctance to accept a broader role in the empire and his renewed willingness to lower the tariff barrier against the United States were denounced by Borden and the Conservatives as "Little Canada" policies. On the domestic level, Borden called Laurier's administration inappropriate, declaring it outmoded as well as immoral.

Robert Laird Borden exemplified the city-dwellers of his generation who were born in rural Canada and had moved to town to profit from the new industrial society that was then taking shape. The town that drew Borden away from his parents' Nova Scotian farm was Halifax, and the career he chose was law: not criminal or private civil disputes but the proceedings of trade and corporate liability. As a corporation lawyer,

Borden developed a spectator's admiration for business that was close to religious zeal. Like the rest of the new middle class, Borden had come to believe that a "progressive" state might profitably imitate business models in all its administrative operations.

Borden had no taste for old-fashioned politics, the artful deception and judicious dispensation of patronage that (judging by their papers) occupied Sir John A. Macdonald and Sir Wilfrid Laurier at least 50 percent of the time. For Borden, old-style politics was corrupt, and the resulting "machinery" of government was hopelessly inefficient. Too frequently, departments overlapped in operations and they were run by amateurs holding their positions as political favours. In 1911, Borden felt he had an opportunity to modernize political practice and the civil service.

Borden's political education had not prepared him, however, for the tasks he wished to perform. He began late, at age 42, when Charles Tupper dealt him a seat in the House of Commons in 1896. Five years later, the pace of Borden's education admittedly quickened when the same person handed him the leadership of the Conservative party and the new leader struggled to develop policy alternatives to those of Laurier's Liberals. Borden decided in 1907 that it was time for a national party to promote what other civic-minded Canadians were advocating on a more local level. Like the municipal reformers, Borden saw tangible benefits in public ownership of the utility base; and he believed government should exercise more vigorous "police" powers and provide a broader range of social services through a more efficient bureaucracy. On a national level, the utilities were the railways, the police were the armed forces (or various regulatory commissions), and the new social services were operations such as free rural delivery of mail to that half of the country that had not yet moved to town.

Once he became Prime Minister, Borden dissociated himself from the old-fashioned considerations of patronage and party organization, and tried to devote his 12-hour working days to fulfilling the reform promises he had been making since 1907. In 1912 and 1913, the civil service was examined for ways to increase its efficiency; farmers were given free rural mail delivery; and innovations were attempted in federal-provincial cooperation for sharing the costs of improving country roads and agricultural education. Finally, preliminary and somewhat halting steps were taken towards nationalizing the as yet uncompleted and faltering transcontinental railways authorized by Laurier in 1903. Thus, Borden moved to reorganize the political superstructure; but like the other middle-class reformers of his day, the Prime Minister did not believe that there were any cracks in the foundation of Canadian capitalism. The intended changes were not sweeping. Moreover, even within the limited scope of hoped-for innovation, the record of accomplishment was disappointing.

According to Borden's biographer, R.C. Brown, the new Prime Minister's record of legislative accomplishment was impeded by the Liberal-dominated Senate that kept recommending amendments to his reform proposals. For this reason, Brown blames Senate obstructionism for preventing Borden from achieving more. John English offers a slightly different explanation. In his view, there was more to Borden's legislative failures than Liberal partisanship in the upper house. According to English, Borden's conviction that there was "an objective and definable general interest" (the validity of which was unquestionable), and his contempt for old-fashioned "brokerage politics" meant that "compromises came grudgingly from him and were abandoned hastily if opportunity arose." In other words, Borden was inclined to believe that there was only one truth—his own—and he pursued his vision without due regard for accommodating opposing points of view. Inflexibility, according to English, is what derailed Borden's domestic policies, and what led to the even greater failure of his imperialist defence policy.

— 2. Imperialism With a Vengeance —

Borden came to power intending to bring Canada closer to Great Britain by contributing in some meaningful way to imperial defence, and by gaining a voice in the determination of the objectives for which such strengthened imperial forces might by used. In this sense, Robert Borden offered precisely the kind of cooperation in 1911 that Joseph Chamberlain had sought in 1897. But after six months in office, Borden was still uncertain about the defence policy that would be most mutually beneficial for the two countries. He did not wish to implement Laurier's Naval Service Act. At the same time, Borden was reluctant to make a cash contribution to Britain without assurances of shared control of imperial defence. As a result of both considerations, Borden announced on March 18, 1912 that the government was suspending the implementation of the Naval Service Act. When a more appropriate permanent policy was determined, he said, it would be submitted to the people for their approval prior to enactment.

On the same day that Borden made his defence policy announcement, the First Lord of the Admiralty, Winston Churchill, announced that a renewed naval crisis was forcing Britain to proceed with yet another crash program of dreadnought construction. Since the situation was an emergency, Borden thought that the appropriate response of Canada would be a direct cash contribution to the Admiralty. The leader of the anti-Laurier, French-Canadian contingent in Parliament, Frederick Monk, refused, however, to consider Churchill's announcement sufficient justification. After Borden conceded that more substantial confirmation was obtainable in Britain, he urged Monk to join him in such a mission. When Monk demurred, another anti-Laurier French-Canadian, Louis-Philippe Pelletier, agreed to go in his place. Thus, a party of Canadian officials boarded ship for Britain on June 26, 1912.

The important meetings that followed were private conferences between Borden and Churchill, with the spokesman for Britain confirming that the situation was "very serious." The First Lord of the Admiralty agreed to put his opinion in writing for presentation to key personnel in Canada. "He is quite willing to play the game," Borden noted later in his diary. "Will give assurance in writing as to necessity."

Upon Borden's return to Canada, he confronted Monk with the letter signed by Churchill. Monk was impressed. In his view, the Prime Minister was now justified in setting a policy and presenting it to the electorate in the form of a plebiscite. If the proposed contribution did not divide the country, Monk promised to support it. Without such prior consultation, however, he said he would "retire" and, by implication, take the rest of the French-Canadian, anti-Laurier contingent with him.

Borden wanted—but did not need—the support of the French-Canadians. Moreover, he believed that a plebiscite would be "fatal" to the Tories in the rest of Canada: it would be too readily apparent that the issue was a problem only in Quebec. Why, then, had Borden suggested earlier that his policy be submitted to the people before implementation? It would appear that the earlier assurance was a gesture, grudgingly offered, and applied only to the permanent policy. The present crisis was apparently a passing phenomenon calling for emergency treatment; Borden therefore had an opportunity to abandon his previous commitment. It was suddenly dropped.

The Prime Minister's resolve to proceed without a plebiscite (or a general election) was reinforced by his discovery that the "variable" and "unstable" French-Canadians were not going to follow Monk. Only seven of the 16 were willing to join Laurier to oppose Borden. The rest stood with the government like ordinary, back-bench Conservatives. Bourassa's *autonomistes* thus reverted to their Parti Bleu origins. Their anti-Laurier, anti-Liberal sentiments proved stronger than their anti-imperialist orientation. Since they had their hatreds out of order, Bourassa eventually denounced the group that he had done so much to create; it was Laurier's party that almost singlehandedly fought Borden's naval aid bill once the matter came before Parliament in December 1912.

The proposed law was to authorize the Government of Canada to spend $35 million for the "construction and equipment of battleships or armoured cruisers of the most modern and powerful type" to be used by "His Majesty for the common defence of the Empire." Laurier opposed the contribution because it did nothing for the Canadian navy. Were he in power, Laurier said, he would proceed in accordance with the Naval Service Act and construct two small fleets to defend Canada's Atlantic and Pacific coasts.

In the end, Borden followed neither course. Having suspended the Naval Service Act, he refused to reinstate it, and the interim policy of aid to Britain failed to pass the full legislative process. Laurier's opposition to Borden's Naval Aid Bill was the longest, most acrimonious in the nation's history. The debate began early in December 1912 and did not cease until May 15, 1913. That day, the government ended the dispute with a device rather common in the proceedings of the British Parliament, but new to the Canadian House of Commons. A new rule empowered the majority to terminate debate and bring a matter to a vote once opposition proved to be "merely obstructionist."

For those, like Borden, who viewed Parliament as similar to a factory whose product was legislation, closure was a sensible streamlining of outmoded procedures. Without time limitation, a howling minority could stop the assembly line by sheer talk and delay the "business" of the House, perhaps to the point of dissolution. In an election thus forced, if the voters agreed that the opposition had been merely obstructionist, there could be severe punishment for the "filibuster." On the other hand, an appeal to the people could also defeat a ministry. In this sense, prolonging a debate to dissolution could be a great majority-minority equalizer in Parliamentary politics. It was how Laurier had prepared the way for his grand entrance in 1896, and how Borden had come to power in 1911.

Borden's use of the new "gag rule" arose from his uncertainty that the Conservatives could win an election in the spring of 1913. But Laurier had another weapon under the old system, a weapon not yet neutralized by Borden. The Constitution of Canada required passage by both "Houses of Parliament" before any measure could receive royal assent and come into effect. By convention, the upper house had developed into a "chamber of sober second thought" offering amendments to measures that the House of Commons would sometimes accept. And yet the Senate never imposed its will on the Commons by insisting upon a course unacceptable to the lower house. The chamber of sober second thought was not "a house of partisan second chance"—not until its outright rejection of Borden's Naval Aid Bill. At the end of May 1913, the Senate returned the measure to the House of Commons stating that the senators refused to concur: "This House is not justified in giving its assent to the Bill until it is submitted to the judgement of the country."

Here was another direct challenge to Borden for a general election; he refused the bait then as previously. Rather than becoming caught in Laurier's net, Borden turned away from defence policy and pushed his domestic "equality of opportunity" program, particularly those measures that were intended to rescue farmers from rural isolation. By the spring of 1914, Borden seemed well prepared to meet Laurier's challenge for an early election in the sense that he was ready to confront the electorate with a list of reforms achieved and intentions obstructed; he claimed that the Liberal Senate was to blame for the latter. Here, to be consistent with the more general call for reform, Borden might have added the demand for a restructuring of the upper house of Parliament.

Other developments deflected Borden from seeking a dissolution, however. One was recession, an economic downturn that began in 1913 and worsened the next year. The acreage of crops sown was lower in 1914 than in any year since 1910 because expected prices were so low. In town, factories were working at only 50 to 75 percent capacity. There were also political discouragements, since the Conservative organizations in both Ontario and Manitoba had fallen into disarray. In Quebec, of course, the situation was even more hopeless for the Tories. Consequently, Borden chose to take a long vacation rather than to enter an election campaign. He went with his wife, Laura, to the lake country northwest of Toronto to enjoy the pleasant company of Canada's wealthiest cottagers: the Eatons, the Sanfords, and the Macleans. Only the daily press found its way to Borden's Port Carling retreat. In this way, he learned on July 27 that, as a result of the Austrian heir presumptive's murder by a Serbian nationalist, Austria was declaring war on Serbia. The news did not deter Borden from playing golf that day. Soon, however, he was urgently requested to return to Ottawa because it appeared that the rest of Europe, including Great Britain, was also going to war; therefore, Canada too was on the eve of a great adventure. Britain's war declaration on August 4 dissolved the

Conservatives' political crisis at once. Borden knew that his government was saved for the duration.

— 3. The Unifying Impact of the War —

As with the response to the call for volunteers to fight in the Boer War, there were more recruits, initially, than places in the ranks of the contingent to be sent to Europe in 1914. No one suspected that the new adventure would be any less exciting than the South African affair. No one foresaw that Canada was plunging into the most tragic episode of its history.

Participation in what soon became known as the Great War led to two kinds of tragedy, quite different in their results. The first was the tragedy of the sacrifice itself, the numbing effect of the slaughter that continued for four years. But from that collective injury it was possible to extract a "sense of power" and national achievement: Canada had made a distinguished contribution to an important moment in the history of the world; the contribution had been at the limit of the country's ability; Canada had survived.

Initially, mobilization for war had the effect of unifying the country around a sense of common danger that was less artificial than anything experienced in the past. Earlier, in the case of John A. Macdonald's attempt to create an atmosphere of national urgency around the building of the CPR, for example, the artificiality of the effort was only too apparent. Later, with the South African war, the episode was only English Canada's adventure. In 1914, however, Germany attacked France through neutral Belgium; Russia, Britain, and eventually Italy joined the conflict. It was clear that there was nothing "secondary" about the new war. The struggle soon became the overriding national preoccupation affecting art, literature, and the new medium of film, as well as politics and the popular press. Borden pledged "every effort and . . . every sacrifice." He believed that "the manhood of Canada stands ready to fight beyond the seas" to the last individual if necessary. Laurier joined in affirming that "when the call goes out, our answer goes at once, and it goes in the classical language of the British answer to the call of Duty: 'Ready, Aye Ready'." The leader of the opposition promised to support the cause fully. Laurier said there would be "no criticism so long as there is danger at the front."

It could be suggested that both affirmations were reckless or hollow in the light of what eventually followed, but no one knew then that they were embarking upon the bloodiest infantry war in human history. Later, even as the brutal reality became dreadfully evident, the spontaneous enthusiasm still held up through the most bloodstained year in the history of warfare. The major signs of disintegration did not become fully apparent until 1917. From this standpoint, there were three years of remarkable unity to face a struggle that demanded more of the country than any prior challenge.

The call for solidarity and self-sacrifice involved more than recruiting young, adventuresome men to join the army. The appeal engaged civilians, as well, to make voluntary contributions of both time and money for the war effort at home. Women replaced men at the workplace. Every association, from the IODE to the YMCA, had wartime projects. Children mobilized for fund raising and victory gardens. But the voluntarism of greatest significance was perhaps the work of the Canadian Patriotic Fund, an association chartered in 1914 for the purpose of "preserving the families' economic status in comfort and decency, as a partial recognition of the services of the soldiers overseas." The idea was to raise and distribute money to the families of enlisted men in the hope of bridging the discrepancy between what a man could expect from his peacetime work and the $1.10 per day that he received as soldier's pay. Although the project was ambitious to the point of pretension, the volunteer workers and contributors almost realized their goal. Before the war, the average pay for a factory worker was about $80 per month, the minimum that the Canadian Patriotic Fund did nearly succeed in guaranteeing to the dependent families of men overseas.

Voluntary contributions were enormous at home because the sacrifices of the men at the front were indescribable. In a sense, the war that began in 1914 was a new kind of conflict; but since no infantry war like it has occurred since, the conflict is deservedly called the Great War. Men on horseback attempted cavalry charges, and infantry units marched against opposing forces as in the days of Napoleon. But in 1914, there were new weapons such as the machine gun, poison gas, and improved artillery. Their killing power was horrendous. The new weapons forced men to dig kilometres of trenches for the protective cover of earth, but to the commanders, whose brilliance stopped at their boot tops, deadlock was demoralizing. Periodically, they would order their forces to rush the other side on the bizarre assumption that decimation was less discouraging than stalemate. During such suicidal frontal assaults, the men were frequently cut down by machine-gun fire even before they had cleared their own defences, and the troops who refused to go "over the top" were shot by their own side for the crime of "cowardice." Such were the conditions Canadians encountered as "civilians in uniform" in April 1915 when the first contingent, organized into a division, was ordered to counter a German attack. In one day, 60 percent were killed or wounded. They did gain their objective, however, and no one knows why they fought so well. Their training was slight. They did not come from a country with a strong military tradition. Their equipment was defective (especially their rifles that were superb target weapons but devices that invariably jammed in the gritty conditions of trench war in France). Despite the conditions that should have led to mutiny or total annihilation, everyone agreed that Canadians fought "second to none" and they quickly earned a reputation for being an elite corps of shock troops. Indeed, for this reason, their movements had to be carefully concealed. According to David Lloyd George, the British Prime Minister, "whenever the Germans found the Canadian Corps coming into the line, they prepared for the worst."

By September 1915, the second contingent arrived in Europe, and Canada was able to place a force of about 42 000 men in combat. Since the ranks could be depleted by as much as 50 percent in a single day's fighting, the Army attempted to maintain one soldier in reserve nearby in Britain for every two on the line. Once it appeared that Canada could maintain two divisions easily, even with such a high level of reserve forces, the War Office asked for a third division. Recruiting in Canada proceeded better than expected, and by the end of the year, it was thought that a Canadian Corps of four divisions was quite feasible. Altogether, a four-division corps represented a manpower commitment of nearly 100 000 men in France and Britain, with an even larger group in the pipeline from the points of recruitment in Canada. On the eve of 1916, Borden announced that he thought the country might do even better, and perhaps double the number of men in uniform. His goal of 500 000 was never reached, but the number was a good indication of Borden's faith in the durability of the spirit of voluntarism that had been attained. Moreover, because the announcement was met with surprise but not outrage, the declaration and its reception were good gauges of the degree of unity that had persisted through the first year of the war.

Bloody though the fighting had been in 1915, that of 1916 was worse. In the protracted "battle" of the Somme, a two-and-a-half month period of mass slaughter, three million men were engaged on the two sides, and one million combatants were killed, wounded, or disappeared into the ooze of the battlefield. In one engagement of the Canadians, 77 000 men were ordered to advance their part of the line 2 700 metres. They did; but this one small gain cost the Canadian Corps 24 029 casualties.

Later in the campaign, near the end of 1916, Canadians began to experiment with covering the infantry by a "creeping barrage" of gunfire. Past practice had been to daze the enemy by artillery bombardment far ahead of advancing infantry, but by the time the attackers reached the German trenches, the defenders were back in the open at their machine guns halting the advance. The new tactic called for a curtain of protective fire just ahead of the troops: a minute of shelling, a three-minute dash by the troops. These actions, immediately following one another, meant that the enemy had no time to recover. The Canadians used the technique successfully with one division in September, 1916 at Courcelette. In January, 1917, the British high command ordered them to perfect the method to achieve a major breakthrough using all four divisions together sometime during the spring offensive of the new year.

The assignment was to take a low, 11-kilometre escarpment with a commanding view of the Canadians in front and the British and French on either side. Fully appreciating the strategic importance of their high ground, the Germans had fortified Vimy Ridge with three lines of trenches, machine guns in steel and concrete pill boxes, and heavy artillery supplied by subterranean railway.

The Canadian Senior Divisional Commander charged with planning the creeping barrage assault to fullest advantage was Sir Arthur Currie. The former insurance man from Victoria devised a plan that placed all units at exact locations at precise predetermined times. That meant every man from the lowest private had to know his own position and the timing in the intended battle. What followed in February and March 1917 was "entirely new," according to Pierre Berton, because whole divisions were taken to rearward areas to practice the "Vimy glide." Again and again they played out the battle, literally in dress rehearsal, to perfect the precise timing of each expected advance and halt. All were prepared for Easter Monday, 1917. That morning, just before light, 1 000 artillery pieces (almost 400 of which were guns hurling shells weighing nearly a tonne) aimed their fire on this one concentration of enemy strength. At 5:30 a.m., the artillery stopped, and all four divisions of the Canadian Corp ran 100 metres towards their objective. Three minutes later, everyone fell to the ground and the most colossal artillery bombardment ever let loose on a battlefront resumed. Soon it lifted, and the Canadians, shivering in the sleet and from the proximity of the explosions, continued their uphill rush, occupying the ground that the artillery had just cleared and fighting their way successfully through the system of three lines of trenches, seizing the guns at the top two hours after having begun the assault. At 7:30 a.m., looking down at the other side of Vimy Ridge, they saw a peaceful scene of green pastures and picturesque farmers' cottages. Behind them, the ground over which the Canadians had just advanced was strewn with more than 3 000 comrades in the "awkward humpback-ed posture of death," and the terrain itself "looked like nothing so much as a rich plum-pudding before it goes to boiling."

Relative to other encounters, the casualties at Vimy Ridge were light. Of more significance were the gains that included the ridge and 54 guns, 104 mortars, 124 machine guns, and more than 4 000 prisoners. These made the victory of Vimy Ridge one of the most dramatic successes of the war. As such, the Canadian achievement was a source of enormous pride for everyone who believed that the athletic accomplishments of war can have deep meaning. Writers looking for cosmic significance in military victory say that the success at Vimy Ridge signified Canada's coming of age. D.L. Goodspeed (and a score of others) have affirmed and reaffirmed that "it was on Easter Monday, April 9, 1917, and not on any other date, that Canada became a nation." Vimy was a fiery ordeal such as the Canada Firsters had imagined, and it worked some of the magic such action was supposed to engender. As one veteran put it: "We went up Vimy Ridge as Albertans and Nova Scotians. We came down as Canadians."

Regrettably, Vimy was not the first success in a larger breakthrough. The British and French to the left and right of the Canadians both failed in their advances. Another more costly offensive followed in 1917, and 1918 was yet bloodier. Inevitably, casualties outnumbered enlistments. Conscription was imposed. Then scandals in war profiteering captured headlines. The government moved to offset claims that the country was involved in a rich man's war but a poor man's fight by introducing taxes on business on an ability-to-pay basis. The Minister of Finance, Sir Thomas White, introduced Canada to the income tax in 1917, saying: "There has arisen . . . a very natural and, in my view a very just, sentiment that those who are in the enjoyment of substantial incomes should substantially and directly contribute to the growing war expenditure . . . ." Those with average incomes were not to be affected but those with incomes of $10 000 per year were to pay $420 annual tax, and the upper-most group, receiving at least $200 000, were expected to pay about one fourth of their income in direct taxation.

The shift from voluntary enlistment and voluntary cash contributions to conscription and the income tax signified the breakdown of voluntarism. The income tax tended to blunt some of the class antagonism that conscription had triggered. But such a gesture was too small to be cathartic for long. Still, at the time of its imposition, the war was drawing towards its final awful phase.

In the spring of 1918, the German command launched one last desperate offensive that drove the Allies almost to Paris. Then they counterattacked. By early August, the Allies had so thoroughly exhausted the German reserves that they knew they were beaten. Germany initiated proceedings for an armistice, and the guns finally fell unceremoniously silent at 11:00 a.m. on November 11.

For a few returned soldiers, the preceding four years had been devastating; "the things that were glorious had no glory," and the sacrifices were like those of stockyards "if nothing was done with the meat except to bury it." For most of the others, however, too much had been expended to dwell on the essential senselessness of the struggle. Simpler truths were more reassuring. A country of less than eight million had placed perhaps 40 percent of its able-bodied, fighting-age men in uniform and 61 326 had died while in the service of their country—56 634 in combat. Another 172 950 did return, but with empty sleeves or other signs of permanent disability. No country can sacrifice so much and consider it futile.

Canadians in 1918, and most of the country's historians since, have affirmed and reaffirmed every November 11 that the tragic deaths of the 61 326 and the inestimable ruin of the lives of the others were necessary costs for the equally immeasurable, valuable prize of international recognition. Having fought so well and having contributed so generously, Canada was no longer a colony in fact or in image. Canada was a nation among the others and worthy of every honour to be accorded a nation-state. In 1919, it was thus proper and uncontroversial for Canada to join the new international body called the League of Nations and to do so as a full and independent member.

In this sense, the Great War was "Canada's equivalent of the War of Independence." But such a conclusion follows from only half the story. There was another less widely-publicized pattern of tragedy that contributed nothing positive to even the most imaginative of the nation's myth-makers. Indeed the second record of tragedy tends to impugn the somewhat boastful conclusion of the first, because the impact of the second was the near destruction of the precarious balance that was the basis of Confederation itself.

— 4. National Disunity —

Among the first to experience faltering enthusiasm for the cause of war was Prime Minister Borden when he was forced to realize that Canada had chosen to participate as a principal without receiving a proportionate share of the war's direction. In the summer of 1915, Borden went to Britain to resolve the question. Rather than resolution, the Canadian Prime Minister found even more problems. Overall, there seemed a frustrating lack of competence in the British approach to the war and Borden was insulted by the supercilious evasion of his questions. He returned to Canada hurt and angered; but his subsequent actions were curious, if not childish, in light of what went before. Rather than deciding to curtail Canada's involvement on the grounds that limited control warranted proportional liability, Borden decided to double the commitment that had already grown about ten times over the original call to arms. The first call in August 1914 was for 25 000 volunteers (three times more than the Canadian contingent in the South African war). But even before Borden's trip abroad, the call was rising to the 250 000 mark. Then, at the end of 1915, the Prime Minister made his promise of raising a 500 000-man army. By this tragic pledge, Sir Robert hoped to prove that Canada was too important to be treated lightly. He would show Britain—and the world—that his country was no mere colony.

Of course, Canada never attained the manpower objective set by the Prime Minister. The reason was simple: it defied reality. The total population then was just under eight million. The total number of 20- to 39-year-old males according to the 1911 census was 1 692 000. If half were engaged in essential services such as food production, running the transportation network, and producing munitions (1 500 such factories in 90 different towns were created between 1915 and 1918), then there were barely 850 000 left for military service. Almost 300 000 had already put on khaki to maintain four divisions at strength. Where were the additional 300 000 volunteers to double the commitment in 1916? And where were the many hundreds of thousands more to take the places of the fallen if the fighting continued as in 1915?

The numbers that impressed Borden and many others were the levels of enlistments before New Year's Day, 1916. But even those figures gave ample reason for caution. Most of the early enlistments were of unmarried immigrants from the British Isles. Less than one third of the first volunteers were Canadian-born; nor was the Canadian portion evenly distributed over the whole country. The Canadians who were most likely to

143

volunteer were the unemployed single men of urban Ontario. Thus, the unity that was apparent in the first rush to enlist was somewhat illusory. The principle that Canada was involved to the maximum, however, remained a commitment that Borden refused to compromise.

Eventually, the need for replacements exhausted the number of able-bodied volunteers. Urban Ontario began to wonder about the rest of the country, and similar distress was echoed by Winnipeggers who expressed concern that "enemy alien" immigrants seemed only to have developed a love of Canada and no proportionate affection for the British Empire. Consequently, the Laurier-Greenway compromise of the Manitoba Schools Question was abandoned by the recently-elected government of T.C. Norris in 1916. In the new system, the guiding premise was that "in an English-speaking country, as this is, a knowledge of English is more necessary than a knowledge of arithmetic . . . ." Earlier, at the height of pre-war enthusiasm for imperialism, in 1912, a similar step had been taken in Ontario to restrict French as a language of instruction, notwithstanding Section 93 of the BNA Act. In 1915, the controversial "Regulation XVII" passed from the status of a directory to an act of the Provincial Parliament, and the Judicial Committee of the Privy Council upheld the law in 1916. In the same year, Robert Seller, an Ontario newspaper editor, reiterated the rationale for unilingualism in the fourth edition of his book called *The Tragedy of Quebec*. In the 1916 printing, Seller asserted:

> The issue . . . is fundamental and admits of no compromise, it is one that is not local but affects the future of the entire Dominion. It is simply whether this Canada of ours is to be British, and nothing else than British, or whether it is to be a mongrel land, with two official languages and ruled by a divided authority. (Quoted in R.C. Brown and R. Cook, *Canada, 1896-1921: A Nation Transformed* [1974], p. 259.)

Such bigotry—inflamed by the passion of war—was bound to provoke a fight with those who envisioned a different country. French-speaking Canadians, in particular, questioned the fundamental premise on which unlimited involvement in the Great War was supposed to have found its ultimate and unanswerable justification. Borden and his party had gone to war initially because Britain was at war. Later, somewhat lamely, they asserted that the cause was just—a holy war of the civilized nations of the world standing together to resist "Prussianism," meaning belligerent, autocratic, and repressive government. French-Canadians began to wonder in 1916 whether the overt discrimination against themselves in

Manitoba and Ontario and a War Measures Act that sanctioned government by decree did not prove that "Prussianism" was rampant in Canada as well.

Another reason that the minorities approached the war with something less than enthusiasm was the absence of anything but English-speaking units in the Canadian Corps. The Royal 22nd Regiment was created, ostensibly to fill the need for Quebeckers, but with few French-speaking officers, the unit became a regiment like the others. The crowning insult to Quebec was commissioning a Protestant clergyman to supervise recruiting in that province.

Not having units of their own, and sceptical that the war aims touched them directly, French-speaking Canadians launched an informal boycott of enlistments in 1916. By 1917, the number of volunteers elsewhere had fallen sharply as well. The result was that the number of recruits fell sadly behind the record of casualties in each month of the first half of 1917. Borden then faced a difficult choice. He could reduce the level of Canada's commitment proportionate to what was possible given the new rate of enlistments, or he could respond to British and English-Canadian pressure and resort to further "Prussianism" by imposing conscription. The Prime Minister opted for the more tragic of the two alternatives.

On May 18, 1917, Borden announced the necessity of conscription to the House of Commons; anti-conscriptionists in Montreal rioted in protest on May 24. The next day, Borden tried to make conscription less bitter by bringing Laurier into a coalition government. But Sir Wilfrid believed that unlimited liability was unwise and conscription worse. Sir Robert was therefore left to pursue his tragic course without the Liberal leader's assistance.

Laurier then made plain that he thought it was time for the voters of Canada to pass their judgement on Borden's record since 1911. An election was constitutionally required in 1916, but the life of Parliament had been extended one year by consent of the opposition. As the extension ran out, Borden sought another, but was refused.

Political parties usually believe that the country's survival hangs upon the defeat of their rivals. Such self-importance was especially the case in 1917. The heart of the matter was the conscription issue. Borden reconciled himself to compulsory service by fervently believing that "the country could not set any limits to its exertions that fell short of the totality of its powers." Laurier agreed. In his view, however, totality meant the utmost of voluntarism. To conscriptionists, such a qualification meant "the virtual withdrawal of Canada from the war, the desertion of her

145

soldiers overseas, the abject surrender of her honour, and the utter loss of her pride." Thus, Borden decided that the election that could not be avoided had to be rigged so that the contest would not be lost. "Our first duty is to win," he confided to his diary. And since the domestic victory had to be won regardless of cost, the election could not be called "until the ground has been carefully and completely prepared."

Borden's spade work was done by the architect of closure, the Solicitor General, Arthur Meighen of Manitoba. His first preparation was a Military Voters Act that provided means for those in uniform to vote overseas. Service personnel would vote by indicating a simple "yes" or "no" to record their support or opposition to the government; but voters who knew the names of individual candidates could vote for them by entering names—the name of any candidate—in space provided on the ballots. Lists of government candidates were taken to the soldiers along with the ballots; in practice then, the one kind of vote was as portable as the other. By this means, the government was given the power to manipulate approximately 25 percent of the vote to its own best advantage.

There was more. Meighen's additional pre-election fixing made even more sweeping changes. For the purpose of the coming election, the wives, mothers, sisters, and widows of military personnel were given voting privileges. Conversely, all conscientious objectors and all newcomers who took the oath of allegiance after 1902 had their voting rights withdrawn if natives of one of the countries fighting with the enemy and if not themselves in uniform for Canada, or if not women related to soldiers overseas. The purpose of the Wartime Elections Act, according to Arthur Meighen, was to "shift the franchise from the doubtful British or anti-British of the male sex and to extend it at the same time to our patriotic women . . . ." On this basis, Meighen thought it a "splendid stroke."

Most of the Liberals did not agree, of course. "It would have been more direct and at the same time more honest," one critic observed, "if the bill simply stated that all who did not pledge themselves to vote Conservative would be disfranchised." Not surprisingly, closure was needed to end the debate. Then, because the Senate had been enlarged with Conservatives in 1915, the manipulation of the franchise received assent from that body too. Borden's spade work convinced many Liberals that they could not survive opposition, and they stampeded to join a coalition called a Unionist government, leaving Laurier and a handful of anti-conscriptionists on the outside.

By mid-November 1917, everything was apparently in order for a Unionist victory, so Borden called the election for December 17. He appealed for unity and harmony on the grounds that he led a nonpartisan coalition dedicated to goals that every "red-blooded" Canadian wanted. There was thus a conscious attempt to stigmatize the opposition as seditious. Although the former Prime Minister was not arrested on a charge of giving aid and comfort to the enemy, Sir George Foster, Laurier's old defence critic, did not hesitate to make the accusation when he told a Toronto audience that "Every alien sympathizer, every man of alien blood born in an alien country with few exceptions, is with Sir Wilfrid Laurier, and every Hun sympathizer from Berlin to the trenches, from Berlin to the Cameroons, wishes success to Laurier, with his anti-conscriptionist campaign."

Since the outcome of the election had been cooked in advance, the victory of Borden's Unionist party was never in doubt. Even so, the results did underscore the extent to which the country was divided over the question of unlimited involvement. Seventy-five percent of the electorate in Quebec voted one way, 64 percent of the electorate in the rest of Canada voted the other. The enormous discrepancy on such a vital issue led Henri Bourassa to wonder whether Canada would ever develop a sense of national interest. "So long as English Canadians remain more British than Canadian," Bourassa predicted that "these differences are bound to happen every time there is a conflict between the demands of British imperialism and the resistance of Canadian nationalism."

Of course, Borden's supporters considered themselves no less patriotic than Bourassa. But their patriotism was entrenched in the other nationalism, the notion that Canada's strength was realized best by close alliance with Britain. In 1917, the cost of the British connection seemed to be conscription regardless of the consequences. There was rioting; Quebec was brought near to secession; civil rights were systematically suspended by the War Measures Act; and the oath of allegiance of the non-British immigrants was cynically disregarded by the Wartime Elections Act. Here were the bitter tragedies, the experience of the war that English-speaking Canadians wanted quickly forgotten.

Suggested Reading

General histories that cover the period from Laurier's defeat in 1911 to the end of the Great War include R.C. Brown and R. Cook, Canada, *1896-1921: A Nation Transformed* (1974), and Robert Bothwell, *et al., Canada, 1900-1945* (1987).

Two works providing useful interpretations of Borden's pre-war reform program are R.C. Brown's *Robert Laird Borden: A Biography*, vol. 1, *1854-1914* (1975), and the more analytical interpretation of Borden's departure from traditional political style in John English, *The Decline of Politics: The Conservatives and the Party System* (1977).

Readers interested in more detailed descriptions of the agonies of the combat in France and Flanders will find evocative portrayals in two books that provide sympathetic treatment that still do not glorify the war itself. Pierre Berton's *Vimy* (1986), offers a personal narrative of the most dramatic Canadian action, repeats the view that victory there confirmed that Canada had at last come of age, but ends in the assertion that if such was the cost of international recognition, the price was too high. D.L. Goodspeed offers a more comprehensive history of the war in fewer pages in *The Road Past Vimy: The Canadian Corps, 1914-1918* (1969). His brief account (only 174 pages of text), is a masterpiece of condensation showing that history need not be verbose to be comprehensive, and closes with the wise suggestion that the "futilities" of war are no sound justification for neglecting its study.

Of course, futility affected those who remained in Canada as well. Several works have appeared recently in a serious attempt to understand the war in its domestic impact. Graham Metson's edition of Archibald MacMechan, *The Halifax Explosion, December 6, 1917* (1978), describes what was perhaps the most dramatic incident on the domestic front: an explosion following the collision of two ships in the harbour that leveled most of the waterfront. No other part of Canada suffered the same kind of destruction, but other wounds were somewhat less reparable. Barbara M. Wilson, ed., *Ontario and the First World War* (1977), offers a book-length introduction to the development of war fever in the most British province, and J.H. Thompson, *The Harvests of War: the Prairie West, 1914-1918* (1978), surveys the impact of the war on the region that was most ethnically diverse. Thomas Socknat, *Witness Against War: Pacifism in Canada, 1900-1945* (1987), shows the diversity of anti-war sentiment. J.M. Hitsman and J.L. Granatstein, *Broken Promises: A History of Conscription in Canada* (1977), is the latest of several works on the "pointless" attempt to bring Quebec to heel by force. For the election that followed, see Desmond Morton, "Polling the Soldier Vote: The Overseas Campaign in the Canadian General Election of 1917," *JCS* (1975).

**Special police marching
against strikers, Winnipeg, 1919.**

"What kind of war was this?"

CHAPTER 8
SOCIAL FERMENT, 1919-1921

— 1. War Fever As a Reform Impulse —

Canadians went to war in 1914, initially, because Britain was at war. That was sufficient justification for raising the first contingent of volunteers. By the time involvement was proclaimed to be total, however, such a justification, by itself, was vulnerable to the charge of jingoism. There had to be more at stake than duty to the mother country. Consequently, two other war aims came to the fore, sometimes separately, sometimes together. One was proving that Canada was a power in the world. The other was vindicating the cause of liberty and democracy. Thus, Clifford Sifton asserted that the experience was a baptism in "nationhood with the blood of our sons . . . shed for the greatest struggle the world has ever seen and in the noblest cause for which men have ever fought. Canada's struggle was supposed to win international recognition and to advance the well-being of mankind as a whole.

Where the population was sufficiently British, there was no need to overemphasize the disinterested advancement of humanity as a war aim. In provinces such as Ontario, it was nearly sufficient to stress the "needs of the Empire" and to play to "British patriotism and loyalty." In Ontario, the central war aim could be proving that Canada was a strong "self-governing state of the Empire." The emphasis was upon Canada's character as a dedicated part of the wider British nation. The Chief Inspector of Schools in Toronto, Robert Crowley, illustrated this mood in his justification for censoring students' music books. Referring to some melodies by German authors, Crowley said:

> The music reader contains at least some selections that should never be sung in a British school, and whatever may have been the opinion as to their general merit at the time they were introduced, they cannot be regarded as a medium fit to develop the high moral and patriotic ideals of British Citizenship. (Quoted in B.M. Wilson, ed., *Ontario and the First World War* [1977], p. xciv.)

In the West, by contrast, because of the different ethnic mix, it was necessary to stress the international reform aspect as well. Illustrating the theme was the work of a Winnipeg clergyman, C.W. Gordon (writing sermons in the guise of novels under the pen-name of Ralph Connor). One of his characters in *The Sky Pilot in No Man's Land* made plain that "the biggest thing . . . is not that the motherland is in need of help, though, of course, we all feel that, but that the freedom of the world is threatened, and that Canada, as one of the free nations of the world, must do her part in its defence." Conveniently ignoring that one of the Allies was Russia, every bit as autocratic as Germany, those who stressed that the war would make mankind more free focused only on Germany. By force of arms, the civilized nations of the world (on the western front) were engaged in a great crusade to make certain that "when the war is over Germany will become a democracy . . . instead of being ruled by a wicked Emperor." As such sentiment was also a reform impulse, it was natural that there would be a domestic as well as an international focus for that energy, and that the zeal would outlast the fighting in Europe.

But just as there was a lack of national unity on the issue of unlimited involvement in military action and the degree to which the war was aimed at reform in the first place, so too was there a lack of national consensus on the proper direction for the non-military domestic crusades. In the West, where the Great War was perhaps most frequently advertised as an international purification struggle, the demand for "uplifting" reforms was strongest. Ontario and the Maritime provinces, the most British parts of Canada, were less keen to embrace the other crusades. And in Quebec, the prevailing mood was resentment of social change in general, and reforms initiated by the rest of Canada in particular.

— 2. Postwar Quebec —

Early in 1918, the Legislative Assembly of Quebec debated a resolution to the effect that "this House . . . would be disposed to accept the breaking of the Confederation Pact of 1867 if, in the other provinces, it is believed that she is an obstacle to the union, progress and development of Canada." The debate provided an opportunity for many speakers to air their dissatisfaction with conscription, the Manitoba and Ontario school questions, and the manipulated franchise in the recent general election. Eventually, however, the motion was withdrawn before it came to a vote. In the retreat, fear of change became more visible than dissatisfaction with Confederation.

The sudden emergence of a separatism that was only rhetorical suggested that French-Canadian nationalism had changed a great deal since the days of its first outburst in the 1830s. Then and later, there were republicans willing to defend the integrity of their province by direct action out-of-doors as well as in the Legislative Assembly. At the same time, there were clerical spokesmen who were no less nationalist, but who were less keen to lead the people to the barricades in the name of republicanism and liberty. The clerical leaders usually preferred a quieter—at times almost a passive—resistance as the sounder course, and so also, it seemed, did the general public of Quebec. Consequently, on the occasions of the most strident nationalism, the secular nationalists trumpeted anti-clerical denunciations as well as their anti-British slogans, and each time the Church emerged the stronger voice of *survivance*. By 1917, French-Canadian nationalism still had its proponents, but its main pivot—its dominant style—was that of the clerical leaders. Since anti-clerical firebrands were no longer of any consequence, the French-Canadian nationalism that arose from the wake of domestic war injuries was quietly inward-turning, not poised for a mass movement for direct action along the lines of the rebels of the 1830s. But the resentment was real, and the consciousness Quebeckers had as a people unto themselves could be gauged by the manner in which they held on to their past, even as they tried all the harder to promote modern capitalism.

One clear indication of Quebec's sense that its refuge was the past was romanticization of agrarianism, a sentiment, expressed many times before by urban writers, that the rural life was morally superior to that of the

153

cities. Such a notion was expressed simultaneously by farmers' movements in Ontario and the West. But the peculiar twist in the Quebec case was the idea that the very survival of the province culturally depended upon pastoral simplicity. When Lionel Groulx said, "we must sow or go jobless, our people must be agricultural or perish," he was saying a great deal more than that the farmer's vocation was the most noble. Groulx fervently believed that Quebeckers' language and religion would perish in the industrial cauldrons of Montreal. He therefore called his people back to the land, even though most had already fled to town. Moreover, the new government that came to power in 1920 did so on the strength of the popularity of its promise to promote yet more industrialism.

Louis-Alexandre Taschereau rose to the premiership of Quebec by promising to make Quebec a leader in the competition for foreign capital investment with a rural thrust to the resource-based industrialism he promised. He appeared to promote a happy compromise of the rural ideal in 1920 since his stated motive was to gain development that would create employment opportunities to keep people in the villages of their birth, to spare them migration and the deracination that was expected to follow. Taschereau's program was promoted as a means of preserving the character of traditional society while progressing beyond the old means of production; in the transition from agricultural village to company town oriented to mining or pulp and paper production, the parish priest would care for his parishioners as always. The people affected would see the pattern of their employment shift from agricultural to industrial work, their incomes would rise, and all such benefits would occur without their leaving home. Here was industrialization that posed less of a threat to "our doctrine."

In a similar, clerically-led manner, there might also be labour organization without deracination or radicalism. Prior to 1920, the unions that had arisen were English-Canadian or American in origin, and clerical authorities had not looked favourably upon either. When a bitter strike at the Thetford Mines in 1915 raised the spectre of radical unionism, the Church moved to head off such a development. A quiescent Roman Catholic union was organized in its place. The initiative was extended and in 1921, the Confédération de travailleurs catholiques du Canada (CTCC), a primarily Quebec-based labour movement, was born.

The Catholic unions intended to diminish "foreign" influence and to counter the "claim that capital, capitalists, and employers are born enemies of labour." The theory of the new organizations was that every union would have its moderating chaplain, or *aumônier*, and the clerical

154

leader, answerable to his bishop, would guarantee harmony between employers and workers. In the 1920s, both objectives were largely realized. The unions of "strangers" made little headway and where the exceptional chaplain misled his flock into labour militancy he was subject to the corrective action of his superiors. John Thompson and Allen Seager have argued that "the gap between CTCC practice and its corporatist theory was wide and growing," but that contradiction did not result in significant consequences until the next generation. In the postwar period of the 1920s, Quebec had drawn inward and found refuge in its ultra-clerical, corporate conception of political community. Whether in the country or in the factory, Quebeckers were told again and again that they had a purpose that transcended materialism or individual well-being. Former politician, Henri Bourassa, editor of *Le Devoir*, expressed the ideal perhaps better than any other spokesman in 1918:

> Our special task, as French Canadians, is to insert into America the spirit of Christian France. It is to defend against all comers, perhaps even against France herself, our religious and national heritage. This heritage does not belong to us alone. It belongs to all Catholic America. It belongs to the whole Church, and it is the basic foundation of the Church in this part of the world. It belongs to all French civilization of which it is the refuge and fortress and anchor amid the immense sea of saxonizing Americanism. (Quoted in George Grant, *Lament for a Nation* [1965], pp. 80-81.)

Like the rhetorical separatism that surfaced at the same time—or the rural industrialism promoted by Taschereau—Bourassa's nationalism translated easily into a veneration of tradition. The discontent in Quebec generated by the war thus heightened a nationalism that romanticized the past even as it embraced and hastened the destruction of the traditional rural basis of Quebec society.

— 3. Nostalgia in the Maritimes —

A similar retreat occurred in the Maritime provinces after the war, although its origins were not to be found in disenchantment with the combat in Europe or disgruntlement over the fanaticism with which the conflict had been supported by Ontario. Indeed, the people of Halifax, for example, had sacrificed more for the cause than any other community in the country. In addition to the loss of its fighting men, Halifax suffered thousands of civilian casualties. On December 6, 1917, two ships collided in the harbour. One, the *Mont Blanc*, a munitions ship loaded with highly-explosive gun cotton (the propellent for heavy artillery), caught fire. When the flames reached the explosive cargo, the entire vessel ignited in a split second, reduced the ship to atoms and levelled about one third of the nearby town with casualties comparable to those of a major engagement of the Canadian Corps. More than 400 of the dead were so completely consumed by the force of the blast that they vanished without a trace. Weeks later, in the election that was also a plebiscite on the war, the majority of Maritimers supported the Unionist government, conscription, and a continuation of the struggle on the level of total commitment. Moreover, they did so without any great promise of wholesale reforms. According to C.M. Wallace, it was enough that the conflict was an important "imperial event." Like most of the people of Ontario, the majority of Maritimers saw their Canadian citizenship in British terms.

Another reason that the war appeared to be supported almost without question was that it sustained a level of prosperity in little factory towns such as Amherst, Nova Scotia, towns that otherwise were beginning to suffer from a process of deindustrialization following the consolidation of industry in central Canada. At the war's end, with the imminent loss of munitions works, some factories on the verge of closing in 1914 faced the prospect of a complete shutdown. At the same time, however, it was clear that the rest of the country expected a "new era" of prosperity. Consequently, once postwar recession hit the Maritimes in the summer of 1920, mass protest developed as local politicians urged everyone to forget parochial differences and unite in demanding relief from Ottawa.

The "Maritime Rights" movement of the 1920s resembled at least two other such exercises that had occurred since 1867. In both preceding movements, the impulse to preserve or restore a prosperity that was imagined to have depended upon independence from Upper Canadian interference motivated Maritimers to protest. Since their complaints arose from national-political causes, the remedy was also expected from the same source. Rhetoricians skilled in projecting their personal frustrations as public problems established prominence by tapping a reservoir of shared resentment, aroused the electorate with accusations that everyone's status was imperiled, and united their compatriots to threaten separation if better terms were not forthcoming from Canada. Such protest was a defensive nationalism that was nearly as strident as Quebec's. Moreover, unity in resistance was sufficient catharsis. Little did the voters seem to notice or to care that their saviours made almost no difference once they were elected. Thus it was with Joseph Howe and his "Repealers"in 1868 and W.S. Fielding and the "Secessionists" in 1886.

In the new movement, however, the cycle of protest unfolded with a special twist; in Nova Scotia and New Brunswick there were specific and local socio-economic definitions of public problems that were leading thousands of workers into a labour movement that was both militant and political. On Cape Breton Island, the great coal-mining part of the region, the miners had successfully formed the largest union in the country. Local District No. 26 of the United Mine Workers boasted more than 13 000 members. Other workers, for instance, the factory-hands of the numerous manufacturing establishments in Amherst (a small Nova Scotia town of 10 000) were also organizing "one great union."

The Amherst Federation of Labour was intended as a union of all industrial workers in the community. Whether they worked in Stanfield's textile mill or Robb's machinery works, they recognized that they shared similar grievances concerning work conditions and pay rates. Their common interest led them to strike in May 1919 to secure a reduction of hours with no reduction in wages. In the face of such solid resistance, strikebreakers could not effectively replace them. Stanfield refused to talk to the union, but other owners did make concessions, eventually. The Amherst General Strike was a partial success.

Elsewhere in the Maritimes, labour made similar gains. At the same time, the new labour movement became openly political in its goals. Labour conventions in New Brunswick and Nova Scotia declared that they would attempt to influence the two established political parties, but they also indicated that their greater hope was with independent labour parties. In this trend, Amherst, the same community that successfully struck in 1919, elected a labour candidate to the provincial legislature in 1920. Since there were a number of other Amhersts in Nova Scotia, and since the politically active farmers defined themselves as a social class that was poorly represented by the two old parties, the Conservatives of Nova Scotia found themselves in third-place position behind a Farmer-Labour Party coalition.

Unfortunately for the labour movement, the war-sustained prosperity collapsed soon after the election. With the rate of unemployment running at ten percent by 1921 and some plants closing permanently, union membership fell almost 50 percent as soon as the recession deepened. The Liberal governments in Nova Scotia and New Brunswick groped for recovery measures by blaming the depression on the recent tariff and freight-rate policies of the Conservatives in Ottawa, but once the national

Liberals defeated the Tories, it became more difficult for the Liberal premiers in the Atlantic provinces to continue the same line of denunciation. At this point, according to one prominent Liberal, the Conservatives broke into "our pantry and stole our prize bone." The Nova Scotia Conservative House Leader, H.W. Corning, demanded better terms from Ottawa and if they were not forthcoming, he claimed that the Maritimers would be justified in separating from the rest of Canada. By the spring of 1923, with such sentiment widespread in New Brunswick and Nova Scotia, Corning proposed a referendum to pull his province out of Confederation to become an "independent, self-governing British dominion" like Newfoundland. Of course, no such referendum was taken, and Corning was subsequently displaced by another Conservative sounding the same note without proposing such specific reprisal if the demands of the "Maritime Rights Movement" were not met.

In Nova Scotia and New Brunswick, the rights demanded had to do with federal policies concerning subsidies, the tariff, and transportation. Since everyone was urged to forget all local fights in the struggle against the common enemy in Ottawa, and since such persuasion was effective, the third-party movements of both provinces were swallowed up by a restored faith in the Conservatives who led the demand for better terms from Ottawa. In 1925, the Liberal governments of both provinces were defeated. The Conservatives attracted 60 percent of the popular vote in Nova Scotia, winning 40 of the 43 seats in the legislature. The Farmer-Labour coalition was wiped out. In New Brunswick, the margin of victory was almost as complete (37 of 48 seats), with the same devastating impact on the labour party. Thus, a genuine radical protest in the region was absorbed by a more facile, old-style provincial rights crusade.

According to George Rawlyk, the election results of 1925 signified the success of another movement by Maritimers to express their disenchantment "in words rather than effective action." Answering that the region did suffer from Ottawa's adverse fiscal and transportation policies, E.R. Forbes has been less harsh in his judgement and suggests that the movement "went much deeper than mere political maneuvering or . . . the attempt by the local 'Establishment' to undercut other forms of social protest." Forbes argues that because all "classes" had reason to be discontented, and because the "Maritime rights agitation . . . saw all classes united in their demands upon the rest of the country," the Maritime Rights Movement was a positive development. That the rest of Canada was unwilling to grant sufficient tariff protection to Maritime products or subsidize freight rates to give Maritimers better access to the wider

Canadian market is no fault of the Conservative leaders of the movement, according to Forbes.

Even so, Forbes does leave a major question unanswered. He does not explain why the Conservatives failed to take more radical action once they lost their war of words with Ottawa. The possibility remains that, notwithstanding Forbe's assertions to the contrary, the greater enemy all along may have been the more local group that humiliated the Conservatives in 1920, because against labour the victory was total. In communities such as Amherst, according to Nolan Reilly, "by the middle of the 1920s, the formal presence of a trade union movement . . . had all but disappeared." Having been checked first by recession and then coopted into a larger movement that brought the people of the region only slight, tangible benefits, the ordinary voters of the Maritimes, like those of Quebec in the same decade, were left stunned by apathy and cynicism. With lower wages and higher levels of unemployment, they had the highest rate of outmigration in the nation. In the meantime, managers and millowners, newspaper editors, and "responsible" leaders of labour continued to sit on Boards of Trade, merely talking about "Maritime Rights."

— 4. The Purification of the Prairies —

The prairie provinces accumulated a different set of Pyrrhic victories in the area of war-accentuated social reform. Indeed, the West led the nation in the cause of domestic purification. Three crusades were central to the reformers' drive to cleanse and purify the country from bottom up. One was the prohibition of the importation and sale of alcoholic beverages. Another was the enfranchisement of women. The third addressed the "problem" of unifying the country around a common cultural standard.

The compelling rationale for the first drive was that the production and consumption of alcohol hampered the war effort. Intoxication threatened productivity and contributed to crime. Grains consumed by breweries or distilleries were better utilized as food for people or livestock. Also, a growing minority simply believed that alcohol was the root of all evil (including poverty). The prairie provinces took the lead in outlawing alcoholic beverages in 1915. The others (except Quebec) followed thereafter. Ultimately, in April 1918, the Government of Canada followed with an Order in Council prohibiting the importation of liquor for the duration of the war. After the Armistice, the importation resumed and Quebec was as wet as ever. British Columbia moved from prohibition to government-encouraged temperance in 1920; Manitoba and Alberta followed British Columbia's lead in 1923; then came Saskatchewan in 1924. Ontario and the Atlantic provinces made their moves to temperance between 1925 and 1929.

By 1930, the typical Canadian "control" of alcohol was to sell spirits in government-owned "dispensaries" to licensed customers. Liquor was not consumed in public. The only public drinking in a typical Canadian province was in the tightly regulated, men-only "beer parlours" whose decor was defined as rigidly as the hours of operation. Such establishments were windowless caverns concealing an activity the state chose to endure but not to condone; they were intended to be joyless "premises" where eating was as forbidden as entertainment, and working men might sit for only a pint or two on the way home from the factory. He who consumed too much was not to be served another, and the wretch who nursed a glass slowly was still shown the door in the early evening because one of the periods of forbidden operation was over the 6:30 p.m. to 8:00 p.m. supper time, when every man was supposed to be home with his wife and "kiddies."

Such temperance—rather than total prohibition—was all that many reformers had sought in the first place. On this account, prohibition exemplified a reform that was tested in an extreme form under wartime conditions, then adopted in moderation in the postwar period. The Pyrrhic victory aspect is that despite the measurable drop in crime that accompanied prohibition, poverty continued as ever. Clearly, drink was merely one of the symptoms of a larger problem, and there were few middle-class reformers who wanted to face the more difficult issue of the inequitable distribution of income. Consequently, one class-biased reform achievement did not lead to the larger social question so much as what John Thompson has called the "end of idealism" in the 1920s.

The same pattern of winning a reform victory in an extreme way during the war, then relaxing the achievement in the post-war period only to discover that victory made little difference, becomes evident in an examination of the two other western reform movements. Female suffrage for example, had been actively agitated in the West since 1912, when a mainly Protestant, English-speaking middle-class women's movement established the Political Equality League in Manitoba. It recruited almost 1 200 members at once, and increased its strength 30-fold over the next three years. Finally, the Manitoba suffragists succeeded in January 1916; two months later, those of Saskatchewan and Alberta won their victory, and the federal concession came in the grotesque distortion of the Wartime

Elections Act of 1917, discussed in the previous chapter. What was expected by the wartime enfranchisement of women?

In the prewar years, middle-class, Protestant Canadians, regardless of gender, had several keen preoccupations and anxieties. They worried about urban poverty, ethnic diversification, and signs of physical degeneration of the human race. The three were related in the sense that "foreigners" were believed to be the most likely to prevent children from attending school, the most likely to drink, and the most tempted to buy the services of street prostitutes, allegedly, the prime source of "social disease"—syphilis and gonorrhea. Given the state of prewar medical science, neither was curable; gonorrhea was untreatable. A much-quoted study of New York City concluded that roughly one in five adults was infected with one or both diseases; the two combined accounted for one quarter of all blindess and sterility, nearly three quarters of miscarriages, and half of something called "terminal brain disease." Where would it end? What was the solution?

The respectable middle-class position was to abolish prostitution and teach chastity at home. The inadequacy of such an approach was that neither alternative remedied sources of contagion from the allegedly ignorant, promiscuous foreigners. Worse yet, since the good fight against poverty by child-saving through compulsory education and anti-child labour laws was supposedly thwarted by the foreign, working-class voter, the growing frustration of the middle class (especially in the West) was that even if every upright, Protestant male refused to vote for any but God-fearing, uncorruptible, decent fellow businessmen, their numbers were still too few to turn the tide. Suspecting that the same hard-drinking, child-exploiting, Pope-worshipping, ignorant foreigners would take a similarly "unprogressive" attitude towards their women voting, female enfranchisement appeared a neat strategy for doubling the middle-class, Protestant vote. According to Carol Bacchi, women's suffrage was a means to an end that had almost nothing to do with women's issues, regardless of class, or the enhancement of the status of women in general. Of course, the same interpretation applies to the suffrage issue in Canada's manipulation of the franchise for winning the election of 1917. Indeed, before proceeding with the matter, the government polled the leading, middle-class women's groups for their opinions on the probable effectiveness of the measure, and then proceeded with the leaders' approval and support.

Later, every province with a Protestant majority adopted the new device for inflating the vote of its middle class: Ontario in 1917, the

Atlantic provinces between 1918 and 1922. Conversely, the one province with a Roman Catholic majority did not move on the question (women were not added to the franchise in Quebec until 1940, after the rest of Canada made the discovery that the innovation had almost no impact on the ethnic and class balance in politics). By that time, of course, the enfranchisement of women at the federal level had been relaxed, in 1918, from the selective aspect of enfranchising only certain women, to the prewar demand of granting all women the vote.

In the meantime, draconian measures were proposed on the Prairies to deal with the "race suicide" concern of Protestant, British-origin Canadians, who believed that they were in danger of becoming a power- less minority in their home provinces. Reformers not caught up in the phobia of "racial degeneration" still worried that a "mongrel" culture was emerging. During the war, they gained an important ally in the Govern- ment of Canada as the Department of Justice began closely monitoring the activities of persons of "enemy-alien" origin.

After the Armistice, indicative of the ill-feeling sustained by the pre- vious four years, Borden received a deluge of petitions demanding the expulsion of everyone disfranchised in the recent election. At about the same time, a Methodist minister in Winnipeg completed a history of western settlement that purportedly documented the preceding 20 years of western development to expose as mistaken the faith that had been placed in central Europeans even as "guest workers." Wellington Bridgman's *Breaking Prairie Sod* asserted that the central Europeans were a violent and disruptive group before the war and a disloyal population during the conflict. With soldiers coming home to Canada by the thousands in 1919, many were finding it difficult to secure peacetime employment. Bridgman argued that the "enemy aliens" ought to be expelled from the country and their property turned over to veterans. The procedure he recommended was as follows: "We would ask the Dominion government to appoint a commission of returned soldiers in each province to adjudicate and settle the amount that will be allowed each enemy alien and enemy alien family" before they were returned to Europe. Suggesting that such a policy was consistent with government action to date, referring to the Wartime Elec- tions Act, Bridgman reminded the government that Canada had already "claimed the right and the authority to disfranchise all the enemy aliens in the Dominion . . . and on appealing to the country, were endorsed by the largest majorities that ever sent men to Parliament." Since harsh measures were evidently popular, he suggested that his scheme would receive wide acceptence, and the returning veterans were the ideal persons to dispossess the disfranchised because "the returned soldier . . . knows the Austro-Hun, our enemy over the sea, and he knows the enemy alien better than any other man. His judgement will not be spoiled by prejudice, nor can he ever be tempted to show favouritism." The returned man would have no scruples against the expropriation of the aliens' property at "one fourth of its value or less"—just enough to pay their return passage to Europe.

Bridgman's scheme was seriously considered but dropped because the government was already too preoccupied with the problems of demobilization, according to Donald Avery. A less extreme remedy was found in deportation on a case-by-case basis: groups were declared illegal, membership in which was cause for internment, and any "enemy alien" interned during the war could be deported at the Immigration Department's discretion between 1918 and 1922. In 1923, the federal government did agree to an outright ban on any further immigration from China, and followed the United States in adopting a generally more restrictive policy concerning the immigration of southern and eastern Europeans. The "docile foreigners" already in Canada were left to the assimilationist programs of the provinces. Assimilationists shared Bridgman's zeal for making "this Dominion mainly British in spirit," but they were more optimistic that the "inferior races" could be trained into an "attachment to British ideals and institutions." What the assimilationists shared with the expulsionists, however, was a profound fear that Canada might develop into a multicultural country.

The new, strident affirmation that Canada was British or nothing was, in a sense, simply a harsher, broader repudiation of collective minority rights, such as the earlier repudiations of dualism in Manitoba in the 1890s, and the other two prairie provinces after 1905. There was nothing new in the distrust of diversity and the suspicion that toleration of minority rights was a sign of national weakness. The novelty of the bigotry of the 1920s was its virulence: many Orangemen on the Prairies donned the traditional sash for the "glorious twelfth" and the white hood of the Ku Klux Klan for other public occasions, declaring that the "major principles propounded were, in the main, such as we had always held . . . ."

— 5. The Winnipeg General Strike —

The passion behind the nonmilitary, domestic crusades was bound to generate conflict between regions, nationalities, and classes. The first and most dramatic clash after the war involved industry and labour. Labour unrest was universal in 1919—in Europe, Britain, and the United States as well as in every region of Canada. The basic problem was resentment over bans on strikes in the face of rapid inflation in 1918. After the Armistice, Canada and the others lifted their strike-bans and inflation continued. By 1919, it cost Canadians at least $1.60 to buy what $1 had purchased in 1913. Some workers such as farm labourers and some railway employees had enjoyed proportionate wage increases, but most workers had not kept up. For most, the rate of inflation between 1916 and 1919 was about twice that of wage increases. To remedy the situation, workers resorted to organized action—almost twice as many were unionized in 1919 as in 1917 (370 000 in comparison with 205 000), and unionized workers almost invariably went on strike (3.5 million working days were lost in 459 strikes in 1919). But here the universality of response ended. In some places, the form and purpose of organization were remarkably radical. And, there was considerable difference in the kinds of responses by government to labour militancy and radicalism.

A militant union was prone to strike; a radical organization was one that attempted to organize the unskilled as well as the skilled, and to organize such workers along the lines of an entire industry or community with one council operating as the exclusive bargaining agent for all the workers thus joined. Within these criteria, the Amherst Federation of Labour described earlier and its use of the "general strike" weapon were both militant and radical. But the Amherst action involved no more than 3 000 workers in a town of 10 000, and the Town Council stepped forward to play a role as honest broker to mediate the dispute without frustration by intervening provincial and federal authorities. In Winnipeg, ten times as many workers were involved in a similar organization and action, and every level of jurisdiction played a part. All government initiatives were repressive. Such action and reaction raise two issues. First, why did maritime and western Canadian workers appear to be more radical than their equally militant counterparts elsewhere in Canada? And what accounts for the evident difference in the responses of those in government?

The key to the first problem may be that the workers of the Maritimes and the West, having missed the demoralizing experience of the defeat of the Knights of Labor in central Canada in the 1890s, were less willing to consider such industrial unionism inherently futile. The leaders of the craft unions in central Canada survived the earlier era by establishing a set practice of negotiation with managers and government that was essentially conservative. Moreover, as James Naylor has shown, the work of such labour bosses was to manage their unions rather than to work at trades or on the factory floor. By contrast, the "One Big Union" concept and the weapon of the general strike were most likely to compel action where leaders were in closer touch with the men and women in their work places and where there were no inhibiting memories of prior similar action. Government reaction to such radical syndicalism appears to have depended upon how polarized the political community was at the time of general strike action. Certainly the Amherst and Winnipeg cases sustain such an interpretation. In Amherst, the local government could intervene with an olive branch, and prepare the way for a negotiated settlement. Then the same leaders could persuade workers to abandon their union altogether, to make common cause against Ottawa in the Maritime Rights Movement. In Winnipeg, by contrast, the government had no such subtle control devices. The community was divided and distrustful before the strike, and, of course, more so after the dispute.

As early as 1913, there were indications that the Winnipeg working class was turning away from the traditional governing elite in favour of working-class leaders. That year, despite a property franchise, R.A. Rigg, the business agent for the Winnipeg Trades and Labour Council, was elected to office as a city alderman. Then in 1914, W.B. Simpson, a mere truck driver, was elected to the body that was supposed to be made up of 18 governing businessmen.

By 1915, it was possible to imagine that men of property might some-day lose control of the government of Winnipeg if they did not set aside their differences and defeat the democracy that put labour's bookkeeper and a socialist teamster in the sanctity of city hall. Hard measures, if necessary, would be justified to preserve the proper social boundaries between workers and managers. In this spirit, the Winnipeg business community joined to move a variety of issues, significant as well as petty. One of the latter, during the war, was a proposal to start a military flying school on the justification that "Winnipeg could help the cause in no better way than in training pilots for air scouting." To this end, $5 000 of public revenue was voted to be added to $40 000 to be raised by private subscription. Tuition for the university-graduate entrants to the flying school was $400. When labour members of council denounced the scheme for its obvious elitism, the businessmen voted in a block to override their objections.

With each subsequent municipal election, an additional one or two labour members were added to the growing labour party on Winnipeg City Council. By 1918, the labour group consisted of five members, roughly one third of the council. The labour group seized the initiative, moving for instance for the reduction of the high cost of a pedlar's licence to make it easier for someone to hawk merchandise in the streets, to the possible disadvantage of established merchants. All but one of the businessmen on Council opposed the labour initiative, and the matter was defeated 11 to six. But on another issue, curiously, a labour motion passed.

Winnipeg's police force had recently formed a union and the city hesitated to recognize it as their collective bargaining agent. The labour members of council took up the cause with a motion to "recognize and deal with the newly formed Policemen's Union, following a policy that employees in the service of the public shall have the right to form unions." The motion carried, but Alderman Frank Fowler spoke for the business minority in opposition when he said that the police were the ultimate security of property. If they had a union, the middle class would lose its last defence. Fowler asserted that the constables must decide whether they were on the side of their "sworn duty" or that of organized labour because, in his view, "they cannot serve both trade unions and the persons whose property they protect." Perhaps the other businessmen on Council felt that since the police were so important to their protection they deserved special consideration and found it easier to oppose cheaper pedlars' licences than collective bargaining for the police force accordingly. Whatever the various reasons, the incident showed that an interesting dichotomy was developing between labour and property, and that the city was well polarized and poised for a dramatic confrontation by 1918.

When representatives of Winnipeg's labour unions attended the annual meeting of the Trades and Labour Congress of Canada in Quebec shortly thereafter, Westerners discovered that there was almost as much difference between themselves and the professional leaders of eastern craft unions as between themselves and the Frank Fowlers of Winnipeg. Complaining that the "labour movement of the east is reactionary and servile to its core," they decided that the appropriate response was to divorce west from east and to pursue bolder action independently. The leaders of western labour met in Calgary in March 1919, and endorsed the concept of industrial unionism without limits on the organization or scope of the application of the strike weapon. They endorsed the idea of One Big Union that would resort to general strikes whenever necessary.

The first test of the new strategy came two months later in Winnipeg. A dispute for improved wages and hours in the building trades joined with a more fundamental struggle by iron workers to win recognition for the Metal Trades Council as their bargaining agent. Soon the building trades and metal workers appealed to the 70 other unions in the city for sympathetic action. Under the auspices of the Winnipeg Trades and Labour

Council, all were polled one by one and the membership indicated over-whelming support for calling a general strike if employers continued to withhold bargaining rights from the Metal Trades Council.

At midday on May 15, 1919, the business of Canada's third largest city came to a halt when about 30 000 workers (one third of whom were not even members of unions) walked off their jobs. Everything from movie houses to bakeries closed. No streetcars ran. The telegraph and telephone services were halted. Even some toilets stopped flushing as the skeletal staff maintaining water pressure held it too low to rise above the first floor of most buildings.

Although the regular institutions of city government continued to function, the actual day-to-day administration of the city passed to the strike committee in a broad variety of matters. For instance, even though the Winnipeg police had voted to strike, they stayed on the job because they were ordered to do so by the committee. Similarly, milk and bread deliveries were permitted, also, "by authority of the strike committee."

To Winnipeg's business elite, the issue was no longer one of collective bargaining or of the legitimacy of industrial unionism. What was at stake was the larger question of the control of the community because, in their view, the socialist revolution in Russia in 1917 had begun similarly. Consequently, they reacted to the strike committee's extra-legal action by forming a body of their own, a kind of vigilante organization called the Committee of One Thousand—"Citizens' Committee" for short. It was their aim to unite voters still loyal to the old political parties into one non-partisan front to break the strike with a union of their own. They deputized "special" firemen, then police, and waited for action. Given the array of competing extra-legal authorities—and the explosiveness of the control issue—it is surprising that the situation did not disintegrate into generalized disorder at once. But the strikers were careful to prevent any appearance of anarchy because they expected that even a small distur-bance would be met with force and martial law. For three weeks, the strike committee worked with cooperative regular police to prevent any such pretext from occurring; for three weeks there was uneasy peace.

As soon as the strike began, however, there were unrelenting calls for government intervention from newspapers across the country on the grounds that the Winnipeg situation resembled a revolution. "Canada must not become a second Russia," they warned. On the same theme, it was asserted that the "revolutionary agitators" who were taking over Winnipeg were mainly "enemy aliens." But judging by their surnames, the most prominent leaders in the movement were eminently Anglo-Saxon. Indeed, some of the strike leaders were prominent Protestant clergymen, such as J.S. Woodsworth who found the strike a glorious outpouring of the "social gospel," a Christianity that was concerned with life on earth and the "Brotherhood of Man," rather than with theology or creed.

Far from being an attempt to take over Winnipeg by foreign (or native-born) communists, the simplest description of the strike was that it was little more than an attempt by the Metal Trades Council to win recognition from three large metal fabricating companies to be the exclusive bargaining agent for all employees in their type of work. The companies, on the other hand, had not yet adjusted to the notion that the several different classes of skilled workers in their firms might bargain collectively. The companies' idea of bargaining was strictly individual or by *ad hoc* committee: "We . . . believe that any man has a right to make a living whether he is a member of a union or not . . . we have agreed to meet with any of our Employees that have any grievance, or with a committee of our Employees if they desire to discuss any conditions that may not be satisfactory." What the companies would not condone was organized negotiation—especially the idea of one large union speaking for the entire industry.

The Government of Canada shared the employers' fear of industrial unionism. The Minister of Labour, Gideon Robertson (a trade unionist himself), had no difficulty with craft unions negotiating, for example, with railways. But the Winnipeg development was industrial unionism on a vast scale, and the general strike, in his opinion, was simply social revolution by another name. Arthur Meighen agreed: "If collective bargaining is to be granted as a principle," he said, "there must be some unit to which the principle . . . is to apply, and beyond which it cannot go." Meighen attacked the idea that there could be "unlimited and heterogeneous collection of all classes of labour that may get together . . . *ad infinitum* . . . ." What Meighen feared was the possibility of a united front of all labour with the collective power of universal strike action—One Big Union, a "seditious conspiracy," or crime in his opinion.

Early in June, almost without debate, the House of Commons approved (after consultation with the eastern Trades and Labour Council of Canada) amendments to the Immigration Act to provide appropriate penalties for the new offense (long jail sentences for British subjects, summary deportation for offending foreigners). Then the mayor of Winnipeg took steps to break the strike by putting the Citizens' Committee in charge of civil order. He dismissed the regular police and replaced them with the citizens' "specials." Within days there was a violent confrontation between "citizens" and strikers, and the federal government had its pretext for intervention. In the middle of the night of June 16/17, the strike leaders were rousted from their homes, charged with the new crime of seditious conspiracy, and jailed in the federal penitentiary at nearby Stony Mountain. Leaderless, the strike collapsed.

As people began to drift back to work, a group of war veterans called upon other "returned men" to parade in protest against the partiality of Ottawa's action. The mayor responded by reiterating a warning that there was a ban on all parades, but the veterans decided to make their protest regardless. On Saturday morning, June 21, 1919, they gathered at the corner of Portage Avenue and Main Street and began to march. Then, specials and the Royal North West Mounted Police moved back and forth through the crowd until one of the "Mounties" fell or was pulled from his horse, and a demonstrator began to beat him. At that moment, the police moved back into the crowd at a gallop, revolvers blazing and clubs swinging. Men who had survived years of war in Flanders fell wounded on the pavement of their home town. Thirty-four of the marchers were injured; one fell dead on the spot with a bullet through his head. Another died later in hospital. Eighty were arrested.

On Monday morning, June 23, Winnipeggers went to work in the shadow of 30-calibre machine guns mounted on trucks ready to silence any recurrence of protest. Not since the conscription riots in Quebec had a popular demonstration been defeated with such brutal swiftness and determination. Then, however, the action was justified as upholding the war effort. What kind of war was this?

Suggested Reading

General histories that cover the social ferment of the war and its immediate aftermath include R.C. Craig and R. Cook, *Canada, 1896-1921: A Nation Transformed* (1974), Robert Bothwell, *et al., Canada, 1900-1945* (1987), and John Herd Thompson and Allen Seager, *Canada, 1922-1939: Decades of Discord* (1985).

Quebec's entry to the 1920s is addressed first by the literature on the conscription crisis (cited in the bibliography for the previous chapter). General issues are covered by S.M. Trofimenkoff in the relevant chapters of *The Dream of Nation: Social and Intellectual History of Quebec*

(1982), and in the political biography of Premier Taschereau by Bernard Vigod, *Quebec Before Duplessis* (1985).

Regarding the Maritimes, the most comprehensive recent work is that of E.R. Forbes, *The Maritime Rights Movement, 1919-1927: A Study in Canadian Regionalism* (1979). An article by Forbes, "The Origins of the Maritme Rights Movement," *Acadiensis* (1975), dismisses too readily the interpretation suggested by George Rawlyk, "Nova Scotia's Regional Protest, 1867-1967," *Queen's Quarterly* (1968), particularly in light of the aftermath of the episode described by Nolan Reilly in "The General Strike in Amherst, Nova Scotia, 1919," - *Acadiensis* (1980). For the enduring "British" outlook of Maritimers, see C.M. Wallace, "The Nationalization of the Maritimes," in J.M. Bumsted, ed., *Documentary Problems in Canadian History* (1969).

Several works address the wartime reforms spearheaded from the Prairies. John Herd Thompson's *The Harvests of War: The Prairie West, 1914-1918* (1978); James Gray, *Booze* (1972); and Carol Bacchi, *Liberation Deferred* (1983), consider prohibition and women's suffrage. Donald Avery, *Dangerous Foreigners* (1977), and Barbara Roberts, "Shovelling Out the 'Mutinous': Political Deportation from Canada before 1936," *Labour/Le Travail* (1986), show how the Immigration Branch and NWMP became security services preoccupied with "enemy aliens." A good chapter in Gerald Friesen, *The Canadian Prairies* (1984), addresses the issue of ethnic diversity and its tensions in the West. William Calderwood, "Pulpit, Press and Political Reaction to the Ku Klux Klan in Saskatchewan," in S.M. Trofimenkoff, ed., *The Twenties in Canada* (1972), describes the situation in which the Klan found its greatest, longest lasting, success.

Of course, the social ferment theme that has received the greatest attention of historians to date is in the area of labour history, particularly as it came to a focus in the Winnipeg General Strike. Gregory S. Kealey, "1919: The Canadian Labour Revolt," *Labour/Le Travail* (1984), attempts to find a national trend in labour militancy, as does James Naylor in "Toronto, 1919," CHA *Papers* (1986). For the Winnipeg strike in its detail, a series of volumes have appeared, primarily from the work of D.J. Bercuson. A survey by Bercuson with Kenneth McNaught, *The Winnipeg Strike: 1919* (1974), is a brief and nicely illustrated overview. Two other books and an article by Bercuson provide rather complete proof that the revolutionary aspect of the strike was more in the reactions of the governments involved than from the aims of the strikers. See Bercuson's "Winnipeg General Strike,

Collective Bargaining and the One Big Union Issue," *CHR* (1970); *Confrontation at Winnipeg: Labour, Industrial Relations and the General Strike* (1974); and *Fools and Wise Men: The Rise and Fall of the One Big Union* (1978).

**Mackenzie King outside
Liberal leadership convention, 1919.**

SOURCE: NATIONAL ARCHIVES OF CANADA/C-24305

*"King posed always as the friend of
humanity."*

CHAPTER 9

THE DISINTEGRATION OF NATIONAL POLITICS, 1919-1926

— 1. The Illusion of Union —

In the last year of the war, Robert Borden imagined that he was launching a new era in national politics. A wartime union of the Conservatives and conscriptionist Liberals was a coalition that he and some other Canadians believed might survive the Armistice. At the same time, many idealists imagined that the Unionist government's electoral triumph in 1917 was a victory for reform because Borden's platform contained a great deal more than the conscription plank. At Westerners' insistence, there were references as well to prohibition, women's suffrage, and a civil service commission to eliminate political patronage. Some visionaries speculated that the old days of two-party bickering might be coming to an end, and that Canada was moving towards nonpartisan rule. Indeed, the country had not divided on party lines in the election of 1917. The electorate returned a Parliament that was not divided as Liberals and Conservatives but as Quebeckers against the rest.

After the Unionist victory, Borden did implement many of the reforms that were promised along with conscription. A broad range of innovation was enacted by legislation or Order in Council (before the extended war powers lapsed in November 1919). Civil service reform made it more difficult for politicians to reward the party faithful; prohibition banned the bar; women were accepted into the franchise for future federal elections; the transcontinental railways (except the CPR) were transformed into a public utility; and legislation was enacted to assist "soldier settlement" (mainly by taking "surplus" land from Indian reserves). These innovations and some new approaches to business-government relations (discussed in the next chapter), showed that Borden's Unionist government was interested in significant change as well as conscription.

But all the Unionist tinkerings with the political superstructure contributed nothing to settle the unrest of labour in 1919. Indeed, the reforms that pertained to labour were intended to secure the manufacturers and the middle class rather than to protect organized workers. The amendments to the Criminal Code and the Immigration Act (together with long-standing Militia Act provisions) made it relatively simple to break strikes by equating such action with sedition, jailing the leaders, and calling out the army to intimidate the rank and file, or suppressing strikes even before their occurrence through the weapon of court injunctions. Thus, the unity of the coalition that governed in Ottawa was an illusion as much by its failure to take labour into account as by its isolation of Quebec. Anyone who sincerely believed that a period of bitter party strife was not about to resume was sadly deluded.

The Liberal Party might have been expected to be the instrument for defeating the Unionists in the postwar period. But such a victory was not possible as long as Sir Wilfrid Laurier continued as leader. He was identified with opposition to conscription and therefore with weak patriotism in English-speaking Canada. By the same token, Laurier could not be dropped from the leadership without alienating Quebec. Conveniently, he died in February 1919. The problem of finding a replacement leader was so serious that the Liberals held a convention to choose a successor—the first leadership convention in Canadian history. At the meeting in August 1919, 1 200 delegates from across the country sought a candidate loyal to Laurier and therefore to Quebec, but not outspokenly anti-conscriptionist and therefore unpatriotic in the sight of the rest of Canada. At the same time, the delegates appeared to seek a leader who might win the affection of the Canadian working class without too severely offending the anti-radical supporters of the Unionist coalition. The impossible combination was found in William Lyon Mackenzie King, grandson of the firebrand who led rebellion in Upper Canada in 1837, former Minister of Labour in 1909, and published author in 1918.

King's book was a vaguely utopian inquiry into *Industry and Humanity*, more philosophical than factual, and more Christian than either socialist or capitalist. For anyone bothing to read the work, it seemed to establish that the 43-year-old bachelor who assumed the leadership of the Liberal Party was a genuine lover of humanity, at least in principle. Perhaps for this reason, the Liberals built some interesting reform propositions (most of which were already enacted in Britain) into their 1919 platform. They called for a minimum wage for workers, unemployment insurance, old age pensions, mothers' allowances, and the eight-hour work day. For King, the social security promises were grand evidence that a great party had a clear course to steer in the future. For other Liberals and most Conservatives, the platform only provided further proof that "the world is in ferment" and there were "doctors and quacks innumerable" to cure its ills.

— 2. Repudiation of Union in the Heartland — of Canadian Conservatism

Since the Conservatives imagined their's was the legitimate voice of "real democracy" rather than demagogic appeals for class domination, and since they tended to regard Ontario as the most sensible as well as the dominant province in the nation, they were understandably shaken by the outcome of a provincial election in Canada's largest province on October 20, 1919. The voters appeared to have rejected political sanity and opted for "class rule"; in the Ontario case, farmers were the "class" that came to power. Their party, the United Farmers of Ontario (UFO), ran 63 candidates for the 83-seat legislature. Forty-five were elected.

Ironically, the farmers of Ontario took control of their province because they feared that they were no longer strong enough to influence the government through the established parties. Since 1880, most of the rural counties had been losing population to the Prairies and the cities faster than was being replaced by immigration or reproduction. In the decade before the war, two thirds of the counties experienced an absolute decline in total population. As the rural parts of Ontario diminished and the urban areas grew, did it not follow that the once dominant part of the still dominant province would be subordinated to the cities and governed by politicians who knew little about agriculture and cared less about farmers?

Agrarian status anxiety was apparent as early as 1911 but increased during the war in the face of Premier William Hearst's oft-repeated assertion that "the full strength of every arm and heart and brain is demanded in the Empire's cause." The farmers were quite willing to comply, but they could not be in two places at once. The problem farmers faced was that the demands on their service were contradictory. They were urged to produce more livestock, butter, and cheese to feed the forces in the field and in industry. At the same time, they were told to send all their sons into military service. The Unionists promised farm lads an exemption from conscription in 1917, then broke the promise almost immediately after the election. Pinched by their own labour shortage and pained by a sense of betrayal in Ottawa, as well as by the charge that farmers were unwilling to do their share in the fighting, rural Ontarians became increasingly dissatisfied with established political leaders at all levels. The local government of William Hearst seemed more "carried away with the interested cry of uplift" than in looking after the more immediate difficulties of the wartime labour shortage or implementing a program for reversing rural depopulation. As a result, farmers felt completely justified in forming their own party to defeat the "big interests."

The Conservative premier thought that the farmers' revolt was futile as well as unreasonable. In the first place, conscription was a federal matter. On the rural depopulation issue, all was being done that could be reasonably expected. Hearst was promoting a program to develop rural amenities, such as better roads. He was also behind a program to replace horse and human labour with more machinery, gasoline tractors in particular. But he refused to pressure Ottawa to exempt farm workers from military service. In his opinion, such a policy would have resulted in a stampede of young men to the country until the war was over. In the present circumstances, if people chose to work and live in the cities, that stampede could not be reversed by any reasonable policy of government. Farmers were unpersuaded. In every county that was losing population, they ran a UFO candidate; two thirds were elected. Nobody was clear how the UFO might "restore agriculture to its former Canadian supremacy" but that was the declared aim of the new government led by E.C. Drury.

— 3. The Carcass of Union —

Ontario's evident degeneration to class domination and the dementia of the rest of the Canadian domestic scene led Robert Borden to spend increasing time looking for order in international politics. Wearied by domestic issues, he was abroad through most of 1919 and 1920, and few instructions were left for colleagues in his absence. By default, ministers left behind filled prime ministerial functions as well as a growing number of portfolios coming vacant by a plague of resignations in 1919.

The Conservative politician who rose to the top of the cauldron of trouble was Arthur Meighen. The leader by default was the same age as Mackenzie King, also born in Ontario, and like the Liberal leader, first elected to Parliament in 1908. There the similarities ended. In nearly every other respect, the two politicians were almost perfect opposites. Where King preferred to wander in vague generalities, generally accepted, in all public utterances, Meighen stated his positions with such stark clarity that he appeared dogmatic to the point of eccentricity. Where King tended to be so indecisive that he appeared to believe most problems would simply dissolve if delayed long enough, Meighen "could turn a corner so fast you could hear his shirt tails snap." Meighen was overtly ruthless. King's ruthlessness was secretive. Meighen, more open in his dealings, behaved as if he wished to be feared; King posed always as the friend of humanity.

The many contrasts between King and Meighen were fully evident in the two politicians' differing attitudes towards radicalism. With regard to the Russian Revolution, for example, King suggested that there was a theme of humanity struggling to become free evident in the epic drama, but Meighen declared: "There is nothing there but a disordered, dishevelled, suffering, seething chaos of humanity, with assassination on top and starvation underneath." There was certainly no reason, Meighen believed, to approve any such "Socialistic, Bolshevik, and Soviet non-sense" for inclusion in the platform of a Canadian political party: "Thousands of people are mentally chasing rainbows, striving for the unattainable, anxious to better their lot and seemingly unwilling to do it in the old fashioned way by hard, honest intelligent effort," he complained. "Dangerous doctrines taught by dangerous men, enemies of the State, poison and pollute the air."

Arthur Meighen sincerely believed that the Canadian political atmosphere was dangerously full of insidious doctrines taught by absurd, hypocritical, and contemptible teachers, not the least of whom was

Mackenzie King. With his mathematician's logic and his lawyer's skill in argument, Meighen demonstrated in Parliament that he was the party's best defender of the "old fashioned way." Consequently, despite his severe political liabilities (identification with closure, conscription, disfranchisement of immigrants, and strike-breaking), the Unionist caucus chose Arthur Meighen to receive the carcass of the Liberal-Conservative coalition abandoned by Robert Borden when he finally resigned from public life on July 10, 1920.

To maintain the fiction that a nonpartisan organization continued, Meighen's group decided to call itself the "National Liberal-Conservative Party." But just as the government's nonpartisanship was hollow, so also—according to King—was the propriety of its continuing in power. In King's view, the Unionist government was a wartime expedient elected by an extraordinary franchise; therefore, its right to continue in office expired the day the war was won. Given that King did not have a seat in the House of Commons when he became Liberal leader, Meighen dismissed his criticism as the nagging of "the outside leader of the outside party." But eventually, in September 1921, he did grant King his chance for victory in a general election. The date was set for December.

— 4. The Revolt of the Prairies —

Meighen entered a contest no Conservative could win. The line of groups seeking revenge in 1921 was simply too long: Quebeckers were anxious to punish the "blood stained" author of conscription; the disfranchised voters of 1917 were eager to punish the "usurper" of their voting rights. And these represented only the wartime offences. The lengthening line of offended voters in the postwar period—farmers and workers—had grievances that were economic, either because Meighen had broken their strikes, or controlled the price of grain, or allowed freight and interest rates to float higher for the benefit of the banks and the railways. The wonder of the election of 1921 was not that Arthur Meighen was defeated; the shocking outcome was that Mackenzie King was also denied victory.

The Liberals took every seat in Quebec and swept the Maritimes but did not win the support of the West and rural Ontario. The spoilers of King's victory in 1921 called themselves the National Progressive Party, an outgrowth of the farmer movements that had developed in every province, but especially in Ontario and on the Prairies. The person primarily responsible for giving them a national focus was Thomas Crerar, a Manitoba Liberal with a longstanding interest in innovations dealing with direct democracy and tax reform. In 1917 he accepted the position of Minister of Agriculture in the Unionist government. Then, at the end of the war (like many other Liberals), Crerar found himself increasingly uncomfortable sitting with the Conservatives. In his case, the point of particular dissatisfaction was with the high tariff policy. As a result, he crossed the floor of the House in May 1919 and took eight other western Liberals with him.

Since the farmers' organizations were calling for a new National Policy that touched on all the reform causes that were dear to Crerar, they naturally turned to him when seeking a national leader. At first, Crerar was sceptical about independent action and hoped to realize his aims through the Liberal Party. By March 1920, however, he was reconciled to the third-party option, began calling his parliamentary group the National Progressive Party, and insisted that he and his colleagues were seeking a broad base of support. "Our appeal is not class, not sectional, not religious," he claimed. Crerar said the National Progressive Party was for "all . . . who desire to see purity in the government restored, who desire to see public morality supplant public corruption, who desire to sweep away abuse of the function of government for the advancement of the interest of the privileged few."

Affirmations of general principles notwithstanding, there was a distinct agrarianism to the specific policies the Progressives advocated. They stressed the need for reform in the system for marketing grain, restoration of the Crow's Nest Pass freight rates agreed to by Laurier and the CPR in 1897 (but suspended by Borden in 1918 and 1919), easier credit for farmers, free trade, and concession of provincial control of natural resources to the three prairie provinces. The Progressives said they opposed use of the militia for strike-breaking and advocated electoral reforms consistent with the direct democracy demand; their platform, therefore, contained something for an urban constituency as well. But the unmistakable fact, no matter what Crerar said to the contrary, was that the National Progressive Party was primarily the national face of the four separate farmer revolts that had developed in Ontario and the West.

Arthur Meighen had imagined that most people, including many farmers, approved his handling of radicals in the strikes of 1919. And he knew that most people, including some farmers, regarded opposition to the tariff as tantamount to treason. Meighen thought that if he could focus the electorate's attention on "Protection or no Protection," the battle would be won. Crerar was willing to fight on the free-trade issue; King (afraid that such a debate would divide the protectionist eastern wing of his party from the free trade West) insisted that "the issue is the Prime Minister himself and what he and his colleagues represent of autocracy and extravagance in the management of public affairs." King's focus on Meighen was an excellent way of furthering everyone's discontent with the reigning Tories, but a poor strategy for convincing voters that his confusion was preferable. Meighen kept trying to draw the electorate's attention to the tariff, saying King's policy was "Protection on apples in British Columbia, Free Trade in the Prairie provinces and the rural parts of Ontario, Protection in the industrial centres in Ontario, Conscription in Quebec and humbug in the Maritime Provinces."

In the end, the electorate repudiated both of the old parties. Seventy percent of all votes cast went against Meighen's party, 60 percent were votes against King's Liberals. Arthur Meighen's Conservatives were reduced to a mere 50 seats, and Mackenzie King's Liberals were hardly victorious with their plurality of 116—two members short of a majority. There were 64 Progressives who could be expected to oppose the Conservatives more often than the Liberals, but the outcome on any question would be uncertain. For the first time in Canadian political history, no party received a majority. A new dynamic entered into the affairs of the House of Commons.

As in the case of federalism, Canadians discovered multi-party politics after the fact; the system of major and minor parties was neither planned nor preferred at its inception. For the first session of the "parliament of minorities," an effort was made to deny its reality—ironically, by the Progressives themselves. Crerar tended to view the situation as a revolt of voters whose true political home was with the Liberal Party. Once King's Liberals had "come to their senses" on such key issues as the tariff, Crerar expected that the Progressive Party would cease to exist (like the Populists in relation to the Democrats in the United States during the 1890s). But another faction within the Progressives, the Alberta group, was opposed to the very idea of political parties. Henry Wise Wood, the chief spokesman for this point of view (but not himself a member of Parliament), regarded legislators as delegates representing interest groups (such as farmers, labour organizations, and so on). He refused to endorse the idea that any coalition should be permanent. Wood's preference was for a constant shifting of allegiances among loosely-integrated groups as they voted on the merits of each issue. Yet another faction (mainly from Saskatchewan and less than one third of the entire Progressive contingent) saw the movement as a party in the sense of a solid block permanently offering a fresh flow of alternatives acceptable to its own constituencies. But since they were only one of three factions and a minority at that, Meighen's Conservatives formed the official opposition. The real number-two group in Parliament was unwilling to behave in the manner of a political party.

The unwillingness of the Progressives to play the game of party politics at first frustrated the dynamics of minority government, and gave Mackenzie King an ideal opportunity to dismiss the farmers' protest as nothing more than a lot of Liberals in a hurry. Building policy bridges for the Progressives to cross home to Liberalism, he reinstated the Crow's Nest Pass rates and tinkered with the tariff to eliminate the duties on farm machinery. As early as 1923, the strategy began to show signs of success. By the end of the first session of Parliament, two Ontario Progressives had crossed the floor, giving King a bare majority. The others, though still opposite, were more likely to vote with the government than with the true opposition. Crerar retired from the party's leadership in November 1922 and King began to speculate about the next election that would bring the Liberals "back into power by getting the Progressive forces and ours united." Interestingly, he also believed that the minor changes that reconciled Crerar-type Progressives were "true to the platform of the 1919 convention, true to the pledges I gave the electors in 1921 . . . . "

Angered by King's leaning towards the Progressives, Arthur Meighen denounced the government for having no policy of its own. In 1922, he complained that the government "listens for the threats and growls . . . then all these noises are gathered together, fused into one and the conglomerate emission becomes the tune that he calls the government policy." From a less critical point of view, such commentary only confirms what King's principal biographers suggest was a major strength of his leadership—that King was a pragmatist like Macdonald or Laurier, but all the more so because of the necessities of minority government. How well, though, was he listening? And how broad was his audible range?

— 5. Missed Opportunities —

It is clear that Mackenzie King heard some of the Progressives' demands but ignored other Members of Parliament, even though the latter advocated social reform policies that were closer to his own party's 1919 platform. The principal spokesman for the new members who were interested in the most significant innovations was J.S. Woodsworth, a Labour member elected by working-class outrage in Winnipeg. In his first speech in Parliament in 1922, Woodsworth asserted that "we have come to a period in the history of our country when we must decide once and for all which shall prevail, profits or human welfare." Knowing that there was more to progressivism than what Crerar would promise, Woodsworth went further and asserted that "there is a group of men here, new Members of the House . . . who have clearly made up their minds that, insofar as they can decide it, human welfare is to be given precedence." The kinds of action that followed from Woodsworth's reform direction pertained to tax reform that went beyond the tariff, enlargement of the public utility sector beyond the existing national railway system, and the provision of social security by national policy.

The tax reforms Woodsworth advocated were increased personal income and business profits taxes to replace the tariff as the prime revenue-generating device. Spending for the Great War had added more than $2 billion to the national debt. So great was the burden of war expenditure that roughly one third of each budget in the 1920s was expended towards interest charges. The wartime novelties of profit and income taxes generated only ten percent of the annual revenue, and, therefore, the rest of the government's income came mainly from the tax on consumer imports. Woodsworth claimed that the people who benefited most by the wartime expenditure were Canada's rich; he suggested that they should play a larger role in retiring the debt, hence his call for steeper income and business profits taxes to "recover from the profiteers the blood money which they laid up during the time of the war."

Woodsworth regarded the leading industrialists as a new "family compact" in control of the economy for their private benefit more than for the public interest. Pursuing the issue one step further, he criticized the government for not including the Canadian Pacific in the Canadian National Railway system. Reasoning that other monopolies or near monopolies ought to operate for the promotion of the general welfare rather than for private greed, he advocated nationalization of other basic industries as well. Finally, Woodsworth claimed that public insurance schemes were justified as protection against poverty in old age or privation in the event of unemployment.

Naturally, Meighen dismissed Woodsworth's proposals as "socialist nonsense." Another Tory, John Baxter, the member for Saint John, was so angered to hear socialism proposed in the Canadian House of Commons that he demanded a vote on the question so that everyone could "stand up either for the reds or against them." The "reds" lost 47 to 108, suggesting that 1922 was not a year to expect the enactment of a great deal of

Woodsworth's program. But with so many "reds" in the House, was it not possible for King to have enacted at least part of the Liberal platform of 1919?

Bolder action may have been possible given the mix of parties in Parliament, but it was not feasible given the personality of Mackenzie King, a compulsive avoider of unnecessary risk. He viewed necessity as anything that kept the Liberal Party in power. A risk was seen as anything that could lead to controversy. King's temerity was well illustrated by his reluctance to provide the protection to organized labour in 1922 that he had promised before the election—even though such protection was manifestly warranted. In January 1922, the British Empire Steel Company (BESCO) announced a one-third reduction in the wages of workers in the mines and mills of Cape Breton Island. The average Cape Breton miner's income fell to about three quarters of an Alberta coal miner even though the cost of living was significantly higher on Cape Breton Island. The matter attracted national attention because near famine conditions resulted. Clearly, if the "living wage" plank in the Liberal Party platform of 1919 meant anything at all, the Cape Breton miners were worthy of the government's attention. When Woodsworth raised the issue in the House of Commons, King pointed out that the only coercive power in existing statutes was of the workers under the provisions of the Militia Act, and pleaded constitutional inability to enact legislation that would make federal conciliation reports binding. After conciliators agreed that the workers were underpaid and BESCO ignored their report, the workers struck. BESCO demanded protection, and the army was sent in to maintain order. But the dispute was so bitter, the officer commanding on the scene asked for air support and proposed a contingency plan to land additional forces from British battleships if existing Canadian forces proved inadequate to the task. Finally, in August 1922, the miners agreed to the new wage schedule "under the muzzle of rifles, machine guns and gleaming bayonets," in the words of the union president.

King's handling of the Cape Breton miners' dispute was confirmation that he listened only to the bloc whose support cost him the least. It was cheaper for him to buy the support of the conservative Progressives with miniscule tariff concessions and the restoration of the Crow's Nest Pass rates for the shipment of grain than to "hear" anything the radical Progressives demanded. As a result, Woodsworth was frustrated by the timidity of most Progressives. To dramatize their conservatism in 1924, he proposed an amendment to the budget, one that the Progressives should have initiated themselves since it called for the kind of tax reform that was

183

supposed to be the main reason for their election in 1921. But the Progressives' leader, Robert Forke (successor to Crerar in 1923), did not wish to reveal how much of his party had been reconciled with King. Thus, he dared not support further reductions in the tariff or higher taxes on large personal incomes. When Woodsworth did propose precisely such changes, he forced the Progressives to vote against their own declared principles or support him against King and Forke. On May 16, 1924, 15 Progressives defied their leader and voted with Woodsworth. At the time, Forke indicated that "there will be a certain amount of what I may call unholy glee on the part of some who think this places the Progressives in a rather difficult position." Actually, Forke's apology was a gross understatement of his embarrassment. The Toronto *Telegram* cynically but correctly described the vote as an "explosion" that destroyed the party. Progressives had to decide "whether they should vote for the principles they pretend to love or for the government that has bought them at a price." Most voted with the Liberals and for all practical future electoral purposes, they killed the Progressive Party.

— 6. The Revolt of the Atlantic Provinces —

In the election of 1925, the Progressive contingent from Ontario and the Prairies was reduced by more than half, to just 24 members. Of this group, most were the "co-operating independents" working with J.S. Woodsworth. By shifting most of the prairie Progressive vote back to the Liberal Party, Mackenzie King had expected to return to power with a comfortable majority. His party did recover on the Prairies. But King still failed to win a majority overall. In 1925, it was the Atlantic Provinces that spoiled the Liberal victory.

In the previous chapter, it was suggested that the immediate enemy of the leaders of the Maritime Rights Movement was the local Farmer-Labour revolt that had reduced the Conservatives to third-place position in Nova Scotia by 1920. Given that the main task of the Maritime Tories was to show that they were more credible than the Farmer-Labour coalition and eventually also the Liberals, they were fortunate in having Liberal governments in power on the provincial and national levels during their most energetic period, 1921-25. Persuading most Maritimers that the root of their troubles was government by people who shunned the truth as preached by Arthur Meighen, the Maritime Tories fancied that they were about to shake a lethargic federation to its foundations.

The Maritime Conservatives' main demand was for a national policy to develop their region just as the "so called National Policy" of Macdonald had promoted Ontario and the Prairies. The logic of their argument was compelling to Meighen. He promised higher duties on coal and steel since most of both commodities consumed in Ontario were imported from the United States. The idea that the Maritimes could be Ontario's alternative supplier prompted yeasty visions of empire in Nova Scotia. Meighen nurtured these further by suggesting that he was prepared to adjust freight rates for the Maritimes in the way King had recently restored subsidized transportation of grain for the Prairies.

Coal and steel made more expensive by tariff increases was bound to be unpopular in Ontario, the province that gave the Conservatives their largest number of seats in Parliament. For that reason, it remained unclear how Meighen could accommodate the Maritime Rights Movement without arousing the ire of Ontario. Mackenzie King avoided any such embarrassment by asking questions rather than promising solutions. His approach was to suggest that the Maritimers had failed to make clear their grievances over the previous four years. "What are Maritime Rights?" he asked. "Let us know and we will fight for them," he promised. Meighen acknowledged that the Maritimers already had a legitimate case and agreed to implement what local Conservatives said they needed; the Tories swept Nova Scotia and New Brunswick with record majorities in both provinces in the voting on October 29, 1925.

The Maritime Rights Conservatives then encountered two problems. One was that they were a bloc of about 20 members in a caucus of 116. How were they to persuade 68 members from Ontario that Maritime rights required that they give up their cheap American coal and steel? But the first problem was not as frustrating as the second: King held on to power even though his party had only 99 seats in the new Parliament. Support from the Progressives and Woodsworth's Ginger Group of "co-operating independents" had kept King's government from falling.

Sustaining King was not Woodsworth's preferred alternative. He tried to get the party leaders to form a new council in lieu of the old cabinet, a council that would not represent any party in particular but would nonetheless be responsible to a parliamentary majority. Of course, King would not consent to such an arrangement. As a result, Woodsworth and Forke each presented King and Meighen with shopping lists of issues from which to decide which was the lesser of two evils. Meighen responded to his letter from Forke by telling him that "the stand of the Conservative Party has been fully and repeatedly outlined by myself in the House of

Commons . . . . So far as I know it has never been charged that my attitude as Leader on any of these subjects has been equivocal or obscure." The Meighen reply to Woodsworth's offer of support for unemployment insurance and old age pensions was the assertion that "the thing to do for the unemployed is to get them work," and this could be accomplished by stiff tariff increases. To be sure, the aged would not be well served by Meighen's unemployment cure, but he thought other matters "more pressing" than federal assistance to pensioners.

Woodsworth and Forke received a friendlier reception from King. In Woodsworth's case, the letter led to a dinner invitation, at which occasion he was offered the position of Minister of Labour. Woodsworth declined, indicating that he would prefer to see the enactment of the social legislation mentioned in his letter and also some law reform removing the Meighen amendments to the Criminal Code and the Immigration Act. King protested that the country could ill afford unemployment insurance, but would Woodsworth settle for the rest of the package? Woodsworth agreed, but he wanted the arrangement in writing. Then, after the first session of the new Parliament opened late in January 1926, Woodsworth read the text of King's letter into Hansard, in a sense as an appendix to the Throne Speech. For Meighen, the bargain was "a shameless brutal assault not only on the most sacred principles of British constitutional government but on common honesty."

It was not, however, Meighen's attack that shook the new government. Much more serious was the allegation made by the Conservative, H.H. Stevens, that the Department of Customs was rife with corruption. He demanded an all-party committee to investigate his specific charges.

The Liberal strategy for dealing with the threat of scandal and legislative unpreparedness was to seek a six-week adjournment. Naturally, Meighen denounced the manoeuvre as "without parallel or approach in the history of this most extraordinary administration." Meighen's complaint was that "the government comes to Parliament, convened at its own instance, brought here under its own auspices and before any business is despatched suggests that we go to our homes for six weeks because it is not in a position to carry on . . . . " Meighen's complaint notwithstanding, the House did adjourn for the period requested.

Six weeks later, the ramshackle government reconvened and King unveiled his program for making peace with the "co-operating independents" and the Atlantic provinces. In addition to the old age pension scheme and law reforms promised to Woodsworth, there was the completely free gift of a royal commission to investigate maritime rights. For anyone who did not have a special sectional or economic interest, there were many other favours of a more general nature: reductions in the income tax, lower tariffs on many items including automobiles, and a lowering of postal rates.

When at last the whole package was opened, Meighen wanted to know what it would cost. He stated sarcastically that he did not expect a precise figure but would be satisfied with even a rough estimate, "say, within a hundred million dollars."

Apparently, King expected one short session and then an election, perhaps as early as September, the date the report was demanded from the Maritime Claims Commission (soon known as the Duncan Commission after its principal commissioner, Sir Andrew Rae Duncan). King's timetable was interrupted in June, however, when the Parliamentary Committee reported on the customs matters Stevens had raised before the adjournment. The evidence was unmistakable. It appeared that every port in Canada was staffed by customs officers who were cooperating with smugglers, especially those engaged in the illegal liquor traffic with the United States (where prohibition was still in force). In Lunenburg, Nova Scotia, for example, schooners loaded with whiskey would leave for the Caribbean or South America and return home from their south Atlantic destinations 48 hours later, only to depart again with the same cargo for the same customers. That the port officials failed to act against such fraud suggested an active connivance between themselves and the smugglers. But was the corruption a function of the system or of the government of the day?

Meighen's party claimed that the abuses were the unique result of an especially corrupt Liberal patronage machine. Woodsworth argued that a fuller investigation would show that the real fault lay with the system itself, and recommended that a royal commission be struck to find practicable remedies in the same way that a similar team was investigating maritime rights. Clearly, Woodsworth believed that the Liberals were beginning to embark upon a worthwhile program and ought to continue in office until their work was finished. Other members of Woodsworth's group were not so pragmatic. For example, M.N. Campbell of Saskatchewan denounced the Liberal government for what he called "one of the worst scandals in the whole history of Canada." He, for one, would not condone its continuation "on the ground of political expediency." Of course, Meighen's Tories agreed. Under attack from all sides, it was clear that King's government would be defeated on a non-confidence motion late in June.

King hoped to avoid the humiliation of defeat by seeking a dissolution of the House before the vote could be taken. But the Governor General, Lord Byng, refused to grant his request, and King resigned on June 28. Given that a general election had occurred quite recently, and that the plurality party had not yet had a chance to govern, Byng turned to Meighen. Once in power, the Conservative leader could not retain sufficient third-party backing and was soon defeated. Then Parliament had to be dissolved, and King rejoiced in the alleged constitutional crisis that launched his campaign. He said the Governor General's action amounted to a breach of responsible government. Of course, Byng had operated within the bounds of the royal prerogative as it was defined in 1926. Byng's real crime was that he was English and an aristocrat; that allowed King to claim that the country's recently-won independence was in jeopardy, and to articulate a novel but popular principle when he went into the election saying the matter of dissolution was always "for Parliament to decide." When Meighen attempted to neutralize King's position with the assertion that "the Governor General acted correctly . . . the hysterical platform utterances of Mackenzie King . . . should only serve to amuse," it could be argued that his laughter was directed at the country's aspirations for fuller autonomy as much as at King himself. In this sense, the constitutional issue was more genuine than Meighen perceived, as King rejoiced in his diary: "I go into the battle of another election believing we have an issue that the people will respond to." Where the alleged constitutional crisis did not inspire the electorate, King still had his sunshine budget and the just-completed report of the Duncan Commission which had several practical remedies bound to be popular in the Maritimes (including a 20 percent reduction on freight rates for railway traffic in or out of the Atlantic region). The result, in September 1926, was that the voters gave King the majority he had been expecting since becoming leader of his party in 1919.

— 7. Return to Politics as Usual —

The Liberal victory in 1926 could be interpreted as a return to politics as usual in the sense that majority standing enabled one party to govern on its own. King's period of listening was over. In another sense, 1926 marked the completion of a transformation begun in 1911 with the repudiation of the old Macdonald-Laurier tradition of forming a national consensus through patronage and barter between diverse regional and class interests.

By 1911, the majority consensus was that such compromises limited the country to "Little Canada" policies. Borden's Conservatives gained popularity with the promise of promoting a progressive, national design. But by 1919, it was only too clear that Borden's nation was Empire Ontario and its satellites. Worse still, the satellites were in revolt and special interest groups were adding their voice to politics. The 1919 platform of the Liberal Party aimed for a new national coalition with a special orientation to Quebec and the discontented working class in the rest of Canada by its endorsement of the minimum wage, unemployment compensation, the eight-hour work day, and more, in principle. Meighen responded by appealing to Canadians' sense of tradition and asked voters to join him in returning to first principles: "the National Policy as Macdonald had shaped it, and as it has since endured." But King would not be caught. Instead of posing an alternative tariff policy, or insisting upon his party's 1919 platform, he retreated, as Roger Graham has argued, into "soft, shapeless, confusing, meaningless verbiage." It is not correct, however, to conclude with Graham that King had "nothing to offer but confusion."

To be sure, King did lay down a verbal smoke screen where national policies were concerned, but he sensed better than Meighen (or any other politician) that the key to success was a return to barter—with a difference. In the new brokerage politics, all the transactions would take place on a regional level. Thus, he pacified the Prairies with the restoration of lower freight rates on grain and minor tinkering with the tariff; he hung on to a fragment of Ontario by asserting that his revenue tariff provided a measure of industrial protection; he kept Quebec support by feeding their resentment of conscription and Meighen's autocracy; finally (after 1926), he pacified the Maritimes by conceding some of the recommendations of the Duncan Commission (freight rate reductions, subsidy increases, and regional development schemes)—all of which indicated a return to the politics of accommodation, but without the bother of developing *national* policies. The nearest he came to that exercise was the pension scheme that Woodsworth demanded in 1926. But even here, the little that was conceded was contingent upon provincial cooperation. The new brokerage politics was thus a positive step in the sense that some real issues were addressed, but the new accommodation was unfortunate in the sense that pressing national problems were shelved by an approach to politics that made the country more regional than ever. In the 1920s, the government in Ottawa became little more than a clearing house for the aspirations of regional principalities. Had the provinces shown concern with the social issues that had first impelled persons such as J.S. Woodsworth into politics, the devolution of authority would have been a harmless trade-off. But they were no more prepared than Ottawa to implement their own unemployment insurance schemes, for example. Consequently, the country fared all the more poorly with the problems of the Great Depression in the 1930s.

Suggested Reading

General histories that cover the subject of national politics in the 1920s include John Herd Thompson and Allen Seager, *Canada, 1922-1929: Decades of Discord* (1925), and Robert Bothwell, *et al., Canada, 1900-1945* (1985). J.M. Beck, *Pendulum of Power: Canada's Federal Elections* (1968), has useful chapters on the several electoral contests of the decade; and, although John English, *The Decline of Politics: The Conservatives and the Party System* (1977), is not intended as a history beyond 1921, the book concludes with profound insights into the rest of the decade with reference to King's manner of government in relation to his predecessors.

Until other political monographs become available, the most comprehensive works on national politics in the 1920s must continue to be the multi-volume biographical accounts of the most important leaders of the decade. Roger Graham's *Arthur Meighen: And Fortune Fled*, vol. 2 (1963), is a sympathetic account of the leader who has received perhaps the least sympathy of the three. R.M. Dawson and H.B. Neatby have written the commemorative work on Mackenzie King. Dawson's *William Lyon Mackenzie King*, vol. 1 (1958), ends in 1923. Neatby's *William Lyon Mackenzie King*, vol. 2 (1963), covers the period from 1924 to 1932. The comprehensive work on J.S. Woodsworth—and a masterpiece in intellectual history—is Kenneth McNaught, *A Prophet in Politics* (1959). Part 2 of McNaught's work, covering Woodsworth's activity between 1922 and 1927, is indispensable reading for anyone interested in the origins of the multi-party system.

For readers who tire of Graham's partisan defence of Meighen or Neatby's meticulous unraveling of King's tedium, shorter biographies are available by other scholars. *Arthur Meighen* (1977), by John English, and *Mackenzie King* (1976), by J.L. Granatstein are both readable accounts and profusely illustrated.

Although biographies are the present, most accessible, detailed approaches to the study of national politics in the 1920s, the regional protests that had such an important impact on the national scene have long held the attention of historians interested in local history. The farmers' revolt in Ontario, for example, is well covered by Peter Oliver, "Sir William Hearst and the Collapse of the Ontario Conservative Party," *CHR* (1972), and W.R. Young, "Conscription, Rural Depopulation and the Farmers of Ontario, 1917-1919," *CHR* (1972). The unravelling of the UFO government, 1919-1923, is described by Charles M. Johnston, *E.C. Drury: Agrarian Idealist* (1986). W.L. Morton, *The Progressive Party in Canada* (1950), examines the national expression of the farmers' revolt not only for its regional origins but also for its operation in the House of Commons. Some readers, however, will dislike Morton's conclusions since he tends to assume that third parties are inherently ephemeral and irresponsible. Thus, Morton would consider that the Maritimers launched a more reasonable protest because theirs was a regional movement that was content to express itself through the national Conservative organization. To test such an assertion, readers may wish to compare the *Maritime Rights Movement, 1919-1927: A Study in Canadian Regionalism* (1979), by E.R. Forbes, with the preliminary section of W. Young's *Democracy and Discontent* (1969), a view of the Progressives that challenges Morton's.

**Strikers outside factory,
Stratford, Ontario, 1934.**

*". . . . nearly half of the Canadian people
were not very interested in innovative
approaches to the problems of the
unemployed."*

CHAPTER 10

PROSPERITY, DEPRESSION, AND THE QUEST FOR RESTORATION, 1926-1939

— 1. Slide Into Depression —

The emergence of multi-party politics in the 1920s was a source of considerable anxiety to business people who preferred the simpler, apparently more stable, two-party state. In the new pattern, the Prime Minister (or his alternate, the leader of the opposition) was vulnerable to newly organized interests in Parliament. And since the new parties tended to be critical of the traditional partner relationship between corporations and the state, business-government relations became exceedingly more complicated in the 1920s. That disturbing development appeared just as business groups became extraordinarily active in their quest for new favours from government.

The basic problems faced by manufacturers were over-extension in prosperity, and cut-throat competition in recession. Between 1909-13, they had employed a remedial strategy of pursuing mergers that might insure stability be sheer domination of the market. Fifty-eight large companies absorbed 217 competitors. Such conglomerates as the Steel Company of Canada, Dominion Canners, and Canada Cement came into being. But the trend towards bigness had not prevented the recession of 1913-15; nor did its continuation through the war years disguise the problem that a return to peacetime economy would lead to renewed instability.

To curb "unfair" competition in the period of postwar adjustment, the Borden government created a regulatory agency called the Board of Commerce (BOC) in the autumn of 1919. Since the BOC also had authority to regulate profits and prices, there was a theoretical possibility that the agency would not serve business as well as the public. Still, the Canadian Manufacturers Association was satisfied that if regulation were "administered sanely there can be no great object." The first requirement was that the BOC be run by personnel with "business experience" rather than by "visionaries and theorists." Properly staffed, the agency could be the culmination of the search for security through regulation, and thus an escape from "destructive" competition. But more than half of the economy still consisted of small-scale or old-fashioned business people who regarded any kind of regulation as unnecessary interference. Consequently, the Board of Commerce rapidly disintegrated into symbolic actions rather than real control over prices or allocation of the market. The experiment ended in 1920.

Another remarkable failure that occurred at the same time pertained to an abortive experiment in business-government labour management. A wartime agency, the Employment Service of Canada (ESC), had come into existence in 1918 to monitor employment patterns and to provide labour exchanges. In both functions, the ESC reflected the idea that government responsibility for unemployment was indirect. But the head of the agency, Bryce Stewart, imagined that his office ought to continue after the war and to extend its activities to include industrial training, immigration policy, and even unemployment insurance. Stewart was not alone in such hope. A provincial commission on unemployment in Ontario during the prewar recession had reported in 1916 that the "personal causes" of unemployment (laziness and alcoholism) were not nearly as significant as impersonal fluctuations of the business cycle, "alternating between inflation and depression." Some form of voluntary, contributory unemployment insurance was the appropriate remedy. Business leaders agreed as long as such a scheme collected the premiums from workers, and paid benefits that were well below wage levels.

After a Royal Commission on Industrial Relations made the same recommendation to the national government in 1919, the concept of government-sponsored unemployment insurance was referred to the Department of Justice and found to be well within the "peace, order and good government powers" of the Constitution. But Arthur Meighen and Gideon Robertson rejected the propriety of the plan. After 1921, Mackenzie King rejected its expediency.

King's difficulty with the plan was that most farmers considered industrialization to have created a rural labour problem, and they believed that urban unemployment was their best hope for recovering cheap labour on the farms. From the standpoint of Thomas Crerar (and other agrarians in Parliament), farmers had been unable, in recent years, to compete with factories for labour because of the abnormally high demand for unskilled workers during the war. The result was that country producers were left with only "one quarter of the labour needed," according to Crerar. It followed, from his reasoning, that if people were out of work in the postwar economy, it was because "they will not do the work which is to be done." He and the Canadian Council of Agriculture demanded that the government "shovel" the unskilled "back into the country" rather than put a "premium on idleness." They were opposed to the continuation of the Employment Service of Canada and the fulfillment of Stewart's larger ambitions. The Parliamentary spokesmen for the farmers of Canada declared that they wanted to "make conditions more difficult in the cities." Otherwise, they said, "we cannot hope to hold our people on the farms."

Mackenzie King's first priority after 1921 was to solidify "an alliance with the rural elements." The author of *Industry and Humanity* oversaw the destruction of the ESC on the grounds that it represented too much of that "centralizing tendency" that had accompanied the war. To those who persisted in the demand for unemployment insurance, as an indispensable amelioration of a serious problem that was a continuing by-product of industrialization, King pleaded constitutional inability to act. Here, however, the BNA Act was more his shield from criticism than his barrier to action. As his own Minister of Labour, James Murdock, reminded King in 1924, there were sound legal reasons for believing that the "Dominion Parliament has power to enact a national system of unemployment insurance should it desire to do so." But Murdock agreed with King that there were more compelling political reasons to reject such a course. By then, the agrarians had been tamed. The new fear was simply the cost: better to leave the municipalities with the responsibility for "relief" in "normal times." But what was normal?

In the 1920s, municipal officials were claiming that every year was a critical one because unemployment reached levels of about 16 percent each winter. The Government of Canada insisted that in order for federal authorities to assume more responsibility for relief, there would have to be better evidence that such "unemployment was to be permanent." In that event, federal officials would "sit down . . . and work for years until we have found a remedy." The "temporary" difficulties had to be met by the cities themselves. To do otherwise would "shelve responsibility which for fifty years has been theirs."

The consensus that prevailed on the unemployment of the 1920s was the "rugged individualism" of small business and farmers and the "fiscal responsibility" of government. As a result, workers were left to fend for themselves—in the traditional way of attempting to gain more than one source of income per family. At the managerial level, corporations sought their security in a second merger movement that led Canada Cement, Canadian General Electric, Canadian Industries Limited, and Imperial Tobacco to develop "near monopolies" in their fields. But neither the trend towards monopoly nor the abandonment of the unemployed was generally considered dangerous, because the years between 1925 and 1928 appeared to "boom" like those of Laurier.

During the Laurier boom, the developments that had attracted attention were the settlement of the West, the building of the railways, and the rise of the metropolitan industrial centres. In the short boom of the later 1920s, the focus was on the automobile and on building a system of roads that would carry the new method of personal transportation. From 1925 to 1929, the amount of surfaced roads almost doubled, increasing from 76 000 to nearly 130 000 kilometres, accommodating about one million motor vehicles by the end of the decade. Naturally, the country's ability to produce the new machines grew at an even faster rate. By 1926, 11 huge factories, employing 12 000 workers, turned out 200 000 cars per year.

Indigenous makes such as the "Russell" produced by Canadian Cycle and Motor (CCM) were enormous luxury sedans, built "Up to a Standard—Not Down to a Price." Notwithstanding their quality, they did not emerge as the leaders of the 1920s automotive boom. The dominant makes were more affordable to the middle-class in Canada and the global British market. The result was an enormous boom for General Motors and Ford of Canada.

In 1904, Gordon M. McGregor of Windsor had secured rights to produce the cheap American Ford for every country in the British Empire except the United Kingdom. Sam McLaughlin of Oshawa attempted a similar scheme in association with General Motors, starting in 1908. But the volume of Fords being produced at Macgregor's Walkerville Wagon Company continued to exceed the most optimistic plans made at McLaughlin's Oshawa carriage works—until 1918. In that year, General Motors orchestrated a merger with the lagging company and broadened the product line. By the early 1920s, the Oshawa plant was assembling Oldsmobiles and Chevrolets as well as Buicks, and soon surpassed Ford's production. At the end of the decade, General Motors of Canada turned out more cars than all of its Canadian competitors combined. Some, such as the Russell, went out of production. Others, such as the Ford, continued to prosper on the basis of their original formula for success. In fact, through the 1920s, Ford of Canada still built more cars than any other plant in the British Empire outside Canada. Since nearly half of all Canadian production was for the Imperial market, the industry was second only to pulp and paper for export earnings in the late 1920s. The plants at Oshawa and Windsor turned out roughly 500 000 autos per year, even though the domestic market at its most bouyant was less than 300 000 per year. The cheapest models still cost almost as much as a factory worker's entire annual income. Consequently, the urban working class still rode the "street railways" on workdays and took the train (along with car owners) for longer trips. Indeed, the automobile option for long-distance travel did not become practical for another 30 years.

To improve the transportation of railway passengers, and to facilitate the movement of staples for export, an additional 8 000 kilometres of track were laid in the 1920s, including a line to Manitoba's port of Churchill on Hudson Bay. Such expansion reflected the scope of the surge of other sectors of the economy, especially the production of paper, metals, and grain. In 1928, the wheat farmers of Canada brought in their largest crop to date, almost 600 million bushels. But that was 127 million bushels more than the world market would absorb, just as Canadian mines and paper mills were out-running world demand for nonferrous metals and newsprint. Prices declined; volume traded diminished. As the trade in staples declined, the work for the country's largest employers, the railways, also declined. The two shocks that began in 1928—one to the staple trades, the other to the transportation system—were then transmitted to the rest of the economy. The automobile manufacturers found it more difficult to sell their cars, at home and abroad; builders started fewer houses; and the rest of the domestic manufacturing sector followed in recession. By 1930, unemployment was greater than during the "hard times of 1921-22" and one third of those classified as employed, the farmers, were so locked between fixed debts and low prices that they suffered a kind of unemployment of their own. Thus began the worst economic crisis since 1873, a depression that unfolded as a ten-year object lesson in the vulnerability of an economy overcommitted to the production of a few staple products and ill-prepared to cope with industrial unemployment.

— 2. Apparent Need For a "New Deal" —

For the first time in the history of Canada, farmers as well as industrial workers were forced to ask for government "relief" and to go through the degrading process by which the heads of households swore that they had utterly failed in their attempts to provide for their families, and to swear also that all relatives were equally incompetent to serve as alternate providers. Rural and urban municipalities provided vouchers to such families for rations to prevent death by starvation. But even such minimal support rapidly exhausted the resources of municipalities. They sought help from the provinces. Provincial jurisdictions, in turn, appealed for help from Ottawa.

In 1930, all but two of the provincial premiers were Conservatives. Mackenzie King did not wish to comfort his political enemies by shouldering their financial burdens; he therefore indicated that he "might be prepared to go a certain length possibly in meeting one or two western provinces that have progressive premiers at the head of their governments, but I would not give a single cent to any Tory government." King wanted to avoid the crisis. He had no program of action. Claiming constitutional inability to innovate, he refused to propose amendments to the BNA Act. Knowing that the provinces needed larger subsidies, he refused to help there as well.

Then the Prime Minister chose the summer of 1930 as the most propitious moment for renewing his party's mandate. King was confident that most voters wanted their central government to meet the crisis cautiously. Most Canadians were not suffering unemployment, and all could hope that prosperity was on the near horizon. Perhaps that was why his confidence was not misplaced. In 1930, the Liberals fell only one percent behind their 1926 total when they won a Parliamentary majority with 46 percent of the vote. But in 1926, the minor parties still maintained significant popularity. In the deepening depression, they had lost ground;

their loss was the Conservatives' gain. With 49 percent of the vote, the Tories won 56 percent of the seats.

The key to the Conservatives' success may have been that they appeared even more cautious than King. The Conservative leader, R.B. Bennett (successor to Arthur Meighen at the party's first-ever leadership convention in 1927), gave the impression that he would restore lost prosperity by traditional means—a heavier dose of the policy that Canadians were no longer holding as dear as they ought, according to Bennett. He said: "You have been taught to mock at tariffs and to applaud free trade." But he challenged the voters to tell him, "when did free trade fight for you? Tell me, when did free trade fight for you? You say our tariffs are only for our manufacturers; I will make them fight for you as well. I will use them to blast a way into the markets that have been closed to you."

After the election, Bennett kept his promise in a special session of Parliament. He adjusted the tariff with the sharpest increase since Macdonald's imposition of the National Policy in 1879. Although Bennett's medicine was no more than what he had promised (in this sense, what the electorate expected), the move to prevent dumping of cheap foreign goods in Canada stabilized falling prices, but tended to increase the deprivation of the unemployed without giving them work. In response to the latter, Bennett introduced an emergency relief appropriation of $20 million.

But the crisis continued to worsen (not reaching rock bottom until 1933; by that time, Bennett had begun to feel that he was struggling against a conspiracy of impossible forces). Legislation providing for federal aid to match local relief expenditures in 1931, and an agreement to pay one third in 1932 led to denunciations by King for "fiscal irresponsibility." When Bennett refused to go further, critics on the left complained of his heartlessness. Bennett responded that too many Canadians were looking to government to "take care of them." He said that the "fibre of some of our people has grown softer and they are not willing to turn in and save themselves." But what could they do? It was clear from Bennett's own mail that a large number of Canadians—independent producers— were powerless to avoid the destitution into which they had fallen. A man wrote from New Brunswick that the family fishing schooner had been sold because the price of fish had fallen too low to repay the cost of fishing. Another from Saskatchewan said he had to grow six times the wheat in 1932 to get the same dollar return as in the 1920s. But in the 1930s, because of disastrous drought, he grew nothing. For such personal reports of hardship, there was a note of sympathy and sometimes money from Bennett's own pocket as token consolation.

Bennett did care. He could show compassion for the individual testimonials of privation. But Bennett was angered by critics who seemed to hold him personally responsible for the Depression. He was hurt by farmers calling their horse-drawn Fords "Bennett buggies" because they could not afford the price of gasoline. And he was angered by the urban unemployed who named their shanty towns in garbage dumps "Bennett boroughs." He continued to believe that he was doing everything possible to meet the crisis, and became angry that unscrupulous opportunists seemed to exaggerate the trouble for their own advantage.

As early as 1932, Bennett was ready to shift the emphasis of his strategy from "blasting a way into the markets that have been closed" to blasting radicals. When 600 delegates to a Workers' Economic Conference in Ottawa attempted to address the public on Wellington Street in front of Parliament, they were met by city police, the RCMP, and a military armored car. So violent was their dispersal, even Conservative newspapers such as the Ottawa *Journal* described the encounter as a "scene that smacks more of fascism than of Canadian constitutional authority." But the repression of radicalism did not diminish.

Fear of communism led the federal government to resume the wartime censorship of books, to increase the postwar deportation of "dangerous foreigners," and to prosecute communists under the "seditious conspiracy" provisions of the Canadian Criminal Code. When socialists such as J.S. Woodsworth attacked the government's anti-radical campaign and demanded repeal of the relevant provisions of the Criminal Code and the Immigration Act, the Conservatives at first refused to debate the justice of repression, then answered that the laws on sedition were "not in any sense a hindrance to any right-thinking person."

But a vocal minority of Canadians who denounced communists for their refusal to seek change through the electoral-parliamentary process still shared the jailed communists' view that the country needed socialism to establish economic justice as well as recovery. Repudiating the basic premises of acquisitive individualism, they demanded an economy geared towards "the supplying of human needs instead of the making of profits."

Such criticism was common in the 1920s, as was shown in the previous chapter. But in that more prosperous decade, radicals struck at a system that was better able to withstand the assault. Then the critics of capitalism were more likely to be denounced as "visionaries" and their organizations endured, if not tolerated. In Toronto alone there were a dozen socialist parties. British Columbia supported three. But during the Depression, the possibility of proscription of radicals loomed ever larger as growing numbers of the middle class demanded that fundamental criticism of capitalism be postponed until the economy recovered.

Fear of repression, as much as the hope of recouping losses, prompted the leaders of the various radical groups to agree that their survival depended upon forgetting their many past differences and working together in a federation of the whole non-communist left. As early as 1930, the "Ginger Group" of "co-operating independents" and Labour members stopped calling themselves by their separate labels. The minor-party coalition led by J.S. Woodsworth began calling itself the Canadian Commonwealth Party. In 1932, a broader coalition of labourites, agrarian radicals, secular and social-gospel socialists met in Calgary to discuss federation. One observer of the gathering commented that the delegates "oozed idealism to the detriment of practical experience." Despite the diversity of background, they still seemed committed to a common thread of political philosophy. Moreover, the name that most of the delegates gave to their philosophy was *socialism*.

Over the winter of 1932-33, the new union of the non-communist left proceeded to define its intended program. A draft platform was acquired when Frank Underhill, a Toronto university professor, wrote a document to present to a convention to be held in Regina in August 1933. In final form, the platform of the new Co-operative Commonwealth Federation began with a ringing affirmation that capitalism was bankrupt:

> We aim to replace the present capitalist system, with its inherent injustice and inhumanity, by a social order from which the domination and exploitation of one class by another will be eliminated, in which economic planning will supersede unregulated private enterprise and competition, and in which genuine democratic self-government, based on economic equality will be possible. (Quoted in K. McNaught, *A Prophet in Politics: A Biography of J.S. Woodsworth* [1959], p. 321.)

The platform closed with the lofty promise the "No CCF government will rest content until it has eradicated capitalism and put into operation the full program of socialized planning which will lead to the establishment in Canada of the Co-operative Commonwealth."

Subsequently, the CCF was denounced by unrepentant capitalists for alleged communism. But the CCF's indisputable commitment to a

201

reformist strategy made it difficult to prosecute its leaders for "seditious conspiracy." More importantly, the national chairman of the party was J.S. Woodsworth, a member of the House of Commons of 12 years' standing. Saint or subversive, Woodsworth was too prominent to turn into a martyr. For both reasons, his presence in the leadership gave the CCF a legitimizing focus.

Even so, it was one thing to unite radical movements and make them safe from criminal prosecution and quite another to persuade a majority of the voters to adopt their point of view. On the other hand, the economic crisis of the 1930s was so peristent that it might have seemed the most likely occasion for the unemployed to have responded to radical criticism of their former employers' economic system. When the CCF emerged in 1933, perhaps as many as half of the *industrial* labour force was unemployed. Workers who did have jobs found that their average hourly pay had fallen by roughly two thirds, but the tariff had stabilized prices at about three fourths of pre-Depression levels. The unskilled who could find employment worked longer days (the 65-hour week for ten cents per hour was fairly common). Then there was the plight of fishermen and farmers, supposedly better off than the jobless because they were classified as "employed." But prices of their commodities were so low that their work was almost totally unremunerative. Not surprisingly, hundreds of CCF associations were formed across the country within a few months of the establishment of the party that promised to eliminate economic hardship forever. By late 1934, the CCF had become the number two party in both British Columbia and Saskatchewan. There were CCF members sitting in other provincial legislatures, and the party was winning municipal elections.

R.B. Bennett feared that a CCF snowball might develop into a socialist avalanche, and decided to halt its momentum by moving his own party in the direction of reform. By 1934, he had already taken a few short steps to the left by launching some reorganization of the banking industry, stabilizing farm credit, and promoting a new system for marketing natural products that was reminiscent of one employed during the war to sell wheat through a government board. But all such changes signified a piecemeal approach and avoided the wage-price spread that had become an issue in Bennett's own party. Some Conservatives (led by H.H. Stevens) were preparing to abandon the Tories in the name of securing a more thorough "Social Reconstruction."

In January 1935, Bennett made his move to reclaim leadership by taking to the air waves without prior consultation with cabinet or caucus and announced: "The old order is gone." He declared, "It will not return . . . I am for reform." With the loftiness of a Woodsworth, Bennett asserted that "There can be no permanent recovery without reform." Then came his message describing a fresh deal of the cards for the Canadian people: unemployment and health insurance, legislated minimum wages, and maximum work hours.

Some members of Bennett's party thought that their leader had converted to socialism, a sensitivity Bennett turned into a less-than-amusing joke when he began greeting certain cabinet colleagues as "comrade." But, in fact, the Prime Minister was careful to make clear that he was trying to free capitalism of its "harmful imperfections," to preserve the system, not to repudiate it. Unconvinced by Bennett's recent conversion, Liberals denounced his New Deal as little more than a pre-election ploy, legislation with which to charm the voters, regain a mandate, and then apologize later that it was all unconstitutional. Thus, Mackenzie King—in his usual indirect manner—asked Bennett to

> tell this House whether as leader of the government, knowing that a question will come up immediately as to the jurisdiction of this Parliament and of the provincial legislatures in matters of social legislation, he has secured an opinion from the law officers of the crown or from the Supreme Court of Canada which will be a sufficient guarantee to this House to proceed with these measures as being without question within its jurisdiction. (Quoted in J.M.S. Careless and R.C. Brown, eds., *The Canadians* [1968], p. 262.)

The question of constitutionality notwithstanding, five measures covering unemployment insurance, minimum wages, maximum work hours, and marketing boards did limp through Parliament before dissolution.

Unfortunately for Bennett, an ugly incident in Regina in the summer of 1935 marred his claim to be the leader with the most sensible and sensitive response to the problems of the unemployed. Since 1932, the single unemployed men of Canada had been recruited from the cities for work at 200 remote bush camps across the country. Since the program's inception, 170 000 men had passed through the facilities under the control of the Department of Defence, working for 20 cents per day at meaningless tasks such as building roads that ran nowhere, or airstrips for aircraft that never landed. The men were not convicts, nor were they held against their will; but upon entering the system, they lost the right to vote, and transport ran one way only: the government would truck them from town to camp, departure was on foot. The lack of transportation did not deter

150 000 from leaving. Those who remained in such warehouses of despair were ready converts to the communist Workers Unity League that organized the men in 1935 in an attempt to humanize the system. When they failed to secure the demanded changes where they lived, thousands of "Royal Twenty Centers" descended from British Columbia camps upon the city of Vancouver in May 1935 and publicized their demands for real wages and work, worker control of the facilities, and re-enfranchisement. When Ottawa seemed unresponsive still, the men decided to take the message directly to the nation's capital, and to recruit more voices to their chorus of resentment along the way. The government decided to stop the "On to Ottawa trek" at Regina.

The interruption of the journey was at first peaceful, even conciliatory, but turned violent on July 1 when the police made a move to arrest the leaders. What followed was a four-hour battle resulting in injuries and death. Bennett denounced the leaders as "bums" and "criminals." He said the use of force at Regina was fully justified, and maintained his belief that he was the true and proper champion of reform. What would the electorate decide?

The range of political choice for the August election was clear and varied. The major alternatives were: the eradication of capitalism by Woodsworth's CCF; changes in the organization of large-scale capitalism following a 15-point program of "social reconstruction" proposed by H.H. Stevens' renegade Conservative Reconstruction Party; the moderate reforms of Bennett's New Deal; or no change at all in Mackenzie King's re-run of the "no precipitate action" stance. Given the voting behaviour of the 1920s, and given the desire for action that might have been inherent in the length and severity of the Depression to 1935, the most likely prospect was for a minority government headed by Bennett. But such did not occur. The more outspoken the party for reform, the more repugnant it was to the electorate. The CCF and Reconstruction groups each received less than ten percent of the vote, the CCF electing only seven members (none east of Manitoba). Bennett's share fell to 30 percent. King's Liberals received 45 percent. The rest went to other minor parties, some to the left of the CCF, some to the right of the Liberals. But the two million votes polled for King's party translated into 173 of the 245 seats in the House of Commons—one of the widest majorities in Canadian history.

What can be inferred most easily from the 1935 election results (interpreting them as a public opinion poll) is that nearly half of the Canadian people were not very interested in innovative approaches to the problems of the unemployed. If nearly half of the people were in dire straits, the other half had jobs; perhaps it was the latter who responded to the Liberal slogan, "It's King or Chaos." In 1935, as in 1930, the electorate showed little support for radical innovation, as evidenced in the drift of national politics. On the provincial level, the voters were even more interested in parties that promised a return to the "good old days" by restoratives rather than by experimentation intended to make a sharp break with the past.

— 3. The Restoration Theme in Alberta —

One of the most interesting variations of the restoration theme in provincial politics was the enthusiastic response of Albertans to Social Credit, an economic theory developed in the 1920s by a British engineer, Major C.H. Douglas. His doctrine was a conscious repudiation of socialist collectivism that at the same time promised to cure capitalism by providing the solution to poverty amidst plenty. The great gear that was askew, according to Douglas, was the tendency of individuals' cash incomes to be less than the aggregate cost of goods for sale, a flaw that he expressed in his "A plus B theorem." Douglas divided (theoretically) all cash flows of society into "A" payments (the payment of money to individuals in the form of wages, salaries, and dividends), and "B" payments (the flow of cash to organizations for raw materials, bank charges, and other costs). Then he reasoned that "The rate of flow of purchasing power to individuals is represented by A, but since all payments go into prices, the rate of flow of prices cannot be less than A plus B." The solution seemed equally clear: "a portion of the product at least equivalent to B must be distributed by a form of purchasing power which is not comprised in the description grouped under A." These were the social credits, the dividends that producers had earned for manufacturing more than they were able to consume.

From the standpoint of the middle class, there was a common sense logic to Social Credit theory in the context of the Depression. It was a point that another British theorist, the economist John Maynard Keynes, appreciated when he argued that in times of recession, the fiscal pump of capitalism ought to be primed by increased government spending to employ people on massive public works, thus restoring consumer purchasing power. In fact, it was application of Keynesian theory through the back door that finally brought about economic recovery through the vast public works project that was the Second World War.

But five years before the war, Albertans were singularly attracted to Social Credit; it was a panacea that they embraced with all the enthusiasm usually associated with religious revival, in part because Major Douglas and his economic theories were woven into the sacred texts of an already influential radio preacher, "Bible Bill" Aberhart.

During the 1930s, Alberta was unusually rural, almost uniformly Protestant, and remarkably homogeneous, given that it was the most recently-settled province. Alberta was also one of the provinces most affected by the Depression; Alberta agrarians were doubly troubled by their fixed indebtedness and drastically falling prices. Albertans' first impulse towards finding escape from the new trouble was to renew faith in the old-time religion: if they promised to forsake drink, dancing, and movies, then the Lord might do his part by improving the weather and the price of wheat and beef. But no miracles followed.

Over the winter of 1932-33, "Bible Bill" began to expound Social Credit doctrine along with his fundamentalist Christianity from the radio studio at the Calgary Prophetic Bible Institute, spreading the Word to thousands of listeners. Study groups organized, and Aberhart became an inspiring teacher as well as the spiritual leader of everyone within radio range—residents of southern Alberta, parts of Saskatchewan, and some areas of Montana.

Throughout 1933, however, Social Credit was still no more than an object of study, not a political movement. The first involvement with organized politics did not come until January 1934. At that time, the governing party of Alberta held a convention at which delegates presented the new theory and urged the government to give it careful consideration as a program for recovery. Several months later, the Committee of the Whole House did consider the idea of social dividends. Aberhart testified. Even Major Douglas made an appearance. But the leaders of the United Farmers of Alberta remained sceptical. Their doubt, and the involvement of the premier in a sex scandal, convinced the star of the Prophetic Bible Institute that it was time to launch a Social Credit movement within the framework of government. Aberhart announced in December 1934 that in the next election "reliable, honourable, bribe-proof businessmen who have definitely laid aside their party political affiliations, will be asked to represent Social Credit in every constituency."

Aberhart's announcement was a significant revelation because it showed his conception of the cause as a nonpartisan crusade. Rather than creating a political party in the conventional sense, Aberhart intended to strike a holy alliance of all right-thinking Albertans to purge the province of corrupt politicians, raise the standard of public morality, and bring about recovery. It was time for "reliable, honourable, bribe-proof businessmen" to succeed where lesser mortals had faltered.

Once Aberhart set his electoral strategy, he dropped the style of the evangelist teacher and stressed his intentions more than the details of the "A plus B theorem" or other doctrinal niceties. "You don't have to know all about Social Credit before you vote for it," he said. Aberhart urged his followers to have faith and trust in the authorities. Reasoning by analogy, he suggested that "you don't have to understand electricity to use it, for you know that the experts have put the system in, and all you have to do is push the button and you get the light." So also with political choices: "all you have to do about Social Credit is to cast your vote for it, and we will get the experts to put the system in."

Many people felt that "Bible Bill" would not knowingly deceive them. He was an authority they could trust. Others, those who decided to read his pamphlet, the *Social Credit Manual*, discovered that the doctrine contained even more benefits than its economic promise. They found a wonderful instrument for abolishing poverty without compromising the purity of the rural ethic. Every adult would receive a monthly $25 dividend but any citizen who "persisted in refusing work" would have dividends "cut off or temporarily suspended." The credits were not to be a premium on idleness; they were therefore touted as a powerful bulwark for the enforcement of the full system of middle-class standards of propriety. Any person who "squandered his dividends . . . or was improperly clothed" would receive a warning from his Inspector, and the offender would reform his habits and shine his shoes or lose his dividends.

For some Albertans, the soft totalitarianism of Social Credit was a major attraction. For others, it was the $25 per month dividend. For still more, Aberhart was simply an attractive novelty. Whatever the precise combination of motives, in August 1935 the electorate awarded his group of "bribe-proof businessmen" a stunning majority of nearly 90 percent of the seats in the provincial legislature, and returned a similar proportion of Social Credit members to Ottawa in the federal election occurring in October.

On the day after the provincial triumph, a number of people called at Calgary City Hall for their first $25 dividend. But it was not forthcoming then or later. By 1936, Aberhart was ready to regret that he had ever heard of Major C.H. Douglas and his "impractical" theories. "Bible Bill" had discovered that there was simply no way to follow Social Credit doctrine without simultaneously freezing prices and repudiating the existing debt of the province. This Aberhart considered immoral. But there were a number of insurgents in "his" legislature who demanded a trial of social dividends regardless of the consequences. Thus emerged the Alberta Social Credit Act of 1937 that provided dividends to the amount of "the unused capacity of industries and people." Later in the year, a variety of other such measures followed. But since most of them pertained to banking, an area beyond provincial jurisdiction, the spurt of Social Credit legislation was subsequently referred to the courts by Ottawa and found to be *ultra vires* before the measures could be implemented. What remained of the doctrine was fiscal orthodoxy and Protestant fundamentalism. On this basis, in the words of Aberhart's chief lieutenant and eventual successor, E.C. Manning, Social Credit provided Alberta with "one of the most genuinely conservative governments in Canada."

— 4. The Restoration Theme in Quebec and Ontario —

Conservatism in the sense of aiming to restore and preserve a pre-1929 status quo was the emphasis of other provincial governments that came to power at the same time as Aberhart's. Quebec and Ontario, together accounting for 60 percent of the country's population, provided variations of the restoration theme that were nearly as striking as the Alberta case. In Quebec, where social strife was ethnic as much as economic, the impulse to escape the Depression by restoring the simplicity of the vanishing past gave rise to a pattern of resentment that was nationalist more than reformist. By 1935, a nonpartisan Roman Catholic social action group, Ecole sociale populaire, proposed a *Programme de restauration sociale* to meet the crisis with diverse restoratives, emphasizing the need to relocate people from the cities to the land (correcting the alleged evil of over-industrialization), and restore public credit by funneling the profits of private utility companies to the public purse through nationalization. When the incumbent Liberal administration of Alexandre Taschereau did not rush to adopt such a program of social restoration, a group of dissident Liberals rallied to Paul Gouin and formed a third party calling itself Action libérale nationale. Since Gouin was himself the son of a former Liberal premier, the movement could not be ignored. But the politician who observed the disintegration of the Liberals with the keenest interest was the leader of the minority Conservatives, Maurice Duplessis. Carefully, step by step, he manoeuvred the Roman Catholic social action group and the dissident Liberals into an alliance with himself, working like

Honoré Mercier to unite Liberals and Conservatives under one nationalist banner. Late in 1935, the Union nationale emerged—a party with no pretensions beyond Quebec and no program other than to govern for the people rather than the "trusts." Duplessis promised to fight nepotism, patronage, and corruption, and became particularly skillful in the use of anti-trust rhetoric without making any specific proposals for nationalization of particular offenders. Once in office in 1936, it was therefore easy for *"le chef"* to set his own course without taking action against Sir Herbert Holt's immensely profitable Montreal Light, Heat and Power (as some had expected), or (as many might have hoped) to move against the predatory giant, International Paper.

A true "trust buster" had good reason to attack both, but especially the latter. Pulp and paper had given Quebec its share of the booming expansion of the mid-1920s, and conditions in the same industry explain much of Quebec's immiseration in the 1930s. Moreover, most of the suffering was needless. According to Bernard Vigod, "there was enough demand to employ 75 percent of the entire industry's capacity" because the main customers, American newspapers, maintained most of their pre-depression demand. But International Paper exploited the crisis of the Depression to seek near monopoly control by undercutting competitors with below-cost prices. The result was that most non-International mills worked at 25 percent capacity or went under, while International plants recruited more orders than they could fill at 100 percent production. The Taschereau government had negotiated a scheme of "prorating" production intending to give each mill 75 percent of its theoretical maximum production, and threatened non-cooperators with punitive stumpage dues. But such a scheme was bound to fail as long as International could obtain adequate supplies from its own land or from other provinces. The opportunity for the radical critic was to suggest that nationalization was the only safe guarantee for effective "prorating."

Unfortunately for workers in Quebec's paper industry, Duplessis was radical in rhetoric only. Once in power, he proved to be as good a friend of enterprise—foreign and free—as any business person could want. The premier did spend a good deal of money promoting new agricultural settlement in keeping with the theme that "our salvation is rooted to the soil." Also consistent with the idea that "we must sow or go jobless, our people will be agricultural or perish," he neglected the problems of the urban poor, especially the suffering unemployed in Montreal, still Canada's largest city.

209

Of course, from another point of view it could be argued that the Union nationale paid a great deal of attention to the urban proletariat because it saved them from Godless socialism. In 1937, Quebec's legislature passed an "Act Respecting Communistic Propaganda"—a measure that empowered the police to lock up any establishment that was used for "propagating Communism or Bolshevism," terms that were left undefined, and which, therefore, were completely dependent upon the interpretive discretion of law enforcement officers. Defenders of *"le chef"* such as Lionel Groulx applauded his action, asserting that the happiest people are those who have "found their dictator," but civil libertarians argued that Quebec's "Padlock Law" was thought-control. Citizens were being prosecuted for the content of their ideas rather than for the violence of their behaviour.

At the time the "Padlock Law" was passed in Quebec, a similarly flamboyant premier, Mitchell F. Hepburn of Ontario, was moving with comparable zeal against radicalism, after having come to power in 1934 as a maverick Liberal defender of "the little guys" against the "big shots," pledging his sympathy to all "victims of circumstance." Examples of those "Mitch" promised to help were the small, independent producers—especially farmers. Addressing one typical audience in 1934, a group of dairy farmers, Hepburn asserted that they were required to live by one set of rules but the "big shots" lived by another. "If any of you farmers water your milk you go to jail. But if you water your stock you get to be Premier of Ontario." Mitch said he would change that as soon as he was in charge.

Of course, Hepburn was not elected so that dairy farmers could water milk; but a dismantling of privilege was expected, and in several superficial ways did follow. The new premier auctioned off some government limousines and he fired all the civil servants hired in the year before his election. He reduced the salaries of the personnel in the remaining civil service and cancelled some contracts with hydroelectric companies. All such moves were bold theatrics, but none assisted "little guys" such as industrial workers or the unemployed. Later, when labour attempted to help itself, Hepburn struck with the same vengeance shown by Duplessis in fighting radicals in Quebec.

The specific episode that provoked Hepburn's rage was the contest that developed in 1937 between the emerging Congress of Industrial Organizations (CIO) and the well-established firm of General Motors. Both were American organizations, one a militant federation of industrial unions, the other a branch-plant auto maker. But when a labour dispute began in Oshawa over management's refusal to recognize the connection of the

United Auto Workers with the CIO, Hepburn came to the side of General Motors in the name of Canadian nationalism. He said that Canada's troubles had never been as bad as outside agitators had made them appear, and denounced the tactic of "sit-down" strikes. Then, despite assurances from the union leaders and the mayor of Oshawa that there would be neither sit-down occupation of the plants nor violence at the gates (as had happened recently in Detroit), Hepburn requested a battalion of RCMP from Ottawa and recruited 400 of his own special police. Then "Hepburn's Hussars" (also called "Sons of Mitches" in the press) moved to break the CIO in Oshawa; but the company came to a settlement acceptable to the union before the conflict erupted in open violence. According to Irving Abella, that was a "great victory" for organized labour in Canada. The Oshawa settlement "created a psychology of success" that was an incentive for organization elsewhere. At the time, however, Hepburn claimed that the peaceful resolution of the strike was the direct result of his intimidation. He went on to victory in a provincial election in October boasting that his position on the CIO was still to be "standing right on top of them, and I'll keep standing there." Thus, in Ontario, as in much of the rest of the country, the spectre of substantial innovation by direct action prompted repression; in this case, repression of action before it had even begun.

— 5. Ten Lost Years —

Here, then, were some of the more striking aspects of Canada's responses to the Great Depression, a period of hardship that generated enormous concern. The flamboyant characters who commanded the greatest popularity had two attributes in common: they saw the economic crisis as a temporary setback in the development of capitalism, and they believed that no recovery could be valid or permanent if it violated the fundamentals of possessive individualism. The dissenters from orthodoxy were a minority without hope of gaining power as long as the paranoid fear that was a function of hard times held Canadians in its icy grip. Radical leaders of the 1920s not only lost ground in the 1930s, some lost their freedom. A few abandoned Canada altogether, including a group of 1 300, mainly participants of the On to Ottawa Trek, who organized the "Mackenzie-Papineau battalion" (after the leaders of the rebellions of 1837), to join the only significant fight against fascism in the 1930s—the Spanish Civil War, from 1936 to 1939. But there as well, the right wing triumphed over the left. In Europe, as well as at home, the 1930s was a time when Canadians, especially the unemployed, were forced to reconsider the structure of their society and the role of their institutions. Some did reason their way to radical criticism. But most Canadians never lost their jobs, and although they were not unaffected by the crisis, they preferred to escape into the wonderful world of the Dionne quintuplets, Walt Disney's *Snow White and the Seven Dwarfs*, Hollywood musicals, or radio entertainments that were designed to soothe a troubled world. Most Canadians remained "right-thinking" people who hoped for a return of the good old days, even though the old days had not been as good as in popular reminiscence, or as easy to recover as nearly every politician promised.

Suggested Reading

General histories that cover the period of the Great Depression include John Herd Thompson and Allen Seager, *Canada, 1922-1939: Decades of Discord* (1985). Other useful general works include H.B. Neatby, *The Politics of Chaos: Canada and the Thirties* (1972), a brief but comprehensive overview, too sympathetic, perhaps, to Mackenzie King, as is Robert Bothwell, *et al., Canada, 1900-1945* (1985). Less general, but more thorough on economic issues, is A.E. Safarian, *The Canadian Economy in the Great Depression* (1959), particularly useful for the relationships that are established between the staple trades and secondary manufacturing. For the general human impact of the Depression, James Gray, *The Winter Years* (1966), L.M. Grayson and M. Bliss, eds., *The Wretched of Canada: Letters to R.B. Bennett, 1930-35* (1971), and M. Horn, ed., *The Dirty Thirties* (1972), all provide richly evocative autobiographical material.

Michael Bliss, *Northern Enterprise* (1987), contains some interesting material on the difficulties of business in the 1920s and 1930s. The subject of business-government relations is covered by Tom Traves, *The State and Enterprise: Canadian Manufacturers and the Federal Government* (1979), and James Struthers in "Prelude to Depression: The Federal Government and Unemployment, 1918-29," *CHR* (1977), and *"No Fault of their Own": Unemployment and the Canadian Welfare State, 1914-1941* (1983). Both provide useful background to the Depression—Traves on the failure to create the regulatory state, and Struthers on the abortive attempt to implement unemployment insurance. After 1929, of course, there were new pressures for both kinds of reform to save capitalism. This theme is developed fully by Alvin Finkel in *Business and Social Reform in the Thirties* (1979). For material on Bennett's "New Deal," in particular, see Donald Forster and Colin Read, "The Politics of Opportunism: The New Deal Broadcasts," *CHR* (1979), and J.R.H. Wilbur, *The Bennett New Deal* (1968).

On the development of radical alternatives, Michiel Horn, "The League for Social Reconstruction and the Development of a Canadian Socialism, 1932-1936," *JCS* (1972), discusses the formation and development of the group that has been called the "brains trust" of the CCF. *Anatomy of a Party* (1969), by W. Young examines the larger aspects of the CCF and its program during the thirties. For the story of radicals to the left of Woodsworth's group, see Irving Abella, *Nationalism, Communism and Canadian Labour: The CIO, the Communist Party and the Canadian Congress of Labour, 1935-1956* (1973).

For radicalism on the other side of the political spectrum, the most useful works are those that are addressed to the appeal of the flamboyant right-wing premiers of the period. C.B. Macpherson, *Democracy in Alberta: Social Credit and the Party System* (1953), is the most penetrating in his analysis of the reasons for Aberhart's success. Duplessis is examined by C. Nish, *Quebec in the Duplessis Era: Dictatorship or Democracy?* (1970), H.F. Quinn, *The Union nationale*, rev. ed. (1979), and Bernard Vigod, *Quebec before Duplessis* (1986). M.F. McKenty, *Mitch Hepburn* (1967), although less analytical than either Nish or Macpherson, is still addressed to the subject of right-wing populism, in this case, in Ontario. M. Ormsby describes the British Columbia variant in "T. Dufferin Patullo and the Little New Deal," *CHR* (1962). The exceptional case was Manitoba where the government of John Bracken was able to enjoy a unique continuity from the 1920s through the 1930s. Since Bracken enjoyed political success without resort to right-wing demagoguery, the Manitoba example invites comparison with Alberta, Ontario, Quebec, or British Columbia. See John Kendle, *John Bracken: A Political Biography* (1979).

**Veronica Foster, the "Bren Gun Girl,"
at lathe, J. Inglis Co., Toronto, 1941.**

SOURCE: NFB/NATIONAL ARCHIVES OF CANADA/PA-51587

*"Thanks to the war, an industrial
worker in 1941 was earning twice as
much as in 1939 . . . ."*

CHAPTER 11
RECOVERY BY WAR, 1940-1945

— 1. Twilight of Depression —

Although the economic crisis of the 1930s made Canadians more aware of the insecurities of life in an industrial society, most continued to view "social security" as an individual responsibility. There was no consensus for the social insurance Bennett proposed. Nor was much credence given to the view that massive government spending on public works was an appropriate means of controlling the fluctuations of the business cycle. Between 1930 and 1937, the interesting legislation pertained to banking, broadcasting, and transportation—the creation of the Canadian Boradcasting Corporation (1932), the Bank of Canada (1935), and Trans-Canada Airlines, the forerunner to Air Canada (1937)—not social welfare.

After his return to power late in 1935, Mackenzie King kept his promise of "no precipitate action" by referring the Bennett New Deal to the Supreme Court and convening a Dominion-provincial conference with the premiers to consider the problem of unemployment. At the meeting in December, the federal government agreed to increase grants for "relief" payments in exchange for provincial cooperation with a National

Employment Commission (NEC) to investigate more appropriate means of handling the realities of unemployment in modern society. Bennett's unemployment insurance scheme was not expected to pass judicial scrutiny. But the Supreme Court soon rendered some surprising decisions to the contrary: the Canadian judges upheld all of the "New Deal" legislation except the Natural Products Marketing Act. Rather than act on their judgement, King's government referred the questions to the anachronistic next level of appeal in Great Britain, and the Judicial Committee of the Privy Council struck down the entire package, ruling that the "peace, order and good government" clause in Section 91 was an emergency power to be used in dire circumstances only. The Dominion could not legislate in any area allotted to the provinces except by reason of war, pestilence, or famine. Instead of asserting the supremacy of the Canadian court, or changing the BNA Act along lines that the premiers seemed to accept in December 1935, King appointed another commission to study the constitution.

Headed by N.W. Rowell (who was soon succeeded by Joseph Sirois because of Rowell's failing health), the Royal Commission on Dominion-Provincial Relations was to examine "the economic and financial basis of Confederation and the distribution of legislative powers in light of the economic and social developments of the last seventy years." With such a broad mandate, the commission's work would never be completed in a matter of months. Consequently, the Prime Minister would gain a period of years, perhaps, in which he would be excused from proceeding with constitutional changes or social legislation.

Unfortunately for King, the National Employment Commission made fiscal recommendations in the interim that had far-reaching implications. The NEC divorced itself from traditional economic theory in an unequivocal endorsement of the novel recovery remedies advocated by the British economist, John Maynard Keynes. The Keynesian formula for dealing with recession involved tax cuts and deficit spending, on the assumption that a modern government should concern itself with balancing the whole economy rather than the budget. A wise government, according to Keynes, would spend more when private investors spent less, and recover deficits by tax increases and budget surpluses as the economy recuperated. When the NEC recommended a Keynesian strategy for Canada, a dangerous split developed in cabinet over the budget of 1938.

Norman Rogers, the Minister of Labour, demanded massive expenditure on public works and threatened to resign if the advice of the National Employment Commission were ignored. Charles Dunning, the Minister of

Finance, was equally insistent that restraint was the only sane policy. With each minister threatening to quit if his own will did not prevail, others took sides accordingly; Mackenzie King imposed a compromise that gave both sides enough to quiet the mutiny. Rogers' demand was met by half, and Dunning was left with a still manageable deficit.

The budget compromise of 1938 emerged thus as a significant step away from traditional practice. According to H.B. Neatby, "it was the most radical and most constructive innovation of that depression decade." But the half-step towards deficit spending on principle was soon dwarfed by enormously greater borrowing for an infinitely vaster, more startling emergency—that of the Second World War. And with that upheaval, the Canadian state underwent its most significant transformation since Confederation.

— 2. Mobilization For War —

Canada's return to a war-footing in September 1939 was somewhat anomalous from a military-history standpoint. In the beginning, as a matter of policy, the country's liability was said to be "limited." The Prime Minister declared that no "great expeditionary forces of infantry" would be sent to Europe as in the Great War. It was hoped—and expected—that the allies would be content to make use of Canada's food and industrial resources more than its human resources. At first, Britain made little use of either. The British responded to the Canadian offer of help in the autumn of 1939 with a modest request for a program to train aviation personnel and token orders for military equipment. But in the spring of 1940, after the Germans' lightning advance across the Low Countries, the fall of France, and abandonment of the British Expeditionary Forces' equipment at Dunkirk, orders for replacement material poured into Canada; and the single division sent to England in 1939, reinforced with one more in January 1940, was bolstered with two additional divisions before the end of the year. To facilitate Canada's growing involvement in the war, a National Resources Mobilization Act provided for complete planning of the economy by the Department of Munitions and Supply, headed by C.D. Howe. Such control extended to the rationalization of labour, of course, to assure that adequate numbers were available for essential industries and the armed forces. With regard to military recruitment, the NRMA permitted conscription for home defence purposes. The personnel going overseas were to be volunteers only.

The voluntary system was expected to be adequate for overseas combat because the troops were not going to be utilized on a full-scale basis. Canada and Britain had approximately the same percentage of their populations in uniform but a significantly smaller percentage of Canada's forces was committed to fighting. The bulk of the army spent most of the war, in the words of their commander, Major-General A.G.L. Mc-Naughton, as a "dagger pointed at the heart of Berlin." But the army was a dagger drawn rather than a weapon bloodied. The men trained and retrained while the fighting went on elsewhere without them.

In the first several years of the war, Canadian combat personnel were to be seen most frequently in the air or escorting convoys across the Atlantic. The two major exceptions were the nearly 2 000 infantrymen killed or captured in the defence of Hong Kong late in 1941, and a similar number who met the same fate in the reconnaissance raid on Dieppe in August 1942. Thus, Canada had mobilized for total war without fighting accordingly. The result was that just one third of Canadian war production was utilized by Canadian forces. Britain was the consumer of two thirds of the tanks, artillery, and rifles made in Canada. To imperialists such as Arthur Meighen, it was disgraceful that Canada had not turned immediately to wholehearted commitment of the infantry to fight with the "Tommies" in North Africa, for instance. In Meighen's view, the reservation of the Canadian army in England demonstrated that the Prime Minister was driven by a cowardly fear of the domestic consequences of imposing conscription for overseas service.

King's avoidance of large-scale infantry combat until the end was in sight was a judicious way to avoid civil war with Quebec, but his commitment to total effort in war production demanded a measure of centralization and control of the economy that did create unrest in Dominion-provincial relations, and led to manoeuvring that reflected anything but cowardice on King's part. In 1940, the Rowell-Sirois Commission finally reported. Its chief recommendation was that Ottawa should assume full responsibility for unemployment compensation in order to ensure a uniform standard of relief in every province. Since the assumption of such a responsibility would cost a great deal, it was also recommended that the provinces surrender their power of direct taxation to Ottawa, with the central government transferring back sufficient funds to maintain provincial administration and other social services. Each province would retain control over its cultural, civil, and educational matters, but in matters of social security, each would become an administrative district of a unitary state. King recommended acceptance of the proposition for the sake of the war.

When the unity he proposed in 1940 proved no more forthcoming than in Macdonald's day, King exploited the wartime emergency to circumvent the disappointing rejection of the Rowell-Sirois Report by the provincial premiers at a conference early in 1941 that broke down after only three days' discussion. The Minister of Finance, J.L. Ilsley, threatened to implement the direct-taxation recommendation on his own—provincial objections notwithstanding. Federal, corporate, and personal income taxes would be raised so much that no province would dare impose its own taxation in excess of the new national levels. The provinces' alternative was to agree to "vacate the field" temporarily for two kinds of compensation: they might receive back from Ottawa the amount collected in direct taxation the year before, or they might claim an amount sufficient to pay the net cost of servicing the provincial debt plus a special subsidy. Thus, the first taxation "rental" agreement emerged late in 1941 as federal blackmail with the provinces settling for what they were given. The consolation to objecting premiers was the knowledge that the central government's monopoly was temporary; it was supposed to terminate one year after the war's end.

The recommendation of the Rowell-Sirois Commission regarding unemployment compensation was implemented through the back door with similar dispatch. King's acceptance of adverse court decisions in the previous decade meant that the BNA Act had to be changed before the unemployment insurance scheme could be implemented. But the change was desired in 1940 because employment was nearly full and the recently re-employed were developing a renewed interest in labour organization, exactly as had occurred during the previous war boom. The question was whether they would become equally restive in the next postwar slump. In preparation for such a development, unemployment insurance was to be instituted during the period of full employment to accumulate a large fund for the expected "hard times" ahead. In preparation for the enabling legislation, the provincial premiers were individually polled in private correspondence. Then, having obtained the premiers' consent for the sake of the war, a joint address of the Senate and House of Commons was submitted to the government of Great Britain and a new power was added to Section 91 of the BNA Act in 1940. With the constitution amended, the appropriate legislation went through the Canadian Parliament without controversy in the summer of 1940.

— 3. Left Turn —

Reform and recovery were proving embarrassingly simple. Between 1939 and 1941, the GNP increased 47 percent as the output of primary commodities doubled and levels of secondary manufacturing trebled. All were directly attributable to federal spending. The government that had spent $322 million on relief during the entire decade of the Depression was spending the same amount in an average month between 1941 and 1943. Thanks to the war, an industrial worker in 1941 was earning twice as much as in 1939, and was twice as likely to be a member of a union. Should such persons suffer the misfortune of layoff after the war, earnings were at least partially insured after 1940.

The war bonanza seemed conclusive proof that a modern government could iron the peaks and troughs out of the business cycle. There was full employment; a blanket price freeze prevented inflation; and rationing moderated scarcities in such commodities as gasoline and tires. To be sure, there was a kind of austerity that followed from shortages of imported liquor and cotton, but such privations were supposed to affect everyone, not just the jobless or destitute farmers and fishermen as in the Depression. The important point was the apparent efficiency with which government took control of collective resources and seemed to manage them competently for the shared goal of victory. Naturally, many Canadians concluded that if a country could spend billions fighting a war and could plan the economy effectively for the good of such a cause, the same bureaucracy might also control production to ensure peacetime prosperity and promote the general welfare by adding other social security programs to unemployment insurance.

There was a dramatic indication that such an opinion had grown to major proportions by 1942 when Arthur Meighen stepped down from the Senate, assumed the leadership of the Conservative party, and sought support from an Ontario riding that had voted Tory in every election since 1904. Meighen staked his fortunes on a supposition of widespread resentment that King had mobilized the country for total war without fighting accordingly. He demanded conscription and coalition government. His opponent, a socialist school teacher named Joseph Noseworthy, suggested that Meighen wanted the same kind of war as in 1914 and would probably administer the same chaotic transition to peace that he had presided over in the 1919 postwar period. Noseworthy countered Meighen's manpower demand with a call for "conscription of wealth," and won 159 of 212 polls

220

in York South—the first CCF victory east of the Prairies (and in Toronto of all places).

Meighen's initial reaction to his defeat was to denounce his opponent for having unfairly smeared him as a defender of predatory capitalism. Meighen felt he had been "pilloried as a cold and burnt-out reactionary." But once he recovered from the sting of personal injury, he speculated that the York South contest could be a fair indicator of the future, especially as the new, non-electoral device for polling public opinion developed by the Gallup organization began to chart the evidently inexorable rise of the CCF nationally. Meighen predicted CCF dominance in industrial areas after the war. He reasoned that if the Liberals could be confined to Quebec, the Conservatives might command a plurality of Parliament by sweeping the West and the rural East. In order for such a strategy to succeed, however, Meighen would have to resign from the leadership in deference to someone with proven popularity in the West; and that some-one might by John Bracken, Premier of Manitoba since 1922.

Other Conservatives feared that Meighen's strategy would turn their party into little more than an echo of the 1920s Progressives. Early in September they met in an unofficial and unauthorized gathering at Port Hope, Ontario to discuss more up-to-date strategies for enabling the Conservatives to lay claim to a middle position between the CCF and the Liberals. They affirmed unwavering faith in capitalism, but still mapped out a program of reforms that went well beyond King's unemployment insurance. The "Port Hopefuls" anticipated a system for assuring every Canadian "a gainful occupation and sufficient income to maintain himself and a family." More specifically, they called for additional "social legislation" in areas such as low-cost housing, collective bargaining rights for organized labour, and medical insurance.

Arthur Meighen subsequently denounced such thinking as the "main cause of the progressive decrepitude of nations," but in a matter of weeks the new eastern Conservatism was being endorsed by Bracken, the old-time agrarian. Since Meighen continued to believe that John Bracken was the only leader who might fulfill his Western strategy, Bracken's evident romance with social legislation would have to be tolerated. Unfortunately, the Manitoba premier laid down other conditions that were equally disturbing. He insisted that the party change its name and that his nomination flow from harmonious consensus rather than a bloody convention battle. Meighen dreaded adopting a platform "merely for the sake of votes," and he also disliked a change of name that suggested the Tories were joining

Bracken rather than *vice versa*. Meighen's dilemma was that Bracken remained the only potential leader who seemed likely to sweep the West. For this reason, Meighen promoted the package to the point of fulfillment, and a newly labeled *Progressive* Conservative Party was born.

— 4. A Comprehensive Strategy —

Meighen's defeat in Toronto in February, the emergence of Progressive Conservatism in Winnipeg in December, and two other influences in 1942 prompted Mackenzie King to move his Liberals with the evident leftward swing of public opinion. The other incentives were external factors, British and American. The British influence was a plan for postwar social reconstruction called the Beveridge Report after its principle author, Sir William Beveridge. The British blueprint for the social security state recommended a complete system of public insurance to protect all aspects of Britons' health, employment, and retirement "from the cradle to the grave."

The public seemed manifestly receptive to the concept, and Mackenzie King expressed private delight that Canadians appeared to be catching up with his own thinking, outlined 25 years earlier in his book, *Industry and Humanity*. There, he believed, one would find "pretty much the whole program that now is being suggested for postwar purposes." It was enormously satisfying for King to believe that his earlier work was finding a rendezvous with destiny.

The other influence in deciding King on the issue of social security was a conversation he had with the American president in December 1942. King discovered that Roosevelt was already acquainted with the Beveridge Report. Moreover, FDR was positive that, "the thought of insurance from the cradle to the grave . . . seems to be a line that will appeal." Both agreed to take up comprehensive social security programs "strongly" as soon as possible.

Before the end of 1942, a social scientist from McGill University was given the assignment of preparing a Beveridge Report for Canada. Leonard Marsh and his team worked day and night to complete a first draft of their *Report on Social Security for Canada* in mid-January 1943. They summarized the main features of existing social programs, suggested improvements of the pension and unemployment insurance acts, and outlined new schemes, including a health insurance plan and the idea of cash allowances for families of so much per child. Altogether, the Marsh

Report was truly a "charter of social security for the whole of Canada," and it created a stir of controversy upon publication in mid-March 1943.

Some of the critics of the plan considered it "socialistic." Indeed, the League for Social Reconstruction (sometimes called the "brains trust" of the CCF) had issued a similar report in 1935 under the title of *Social Planning for Canada*. But there were vast differences between the two approaches to planned intervention for social welfare. The assumption that ran through the Marsh Report was that there was enough wealth in Canada to assure that certain securities that were at present limited to the wealthy and the middle class would be available to everyone. Marsh contended that a minimum universal standard could be assured if the government of Canada were willing to administer "properly integrated" schemes of insurance and public works to protect well-being and "purchasing power." In the Marsh approach to planning, the maldistribution of income and production for profit were both left undisturbed in the sense that there was no declaration of intent to impose a ceiling on incomes (as *Social Planning for Canada* had proposed in 1935); nor was public ownership endorsed as a more efficient means of maintaining levels of investment and therefore employment (another LSR-CCF position in 1935). Since both omissions were painfully evident to socialists, *Canadian Forum* suggested that the Liberals' endorsement of social security on the Marsh plan was simply "the price that Liberalism is willing to pay in order to prevent socialism."

King was forced to focus on socialism in 1943 because the "CCFers" were becoming the Liberals' main rival for popularity. Early in August, the CCF won 34 of the 87 seats in Ontario's legislature. One month later, Canada's socialist party appeared even more popular, a trend that seemed to be spreading across the country. A Gallup poll showed that the CCF had edged one percentage point ahead of the two major parties, with 29 percent of the decided voters.

Mackenzie King secretly enjoyed the leftward swing of public opinion. He wrote in his diary that he was satisfied that "the mass of the people" seemed to be "coming a little more into their own." His only "regret" was that they did not see him as their true champion. But King imagined that defect could be remedied by enacting the right sort of social security legislation before the next general election. He might yet prove to "the great numbers of people that I have been true to them from the beginning of my public life." With that intent, the Prime Minister drafted a Throne Speech in December proclaiming that "a national minimum of social security and human welfare should be advanced as rapidly as possible."

Having pledged his party to specific action, something was needed for the new session of Parliament beginning in January 1944. Where to start? King initially favoured legislation for a national health insurance scheme. But such an innovation would require the cooperation of provincial governments and the medical profession. Its implementation meant negotiation and controversy, and King dreaded both. One by one, other items of social legislation were ruled out for the same reason. Ultimately, he seized upon the family allowances scheme even though it had seemed "sheer folly" to him at first thought.

The main attraction of a "baby bonus" was that it could be implemented without any involvement of the provinces because the grants would be direct payments to individuals at so much per head. Another attraction of the plan was that it provided several ways of confounding the Tory and the socialist opposition. Given that the allowance was to be paid on a per-child basis, socialists could be expected to support it as a suitable method for adjusting incomes by need. But since organized labour, like business, insisted that families should be paid according to their wage-earner's skill—a principle that the Liberals also supported—it was possible that the debate over the general significance of family allowances might confuse the left by provoking divisions between socialists and organized labour. Equally important, the scheme was certain to anger the Tories because families were to be rewarded in proportion to size, and Quebec was still the province with the highest birthrate. The Tories could be expected to denounce the plan as a bribe to keep Quebeckers voting Liberal.

Quebec's loyalty to the Liberal party needed additional support in the spring of 1944; the continuing threat of conscription for overseas service loomed ever larger as the final months of war approached and the government at last committed the whole army to combat. The invasion of Europe was expected at any moment. Once the infantry was committed totally to such a bold venture, casualties would mount and it would be difficult to withdraw forces simply because volunteer reinforcements were not forthcoming. If conscription proved necessary to maintain the strength of the army in Europe, a chain of promises extending back to 1917 would collapse and Quebec would surely hold Mackenzie King responsible for the betrayal. A special gift for the province with the highest birthrate might have been expected to make the difference between success or failure at the next election.

Even so, the event that caused King finally to introduce his family allowance scheme was not a crisis in Quebec. The determinant of King's timing was disaster in Saskatchewan. On June 11, 1944—five days after the allies invaded Europe—the CCF won a clear majority in the province hardest hit by the Depression. Three days after Saskatchewan emerged with the first socialist government in Canada, King brought the family allowance scheme before cabinet. It came before Parliament on July 25.

The opposition parties—especially the Conservatives—were completely cornered. To oppose the scheme would seem to imply a lack of commitment to social reform on their part, but to approve the bill would virtually guarantee the Liberals' re-election. On one hand, they lamely asserted with John Diefenbaker that "We believe in social legislation . . . . No political party has a monopoly in that direction." But on the other, they denounced the measure as "legal bribery." A Toronto Conservative, Herbert Bruce, went furthest in denouncing the proposal by accusing King of "bonusing families who have been unwilling to defend their country." The scheme was a "bribe of the most brazen character," said Bruce, "made chiefly to one province and paid for by the rest."

While it was true that Quebec did have a higher birthrate than the rest of Canada, the government produced evidence that Quebec's expected family allowance allocation would not be disproportionate to its contribution to federal revenue. Quebec contributed 34 percent of the taxes, and was expected to collect just 33 percent of the family allowance benefits. The government did admit that Ontario, contributing 47 percent of the revenue, was likely to collect only 29 percent of the allowances; but the difference would subsidize the Maritimes and the Prairies, not Quebec. In the end, the real issue seemed to be the rectitude of subsidizing motherhood and a happy childhood, and since Herbert Bruce absented himself from the House of Commons the day the crucial vote was taken, the family allowances bill passed unanimously.

The first payments of from five to eight dollars per month (depending upon the age of the child) were scheduled to begin on July 1, 1945 because a general election was expected in the interim. King explained in his diary that he "did not like the idea of spending public money immediately before an election . . . people were likely to be more grateful for what they were about to receive than anything they might be given in advance."

— 5. Right Turn —

By July 1944, the stage was set for the Liberals to make a credible claim to the dominant centre-party position. The government's legislative agenda on social security (completed and in expectancy) placed the Liberals to the left of the Progressive Conservatives but still comfortably to the right of the CCF. The one issue that could spoil an electoral victory in the summer of 1944 was that of conscription. King had worked desperately through the summer of 1944 to avoid such a confrontation but Conn Smyth, a popular sports personality in uniform, returned to his Toronto home in September to convalesce from injuries sustained in the ferocious fighting unfolding since the D-Day invasion of France on June 6. Newspapers naturally seized on Smyth's recovery for its human interest value. At the same time, they printed the hero's explanation of why he and so many others were being wounded. Smyth was quoted as saying that "General Service" volunteers were receiving reinforcements with too little training and that large numbers of "unnecessary casualties" resulted from the more experienced soldiers having to look after the newcomers as well as themselves. Better trained troops were available in Canada but they were not being sent overseas.

The alternative replacements were NRMA men—soldiers conscripted for home defence since 1940 (under the provisions of the National Resources Mobilization Act). Since the home-defence conscripts were legally exempt from service outside the Western Hemisphere, they were literally only half-conscripted and (in the view of a growing number of people in English-speaking Canada), since they were only half-way participating in the war effort, they were only half alive to the world around them, the real world embodiment of the characters in Hollywood horror movies called "zombies." On September 18, 1944, Conn Smyth said that the time had come to send Canada's conscripts overseas.

Others shared the view that the NRMA men were less than "real Canadians." As the country brooded over the dichotomous results of a plebiscite that had been held on conscription in 1942 (three quarters of Quebec rejecting, a similar portion of the rest of Canada approving), the French-Canadians were identified as the prime zombies and a furor developed over the renewed demand to send NRMA men to fight in Europe. The army cooperated by making the number of General Service reinforcements seem dangerously low, because the Prime Minister had said repeatedly that there would be no conscription for overseas duty unless it were necessary. When the cabinet divided on the question of current necessity through October, Mackenzie King forced the resignation of the pro-conscriptionist Minister of Defence, J.L. Ralston on November 1. He replaced him with the former army commander, General A.G.L. McNaughton. Soon, however, the new Minister of Defence was persuaded by district commanders that his predecessor was correct in the conclusion that the supply of General Service replacements was impossible to maintain by volunteers. When McNaughton declared conscription to be necessary at the end of November, King agreed, and conscripts were on their way to Europe before the end of the year.

Was the necessity genuine? It had been estimated that 15 000 reinforcements were needed and there were more than 30 000 available in England and Canada by what Douglas and Greenhouse call energetic remustering and cuts in headquarters personnel (four percent of American combat troops were assigned to generals' staffs with such duties as running the duplicating machines, while Canadian generals used 13.6 percent of their men for the same purpose). From this standpoint, the necessity was more artificial than real. But one general suggested that the troops in Europe would not feel well-supported from home if the government allowed the NRMA men to "sit comfortably" in Canada while the fighting in Europe was reaching its last, most intense, phase. Judging by the public opinion polls of 1944, the majority of the English-speaking electorate agreed. Consequently, King reluctantly gave them what they wanted. In this way, emotionalism determined military necessity and the chain of promises to Quebec was broken.

By 1945 the Tories were convinced that they had King in a corner: if they maintained the pressure to have the government send even more zombies overseas, the Liberals were certain to lose strength to nationalist minor parties in Quebec (such as the quasi-separatist Bloc populaire), while the Conservatives were certain to capture a proportionately larger share of the 75 percent pro-conscriptionist majority in the rest of Canada. Consequently, the "progressive" aspect of Progressive Conservatism receded as the party's emphasis on conscription came ever more to the forefront in 1945. Indeed, the party began to repudiate the basic concept of the social security state as leading to "elaborate and burdensome" bureaucracy, only slightly less undesirable, in its characterization, than the "rationed scarcity" that was certain to follow from the CCF's socialism.

Unfortunately for Bracken, the war in Europe ended before the election. Victory over Hitler occurred on May 7. The Tories' greatly-desired triumph over King was set for June 11. By that time, the only foreign enemy was Japan. Bracken's call to avenge the humiliation of the Canadian defenders of Hong Kong by fighting alongside the Americans in the expected invasion of the home islands proved to be the greatest miscalculation of his long political career.

Bracken and his fellow Tories misjudged the amount of resentment of conscription in Quebec and of the zombies in the rest of Canada. Only 550 000 French-Canadian voters turned their backs on the Liberals as well as the Conservatives; 700 000 still preferred King's party. Moreover, the Liberals did very well in the rest of Canada. Overall, Tories won less than 30 percent of the vote (in Bracken's home province of Manitoba only 24 percent). But the Progressive Conservatives' disastrous showing was still less humiliating than the defeat of Canada's socialists who sank to 16 percent of the vote.

If the Tories' humiliation is explained easily by their dogmatic advocacy of conscription even after the European war—Canada's war— was already over, what explains the CCF's even greater defeat after their spectacular rise in popularity in 1942 and 1943? According to J.L. Granatstein, the CCF was defeated by King's successful reinstatement of the Liberals as the credible centre party. King was the experienced leader, and it was he "who had pushed through the great social reform program that more than anything else secured the Liberals their majority." In large part, however, the program was but one measure, the family allowances scheme. Given that the promise of the Throne Speech of 1944 was still quite unfulfilled, how could the electorate trust King to finish what he had first promised in 1919, completely forgotten during the last postwar period, and also through the Depression?

Gerald Caplan suggests that the evident preferences for King developed despite his past record. In Caplan's view, the CCF was defeated because it was victimized by the "most formidable and devastating campaign in Canadian history." In the autumn of 1943, Canadian business began an expensive and well-organized advertising blitz to convince the public that the CCF was a party completely unlike the others. Canada's socialists were depicted as advocates of "the sort of system they have in Germany and Russia, where the government takes everything away from you and tells everybody what to do." The climate of fear generated was so all-pervasive that even such normally moderate voices of opinion as Maclean's magazine began to hint editorially that the CCFers were totalitarians in disguise. Voters could switch from one legitimate party to another but, in the case of the CCF, Maclean's warned, "you can't 'try' socialism" on the same basis because "it can work only when socialists are permanently in power which means that opposition couldn't be tolerated." Caplan argues that such propaganda systematically frightened voters away from the CCF, even though they did not truly know what they were rejecting.

The irony of the smear campaign is that the CCF was far more moderate in 1945 than in any of the previous elections in which the party was a factor. Under the pragmatic leadership of M.J. Coldwell (successor to Woodsworth after his pacifist refusal to support Canada's entry to the war), it dropped the rhetoric of "eradicating capitalism" completely. Indeed, the socialism

228

of the CCF in 1945 was so muted, some voters might have wondered whether it mattered to vote for them against the Liberals. For this reason, the CCF may have been as damaged by its own voices of moderation as by its "nonpartisan" critics. The end result is that half of the people who said they were going to vote CCF in 1943 voted Liberal in 1945, and the author of *Industry and Humanity* was returned to power with a clear majority.

Subsequently, King did not complete the work that was outlined in the Throne Speech of 1944; no system of cradle-to-grave social security was forthcoming in 1946, or in his lifetime. Moreover, King's new evasiveness was accomplished without criticism except from the CCF. This fact suggests that the country may have been leaning far less to the left than the pools of 1943 seemed to indicate. It may be that the apparent preference for the CCF earlier only indicated a conservative desire to preserve the wartime prosperity that seemed implicit in the social security promise. By 1945, the vast majority of Canadians were probably weary of military discipline, wartime control, high taxes, and enormous government expenditure. Most voters looked forward to a new era of unregulated bonanza. Had the Tories stressed their "opportunity and prosperity" promise (and remained silent on the issue of conscription for the war against Japan), it is possible that the election results would have been remarkably different; after 1945, it was the Tory platform, shorn of conscription, that the Liberals in fact gave the country. The unfinished aspects of the social security state continued to haunt the electorate for the next generation; but the CCF alone expressed the demand, and in each election after 1945 the party lost popularity, slipping to 9.5 percent by 1958. The vast majority of the country seemed content with random prosperity and individual pursuit of security. The Liberal promise of a new social order was thus quietly forgotten and forgiven as everyone scrambled for a share of the postwar boom. What survived the war more than the concept of a comprehensive social security state was the mere centralization of power in Ottawa and a pattern of wartime alliances, which led to increased dependence upon an imperial power.

Suggested Reading

General histories that cover the impact of the Second World War on national politics include Donald Creighton, *The Forked Road: Canada, 1939-1957* (1976), Robert Bothwell, *et al., Canada, 1900-1945* (1985),

W.A.B. Douglas and Brereton Greenhouse, *Out of the Shadows: Canada in the Second World War* (1977).

Works addressed to the prewar constitutional dilemmas and the war-time breakthough include Doug Owram, *The Government Generation: Canadian Intellectuals and the State, 1900-1945* (1986), Frank Scott, *Essays on the Constitution: Aspects of Canadian Law and Politics* (1977), and G.F.G. Stanley, *A Short History of the Canadian Constitution* (1969). Scott's volume contains an excellect essay on "centralization and decentralization" and Stanley's offers a useful summary of the Rowell-Sirois Commission's recommendations and the utility of the war in their promotion after rejection by the premiers.

For the emergence of *Progressive* Conservatism, J.L. Granatstein's *Politics of Survival: The Conservative Party of Canada, 1939-45* (1967), is an account that covers both the background and the futile aftermath. John Kendle's *John Bracken: A Political Biography* (1979), tells substantially the same story, but from the point of view of the groom in the marriage of convenience.

Mackenzie King's drive to restore the Liberal Party to the centre position is developed in another book by Granatstein, *Canada's War: The Politics of the Mackenzie King Government, 1939-45* (1975). The details of his struggle with the conscription issue are found in Granatstein and J.M. Hitsman, *Broken Promises: A History of Conscription in Canada* (1977). Throughout, Granatstein argues that the triumph of the Liberals in the election of 1945 was largely the product of King's personal skill in directing the war and his timely promotion of the social security state. Gerald Caplan attributes more importance to the two year anti-CCF campaign promoted by business in *The Dilemma of Canadian Socialism: The CCF in Ontario* (1973). Two works that confront the issue of the postwar decline of the CCF are Walter Young, *The Anatomy of a Party: The National CCF, 1932-61* (1969), and L. Zakuta, *A Protest Movement Becalmed* (1964).

**Road sign on Yukon
section of Alaska highway, 1942.**

SOURCE: NFB COLLECTION/NICOLAS MORANT/
NATIONAL ARCHIVES OF CANADA/PA-121715

*"Prime Minister King had grown increasing-
ly ill-at-ease with Americans involving themselves in projects on Canadian soil."*

CHAPTER 12
CONTINENTAL SOLIDARITY, 1941-1956

— 1. A New Relationship With Uncle Sam —

The Second World War prompted the implementation of social insurance programs welcomed by many as signs of "social progress." But the emergency that facilitated social development led to regression in external relations in the sense that the country traded sovereignty for security. Moreover, the new dependence outlasted the war because the "Nazi threat" was almost immediately followed by the new danger of "Soviet expansion." Since resistance to both enemies was almost universally accepted in Canada, the new colonialism tended to be advertised as international cooperation rather than subordination. Even so, such celebration was rather muted because the security obtained in a world of balanced terror was more illusory than real, and Canadians prided themselves on having been at the forefront of the development that had led the "autonomous colonies" of Great Britain to become partners in a community of nations. A polite fiction of a British Commonwealth of nations survived.

In 1917, Prime Minister Borden had insisted that the Imperial War Conference of the Great War must change its nature to recognize the constituent members as the equals rather than the subordinates of Britain. It was Borden again who, at the peace talks in Paris, had led in the campaign to have the Dominions sign the Treaties in their own right. And it was Borden's successor, Arthur Meighen, who played the leading role at the Imperial Conference of 1921, causing Britain to abandon the renewal of a treaty between Japan and Britain dating from 1902 that was a pact between countries as empires.

The Liberals were no less hesitant in the further development of Canadian autonomy between 1921 and 1939. It was under Mackenzie King that the Chanack incident took place in 1922. In that year a clash between Turkey and Greece in Asia Minor threatened to provoke British intervention, and Britain simply assumed, as in 1900 and 1914, that Canada would automatically become involved. King decided otherwise and let it be known that his country saw no reason for involvement. A year later, autonomy went one degree further when Canada signed a fisheries treaty with the United States without any imperial input. By 1927, a completely independent Canadian diplomatic presence had been established in Washington as a first step towards making wider ambassadorial links with the world at large.

Such initiatives were accepted without resistance by the former mother country. In 1926, in the wake of the King-Byng affair, the Imperial Conference produced the Balfour Report in which the Dominions were defined as "autonomous communities . . . , equal in status, in no way subordinate one to another in any aspect of their domestic or external affairs . . . ." As if that were not sufficient declaration of independence, the words were embodied in law in 1931 by the Statute of Westminster. Thus, Canada and the other autonomous Dominions won the right to independent foreign policies, having already established their right to independence in domestic politics.

As the likelihood of a second Great War in Europe loomed after 1935, Mackenzie King used the newly-won Canadian autonomy to avoid "entanglements"; he was emphatic that in any future war, Canada would be "at Britain's side" but not necessarily in the trenches. As a result, in 1938, when Britain recommended that Canada cooperate in a joint program for training aviators in anticipation of possible war, King refused. Canada acknowledged a formal liability if the British were to find themselves in another struggle with Germany but the Canadian Prime Minister meant to imply passive belligerence, not participation as a principal as in the 1914 war. It came as no surprise, therefore, that

Canada hesitated before joining Britain and France when they declared war on Germany on September 3, 1939.

Four days elapsed before the Canadian Parliament convened to debate its own war resolution. When Parliament did agree to participate on September 10, King announced that Canada's policy would be "effective cooperation" within stated limits. The primary military effort would be home defence.

Soon, however, Canada's liability was extended as King responded to popular pressure for greater involvement. On September 16, he announced that a division would be sent to England. He followed the first announcement with another, on December 17, indicating that Canada's major contribution to the war was to be the British Commonwealth Air Training Plan.

As was shown in the previous chapter, the war was most immediately important to Canada for its usefulness in bringing about recovery from the Depression. For those Canadians who continued to cling to a strong British orientation and loyalty, the lack of a more robust militarism was regrettable, even cowardly. The foremost such critic was Mitchell Hepburn, the Premier of Ontario, who believed he was speaking for the vast majority of the country when he moved his legislature in January 1940 to condemn the central government for not joining the war in "the vigorous manner the people of Canada desire to see." King responded to Hepburn's jingoism by noting in his diary that it was "just what is needed." Parliament was dissolved on January 24, 1940, and the nineteenth general election, called for March 26, unfolded as a plebiscite on King's policy of limited liability. To Hepburn's surprise, the electorate confirmed King's position rather than the opposition's. Evidently, the voters wanted no repetition of the 1914 war. The Liberals won 52 percent of the votes and three quarters of the seats in Parliament.

But within months of the 1940 election, the nature of the conflict changed dramatically. The "Phony War" during which few hostile acts had occurred was suddenly succeeded by the *Blitzkrieg*, the collapse of France, and the evacuation of the British Army from Dunkirk. Then a torrent of German bombs fell upon British cities, and an expectation of defeat developed when the island nation seemed incapable of holding out for long. It was against such a background that Canada became abruptly receptive to overtures from the United States. On a Friday afternoon in mid-August 1940, Franklin Roosevelt telephoned Mackenzie King and arranged a meeting of the two leaders to take place in Roosevelt's private railway car the next day in nearby Ogdensburg, New York. In their one meeting on August 17, the two leaders agreed to form a joint defence command for North America. The purpose was self-evident, therefore no rationale was elaborated. Similarly, because the accord was so manifestly advantageous for the defence of the whole continent, then and forever, its duration was left open.

Despite the informality of its inception, the Ogdensburg Agreement was of momentous importance. According to Donald Creighton, a single step taken by a Canadian Prime Minister without consultation with cabinet or consent of Parliament "effectively bound Canada to a continental system for the indefinite future." Under the circumstances, however, such a consolidation seemed eminently sensible—at least for the duration of the present crisis. For the same reason, less than one year later—but still before the United States had actively entered the war King and Roosevelt struck another accord that was just as sweeping; the second was to cover economic consolidation. The Hyde Park Declaration of April 1941 was the economic corollary to the Ogdensburg Agreement because it stated that "each country should provide the other with the defence articles which it is best able to produce." The result was that Canadian arms producers could bid on American contracts on the same basis as American firms, and could provide certain kinds of munitions, strategic materials, aluminum, and ships for the Pentagon with access accorded to no "foreign" country. For the purposes of defence production, King and Roosevelt agreed to pretend that the border between the two countries simply did not exist. In effect, Mackenzie King was accorded the status of governor of an American State. Here, also, King has been accused of reckless surrender, while his defenders suggest that the step was as necessary as it was bold. In this case, the necessity was a balance-of-payments crisis.

By late 1940, Canada was producing hundreds of millions of dollars worth of arms per month for shipment to Britain. Given that approximately one third of the components for war materiels had to be imported from the United States, and that Britain was unable to obtain its weapons on a cash-and-carry basis, Canada's loans (later gifts) created a dreadful drain on Canadian dollars to the United States. The solution to the problem was for the Americans to meet many of their own defence needs by purchases in Canada. Since the Hyde Park Declaration provided just such a remedy (see table 12.1), J.L. Granatstein has argued that the agreement "saved Canada's bacon." Still, the continentalism of the arrangement was undeniable.

236

Table 12.1 US-Canada, Import-Export Trade ($ millions)

Years	Imports from US	Exports to US
1938	414	270
1939	485	380
1940	711	442
1941	912	599
1942	1209	881
1943	1410	1147
1944	1435	1296
1945	1183	1193

SOURCE: *Historical Statistics of Canada*, G389-400.

If King had fought like Borden to win a measure of control in the councils of war after the United States entered the conflict as an active belligerent (in December 1941), the subordination inherent in the continentalism of the Ogdensburg Agreement and the Hyde Park Declaration might have been considerably muted. But because Churchill and Roosevelt found it difficult to make even the smallest consultative gestures towards Russia, France, or China, and regarded such consultation with the junior governments of North America as patently absurd as well as unnecessary, the state governments and that of Canada were thus excluded from the Combined Munitions Assignment Board as well as from the Combined Chiefs of Staff. The North American part of the alliance worked more as a merger than as a partnership. Canada was treated more as a wealthy subordinate than as an autonomous equal, and Canadians themselves began to speak of "our leaders, Churchill and the President."

The gestures Mackenzie King made to assert Canadian independence were more theatrical than substantial. A conference occurred at Quebec in 1943 with the flags of the three attending leaders flying side by side; Churchill, Roosevelt, and King were photographed as a controlling threesome. But insofar as any real conferring occurred, it involved the American and the British leaders, not the Canadian. King's role was of a person who "lent his house for a party." Still, the meeting was such "good theatre" that King was well satisfied that a second such exercise would be "quite sufficient to make clear that all three are in conference together." The show was rerun in 1944. There was no need for a third performance. The war that ended in Europe in May 1945 soon came to a conclusion in the Pacific as well. American atomic bombs—with plutonium refined from Canadian uranium—ended the struggle against Japan in August.

— 2. A Bolder Repression of Minorities —

Despite diminished independence, Canadians emerged from the Second World War imagining that they had become "a power in the world." In the Great War, they were told that they had acquired the spirit of a nation; by 1945, they were congratulated for having gained international stature. A country with a relatively small population had emerged in the number three position by industrial production and in the number four position by the strength of its armed forces. Both achievements were a source of pride tending to obscure the less pleasant subordination and proximity to the number one industrial and military power. Another consolation was that Canada had suffered relatively lighter losses than those sustained in the 1914 war. In round numbers, 17 000 airmen, 22 000 soldiers, and 2 000 sailors had been killed. For a country of nearly 12 million, such losses were not large: about one third of one percent of the population overall. But here as well, satisfaction over one fact obscured a less pleasant reality—there were losses on a comparable scale that were not included in the battle casualties, injuries that were not inflicted by the enemy.

The first Canadian residents attacked by Canada were "enemy aliens," the German and Italian-origin immigrants thought to be sympathetic to fascism. Ironically, an even larger number of the 2 400 persons rounded up in 1940 and 1941 were Communists and radicals because, as Reg Whitaker has shown, "the security police identified the Communists as the main enemy within." The pretext for such action was the neutrality of the Soviet Union until the summer of 1941 when Hitler broke his "non-agression pact" with the Soviets and invaded Russia. In 1942, detentions of left-wing Canadians abated, and Canada did make some restitution for seizures of property of previously-banned organizations such as the Ukrainian Labour-Farmer Temples, pro-Communists with approximately 10 000 members in 300 different localities. But the compensation for seized buildings and burned libraries was as low as 14 cents on the dollar and, according to Whitaker, "the government charged back taxes for the years when the halls were in the governments' posession." By the time of the abating repression of Communists, however, the apparatus of detention and confiscation verred off in a new direction with the more massive assault directed against Japanese-Canadians.

238

For generations, British Columbians had been seeking a means of eliminating "orientals" from their province. Asian newcomers were the objects of mob violence in the nineteenth century and legal discrimination in the twentieth. First there were immigration restrictions and for those already in the country there was a denial of basic civil rights, such as the right to vote. Consequently, when war broke out against Japan in December 1941, racism became "patriotic" and a golden opportunity was seized for the complete elimination of the hated minority. The first steps towards solving the "problem" of the Japanese presence were almost reasonable. Thirty-eight persons suspected of being potential subversives were arrested by the RCMP and interned in accordance with the provisions of the War Measures Act. In each case of detention, there were individual causes for confinement. The authorities had obtained certain evidence prior to the arrest of each person involved. But local politicians wanted a broader round-up leading to the internment of the entire population. The army was reluctant to act on such an extreme demand because 13 000 of the 22 000 people of Japanese ancestry in BC were British subjects. To the Chief of the General Staff, Ken Stuart, wholesale internment was excessive as well as unnecessary. "I cannot see that they constitute the slightest menace to national security," Stuart explained. The RCMP agreed. The navy also argued that all persons of Japanese origin were militarily neutralized once they were barred from fishing. Even so, political use of racist extremism prevailed. Beginning in January 1942, the "evacuation" began, and the lives of 22 000 people were disrupted forever. Entire households lost their freedom and property; families were divided; children's educations were interrupted. From 1942 until 1945 the detainees languished in camps that were far inland from the coast. Finally, in the spring of 1945, the prisoners were given the choice of settling "east of the Rockies" or "repatriation" to Japan. Understandably, almost half chose exile to the shattered land of their ancestors.

Later, British Columbia paid a measure of penance for its racism by offering partial reparations for confiscated property to those who had the stamina to go through the elaborate procedures for processing claims. And in 1949, those who returned to BC under the relaxation of the previous exclusion order could do so in the knowledge that they would be able to vote for the first time in the history of British Columbia. Later still, in the autumn of 1988, the Government of Canada gave an official apology and made a pre-election promise to pay $21 000 to each detainee still alive at the time of the announcement (and not necessarily resident in

Canada). A kind of truce was offered at least to the most injured segment of the population—more than 40 years after the war had ended abroad.

No such apology or compensation was ever offered on account of the other serious breach of trust involving one of the two founding nationalities. As was indicated in the previous chapter, the chain of promises extending back to the first imposition of conscription in 1917 was broken for purely political reasons in 1944. Civil war did not erupt. And while it is fair to say that a majority of the voters in Quebec kept faith with the Liberals in the general election of 1945, more than 40 percent turned their backs on the two national parties, having already rejected the national focus just as the conscription issue was becoming controversial late in the summer of 1944.

In the provincial election in August, the voters had a rich array of extraordinarily resentful politicians from which to choose. The most extremely angry was a coalition more nationalist than the Union nationale, and more reformist than the Action libérale nationale. The new group, called the Bloc populaire, was led by Maxime Raymond for federal purposes, and by André Luarendeau, provincially. But in 1944, nationalism was more popular than radicalism; the Liberal administration of Adélard Godbout, elected in 1940 to prevent conscription, was easily defeated for granting the vote to women in 1940, imposing compulsory elementary education in 1943, and working closely with Ottawa on all things military. Since the most popular defender of Quebec nationalism was Maurice Duplessis, the eloquent proponent of Quebec's autonomy in the 1930s, he enjoyed a triumphal return to power after a close autumn election. With his return to the premiership (and that of Camillien Houde to the position of mayor of Montreal), the most colourful anti-Ottawa champions were once again in charge in Quebec, and the conscription crisis at the end of the year seemed to legitimize their presence. On this basis, it might be suggested that the war did irreparable harm at home as well as causing a loss of independence in external affairs. In fact, it might even be correctly asserted that English-speaking Canadians felt closer to the Americans in 1945 than to the people of their own federation in Quebec.

— 3. Continuing Continentalism in External Affairs —

Under normal postwar circumstances, Canada might have worked to restore the independence that had been lost to the United States in the alliance to defeat Hitler. Prime Minister King had grown increasingly ill-at-ease with Americans involving themselves in projects on Canadian soil. One example was the Alaska-Canada (Alcan) highway launched as a cooperative venture in 1942 from north-eastern BC through the southwest Yukon. The road brought real benefits even to Alberta (especially Edmonton). But another, less cooperative undertaking was an authorization by the United States army for the Imperial Oil Company to construct a pipeline from Norman Wells, Northwest Territories, to Whitehorse in the Yukon without prior consent from the Government of Canada or the native people in the area. King understood the disregard of the Indians, but not of his government. Later, after the Americans sent Canada a bill for $60 million to cover the cost of the pipeline, King told his friend Vincent Massey that he thought the "Canadians were looked upon by Americans as a lot of Eskimos." It was King's opinion that "We ought to get the Americans out of further development there and keep control in our own hands." He believed that the "long-range policy of the Americans was to absorb Canada." King asserted that he "would rather have Canada kept within the orbit of the British Commonwealth."

In the immediate postwar period, Canada did seek closer relations with its nearest British neighbour as Newfoundlanders reconsidered their earlier rejection of Confederation. Bravely, they had gone their own way as a separate country even as the traditional mainstay of Newfoundland's economy, the cod fishery, started a deep decline in the 1880s. A trade arrangement negotiated with the United States in 1890 held out promise on the market side of the problem, but Canada pressured Britain to abort the fisheries treaty for the sake of Prince Edward Island and Nova Scotia interests. When Canada then offered the angered Newfoundlanders attractive financial terms for Confederation (including an annual subsidy proposal of millions, and the inevitable railway promise), the response was negative. The island Dominion preferred to seek its own prospects in a redirected economy. The economic directions pursued in the new century involved land-based resource development and hopes for large-scale urban and industrial growth instead of restructuring the cod fishery for the European market as was occurring in Norway and Iceland. Some diversification into mining, and pulp and paper did follow, but the inefficiencies of Newfoundland's "dual economy" and the "wholesale venality" of politicians from 1900 to 1930 meant, according to Terry Campbell and G.A. Rawlyk, that Newfoundland was unusually vulnerable to the Great Depression when diminished revenues and enormous public debt culminated in a financial crisis and the voluntary surrender of Dominion status to government by a British commission in February 1934. Campbell and Rawlyk suggest that "most Newfoundlanders accepted Britain's harsh solution in a spirit of meekness and gratitude," but no one expected Commission rule to be anything more than temporary—only for the duration of the depression, then the war.

Geographical location became Newfoundland's greatest asset during the Second World War. All trans-Atlantic air traffic touched down on North America's easternmost land mass, and Canadian and American forces protected sea convoys from newly-built Newfoundland bases. Who would bring in such revenue after the war? Economic and political union with Canada or the United States were the most obvious sources of continued well-being. Naturally, Britain and Canada preferred the Confederation option.

In 1945, Britain announced that Newfoundlanders would send delegates to a National Convention, discuss their alternatives, then make their choice by referendum. The convention clarified that the traditional aversion to Confederation was still lively. But the "antis" were divided several different ways (some favouring continuation of the status quo, others seeking a return to Dominion status, still others preferring any political alternative that included economic union with the United States). The result was an inconclusive plebiscite on June 3, 1948. A campaign for a second vote led by a popular local radio announcer, Joey Smallwood (emphasizing the enormity of the economic advantages promised by Canada), led to a narrow majority in favour of Confederation; Newfoundland became Canada's tenth province on March 31, 1949.

In the meantime, international developments obscured and superceded Mackenzie King's intentions for strengthening Commonwealth ties in other respects. On September 6, 1945, a cipher clerk from the Russian embassy, Igor Gouzenko, sought asylum in Canada with a great wad of documents proving that the Russians had worked tirelessly to obtain secrets of North American technology almost from the moment the Russian embassy was opened in Ottawa. The documentation also demonstrated that the spy network included Canadian collaborators. Gouzenko's revelations prompted a secret commission of inquiry under the War Measures Act, led to a host of arrests and interrogations, and concluded in official reports naming scores of Canadians as spies and traitors even though most such culprits were never charged or convicted in ordinary court. The net effect was the ruin of many people by investigations that implied guilt. A few, having been turned over for prosecution and punishment, were sent to jail for their crimes. The convicted spies included a nuclear physicist, clerks and secretaries, and a Member of Parliament (Fred Rose, the one Communist in the House of Commons).

The exposure of Soviet espionage in Canada was not the sole cause for the cooling in relations with the Russians, nor, as Reg Whitaker has argued, the first event in the series. "The thread of continuity in official repression of radical left-wing activities runs consistently from World War I through the Great Depression to World War II and on into the Cold War years ahead." But the Gouzenko affair was certainly the most dramatic indication to Canadians that a new era of international crisis was beginning. Consequently, the Liberals had serious reservations about weakening solidarity with the Americans, even though Mackenzie King continued to be sensitive about lost independence.

The Prime Minister displaced his concern about colonial status onto the British by attacking the last "badges of colonialism" from that source. King attempted to rally the country to adopt a "distinctive" flag, to define Canadian citizenship as distinct from British "subjecthood," to drop references to Canada as a "Dominion" in public documents, and to end appeals from the Supreme Court to the British Privy Council. All were overdue assertions of national maturity, but not all were fulfilled in King's lifetime (the flag, for example, was postponed until 1964, and patriation of the Constitution did not occur until 1982). Moreover, none compensated for the continuing dependence on the United States; but in the postwar climate of fear of Soviet treachery, there were few politicians who were willing to identify American influence as colonialism. The proof that such was the case came in 1947 with acquiescence to an American request to exempt its service personnel in Canada from Canadian law. In statutory form, the favour was the Visiting Forces Act. In effect, the law defined American bases in northern Canada as extensions of the United States itself. Stanley Knowles, a CCF member from Winnipeg, wanted to know why the Americans had not been told that the war was over and it was time to go home. Speakers for the government side solemnly replied that President Truman had reason to suspect that the Soviet Union was planning to invade North America sometime before 1950; therefore, the Canadian Arctic was the first line of defence. Under the circumstances, it made sense to continue the Joint Board of Defence and to keep American personnel on watch for the Russians. Knowles persisted: "I think this country at this moment has a supreme opportunity." The chance for Canada was to assert neutrality in the face of bi-polarity. "We can say that we are not going to have United States troops in Canada in peacetime.

That would be the first move of any small power against the Truman policy or the Stalin policy." Unfortunately, the CCF and Conservative members who supported Knowles' non-alignment proposal were a small minority. Parliament approved the Visiting Forces Act overwhelmingly and conceded to the United States in 1947 what had been properly denied to Britain in 1938.

Still, Mackenzie King dreaded the appearance of surrender except as necessary for defence purposes. He halted, for example, a project that Canadian civil servants and their American counterparts had brought close to fulfillment in 1948. The idea was to establish something close to North American free trade. When the story leaked to the American press, *Life* magazine reported in mid-March that a "Customs Union With Canada" was imminent and endorsed the change saying that "Canada needs us and we need Canada in a violently contracting World." The *Globe and Mail* shouted "Not on Your Life" in prompt reply. King then realized that the opposition was about to denounce him in the twilight of his career (exactly as Laurier had been condemned near the end of his days in 1911) and backed away from the free-trade scheme he had previously encouraged.

The defence of the tariff, like the flurry of activity to purge the country of the "badges" of British colonialism, implied a robust nationalism but the demand for independence was not nearly as salient as the fear of communism and the willingness to defer to the United States as imperial leader in the "cold war" that Canadians wanted won. For both reasons, exactly one year after the Canadian opinion makers had denounced free trade because it was supposed to be a prelude to absorption by the United States, they supported a giant step towards surrendering Canada's remaining diplomatic freedom when Parliament ratified the country's membership in the North Atlantic Treaty organization in 1949.

The *Globe and Mail* and others approved NATO because everyone pretended that the treaty was more than a military security pact. Article 2, proposed by Canada, pledged the signers to "make every effort, individually, and collectively, to promote the economic well-being of their peoples and to achieve social justice." A few visionaries interpreted the clause as the first step towards general acceptance of "Atlanticism," the notion of a North Atlantic community of nations that might formally federate in the future. Thus, membership in NATO was not denounced as a furthering of subordination to the United States. All parties—including the CCF—approved Canada's joining.

The Canadian pretension that NATO was a United Nations on a smaller scale was not shared by the Americans. Their sole concern was NATO's potential for military effectiveness. The United States was the dominant member; NATO therefore emerged as the military security pact that the Americans wanted and expected, and all participating countries were badgered to perform duties as determined by the Americans. Given the buffer of the Atlantic and the less complete dependence of the European members on the United States economically, the Europeans were in a better position to resist or withdraw from such aggressiveness than was Canada. As the American Secretary of State, Dean Acheson, explained the facts of life to a stunned Lester Pearson, Acheson had enough trouble with divisions within the United States itself. "If you think that we are going to start all over again with our NATO allies, especially with you moralistic, interfering Canadians, then you're crazy." Pearson did not view Acheson's admission as sufficient cause for Canada to reconsider the NATO affiliation, hoping instead that "quiet diplomacy"—a patient wheedling—might somehow breathe life into the stillborn Article 2. Illusions to the contrary notwithstanding, a diplomatic revolution had been completed. Having traded independence for security, Canada fell dutifully into line as a satellite in the American solar system. Policy regarding China, Korea, the Middle East, and North American air defence between 1949 and 1957 was that of the United States rather than of a country with separate interests, independently pursued.

4. Centralism and Continentalism on the Domestic Scene

The evident extension of the subordination of Canadian diplomacy to the United States after 1945 was accompanied by another continuity that was almost equally important. The other continuing wartime expedient was centralization of administration in Ottawa, a process that transformed the provinces from alleged partners in Confederation into the unwilling "junior governments" of Canada. In large part, the change was nothing more than an adjustment to conditions under Canada's emergency constitution, the War Measures Act, the statute that was passed in 1914 for the sake of the Great War but whose potential was not fully realized until the Second World War when the government's planning and control powers were exercised to the maximum. With no need to worry about provincial obstruction or Parliamentary delay, the typical instruments of government became Orders in Council rather than statutes of Parliament. More than 6 000 such executive orders were approved by cabinet between 1939 and

1945. They revolutionized the scope of the federal government's activity and led to an explosive growth in the Ottawa establishment. The Government of Canada employed 46 000 people in 1939. By 1945, 116 000 were on the federal payroll. As a result, the new strongholds of Confederation became government departments (Finance, Munitions and Supply, and External Affairs), and the new powerbrokers were several flamboyant ministers and their deputies—the Ottawa "Mandarins."

The problem for the Liberal Party and the national bureaucracy in 1945 was that a growing number of Canadians recognized that enlarged bureaucracy led by "expert" advice had diminished the importance of Parliament and had left the task of opposition increasingly to the provinces advised by their own bureaucratic experts. But the federal civil service and the Liberal cabinet fervently believed that centralism was the only way to maintain prosperity in the postwar period. "The modern governmental budget must be the balance wheel of the economy," declared the *White Paper on Employment and Income* (1945). If provinces and municipalities taxed and spent on the same scale as the government in Ottawa, there was real danger that fiscal policies would work at cross purposes.

What the Mandarins needed was a constitutional conference to establish in peacetime that which had been grudgingly conceded for the sake of the war. Since the aging Mackenzie King was still Prime Minister, he would preside at the meeting, flanked by his ministers, supported by the wisdom of the nation arrayed in the row of advisors seated behind them. Even with such high-powered support, could he prevent the conference on "reconstruction" from ending in disaster? King was frightened by the political implications of his assignment. To be sure, he had started his own career as a mandarin; but as King matured, he became less the administrative wizard and ever more the public politician. In 1945, he knew that the premiers would not willingly concede what was offered in the little green book prepared by the wizards on his own administrative team. Ontario and Quebec were particularly adamant in their refusal to consider the centralist design on principle. Others, such as Manitoba, were only too happy to see the federal government assume "full fiscal responsibility for unemployment," but found King unwilling to make the commitment. Consequently, even the ideologically sympathetic found themselves opposing centralism if only to preserve the means for looking after the responsibilities Ottawa wished to share. Not surprisingly, the first conference ended in failure. After a nine-month recess, a second such meeting was held in the spring of 1946. When the second attempt also ended in failure, the Department of Finance proposed reimplementation of the Ilsley tax scheme of 1941. At first, Quebec and Ontario refused to join the new rental arrangement. But in 1952, Ontario accepted "rent" in return for its power of direct taxation, and Quebec joined in 1957 after the carrot of "equalization" was implemented for additional incentive. By the latter scheme, any province could expect up to ten percent of the federal income tax for its own purposes. Then, having determined the per-capita share of the two wealthiest provinces, the others would receive grants from Ottawa to bring the "have not" regions up to standard. In this way, Ottawa was able to maintain its control of—or at least to channel—the bulk of the public revenue.

The desire to dominate taxation in the postwar period reflected a renewed resolve by the central government to create a prosperous and united country by the force of national policy; the increased level of the "rent" reflected a new effectiveness of provincial power as official opposition. When Mackenzie King retired in 1948, to be replaced by Louis St. Laurent, the change was complete. Under St. Laurent, government unfolded in essentially managerial functions, with power distributed broadly throughout a committee of ministers and the leading civil servants. C.D. Howe, the Minister of Trade and Commerce, was hardly less prominent than the Prime Minister himself; Douglas Abbott was supreme in Finance; and Lester Pearson won a Nobel Prize for his service in External Affairs. Behind such elected leaders were the less conspicuous but equally important near-ministers: J.W. Pickersgill, Clerk of the Privy Council, Clifford Clark in Finance, and Mitchell Sharp in Trade and Commerce.

The major purpose of the St. Laurent Team in the domestic arena was to continue the vigorous, centralizing administration that seemed to have won so much favour during the war. Unruffled by premiers' objections, St. Laurent believed that governments with a tangible presence inspired confidence and loyalty. He believed that Quebeckers, for instance, would judge centralism by the successes of specific projects—gargantuan undertakings such as the Trans-Canada Highway begun in 1948 and the St. Lawrence Seaway (a new system of locks and canals to make the Great Lakes fully accessible to trans-oceanic shipping) begun in 1954. Both were intended as major arteries of prosperity, the ultimate justification of centralism. During the war, the economy had grown and changed in ways that the government wished to encourage after "reconversion" to peacetime production. Secondary manufacturing had developed to produce synthetic rubber, sophisticated electronic apparatus, and a vast array of plastics where nothing of the kind had been produced in Canada before. A million newly-formed families needed housing, and everyone wanted automobiles. An enormous surge in all areas of manufacturing and construction, as well as a rush to develop natural resources such as oil in Alberta and iron ore from Newfoundland, resulted in full employment, a doubling of the number of households that owned automobiles, and by the mid-1950s, massive improvement in housing. Canada sustained the highest birthrate of any industrial country in the world, and immigration reached record levels as 30 percent of all the newcomers attracted since 1867 poured into the country between 1945 and 1955. Surely such indicators of growth, along with the nearly annual inflation-fighting budget surpluses and the yearly net increase of the unemployment insurance fund, suggested that Liberal management had led to tangible benefits indeed.

It was in the midst of this mood of somewhat smug satisfaction that Vincent Massey was commissioned in 1949 to survey Canadian attainments in arts and letters, with the purpose of recommending adjustments so that Canadian achievements in the cultural field might blossom proportionately to the country's recent attainments in economic development and population growth. The survey was conducted with the assistance of three academic scholars and a Montreal engineer over the course of two years; the findings however, were less than encouraging. The Massey Report provided a vast amount of evidence in 1951 to indicate that Canadian culture was derivative and subordinate rather than distinctive and thriving: no national library or systematic preservation of public records; no national support for universities, museums, or theatre; and popular entertainments such as cinema were almost entirely American in content, theme, and origin.

The Massey Commission predicted that Canadian culture would be a lost cause without major and immediate support for the country's authors and cultural institutions. Consequently, the commission recommended financial assistance for the provincial universities and the endowment of a council to provide grants to individual scholars or institutions such as the Winnipeg Ballet Company. It was obvious from the commissioners' recommendations that they were most interested in "high" culture. Nothing they recommended touched directly on "mass" culture. Nor was there much demand for such promotion. Canadians seemed completely satisfied with their Hollywood movies and Ellery Queen mystery stories. As for the higher sort of culture, three cities maintained symphony orchestras and two supported permanent ballet companies. Even so, Louis St. Laurent was sceptical that the performing arts were resources that needed developing; as he put it, the Government of Canada had no business "subsidizing ballet dancing."

Grants to the universities were another matter since they emerged in the postwar period as trade schools for the various professions and served an obvious purpose in economic development. Consequently, the Massey Commission's funding proposal for higher education was adopted at once. But six years passed before the central government decided to take an interest in "ballet dancing" as well. By then, with an election approaching, Canadians were alerted to American dominance of another sort.

In 1955, a leading accountant, Walter Gordon, decided to publish his thoughts on the continentalist cost of the economic policies pursued since the war. Later, Gordon said that he had been "worrying about . . . the complacency with which Canadians were witnessing the sellout of our resources and business enterprises to Americans and other enterprising foreigners." Gordon stood against a well-established tradition because foreign investment had been actively encouraged by every government since Confederation. The only prior lament of ruling parties was that the inflowing stream of capital was never quite enough. At the time Gordon began to be concerned about the volume of incoming foreign capital, the stream had become a flood. Since most of the investment was by companies of the country to whom diplomatic autonomy had been conceded, Gordon decided that unregulated foreign ownership posed an unnecessary risk to whatever sovereignty remained.

He sent a draft of an article on the subject to a Liberal friend in the government. Gordon's thesis was not markedly different from that expounded by speakers for various minor parties since the 1920s. The novelty of the warning in 1955 was the source of the alarm: Gordon was an Ontario aristocrat, not a Western populist; he was part of the same circle that had always sought to foster foreign investment; he was a respectable businessman, not a socialist Jeremiah. On this account, Gordon's yet-unpublished article was reviewed by the government with considerable interest, and Gordon was asked if "he would mind very much if the government took over" his idea that Parliament should concern itself with regulating foreign ownership. To do so intelligently, however, Canada would need another Massey Commission, the new one to study economic rather than cultural prospects. Naturally, Walter Gordon seemed the ideal person to take charge of the new commission in 1955.

Later, when Gordon tabled a preliminary report in time for the 1957 election, the government found itself once again on the defensive. The preliminary findings seemed to suggest that the economy was dominated by Americans almost as completely as was diplomacy or culture. Gordon showed that 70 percent of oil and gas, 52 percent of mining, and 56 percent of secondary manufacturing were then controlled by foreigners. What the report failed to uncover, according to William K. Carroll, was the growing divergence of ownership between large- and medium-scale capitalism in Canada. Of Canada's 70 largest industrial corporations (accounting for approximately 50 percent of all industrial assets in Canada in 1956), the overwhelming proportion was in interlocking Canadian hands, a cozy club of the wealthiest Canadians sharing directorships in one another's companies. Carroll suggests that the rapid growth of foreign ownership was at a lower level of capital concentration. "Instead of taking over large indigenous firms and constituting a direct predatory threat to the monopoly fraction of the Canadian bourgeoisie," American investment levels grew fastest by competitive expansion of branch plants, the takeover of smaller Canadian firms, or (most conspicuously to Gordon) in the new glamour sectors of resource development—mining, oil, and gas. To critics of the Liberal management of Canada, such findings were particularly interesting when taken in conjunction with the survey of the Massey Commission and what was common knowledge about external affairs. The evidence seemed to prove that Canada had been "betrayed" by an administration whose approach to national development was so piecemeal that the country was emerging more North American than Canadian. What had gone wrong?

One group of critics suggested that Canada had blundered by turning its back on Britain. Another group had no illusions about the British Commonwealth or diverting attention to Britain, but they did insist that a greater measure of independence from the United States was needed for the same reasons that colonial ties to Britain had been severed.

The Liberal establishment and their apologists since have denied that they were promoting any kind of "colonialism." They argued that the apparent subordination in external affairs was an illusion arising from mutual interest rather than domination, and the "sellout" of the economy was purely a matter of market conditions rather than policy preferences; the overall investment patterns flowed from thousands of private choices as Canadians sought to develop a larger economy in the shortest time possible. The problem with the Liberal defence was that it echoed the apology that the imperialists of an earlier era had used to rationalize the ties to Britain, with the difference that the new imperialists made their apology more by negating the nation than by identifying it on a higher level. The turn-of-the-century collaborators with imperialism had argued that Canada was a stronger country for developing within a larger imperial system and added that every Canadian felt "pride in the British Empire." The latest generation advanced the same major premise (that Canada was stronger for its integration into the larger system), but no one suggested that a Canadian should be proud to be almost American. Unable to provide a remedy for the growing national identity malaise, the Liberals were vulnerable to critics who claimed to know how to nurture Canada's integrity without jeopardizing the postwar prosperity.

Suggested Reading

General histories that cover the subject of Canadian-American relations and centralism in domestic affairs include Donald Creighton, *The Forked Road: Canada, 1939-1957* (1976), and R. Bothwell, *et al., Canada since 1945: Power, Politics, and Provincialism* (1981). Readers seeking a less tendentious approach will find relief in C.P. Stacey, *Canada and the Age of Conflict: A History of Canadian External Policies*, vol. 2, *1921-1948, The Mackenzie King Era* (1981), or (for the domestic aspect) Doug Owram, *The Government Generation: Canadian Intellectuals and the State, 1900-1945* (1986).

Detailed accounts of particular episodes in external affairs are also available. Terry Campbell and G.A. Rawlyk, "The Historical Framework of Newfoundland and Confederation," in G.A. Rawlyk, ed., *The Atlantic Provinces and the Problems of Confederation* (1979), and David Mckenzie, *Inside the Atlantic Triangle: Canada and the Entrance of Newfoundland into Confederation, 1939-1949* (1986), cover the subject of the external province and its entry into the Canadian federation in 1949. J.L. Granatstein and R.D. Cuff have published articles on "The Hyde Park Declaration," *CHR* (1977), and "The Rise and Fall of Canadian-American Free Trade, 1947-48," *CHR* (1977). Other essays by the same authors (including an excellent article on the formation of NATO) appear in the collection edited by Granatstein and Cuff, *Ties That Bind: Canadian American Relations in Wartime From the Great War to the Cold War* (1977). Their treatment of NATO, and also the accounts by Escott Reid, *Time of Fear and Hope: The Making of the North Atlantic Treaty* (1977), and Denis Smith, *Diplomacy of Fear: Canada and the Cold War, 1941-48* (1988), are less critical than the version presented here.

On the subject of the repression of minorities during the war, the accounts of the imposition of conscription on Quebec, and the internment of the Canadians of Japanese ancestry, see W.A.B. Douglas and Brereton Greenhouse, *Out of the Shadows: Canada in the Second World War* (1977), and Reg Whitaker, "Official Repression of Communism During World War II," *Labour/Le Travail* (1986). More detailed work on conscription is the book by J.M. Hitsman and J.L. Granatstein, *Broken Promises: A History of Conscription in Canada* (1977). S.M. Trofimenkoff's relevant chapter in *The Dream of Nation: A Social and Intellectual History of Quebec* (1982), relates conscription (and feminism) to the postwar political ferment in Quebec. For the background to the "oriental issue" in British Columbia, see Donald Avery and Peter Neary, "Laurier, Borden, and a White British Columbia," *JCS* (1977). The same subject through the 1940s is treated briefly by W.P. Ward, "British Columbia and the Japanese Evacuation," *CHR* (1975), and at greater length in Ward's *White Canada Forever: Popular Attitudes and Public Policy Toward Orientals in British Columbia* (1978), and Ann Sunahara, *The Politics of Racism* (1981).

A wealth of material is available, as well, on the subject of foreign ownership of the Canadian economy. Works that purport to describe without seeking to alarm are Harry G. Johnson, *The Canadian Quandary* (1963), and A.E. Safarian, "Foreign Investment in Canada: Some Myths," *JCS* (1971). Works that interpret the issue as a serious national problem are D. Godfrey and M. Watkins, eds., *Gordon to Watkins to You* (1970), and Kari Levitt, *Silent Surrender: The Multi-National Corporation in Canada* (1970). William K. Carroll, *Corporate Power and Canadian Capitalism* (1986), finds the subject more complex than his predecessors of either the Johnson or Levitt schools of interpretation and offers some surprising conclusions about the power of Canadian business at its most concentrated level of development.

**Diefenbaker during
election campaign, April, 1963.**

SOURCE: FISH/FEDERAL NEWS PHOTOS/NATIONAL ARCHIVES OF CANADA/PA-146238

*"His continentalism was even more advanced
than the Liberals'. What went wrong?"*

CHAPTER 13

THE DIEFENBAKER PHENOMENON, 1957-1962

— 1. Televised Sell-Out —

Critics of Liberal continentalism received a dramatic rallying point in March 1956 when the Minister of Trade and Commerce, C.D. Howe, presented Parliament with a project that was to be the crowning achievement of his long career. He announced that the time had come for the construction of a pipeline to conduct natural gas from the oil fields of Alberta to Ontario. The route was to be all-Canadian across the Prairies and over the Shield, but the private company that was to undertake the task was half-American. In 1954, representatives of a Canadian firm had indicated interest in the plan but they balked at the cost of bridging the Shield. They proposed a line that would run east as far as Winnipeg, then turn south to the lucrative and easily-serviced market of the American Midwest. Central Canada would be more economically served by suppliers running lines north from the United States, they said. Howe objected to the continentalism of the Canadian proposal. He preferred to see Alberta gas

255

going to Ontario but refused to use the local private sector's reluctance as sufficient justification to develop the Canadian gas utility through a crown corporation. Instead, he forced a merger of the Canadians with an American firm. In this way, Trans-Canada Pipelines came into existence in 1954—50 percent American in ownership, but east-west in mission.

In 1955, the company informed Howe that they were unable to raise enough capital to finance the most expensive section across the rugged and sparsely-populated Shield. The solution was to create a crown corporation for this third of the project (see map 13.1). Later, once Trans-Canada was on a better footing financially, the government-owned section was to be sold to the private developers. To create such a firm, Parliamentary approval was required.

For C.D. Howe, the "Minister of Everything," the ceremonial appeal to Parliament was always the most tedious part of any project because the opposition behaved as if they had the power to influence decisions that were already made. In Howe's view, all their tactics only served to delay the inevitable and it was regrettable to have to waste valuable time in "useless chit chat." Since he was incapable of disguising his contempt, Howe was the chief (but unintentional) contributor to the myth that the Liberals were a group of centralizers, contemptuous of Parliament.

But the pipeline initiative was handicapped in the House as much by the substance of the proposal as by the impatience of its principal promoter. On March 9, John Diefenbaker, a colourful Conservative critic in Parliament since 1940, spoke on radio to condemn the scheme. He denounced Howe for giving the company the "profitable end of the project" and piling the unprofitable part "on the backs of the Canadian taxpayers." Certainly on that basis the project was vulnerable. Then Howe gave the opposition even more to attack.

Just as the proposal was to be debated in the House of Commons, the directors of Trans-Canada informed the Minister of Trade and Commerce that their credit was not sufficient to buy the quantity of steel pipe they needed to build the Prairie section in the summer of 1956; but the obstacle would vanish if Howe would make two concessions: that the Americans be allowed to assume a controlling interest, and that the Government of Canada issue an $80 million loan to the reorganized firm. Howe agreed, and threats of his resignation brought the outraged "Junior League" of the cabinet into line. The greater difficulty was persuading Parliament that the newly complicated proposal was reasonable.

The CCF insisted that the proposed crown corporation should have control of the entire pipeline, *ad infinitum*. The Tories placed their

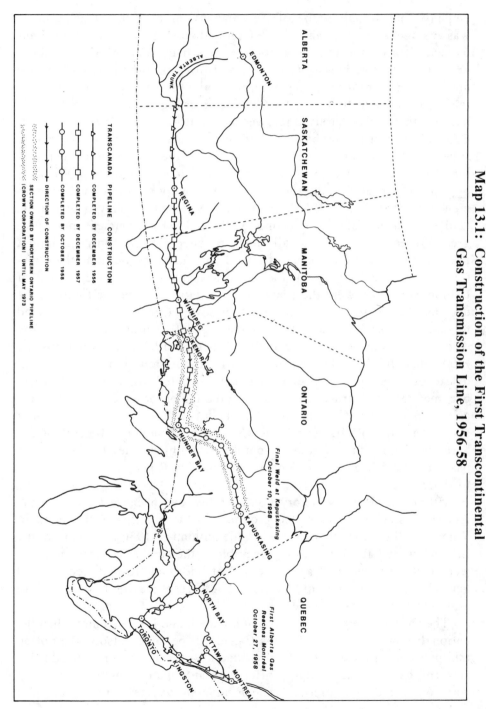

Map 13.1: Construction of the First Transcontinental Gas Transmission Line, 1956-58

emphasis on the nationality of the company, arguing that Trans-Canada was analagous in importance to the CPR and ought to be wholly Canadian-owned. Clearly, the two opposition parties had plenty to dislike about Trans-Canada Pipelines as sponsored by Howe, but their only unity was a common hatred of his scheme. Still, they might unite to kill the project by talking it to death. In March 1956, a filibuster seemed a reasonable tactic because there were barely three weeks of sitting days left before Trans-Canada's option to purchase pipe from American steel mills expired on June 7. Surely a matter almost as important as the debate on the award of the contract for the CPR was worthy of that much consideration. What the opposition parties did not know was that Howe was determined to commence construction in 1956—whatever the cost. He believed that in its "balance wheel" role in the economy, the federal government must have great projects underway at all times to keep the economy humming. Rearmament in the fulfillment of NATO commitments, building the trans-Canada highway and the St. Lawrence seaway, and the development of Labrador iron ore were the centrepiece initiatives of the first half of the decade. The pipeline would round out the roster. Consequently, he decided to impose closure at each stage of the legislative process—even before discussion began. What Howe and the Liberals failed to consider was the established tradition in Canada of using time limitation only after all details of a measure had been exhaustively debated, when further talk had become merely obstructionist. For the pipeline proposal, he served notice as his opening volley in the debate. "This isn't the way to run a peanut stand, let alone Parliament!" one Conservative shouted. But all of the harangues and points of order accomplished nothing. The pipeline bill did pass on June 6, cleared the Senate, and received Royal Assent with hours to spare.

Ultimately, Howe's victory was a hollow one because a strike in the American steel industry halted progress on the pipeline in the summer. When gas did not reach Winnipeg in the autumn of 1956 as promised, the Liberals were left all the more vulnerable to the charge that their methods were ineffective as well as reckless. Not only had Howe failed, he had abused Parliament and sold out a valuable resource for the sake of an arbitrary and useless expediency.

The charge of selling out was complicated, and involved more than the nationality of the owners of Trans-Canada. It pertained also to the notion that public utilities ought to be provided as a service by the state. In this case (probably because large profits were anticipated), public ownership was considered inappropriate. The *Financial Post* tried to explain that public ownership meant political influence, and that would lead to "spur lines to Point Pot Corner and Osmosis Centre" (without indicating why small communities were any less entitled to natural gas than to electricity and why public ownership was suitable for some utilities but not others). Since C.D. Howe appeared indistinguishable from other business people on the public ownership issue, suspicion lingered in objective news reports that something valuable had been given away rather too readily for private advantage. Worst of all, even the people of Osmosis Centre had seen the affair unfold day-to-day on the television news as if they were in Ottawa themselves. On the stage of the country's electronic boxes, the government's critics were a main attraction, and a sympathetic public sensed that the Liberals had begun to grow old and arrogant in power.

— 2. Continentalism on Trial —

In the course of the pipeline debate, the Conservative leader, George Drew, had exhausted himself and had subsequently retired from politics on doctor's orders. At the leadership convention that followed in December 1956, the party elected John Diefenbaker, the seasoned critic from Saskatchewan, whose Western populism made him seem radical to the Tory faithful that had elected Drew. Diefenbaker was no opponent of capitalism, but the ideal government, in his eyes, dispensed no special favours (even to millionaires), looked after the downtrodden, and defended Canada's British heritage. In a number of ways, Diefenbaker was the man Arthur Meighen had wanted in 1942: exactly the person who might have built the Conservatives' strength in the West, rural Ontario, and in the Maritimes. At the convention, Diefenbaker won grass-roots support from all peripheral sections of Canada. He owed no debts to "eastern politicians or rich men from Bay Street and St. James Street." Nor did he owe anything to Conservatives from Quebec. His supporters were almost exclusively rural or from the urban centres of the West and the Maritimes. To bridge the gap in between, Diefenbaker spoke spaciously about a new spirit of unity, "one unhyphenated Canada." Rather like a prophet for the by-passed individuals or regions of the country, he called his "fellow Canadians" to a standard that central Canada had forsaken.

Diefenbaker did not have long to wait to carry his message to the country at large in a great crusade. By the spring of 1957, four years had passed since the last rejuvenation of the government party's mandate. It was time for another application by St. Laurent's team for a renewal of their lease on power. For the sake of the election, the 75-year-old St. Laurent posed once again as "uncle Louis," elderly patriarch, lover of children, and lecturer on the promise of Canadian development. Any question of an alternative approach to government was dismissed out of hand on the grounds that no other party could develop anything that "we are not already developing." The Liberals' slogan in 1957 was "Unity, Security, Freedom." It directed attention to the material achievements of the recent past and the promise of the immediate future. Like the Conservatives of the early 1870s, the Liberals of the 1950s suggested that their politics was their record of achievements.

In most sections of Canada, the Liberals' projects had worked rather well. C.D. Howe never tired of telling the country that Canada's overall standard of living was second only to that of the United States. Since 1945, the country had slipped from fourth to sixth position in world industrial production, but Canada was still number four in the volume of its import-export trade given the booming development of Canadian staples that had followed the war. Ontario and British Columbia garnered the greatest wealth from the new staple exports. Quebec, the Prairies, and the Maritimes were left behind—in the case of the Atlantic provinces and the agricultural West, very far behind. For this reason, many Nova Scotians, for example, may have wondered why the Liberals did not help them develop their steel industry before rushing to build the pipeline with thousands of kilometres of pipe imported from the United States. Similarly, Prairie grain farmers whose net income had dropped by more than 50 percent between 1953 and 1955 probably wondered why the government party (claiming to be developing everything possible) had not devised a plan, perhaps along the lines of the Americans', to support the price of wheat domestically, or to support some of Lester Pearson's declarations of good intentions in external affairs with the gift of wheat that was surplus (relative to price), but in desperately short supply (given the reality of starvation) in the poorest countries of the world. The Liberals were thus vulnerable to attack for their rather smug assertion that nothing warranted action except those government projects that were already underway. Diefenbaker did attack their attitude, but like Alexander Mackenzie's denouncement of Macdonald's corruption in 1874, Diefenbaker's criticism was based on the premise that the Liberals' shortcomings were essentially moral and easily corrected by more rigid adherence to right principles. The values on which Diefenbaker placed particular stress were the rights of Parliament (forgotten or systematically abused) and the principle of Canadian autonomy (also violated). The pipeline debate was

Diefenbaker's great symbolic issue: "Parliament was made a mockery of at the behest of a few American millionaires." Diefenbaker warned that if the Liberals were returned, "don't ask the opposition to stand up for your rights, because there will be no rights left."

In one sense, Diefenbaker's campaign was strongly negative, with the Conservative leader playing the role of a crown attorney seeking the conviction of an especially odious group of offenders. But at the same time, Diefenbaker offered redemption as well as retribution. He spoke of a new sense of purpose and revived the image of a "New National Policy . . . Unity requires it . . . Freedom demands it . . . Vision will ensure it . . . ." There would be "subventions" (cash grants) for Nova Scotia coal miners, cash advances to farmers for farm-stored grain, significant increases in old age pensions, and government encouragement for greater foreign investment which, under his direction, was promised to return greater benefits to Canada. There was no overall coherence to the package and some commentators suggested that the approach was dangerously piecemeal, addressed to symptoms rather than to causes. With regard to foreign investment, for example, it was clear that Diefenbaker considered the Liberals' deals dangerous, but he failed to clarify his own strategy for dealing with "American millionaires."

What did become clear between April and June of 1957 was the intensity of Diefenbaker's indignation and the growing tendency of voters outside Quebec to share his sense of outrage. The degradation of Parliament was the theme that Diefenbaker developed with enormous effectiveness over the course of a speaking tour that covered more than 30 000 kilometres and led him to make approximately the same speech to over 100 different audiences. The enthusiastic crowds and Diefenbaker's phenomenal sincerity looked especially genuine in film excerpts on television; there was just enough on the nightly news to convey the intensity without the incoherence. In this way, those who saw Diefenbaker only on their television screens might have been even more susceptible to his message than those who saw him in person.

The voters to whom Diefenbaker appealed most were English-speaking Canadians of moderate incomes who wanted rapid development of the country's resources without compromising either the national integrity or democratic processes. Such voters were to be found almost everywhere, though Diefenbaker tended to ignore Quebec. Of course, the attitude was reciprocal as the Premier of that province professed apathy concerning the outcome even as the election developed momentum elsewhere. When asked to comment on the relative strengths of the parties in Quebec,

Duplessis would only say that "the party that wins the largest number of seats will win."

In the rest of Canada, excitement developed over the possibility that the winners might not be the Liberals. Diefenbaker felt confident that he had scored something of a moral victory by the end of the campaign, even though he doubted he would win the election. Similarly, the Liberals expected to lose some of their previously overwhelming majority, but having won the last five general elections in succession they, too, had come to imagine that their custody of the managerial state was more or less inevitable. Indeed, they did win the largest share of the votes on June 10, and the CCF did continue its apparently inexorable decline. But the Liberals' share of the seats in the new Parliament fell from 65 to 40 percent: nine Liberal cabinet ministers were defeated, including C.D. Howe. One explained that the "electorate got bored. St. Laurent made it seem so easy to govern Canada that the electorate decided that anybody could do it. And so the people elected anybody." Such smug assurances disguised the more important fact that Liberal representation on the Prairies and in the Maritimes fell from one half to one fifth of their Members of Parliament. Such dissatisfaction in the regions that had benefited least from the postwar boom had to indicate more than boredom. The question in the summer of 1957 was whether the Parliament of minorities under John Diefenbaker (leading 112 Tories against 105 Liberals and 48 members representing other parties) could implement policies that would serve the forgotten regions better than C.D. Howe's leadership on behalf of his cronies in the Toronto and Montreal business communities.

— 3. Government Party Vanquished —

The Conservatives had been in opposition for over a generation. No member of the new cabinet had governed Canada before; there was much for everyone to learn about the exercise of power. But two things helped ease the transition from opposition to government. First, the economic situation aided the Tories, because the enormous expansion of the economy that had followed the Second World War had begun to decelerate by 1957. The Keynesian recipe for recovery called for tax cuts and increases in government spending. The Tories provided both—not because they were committed to the new economics, but because they had promised to spend more on the disadvantaged and to provide tax relief for the able. Taxes were cut by $178 million; old-age pensions were increased from $46 to $55 per month; and farmers were granted a $150-million advance on the sale of farm-stored grain. These steps led to an $800 million deficit in a $5 billion budget—just what the economy needed in Keynesian terms.

The second strength of the new government was the ineptness of the Liberals in opposition. The old team was largely defeated or retired; a new group of younger members that Howe called the "Junior League" remained. Lester Pearson succeeded St. Laurent in the leadership and immediately bungled his new role. As unemployment was on the rise in January 1958 (moving from four percent in 1956 to seven percent in 1958), Pearson felt that it was no time for government by amateurs. He moved that "in view of the desirability at this time of having a government pledged to implement Liberal policies, His Excellency's advisors should . . . submit their resignations forthwith." There would be no need for a dissolution and another campaign. Diefenbaker could yield to Pearson as King had given way to Meighen in 1926. Diefenbaker responded by working himself into a lather on the subject of Liberal arrogance. First, he attacked the Liberals for their apparent desire to govern without the bother of winning support at the polls: "Don't have an election but give us back our jobs" was Diefenbaker's characterization. By the time he had finished, one Member of Parliament was moved to "wonder if the Prime Minister believes in the humane slaughter of animals." Diefenbaker's second line of attack was the disclosure of a "hidden report" produced by civil servants in the Department of Trade and Commerce while the Liberals were still in power. The document warned that unemployment was the principal danger facing the country before the previous election. Since the Liberal Minister of Finance, Walter Harris, had insisted that inflation was the continuing danger and budgeted for restraint in expenditure in 1957, Diefenbaker asserted that Pearson's claims notwithstanding, the Liberals were far from perfect in their economic forecasting.

With apparent proof of Liberal incompetence as well as arrogance, Diefenbaker had no fear in challenging the party to another election. Subsequently, Parliament was dissolved, and Diefenbaker was back at the work he loved best in February-March 1958. Once again, he confronted the country eyeball-to-eyeball in what unfolded as the most emotional campaign in Canada's history. After generations of measuring national health by the growth of the Gross National Product, Diefenbaker asked Canadians to strive for more than their country's material expansion. He invited them "to create a new sense of a national purpose and national destiny." Diefenbaker claimed to know the way to a more unified, self-aware, and independent Canada. He made cash promises that also conveyed a sense of cosmic purpose: "Jobs! Jobs for hundreds of thousands of Canadians. A new vision! A new hope! A new soul for Canada!" The nation could save its character and reap the material promise of unlimited development. "Catch the vision of the kind of Canada this can be! I've seen this vision; I've seen this future of Canada. I ask you to have faith in this land and faith in our people." Elect a few more Conservatives. "We need a clear majority to carry out this long-range plan, this great design, this blueprint for the Canada which her resources make possible."

Of course, some sceptics said that there was no plan, no coherent blueprint, only—in Pearson's words—"quivering clichés or evangelistic exhortations." But others agreed with the Ottawa *Journal* which called the Diefenbaker "vision" an "homage to imagination which makes democracy exciting." They saw a Prime Minister asking Canadians if they wished to have "one country" developed by themselves in accordance with their own destiny. If so, he was the one to lead them there. It was possible—and in the immediate future—through the magic of a Diefenbaker majority. Not since the restoratives promised by the populists of the 1930s or the zeal of Alexander Mackenzie in 1874 had the electorate been promised so much for so little. Eighty percent of the eligible voters turned out on March 31; 54 percent voted for Diefenbaker's Conservatives. Even Quebec seemed to approve the new nationalism by awarding "Dief the Chief" 50 of its 75 seats. The rest of Canada was even more generous. Overall, 208 of the 265-member House were to sit on Diefenbaker's side. The Liberals and the minor parties were routed.

— 4. Continentalism Continued —

It soon became obvious, however, that the high priest of Canadian nationalism could arouse his people to moral indignation more effectively than he could enact the kind of integrated program he asserted without defining. In the 46 days of campaigning in 1958, four central intentions had been indicated: northern development, revitalization of federalism, reduction of continentalism, and restoration of closer relations with Great Britain and the Commonwealth. But in the years that followed, despite his commanding the largest majority to date, Diefenbaker made measurable headway only with the first of his four declared purposes. There was promotion of mineral exploration in the Arctic, and road and railway development that threatened profound disruption of the lives of aboriginal people in the north. Even so, no northern boom followed. Useful and expensive facilities were provided, but they neither transformed nor significantly reoriented the Canadian economy.

Other successes were symbolic or the results of good fortune. In the first category was the Canadian Bill of Rights, a statute of the Parliament of Canada enacted in 1960 and advertised as a guarantee of basic freedoms. But the guarantee applied exclusively to matters under federal jurisdiction, and the protection provided was indirect to say the least. All persons were said to have certain rights unless Parliament declared otherwise. Future discrimination on the basis of religion, sex, or race, for example, would have to be enacted "notwithstanding the Canadian Bill of Rights." The presumption was that Parliament would find it so embarrassing to include such a declaration in future statutes that everyone would be quite free from violation forever. As a Bill of Rights that placed certain freedoms beyond legislative trespass, the law was practically meaningless. The achievement was more symbolic than real.

Another notable success of Diefenbaker after 1958 was a windfall benefit in foreign trade. After two years of crop failure in China, the government of that country sought cereal grains on the world market in 1960. The United States neither recognized nor traded with China; Canada was therefore approached and the Wheat Board negotiated a deal, even though the Canadians, like the Americans, refused to recognize the Communists as the legitimate government of China. Their political differences notwithstanding, the two countries agreed to trade 240 million bushels of wheat and barley in 1961 and 1962. Canada continued to withhold diplomatic recognition, but the $450-million grain sale transformed "Red China" into one of Canada's most important customers. The Wheat Board sold all surplus stocks during the Diefenbaker years and net farm income trebled in the same period. Diefenbaker was not responsible for the crop failure or the embargo that forced the Chinese to seek supplies outside the United States. To his credit, he did agree to guarantee the sale, and he did protest when the United States attempted to intervene to prevent subsidiaries of American firms (such as Imperial Oil) from doing business with the Chinese ships when they called at Canadian ports.

Diefenbaker's successes were more than balanced by actions in areas where government initiatives had been promised but not taken, or areas in which one line of action was indicated but the opposite resulted. Nothing illustrates such tendencies better than the difference between what was promised and what was done in relations with the United States and Great

Britain. Out of a genuine emotional attachment to Britain and real distress over the recent increasing integration of Canadian trade with the United States, Diefenbaker proposed in July of 1957 to divert 15 percent of Canadian imports from the Americans to the British. Britain responded almost immediately with a proposal for free trade between the two countries, but Diefenbaker did not take up their offer, then or later.

Table 13.1 US-British Shares of Canadian Trade,* 1874-1954

Years	Canadian Imports From		Canadian Exports To	
	UK	*US*	*UK*	*US*
1874	49.9	42.0	46.6	43.3
1894	34.0	46.5	58.6	31.4
1914	21.4	64.0	49.9	37.9
1934	24.2	54.9	43.3	33.0
1954	9.6	72.3	16.7	60.0

*Values are percentages.

SOURCE: See Appendix A, Tables 6 and 7.

Rather than attempt to reorient Canada to Britain and the Commonwealth, Diefenbaker furthered the continentalist policies of the Liberals. In 1957, the air forces of Canada and the United States were consolidated under one joint command located under a mountain in Colorado. The NORAD (North American Air Defense) arrangement resembled the Ogdensburg Agreement of 1940 but differed in that it was a peacetime initiative. One year later, the Diefenbaker government approved another understanding— the new one resembling the Hyde Park Declaration of 1941. The Development and Production Sharing Program, approved in 1958, enabled companies in Canada to bid on American defence contracts on the same basis as the firms in the United States. From the standpoint of the rationalization of the manufacturing of the continent, and also to improve Canada's balance of payments with the Americans, the agreement made economic sense. Moreover, the firms most likely to take advantage of the program were already American with respect to ownership. But further integration of the two economies reduced Canada's freedom of action in external affairs. How could the Government of Canada ever claim impartiality in future wars involving the United States and third parties if Canada was a significant supplier to the Pentagon or operated as a branch of the United States Air Force? In this sense, Canada's acceptance of the new arrangement contradicted Diefenbaker's promise that he would lead the country along a more independent course.

Other examples of the same contradiction involved joint utilization of Canadian energy resources. In 1960, the first exports of natural gas to the United States were permitted, and in 1961 Diefenbaker signed a treaty that allowed the Americans to exploit the hydroelectric potential of the Columbia by damming the river near the border and flooding land in BC. The compensation for Canada was a cash settlement. Thus, Diefenbaker not only failed to act as he had promised; his continentalism was even more advanced than the Liberals'. What went wrong?

According to J.L. Granatstein, the unraveling of the "vision" is to be understood by the unfolding of an unfortunate sequence of events: "an extraordinary concatenation of events in foreign policy, in the economy, in financial policy, and in defence questions." But such an analysis begs the larger issue. An historical sequence shows how a chain of events unfolds, not why. Diefenbaker's problem—the problem of his country in microcosm—was his handicap of cross-purposes. Anticommunism neutralized ardent nationalism. A dogmatic commitment to private enterprise and individual liberty was blunted by an equally strong commitment to maintaining public welfare and vigorous government. A fervent desire to promote humanitarian idealism was cancelled by an impulse to maintain fiscal orthodoxy. Thus, Diefenbaker professed do-it-yourself development but acquiesced in subservience to the United States for the sake of a more vigorous stand against communism. He acted one way to promote exploration of the north, but sold out Canadian resources to the Americans as quickly as possible in the south. Or more frequently, Diefenbaker would find himself and his party locked between alternatives and they would not act at all.

Since Diefenbaker had campaigned in 1958 for bold initiatives, and since he had won such an overwhelming majority, he became especially vulnerable to ridicule on the grounds of apparent indecision. The *Globe and Mail* dubbed his majority the "idle Parliament." But he was far from idle. Indeed, his own estimate of his accomplishments since 1957 was that he had made dramatic headway towards the fulfillment of all promises. Campaigning in 1962 for a renewal of his majority, he made no apologies. Diefenbaker said: "Vast as our program has been in the last five years, it will be even greater in the five years ahead." He repeated the vision, but the magic was gone.

The Liberals posed as the "professional team," a group of experts who were well trained in the technique of government and anxious to win power in order to make the machinery of administration hum. Their image was that of a non-ideological party, a group that was unencumbered by visions or rigid moral purposes. They were technicians who promised to get everything moving again and to put an end to "indecision and fumbling."

Given the choice between Diefenbaker's demagoguery and Pearson's espousal of expediency under the banner of professionalism, many voters turned to minor parties. In Quebec, a new version of Social Credit under the tutelage of Real Caouette appeared especially interesting to voters there and won over one-third of the Quebec representation. Elsewhere, the CCF (repackaged and relabeled as the New Democratic Party in order to minimize even the barest hint of socialism) recovered slightly from its slide into oblivion: 15.6 percent of the votes in 1945, 13.4 percent in 1949, 11.3 percent in 1953, 10.7 percent in 1957, and 9.5 percent in 1958. In 1962, the NDP attracted 13.5 percent of the votes, winning 19 seats in Parliament. What remained for Diefenbaker was the rural vote of English-speaking Canada; his majority of 208 was reduced to a plurality of 116.

— 5. Defeat in Defence of Canada —

The return to minority government did not make Diefenbaker more decisive; the position of leading a parliament of minorities merely made him vulnerable to defeat in a crisis of indecision that was already six months old at the time of the 1962 election. The problem was deciding upon an affordable defence policy that was anticommunist without being subserviently pro-American. It has already been mentioned that Diefenbaker's anticommunism led him to accept an extension of continentalist collective security by the NORAD agreement of 1957. Canada would need more sophisticated weaponry for the new commitment; the same anticommunism led Diefenbaker to seek the latest weaponry with which to equip the royal Canadian Air Force. His nationalism encouraged him to think such hardware might be produced in Canada itself.

Since 1953, the Liberals had been supporting the A.V. Roe Company of Malton, Ontario, builders of the first Canadian-designed jet fighter aircraft (appropriately named the "Canuck"), to develop a more

sophisticated fighter-bomber. The result was the "Arrow." By 1957, however, the Liberals had decided that the CF-105 project was not cost-effective and determined that all further development would be cancelled after
the election. Diefenbaker's cabinet was less willing to abandon the
Arrow—not until 1959 when it became clear that each plane would cost
almost $9 million (or ten times more than an American-built alternative
such as the F-104). Diefenbaker's sense of fiscal conservatism rebelled at
the billion dollars it might cost to equip the RCAF with Arrows. Despite
its technical sophistication and the loss of 14 000 jobs in Malton, the
Arrow was scrapped. A partial substitute was found in the BOMARC
interceptor (an unmanned missile manufactured by the Boeing Corporation of the United States). The attraction of the BOMARC was that it was
cheap. Canada would pay for the installation sites, the Americans would
provide the missiles. Moreover, their nuclear warhead meant that just a
few BOMARCs could inflict spectacular damage on entire squadrons of
incoming Russian bombers. And the nuclear depth charges being considered for Canada's warships as well as nuclear tactical weapons for the
brigade of Canadian troops in Germany were attractive for the same
reason, that of obtaining a bigger defensive "bang" per dollar spent.

But a snag developed over the issue of control. American law
prohibited the release of atomic bombs to foreign powers. If the nuclear
arsenal were acquired as planned, Canadian forces would have to be
staffed by Americans as well as Canadians.

Diefenbaker's sense of national pride was incompatible with the idea
of subordination to the United States. Unfortunately, the years after 1959
tested the relationship to the utmost. In the first place, a new Minister of
External Affairs, Howard Green, came into his diplomatic responsibilities
in the summer of 1959 with a deep commitment to nuclear disarmament
and the idea that non-alignment was the most appropriate diplomatic
position from which to pursue the nuclear non-proliferation issue. In the
second place, a new President, John F. Kennedy, succeeded Eisenhower in
1961 in some respects as a youthful and idealistic leader, beckoning his
compatriots to follow him forward to a "New Frontier," but in most other
respects, as simply a younger, more imperious Caesar. Diefenbaker and
Kennedy developed a deep and mutual dislike of one another, a dislike that
increased enormously in the autumn of 1962.

On October 22, Kennedy declared naval war on Cuba and the Soviet
Union to prevent the installation of Russian missiles on Cuban territory.
When NORAD went to "defensive condition" three (on the DEFCON
scale, a five was peace, one meant nuclear war), Canada was expected to

269

follow, but Diefenbaker insisted upon his own assessment of the situation. Although the cabinet went along with his stalling, the Minister of Defence, Colonel Douglas Harkness, quietly put the Canadian forces on alert. After the United States went to DEFCON two on October 24, Harkness successfully badgered the Prime Minister into legalizing what had already occurred in defiance of Cabinet. For two days, however, Diefenbaker thought that he had supported the principle of Canadian independence by refusing immediate and unquestioning compliance. Then, as a further gesture towards an independent Canada, the Prime Minister dug in his heels at accepting nuclear bombs for the BOMARCs or the Canadian NATO forces in Europe and at sea.

The issue of defence, and the BOMARCs in particular, revealed Diefenbaker caught in an agony of indecision. He wanted nuclear weapons in order to have more terrifying sabres to rattle at the Russians. But as he loathed the idea of American controls, he did not find it easy to accept the warheads. Diefenbaker was thus paralysed between "yes" and "no" from February 1962 (the date of completing the first BOMARC site in Canada) to February 1963 (when all parties united to defeat him in the House of Commons).

The beginning of the end was Lester Pearson's announcement on January 12, 1963, that the expedient course was to accept the warheads. Pearson said that maintaining international commitments was of paramount importance. He asserted that the BOMARCs and other nasty bits of military hardware were useless without their nuclear armament, and wondered why the government accepted the delivery devices if there was no intention of taking the warheads as well.

Diefenbaker tried to answer Pearson when the House reconvened on January 25. He repeated his reservations about accepting the warheads immediately, and asked for more time, saying that a decision would follow from the next meeting of the NATO allies in May 1963. For the interim, he suggested that everyone should pray for divine guidance in the matter, adding that "Some may ridicule that belief on my part." Even so, the Prime Minister insisted that "the Western World has been directed by God in the last few years . . . " and he wanted to leave the Government of Canada to the Lord for another several months.

Prayer was not enough for the opposition or Diefenbaker's Minister of Defence. On February 3, a Sunday, the Cabinet met at the Prime Minister's residence. Harkness demanded his leader's resignation. When Diefenbaker agreed, and rose to inform the Governor General of his decision, a large block of other ministers announced that they too would resign. At the end of what J.L. Granatstein has described as the "strangest" cabinet meeting in Canadian history, only one resignation stuck—that of Douglas Harkness. The next day, the former Minister of Defence made his resignation public and Lester Pearson moved non-confidence at once, accusing the government of "lack of leadership, the breakdown of unity in the cabinet, and confusion and indecision in dealing with national and international problems . . . ." The NDP and Social Credit members agreed, and joined the Liberals to defeat the government on February 5.

Diefenbaker's humiliation in the House of Commons was repeated two months later at the polls. His rejection by the electorate seemed even more significant than the defeat in Parliament. Other Prime Ministers had suffered a similar fate in the House, but the election of 1963 was the first time in Canadian history that a dramatic appeal to nationalism failed with the public. Diefenbaker compared the Liberals to the promoters of the Annexation Manifesto of 1849, and taunted them as wantonly unprincipled pursuers of expediency. He called them tools of the Americans and the "sinister interests," while portraying himself as simply "trying to help others," attempting to fulfill the vow that he had made in 1956 when he accepted the Conservative leadership: "I hope it will be said of me when I give up the highest honour that you can confer on any man, as was said of another in public service: 'He wasn't always right; sometimes he was on the wrong side, but never on the side of wrong.' That is my dedication; that is my humble declaration." Diefenbaker was still making the same affirmation in 1963: "I'm not asking for the support of the powerful, the strong and the mighty, but of the average Canadian—the group to which I belong."

In the election of 1963, the old affirmations and paranoid accusations did not work well enough to return even the plurality he had won the year before. The defence question was the central issue, and to some observers, the defeat of Diefenbaker signified the defeat of Canadian nationalism; a "lament for a nation" was called for. But such pessimism, expressed so eloquently by George Grant, failed to appreciate that previous popular nationalists offered more than rigid adherence to conflicting principles. They were also proponents of some wonderful policy to make the nation as well as to affirm it. In that tradition, Diefenbaker was defeated because Canadians still expected a government to provide deliberate actions as well as words. The voter in Halifax who said "he's not the man I thought he was," expressed disappointment similar to the *Globe and Mail* when that paper charged that "there never was a program . . . . Mr. Diefenbaker is barren of constructive ideas and incapable of action."

Nationalism versus continentalism was thus only the most immediate issue in the election of 1963. The other, broader question was whether Canada would have a government whose politics were its principles, or an administration whose politics was its program. The two questions tended to blur, of course. But on both matters, public opinion was quite clear.

Diefenbaker's was the only party that stood upon the ground of pious nationalism exclusively. On that basis, they received a mere 30 percent of the vote. The remaining votes went to the Liberals, the NDP, and the Social Credit Party—groups that differed on what they promised, but who were united in the opinion that principles and pious intentions were not enough. It was time to return to government with projects. By 1963, most of the electorate had little patience with John Diefenbaker and government by platitude. As a result, "Dief the Chief" was returned to oppose a government rather than to lead one, in much the same way as Alexander Mackenzie in 1878—piously to oppose an administration that asked to be judged in accordance with the projects it completed, rather than by the principles it professed.

Suggested Reading

The most recent general history that covers the Diefenbaker phenomenon is J.L. Granatstein, *Canada, 1957-1967: The Years of Uncertainty and Innovation* (1986). Another general work of comparable detail, but without the same level of annotation, is Robert Bothwell, *et al., Canada since 1945: Power, Politics, and Provincialism* (1981). Less comprehensive and now somewhat dated but still eminently readable is Blair Fraser, *The Search for Identity: Canada, 1945-67* (1967). A tract for the times is Peter Newman, *Renegade in Power* (1963). All of the above are sympathetic to the Liberals and their purposes. A general history more sympathetic to Diefenbaker's intentions, if not his accomplishments, is found in Donald Creighton, *Canada's First Century, 1867-1967* (1970).

Some specialized works have appeared recently on select aspects of the period. The biography of *C.D. Howe* (1979), by Robert Bothwell and William Kilbourn, for example, provides excellent material on the twilight of the St. Laurent period; and William Kilbourn's *Pipeline* (1970), offers a comprehensive account of the pipeline debate. For the elections of the period, John Meisel's studies of *The Canadian General Election of 1957* (1962), and *Papers on the 1962 Election* (1964), contain useful survey data. James Dow's book on *The Arrow* (1979), analyses that interesting chapter in the history of Canadian technology, but the relevant chapters in Michael Bliss, *Northern Enterprise: Five Centuries of Canadian Business* (1987), provide a more critical perspective. George Grant's *Lament for a Nation* (1965), is a brilliant, perhaps premature, post-mortem on Canadian nationalism, written in the aftermath of Diefenbaker's defeat in 1963.

Many of the other important questions on the period await the research of future historians. In the meantime, two works that are likely to be important source material for such investigators are the memoirs of the leaders of the two major parties: Diefenbaker's *One Canada*, 3 vols. (1975-7), and Pearson's *Mike*, 2 vols. (1972-5).

(Left to right) Lester Pearson and Pierre Trudeau greeting Daniel Johnson at Federal-Provincial Constitutional Conference, February, 1968.

"Diplomacy set the tone of Pearson's government."

CHAPTER 14
TENTH-DECADE DIPLOMACY, 1963-1967

1. Decisions and Doubts in Canadian-American Relations

When Pearson's "professional team" assumed power in the spring of 1963, the new government promised "sixty days of decision." The principal area of indicated activity was that of international diplomacy: arming the BOMARC missiles and accepting American control of the nuclear warheads. Other promised action included a health insurance plan, improved old-age pensions, federal assistance to municipalities, federal programs to moderate regional disparities, and government discouragement of growing foreign investment. Diplomacy was a factor in such domestic areas as well, because the regulation of foreign ownership had serious implications for relations with the United States, and because new circumstances in federal-provincial relations meant that projects planned in Ottawa were no longer conveyed easily to the public by the vehicle of shared-cost programs. Moreover, the Liberals needed to exercise extraordinary finesse in winning parliamentary approval for any of their initiatives because the party was four members short of a majority in 1963, and two members short in 1965. For all reasons—the nature of the Liberals' policy intentions, a new assertiveness of the provinces, and the lack of a majority in the House of Commons—diplomatic issues and a diplomatic style of administration were central to the Pearson years, 1963 through 1967.

Another reason why diplomacy set the tone of Pearson's government is that the Prime Minister himself was one of Canada's first and finest professional diplomats. In the 1920s (after a stint in the army and the completion of a bachelor degree in history at the University of Toronto), Pearson rejected a career in business or law, traveled to Oxford for more advanced study of history, and settled into his first living as a lecturer at his alma mater in Toronto. In 1928, Pearson abandoned his teaching career to join the small but elite group of diplomat-trainees that had gravitated to the new Department of External Affairs in the decade when Canada's autonomy expanded most dramatically. Pearson continued in that department until the autumn of 1948, then made the move that was so easy for several other mandarins at the same time: he accepted a Liberal nomination for a safe seat in Parliament. Following his by-election victory, Pearson then appeared in the House of Commons, but as a member more interested in government than in politics. Even after he accepted the leadership of the Liberal Party in January 1958, Pearson in no way retired from diplomacy. As he later expressed it: "My whole career, my deepest instincts, have been dedicated to the resolution of disputes . . . ." In his chosen profession, Pearson was remarkably successful; indeed, his proposal to establish a UN peacekeeping force to aid the departure of Britain and France from Egypt won him the Nobel Prize in 1957. But the task of mediation is ever a thankless one. To some, the mediator is simply a person who fears saying anything unpleasant face to face; he is never in control, he only reacts, moving one way and another in the continuous search for common ground between adversaries.

Like Diefenbaker, Pearson was often caught between cross purposes, and usually reacted more often than he led with his own initiatives. But unlike Diefenbaker, Pearson was always in motion, cheerfully going about his diplomat's work because, as he explained in his memoirs, he was "dedicated to . . . the search for agreement, to the avoidance of controversy, and the finding of solutions to difficult problems." His first such effort after the election of 1963 was to give the Minister of Finance, Walter Gordon, a free rein to develop a budget to discourage foreign investment, while Pearson personally visited the American President to assure him that the new

Government of Canada would honour its international commitments and cherish its fraternal association with the United States in other respects.

In the visit to President Kennedy, Pearson chatted about baseball, NATO commitments, and further development of shared resources such as the Columbia River. Canadian-American relations, strained in the Diefenbaker years, were thus repaired almost immediately. "He'll do!," Kennedy remarked afterwards, but what Pearson agreed to "do" was not something Walter Gordon would accept with approving smiles. Still, a rift in Canadian-American relations had been closed by Pearson's affirmation that the BOMARCs would be armed and Canadian NATO forces bolstered. In this manner, there was relief in the ending of the crisis if not in the substance of its resolution.

Walter Gordon's experimentation with economic nationalism unfolded less facilely or cheerfully. The budget, introduced on June 13, included two revolutionary proposals. One was a 30-percent tax on the value of Canadian firms purchased by American corporations. The other was a five percent increase in the 15-percent tax on dividends of wholly foreign-owned firms; or, a five percent reduction for those that were at least one quarter Canadian-owned. For the first time in Canadian history, a government proposed specific measures to discourage foreign investment. There were objections from the Americans, of course, but the Canadian business community (the potential sellers of manufacturing plant) denounced the budget so loudly that the "takeover" tax was withdrawn for "further study" on June 19. Early in July it was dropped entirely, and the tax on dividends was significantly modified. All that remained was the record of the attempt.

For the next two years, continentalism appeared to be a stronger current than economic nationalism. A ripple of continental disharmony did develop in 1964 over Canada's refusal to permit foreign ownership of the chartered banks, but the rest seemed to be goodwill and solidarity, symbolized best, perhaps, by the announcement of an arrangement for quasi-free trade in automobiles. By the "Auto Pact," announced in January 1965, domestic car manufacturers were permitted to develop North America as one integrated market through import-export freedoms for manufacturers. As far as consumers were concerned, the tariff remained and manufacturers continued to price their product to the separate markets. Prices changed very little. What was gained besides greater profits for the companies? From the standpoint of the Government of Canada, the Auto Pact was worthwhile because minimum levels of Canadian production relative to sales were assured without conceding a maximum level of Canadian output. Over the next two years, Canadian production increased more than 30 percent, with a proportional increase in jobs. By 1967, half of all the cars and trucks manufactured in Canada were sold in the United States. The overall balance of payments still favoured the Americans, but the pre-Auto-Pact disparity had been reduced dramatically. On this account, the agreement encouraged exports without conceding protection on domestic manufacturing—a real triumph in "quiet diplomacy."

The auto agreement seemed to indicate that Canada had resolved its fitful doubts concerning the advantages of continentalism. In the year after the Auto-Pact's negotiation, two senior diplomats issued a report on procedures for assuring the compatibility of policies of the two countries in all other respects. Pearson and the President had commissioned the study by Arnold Heeney (for Canada) and Livingston Merchant (for the United States) in 1963 when both leaders agreed that it was important to find ways to "make it easier to avoid divergencies in economic and other policies." Appearing in July 1965, the Heeney-Merchant Principles for Partnership was an unqualified endorsement of "the practice of quiet diplomacy," an approach considered more "neighbourly" and also "far more effective than the alternative of raising a row and being unpleasant in public." The assumption was that the two countries lived similar collective lives on one continent and hoped for the same future in a difficult and troubled world. Such a view seemed wise in 1940 when the world's villains were perfectly villainous; it was also popular in 1948, in the face of the new menace of Stalinism and the fear that an irresponsible dictator might plunge the world into another global conflict. But by 1965, many Canadians were beginning to believe that the United States was no longer the chief proponent of world peace and freedom. By that time, the American Commander in Chief seemed so obsessed with communism that he appeared willing to support any kind of noncommunist regime by any means. The domestic scene was equally disturbing. The televised assassination of President Kennedy in November 1963 and images of Americans violently resisting the civil rights movement for blacks in 1964 were two shocks. Then, "Rolling Thunder," an air war against the Vietnamese launched in 1965, caused even deeper questioning of American leadership by some concerned Canadians.

For Lester Pearson, the American war against Vietnam was a crisis to mediate. In an acceptance speech for a peace award from Temple University in Philadelphia in April 1965, he suggested that a pause in the bombing might be an effective invitation to the other side to negotiate a settlement that could lead to the unification and democracy promised by the French in their withdrawal from Indochina in 1954, an accord that Canada was to supervise from a position on the International Control Commission created to monitor the process at the same time. The address was followed immediately by a meeting with President Lyndon Johnson at his retreat near Washington, D.C., where Pearson discovered that Johnson was outraged by the substance as well as the source of the proposal. Pearson's suggestion had, in effect, preempted U.S. plans to use the halting of bombing as a negotiating device with Vietnam. The President grabbed the Prime Minister by the lapels and scolded him severely for presuming to tell the Americans how to carry their burden of defending world freedom when the Canadians allegedly did so little to shoulder their share of the struggle. Too shocked to reply coherently, Pearson fumbled an answer. From that moment, according to Robert Bothwell, Pearson knew that Johnson was a "bully who threatened, a vulgar manipulator . . . ." Thereafter, Pearson regarded the United States less as a senior partner, and more as a country to be viewed from afar.

The Vietnam War might have been as important for Canada's relations with the United States as the Great War had been in Canada's view of Britain. Both wars provided cause to convince Canadians that a greater measure of independence was both warranted and worthwhile. Robert Fulford, normally a critic of art and literature, thought that he was speaking for a generation of Canadians when he suggested that those born of the Second World War "baby boom" had grown up believing that "if we were very good or very smart, or both, we would surely graduate from Canada." Fulford and others had learned to look beyond Canada much as the imperialists had looked beyond their country between 1900 and 1914. What had made Diefenbaker's nationalism phenomenal was that, 1958 excepted, most people—especially in English-speaking Canada—seemed to accept the popular notion that a Canadian was a North American who had not yet accepted a job in the States. But in 1965—in the face of assassination, race riots, and an obscene war— new critics of continentalism seemed to have tangible proof that greater political distance from the American Empire was necessary. They asserted— they pleaded—for Canada to be different from and independent of the Americans, and discussion of the Canadian-identity malaise resumed with new urgency.

After France pulled out of NATO in 1965, critics of American-dominated collective security questioned Canada's membership in the alliance, especially in its corollary, NORAD. Suggesting that independence was nothing more than the exercise of the right to say "no," one observer, Stephen Clarkson, asserted that a more negative Canada might even receive greater material advantages from the United States, pointing out that "the more truculent General de Gaulle has become, the gentler has been the Americans' treatment of France. With so much direct investment in Canada, it is unlikely that the Americans . . . would want to get rid of a blemish on the finger by amputating the arm." Others disagreed, on the basis of the same economic evidence. Meeker critics suggested that the US presence in the economy was simply too important to jeopardize by foolish posturing in international affairs.

The debate over the possibilities for independence in foreign relations gave the concern over the "branch plant economy" new importance. The more strident critics asserted that the indicators of "lengthening dependence" were undeniable. By Kari Levitt's reckoning, the "long term foreign investment" share of Canadian mining and manufacturing had increased from less than 40 percent before the Second World War to almost 60 percent by 1964; moreover, "foreign" had become virtually synonymous with American. It seemed to follow that bold action was needed to halt the process of "silent surrender" before it reached the point of irreversible dominance.

The intruder, however, was not a single firm, US Inc., but an aggregation of thousands of companies frequently working at cross purposes. What was their immediate and potential "dominance"? In a practical business sense, dominance implies organized action for a defined interest. From such an organizational standpoint, a dominant factor is the predominant firm by the level-of-assets criterion. By that test, William K. Carroll has found that the 70 dominant industrial corporations, 20 dominant financial institutions, and ten dominant merchandizing firms of Canada of 1946, in comparison with 1966, were in fact more "Canadian," controlled a larger percentage of the assets in their respective spheres, and were becoming stronger still after 1966 by aggressive expansion in the United States as well as in Canada. Carroll suggests that his findings "contradict the thesis that an historical trend exists toward silent surrender." Michael Bliss agrees that "the alarm about foreign ownership was not a function of its seriousness as a national problem." In his opinion, "fear of foreign ownership was a perverse expression of Canadians' sense of power in the 1960s."

And yet the "power" and "dominance" affirmed by Bliss and documented by Carroll leave unexplained the other aspects of "dependency" that are even more fundamental to the new mercantilism denounced by Levitt. The issue of colonialism inherent in the continental trade of raw materials for American-made finished goods, the lagging status of indigenous research and development, and the pervasive influence of American media and consumerism were all unrefuted aspects of the overall alarm. On that account, it would appear frivolous to join Bliss in dismissing the larger concern of the 1960s as merely "nationalist hand wringing," particularly when one considers the phenomenon of anti-colonialism in more focused contexts such as the province of Quebec.

— 2. Autonomy With New Purposes in Quebec —

Traditionally, Quebec was the province most willing to resist colonialism, particularly in defence and diplomatic matters. Throughout the centuries, Quebeckers had been told by their leaders that they were a people with a special character and mission: a character to be protected from cultural contamination or extinction, and a mission to preserve the faith, the language, and the pastoral way of life.

During the 1930s and 1940s, in the crises of the Great Depression and wartime conscription (discussed in previous chapters), Quebeckers took refuge in defensive nationalism to protect the ideal of romanticized agrarianism. By 1941, although the population was still overwhelmingly Roman Catholic and French-speaking, the agrarian aspect was exceptional (see table 14.1). Nationalists such as Richard Arès continued to insist that "By tradition, vocation as well as necessity, we are a people of peasants. Everything that takes us away from the land diminishes and weakens us as a people . . ." And in 1956, the Tremblay Commission reporting on cultural survival echoed the same theme in the interest of revitalizing what they called the "old spirit," even though by that time, almost 90 percent of all French-origin Quebeckers were neither farmers nor farm dwellers.

Table 14.1 Rural-Urban Characteristics of Quebec Population, 1941-1961

Origins*

| | *FRENCH* | | | *OTHER* | |
Years	*Rural Non farm*	*Rural Farm*	*Total French*	*All locations*	*Overall Total*
1941	1107	105	1483	1849	3332
1951	714	522	2091	1965	4056
1961	533	699	3009	2250	5259

*Values are in thousands

SOURCE: Adapted from data in D. Posgate and K. McRoberts, *Quebec: Social Change and Political Crisis* (1976), pp. 48-49.

The persistence of the myth of the pastoral French Canadian was thus an indicator of the intensity of a belief rather than a mirror of reality. But while the myth remained strong, governments could use the symbols vocally to resist colonialism and at the same time as an excuse for having no strategies to promote industrial development or to attend to the problems of industrial workers in an urban context. The winning electoral formula developed by Maurice Duplessis in the 1930s—the formula that kept his Union nationale in power almost continuously to 1960—involved local favours rather than sweeping policies. In the 1940s and 1950s, just before an election, advertisements would appear in newspapers recounting the funds that the government had recently expended on public works in the district. If the incumbent candidate happened to be a Liberal, the favours were attributed to the UN organizer. Otherwise, the benefits were listed as the achievement of the local legislative patron. Since the UN was also touted as the party most likely to win the upcoming election, voters were advised to make certain that they elected a member of the ruling party to assure them an even larger share of future patronage. On this basis, as well as by demagogic appeals to elect a government that was "closer to the people," the UN usually won large majorities and maintained the support of the working class, even though Duplessis was demonstrably opposed to militant organized labour.

Workers or organizers who troubled the political scene were vulnerable to harassment under the old Padlock Law that survived the 1930s until the Supreme Court found it unconstitutional in 1957 (because it invaded the exclusive power of the federal government over criminal law). Still, the draconian labour code of Quebec was usually sufficient deterrent. The Minister of Labour was empowered to take bold action against strikes deemed to be illegal or turbulent. The most dramatic such repression occurred in the spring of 1949 when the workers employed in the asbestos mines of the Eastern Townships decided to go on strike, without waiting for conciliation proceedings to run their time-consuming course to the inevitable denial of the union's demands. Duplessis came to the aid of the workers' American employers with police protection for strikebreakers, and enlisted the Church to join him in denouncing the union. Had the event followed the pattern established in previous strikes, the three authorities of Church, state, and company would have been sufficient to dictate terms to the workers. But in 1949, the archbishop of Montreal, Joseph Charbonneau, sided with the Roman Catholic union. The strikers were emboldened by their unexpected support, and the strike became violent before it was ended with the mediation efforts of the archbishop of Quebec. The five-month dispute won the workers a ten-cent raise and assurances of re-employment. Even so, scores of the more outspoken strike leaders were not rehired and Charbonneau found that his superiors thought that he would be more effective in another diocese, transferring him to Victoria, British Columbia. Other clergy were warned to drop their labour activism in 1950; and in 1954, the Duplessis government added a new power to its anti-radical weaponry with a law that empowered the Minister of Labour to decertify unions that even "tolerated communists" or "threatened to strike public services."

In some ways, the Asbestos strike represented little more than a minor setback for the companies and the government of Quebec. In the longer term, however, the episode proved to be a major turning point because it rallied disaffection in three important sectors of Quebec's population. Increasing numbers of workers, business people, clergy and professionals became angered by the contradiction between the rhetoric of anti-colonialism for the sake of cultural survival and bucaneer resource development for the benefit of large corporations. Gradually, other workers would see themselves in approximately the same position as the asbestos miners. More of the traditional leaders in the church and the professions would see the Duplessis regime as a betrayal of the "old spirit." And the francophone business class would become increasingly dissatisfied with its marginal position in relation to the huge corporations engaged in resource development. The elements of a reform coalition grew in strength and awareness of common interests.

The breakthrough for reformers came in 1960. Duplessis died in September 1959; and his successor, Paul Sauvé, died in office just four months later. The loss of both leaders in such rapid succession left the Union nationale disorganized and vulnerable to defeat by the coalition that had gravitated to the Quebec Liberal Party.

The electoral victory of the reformers led by Jean Lesage in June 1960, indicated that the desire for change was irresistible and the slogan, "Things must change" (*Il faut que ça change*) signified more than an electoral stance. The Liberals were determined to move boldly to "catch up" with the rest of Canada. So dramatic was the difference between the new and the old government, in this respect, that a *Globe and Mail* reporter covering events in Quebec called the change of government a "Quiet Revolution." The break with the past was particularly dramatic in the attitudes of the new politicians towards the role of the state in shaping society. The agrarian myth that justified limited government was replaced by the notion that Quebec had to refine its technological proficiency;

Quebeckers looked to the state to set the pace and direction of such refinement.

Nowhere was the effect of the new ideology more evident than in the Liberals' reforms of education. Under the old system, there was one set of institutions for the children of Catholic parents controlled by what was, in effect, a committee of the Roman Catholic church. All other children attended "Protestant" schools controlled by different trustees. Church and state were thus inseparable because the preceding governments had delegated all responsibility for the social development of human resources to religious authorities. The new government operated from the premise that education should be directed by secular institutions because it was regarded as job training more than catechism; the schools were to transfer skills more than beliefs. One of the first official acts of the Liberals was, therefore, to appoint a commission—of secular as well as clerical educators—to survey the existing pattern of schools and recommend changes. The Parent Commission (reporting in 1963) gave the Minister of Youth, Paul Gérin-Lajoie, precisely the information he wanted. In May 1964, the government assumed responsibility for schooling by creating the Ministry of Education under Gérin-Lajoie, and the expensive work of transforming the schools into training grounds for masters of technology began.

Equally ambitious—and expensive—were the projects for the decolonization and development of Quebec's economy. Here too the new government operated from an assumption that was radically different from its predecessors, who had assumed that economic growth was an entirely private matter, and who had left the initiative in the hands of individual farmers and business people. The new regime believed that the state had an active role to play, particularly in the promotion of French-Canadians to the managerial level of the Quebec economy. The most outspoken advocate of such active statism was René Lévesque, the Minister of Natural Resources and, after Lesage and Gérin-Lajoie, the most important person in the government.

Although Lévesque was outspoken in his affirmations of economic nationalism (and considerably left of centre in his economic philosophy), the program he implemented was striking for its pragmatism. Consider, for example, the great headline-maker of 1962-63, the "nationalization" of electrical utilities. Critics of the campaign called it socialist or insanely nationalist because privately-owned companies were bought out by the government, and French-Canadians appeared promptly in the management of the public conglomerate, Hydro-Québec. But the government assumed control of only one third of the private firms, and the process of acquisition employed a pragmatic principle of selection as well as compensation for the owners. A truly radical approach would have insisted upon the takeover of all firms and expropriation without payment. To Lévesque, however, the important goal was to improve service. The private companies in the northwestern part of the province were one target because they provided 25-cycle power in a 60-cycle world. They were nationalized to make the conversion. The other large target, on the Gaspé peninsula, came under the public-utility umbrella to reduce rates from five times those of Montreal to the same standard. But the private companies that produced cheap, 60-cycle power for the American corporations in the Lac St. Jean region were left as they were. In this way, public ownership was instrumental in solving specific problems, not an end in itself.

A similar pragmatism characterized two other initiatives in the area of economic policy, the creation of the Quebec Advisory Council (*Conseil d'orientation économique*) and the establishment of the General Investment Corporation *(La Société générale de financement)*. The first was a planning agency to study "the economic organization of the province with a view to the most complete utilization of its material and human resources . . .," a body to "indicate" the way to a rationalized economy with French-Canadian participation above the level of "cheap and docile labour." The role of the other institution was to offer financial assistance, enabling private enterprise to follow the "indicative planning" of the Advisory Council. The General Investment Corporation was supposed to provide funds (in the form of loans or actual investment) for small firms to consolidate into larger operations and thus achieve economies of scale.

The emergence of the state as the principal promoter of economic and social development led to an enormous growth in the civil service and an astronomical increase in the scale of government expenditure. Between 1960 and 1965, the Liberals created six new ministries and eight public enterprises to begin to deliver a broad spectrum of social services available elsewhere in Canada but previously unknown in Quebec because Duplessis had refused to participate in federal shared-cost programs. Under Duplessis' regime, Quebec had lacked services but taxes had also been low. In 1959, the government of Quebec collected only $556 million in revenue and finished the year with a $23-million surplus. The provincial income tax was so low that one fifth of all wage earners had been exempt. By 1966, the Liberals had imposed a six percent sales tax and had increased the personal income tax so greatly that the government collected nearly $1 billion in revenue, but still completed the year with an enormous deficit.

A reorganized Union nationale seized on the contrast and suggested that the Quiet Revolution was beginning to cost more than people ought to be willing to pay. According to William D. Coleman, the price was becoming too high even for the coalition that brought the Liberals to power in 1960. "The educational reforms held out the promise to workers of better technical training and of greater access to higher education," but it was becoming increasingly clear to organized labour that the new system tended to divert working-class families into vocational training, while maintaining the flow of middle- and upper-class families to universities. That was no cause for concern to the francophone business class who wanted a more skilled labour force and greater access to expansion capital. Their disillusionment was the state's evident tendency to join the ranks of the big companies with its own huge crown corporations. Even so, "after the nationalization of hydro-electric power companies in 1962, no systematic attempts were made to gain majority control over other resources, and the practice of shipping resources out of the province in brute form was not discontinued." The economy expanded largely along the old lines and the nature of the "education reform tended to increase the materialism and consumerism of society rather than decrease it." Thus, the disillusionment of reform-minded clergy and other professionals lay in their hopes for "reunification" and "rejuvenation" of French-Canadian culture. Consequently, the Quiet Revolution spawned its own quiet reaction with many of the Liberals' supporters in 1960 returning to the UN or seeking more radical approaches to Quebec's decolonization. The immediate beneficiary was the UN, led by Daniel Johnson, that came to power in June 1966 with the promise of a slower pace of social innovation and scaled-down expenditure. Pointing to severe strains that had developed in federal-provincial relations since Quebec had started to exercise its full powers under the Constitution, Johnson promised to forge ahead and secure a new relation between Quebec and Canada. Here was a policy that was consistent with the popular autonomy theme, but a program with attractive revenue implications, because the bolder anti-Ottawa stance was supposed to recover the taxing power "usurped" by the government of Canada.

— 3. Federal-Provincial Diplomacy —

Traditionally, the Quebec autonomy demand meant defending (more than exercising) the powers assigned to the provinces under the BNA Act. For Duplessis, the best defence was to denounce each federal encroachment and refuse to participate in shared-cost programs as Ottawa put up funds to confront problems that Duplessis maintained were exclusively provincial. As a result, Quebec was the only province in 1959 that did not take federal money for hospitals and universities, for example. Since the government of Quebec did not choose to launch programs of its own in either field, Duplessis seemed to win his little wars with Ottawa and no blood was shed in the fighting. Moreover, the Government of Canada also emerged victorious because its agenda was not interrupted with the other nine provinces.

An enormous problem developed once the government of Quebec chose to enjoy the same social services as existed in the rest of Canada without sacrificing the autonomy Duplessis defended. At the first federal-provincial conference attended by the Lesage government in July 1960, the new premier proposed compensation for the revenue denied Quebec for non-participation in shared-cost programs and he asked for "abatement" of federal dominance in the field of direct taxation. Diefenbaker conceded some room for Quebec to raise revenue for universities by direct taxation, but the Quebec proposal was rejected because the Prime Minister refused to see the central government impoverished in the name of provincial autonomy. His nationalism was stronger than his other declared commitment to fighting centralism.

If all provinces had united behind the abatement formula advanced by Lesage, it is possible that Diefenbaker's "one Canada" principle would have led to a different outcome in 1960. But the only point on which the others could agree was that every province needed more revenue. They could not agree on the method. Some demanded higher equalization payments; others wanted more federal participation in shared-cost programs. Either position was markedly different from the idea that the central government should make room in the direct taxation field for the provinces to impose higher personal income, corporate, or inheritance taxes of their own. That preoccupation was peculiar to Quebec. Since Lesage refused to back away from his new concept of autonomy, the Quiet Revolution developed rapidly into the "Quebec Problem."

Diefenbaker seemed insensitive to Quebec's aspirations. Equally important, he did not seem to know how to react except to ignore them. In 1962, for instance, one of the few French-Canadian members of the cabinet, Paul Martineau, asked Diefenbaker how he should respond to reporters' persistent questions on the government's policy regarding Quebec. "Look," Diefenbaker replied, "you didn't make too much trouble before you were in the cabinet: I hope you're not going to start making trouble now." For Diefenbaker, the issue of Quebec versus Ottawa was simply troublesome, too complicated for day-to-day or long-range responses.

Lester Pearson viewed the conflict from a diplomat's perspective and also with a different concept of Canada itself. While Diefenbaker insisted that Canada was one "unhyphenated" nation, Pearson believed that the facts of the French-English past made the country binational, like it or not. In December 1962, he called for a commission to investigate not only the realities of past and present French-English relations, but also "the means of developing the bicultural character of Canada" in the future. The country, in his opinion, had to grow beyond the "narrow vision" that promoted bilingualism in Quebec and tolerated English-only for the rest. According to the 1961 census, only 2.2 million of Canada's 18.2 million total population were bilingual, and 64 percent of Canadians speaking both languages were French-origin Quebeckers. More Canadians needed to learn French as well as English. At the same time, Pearson suggested that Canadians in general would have to become more tolerant of Quebeckers "determined to become directors of their economic and cultural destiny in their own changed and changing society . . . ." Pearson promised "the greatest possible constitutional decentralization . . . to strengthen, indeed to establish and maintain unity."

Lesage was not deflected from his original course by Pearson's pronouncements on bilingualism and biculturalism. He persisted with the abatement demand. Three days before the election that confirmed the defeat of Diefenbaker in 1963, Lesage demanded a federal retreat to 75 percent of its current share of the income tax, 75 percent of the corporate-profits tax, and a complete withdrawal from the inheritance tax. If the federal government would not make room for his province's intentions in the field of direct taxation, Lesage threatened double taxation in the next provincial budget. He said: "Twelve months will go by before the next budget speech. Either the federal government . . . will have made use of the 12 months to make allowance for Quebec's needs, or else we in

Quebec will have taken steps on our own side to make the required decisions in fiscal policy."

Once elected, Pearson indicated that he was "prepared to make substantial concessions." But the commitment to symbolic gestures was more readily apparent than substantial fiscal or constitutional decentralization. French became a language of caucus and cabinet discussion. Bilingualism incentives were incorporated into the federal civil service, and in July 1963, Pearson announced the formation of the Royal Commission on Bilingualism and Biculturalism that he had called for the previous December. On the revenue issue, there was every indication that the Pearson government intended to broaden its occupation of the field of direct taxation with new levies to create a Canada pension plan.

Quebec had been working on a pension scheme of its own. That detail was constitutionally important because Ottawa's power to legislate in the field left the provinces with the paramount power. Section 94A of the BNA Act declared that "no law made by the Parliament of Canada in relation to old age pensions shall affect the operation of any law present or future of a Provincial Legislature in relation to old age pensions." The wording of the constitution raised two issues because in addition to the obstacle of provincial paramountcy, the federal proposal was more than an old-age pension. The federal scheme proposed other security in the form of "supplementary benefits" to the disabled and to the survivors of deceased contributors to the pension fund. On either point, the federal government faced defeat by any province refusing to co-operate. Ontario had reservations. More spectacularly, the Quebec legislature voted unanimously to reject the federal plan outright as soon as it became public in 1963.

Having cornered the Government of Canada with the prospect of defeat, the government of Quebec then invited the premiers and Pearson to meet in Quebec City to find an opening in the apparent impasse. The conference that followed, from March 31 to April 3, 1964, was extremely effective in creating a united front against Ottawa, as Lesage unveiled the Quebec plan in lavish detail. It was more generous to contributors in benefits and, equally important from the standpoint of the leaders of the provincial governments, the fund that accrued in the Quebec scheme was a pool of capital that the province could tap to finance its own development schemes—just as private insurance companies invested the money held in trust by them for their policy holders. The effect on Ottawa was devastating. According to one member of the Pearson delegation, "the federal government position was destroyed."

In the diplomacy that followed, Quebec agreed to a constitutional amendment that gave the Government of Canada power to make laws in relation to old-age pensions and supplementary benefits, "including survivors' and disability benefits irrespective of age." The reasons for such a significant concession by Quebec were varied. In the first place, the text of the new version of Section 94A left the provinces still paramount since the amendment kept the language that "no such law shall affect the operation of any law present or future of a provincial legislature in relation to any such matter." Thus, Quebec's power to enact its own plan was not jeopardized. And there was more: Quebec won recognition of its abatement formula in the direct taxation field, plus compensation for non-participation in the other shared-cost programs. Of course, the other provinces had the same right of opt-out should they choose to exercise it. But in the 1960s, only Quebec exercised the option. With respect to pensions, Quebec enacted its own; Ottawa implemented the Quebec plan for the other nine in 1965.

Defenders of Pearson's diplomacy called it "cooperative federalism," and argued that the "opt out" arrangement was proof that Quebec's aspirations could be accommodated within Confederation. In Quebec, however, it was argued by Claude Morin (the Deputy Minister of Intergovernmental Affairs), that "In setting up the Quebec Pension Plan . . . Quebec conquered no new constitutional territory, but simply occupied a field of its own that Ottawa had been preparing to mine." Similarly, in the complicated negotiations by which Quebec "won the right to collect 20 additional tax points instead of getting federal subsidies," there was no concession of new power. In Morin's view, "Quebec was simply repossessing some of its own territory," defined clearly in Section 92 of the BNA Act. But since Quebec's repossession was still Ottawa's loss, critics of Pearson who thought he had conceded too much feared that further retreat would jeopardize the ability of the central legislature to respond to complicated issues with national policies in the future. By 1965, the consensus—even within Pearson's Liberal Party—was that too much had been yielded already. In the future, Quebec would have to be content with the economic benefits of equalizing federalism or find satisfaction in symbolic changes. The first involved federal programs to insure economic development in the less wealthy provinces, the group of "have nots" with which Quebec was usually classified. To avoid the stigma of paternalism, such initiatives were usually summed up simply as "paying federalism." In the area of symbolic concessions, there was a new flag, re-uniformed forces (without British symbolism), and more bilingualism in a program that was supposed to enhance the status of French-speaking Canadians outside Quebec.

Just then (1966) Daniel Johnson entered the scene, demanding 100 percent of personal income, corporate profit, and inheritance taxes collected in Quebec. Johnson demanded more than the recovery of what was constitutionally Quebec's existing legal territory. His hope was to establish exclusive authority over powers that were shared, or share the exclusive terrain of Ottawa.

— 4. Separatism —

Johnson was more cautious than Lesage in social and economic policies, but more daring with respect to Quebec's status in Confederation. In September 1966, he suggested that his constitutional objective was to achieve complete mastery of cultural affairs and human development issues. Theoretically, either goal was attainable under the powers enumerated in Section 92 of the BNA Act; but in practice, such autonomy called for near independence or at least a share of power over banking and external relations—both areas under the exclusive jurisdiction of the central government.

The insistence upon the right to enter into agreements with foreign countries (French-speaking states, in particular) emerged in 1967 as the most contentious attempt by Quebec to assert full autonomy. The issue was made all the more complicated because the foreign power courted by Quebec was France, and France under General Charles de Gaulle fully supported Quebec's attempt to establish quasi-sovereign status in the field of foreign affairs. When Johnson invited de Gaulle to visit Quebec to take part in Canada's centennial celebrations in 1967, the invitation was accepted in 1966 without consulting the Government of Canada. There was no question that de Gaulle would be invited (all heads of state with the remotest ties to Canada attended). The problem was that de Gaulle accepted his invitation from Johnson rather than from Pearson. Subsequently, each leader attempted to outmanoeuvre the other in planning the visit and setting de Gaulle's itinerary. Ultimately, Johnson emerged the winner.

De Gaulle crossed the Atlantic on a French warship rather than by airplane, so he arrived at Quebec City instead of Ottawa on July 23, 1967. From the moment the President stepped ashore, the welcome was thunderous with enormous crowds chanting "*de Gaulle*" and "*Vive la*

France." The next day, over the course of de Gaulle's regal progression from Quebec to Montreal, the people lining the roadway were no less enthusiastic. Finally, the welcome reached a crescendo when de Gaulle arrived at Montreal City Hall and began to address the populace from a balcony. The old man began his few words by telling everyone that his welcome by 500 000 persons representing the survival of the French fact in North America moved him nearly as much as the welcome he received from the Parisiens who greeted him in 1944 on their liberation from Nazi occupation. Then came the climactic phrases whose impact was made all the greater by rhetorical pauses and roars of approval at each phrase: "*Vive Montréal! Vive le Québec! Vive le Québec libre*."

Predictably, the government in Ottawa reacted to de Gaulle's utterances with far less enthusiasm than the Quebeckers. Pearson declared in the evening that the "people of Canada are free. Every province is free. Canadians do not need to be liberated." Then the English-language newspapers rallied to the Prime Minister's side, and openly questioned de Gaulle's sanity. De Gaulle for his part remained unruffled and unrepentant. Having cut short his visit at Canada's request, he returned to France to face the criticism of his compatriots for meddling in delicate Canadian issues; but de Gaulle insisted to his dying day that the welcome he received on July 23 and 24 was "a unanimous and indescribable will for emancipation."

The French-language press in Quebec tended to agree that Quebec was not as free as it wished to be, and denied that de Gaulle's affirmation of goodwill to Quebec was sufficient cause for the hysteria that developed in the rest of Canada. Claude Ryan refused to condemn de Gaulle's visit in *Le Devoir*. And the premier was similarly tolerant. A public opinion poll revealed that Ryan and Johnson were in step with the majority of Quebeckers, as well. Almost three quarters thought that the visit had been worthwhile. Only one fifth believed that de Gaulle intended to encourage separatism.

By the autumn of 1967, however, a growing minority of dissident Liberals and UN supporters were beginning to consider the development of a system in which such a debate would be simply irrelevant. The time had come to abandon any further experimentation with federalism. The most prominent such Liberal was René Lévesque. In the middle of September he confronted his riding association in Montreal with the independence option, arguing that a separate Quebec, in special economic association with Canada, presented the best solution to the recent struggle over fiscal means to control social policy and such matters as the silly wrangle over de Gaulle's Quebec *Libre* speech. Fellow Liberals agreed to the extent of sending the matter to the provincial convention later that autumn, where a huge majority adopted special status in Confederation as the preferred option. Lévesque then left the party to found the sovereignty association movement in October 1967.

Soon Lévesque's separatist "option" appeared at greater length in his book, *An Option for Quebec*, and became an instant best-seller in January 1968. Less notorious, but equally important, was the Canadian rejoinder, a White Paper of the Government of Canada called *Federalism for the Future*. Nothing illustrated better the rift that had developed in conceptions of Canada than the two documents side by side, or, for that matter, the federal document alongside the special status option being promoted by the UN and the Quebec Liberals. Lévesque's Canada of the future was an association of sovereign states in economic community—a North American echo of the European Economic community. The special status option called for a Canada of ten to become a Canada of two. Ottawa's image was of a single national entity, with a strong central administration and ten complementary junior governments. "There are central areas of responsibility to the apparatus of a modern sovereign state," the report declared. Enumerating minimum powers for establishing the necessary central focus, the report mentioned control of "economic policy, the equalization of opportunity, technological and cultural development, and international affairs." Although the report admitted that some "central areas of responsibility" could be "shared with the provinces," *Federalism for the Future* asserted that no *provincial* power could be construed as an exclusive right. "We question whether it is any longer realistic to expect that some neat compartmentalization of powers can be found . . . ."

Clearly, no common ground was immediately evident between separatism and centralizing federalism, or between federalism and special status. According to the new federal Minister of Justice, "we rejected any kind of special status for Quebec." The spokesman for the new, harder line in Ottawa, Pierre Trudeau, declared that "federalism can't work unless all the provinces are in basically the same relation towards the central government . . . ." Lévesque agreed, but such federalism-can't-work commentary was his prime rationale for abandoning the "system conceived by the fathers of Confederation." Soon, the new man in Ottawa, along with the new leader of the independence movement in Quebec, would be the principal headline makers in Canada at large. The decade that began as

293

Pearson's and Diefenbaker's thus ended as Trudeau's and Lévesque's, and pointed the way to a period of especially acute confrontation between irreconcilable visions of the future of Canadian federalism.

Suggested Reading

General histories that cover the Pearson years include J.L. Granatstein, *Canada, 1957-1967: Years of Uncertainty and Innovation* (1986), and Robert Bothwell, *et al., Canada since 1945: Power, Politics, and Provincialism* (1981). A dated but interesting treatment of selected political episodes (particularly those that reflect the obsession with the Canadian identity during the period) is Blair Fraser, *The Search for Identity: Canada, 1945-1967* (1967).

For the diplomacy of the Pearson years, the debate on Canadian-American relations and the new economic nationalism is treated—and reflected—in Stephen Clarkson, ed., *An Independent Foreign Policy for Canada?* (1973), Kari Levitt, *Silent Surrender* (1970), William K. Carroll, *Corporate Power and Canadian Capitalism* (1986), and Michael Bliss, *Northern Enterprise* (1986). The other aspect of the diplomacy of the 1960s, the internal relations between Ottawa and the provinces, is covered by Richard Simeon, *Federal Provincial Diplomacy* (1972). The special concerns of Quebec are elaborated by Claude Morin in *Quebec versus Ottawa* (1976), and, of course, in Lévesque's own manifesto, *An Option for Quebec* (1968). For the sake of comparison, readers may wish to consult Christopher Armstrong, *The Politics of Federalism: Ontario's Relations with the Federal Government, 1867-1942* (1981), for the story of an earlier attempt by a strong province to challenge "Empire Canada."

The phenomenon that led Quebec to resist centralism in new ways is the Quiet Revolution. Excellent background to this development is in Pierre Trudeau, "Quebec on the Eve of the Asbestos Strike," in Ramsay Cook, ed., *French Canadian Nationalism* (1967), and Michael D. Behiels, *Prelude to Quebec's Quiet Revolution: Liberalism vs. Neo- Nationalism* (1985). For developments in the Lesage years, see Richard Jones, *Community in Crisis: French Canadian Nationalism in Perspective* (1967) and Edward M. Corbett, *Quebec Confronts Canada* (1967). More analytical and written from a longer historical perspective are Dale Posgate and Kenneth McRoberts, *Quebec: Social Change and Political Crisis* (1976), and William D. Coleman, *The Independence Movement in Quebec, 1945-1980* (1984).

**René Lévesque, election night
rally in Montreal, October, 1973.**

SOURCE: DUNCAN CAMERON COLLECTION/
NATIONAL ARCHIVES OF CANADA/PA-115039

*"The cause of separatism was becoming
more organized in Quebec."*

CHAPTER 15

NEW ERA OF CONFRONTATION, 1968-1976

— 1. New Century, New Leaders —

By 1965, Quebec's Quiet Revolution had reached its peak and Lester Pearson was fast approaching (some said he had already exceeded) the limit of propriety in the autonomy that the federal government could yield to any province seeking to exercise its full powers in Confederation. The new strategy for discouraging the Quebec government's demand for "special status" or the more extreme alternative of "sovereignty association" was to show that everything Quebeckers could reasonably expect was possible under the existing distribution of powers. The strategies of "paying federalism" and enhancing the status of French were supposed to turn around all but the most disgruntled. On one line, Quebeckers would be shown the tangible benefits of "equalization"; on another, they would see a higher profile for French-speaking Canadians—speaking French—in Parliament and the federal cabinet.

The greatest achievement of equalizing, paying federalism in the post-1965 period was the delivery of a guaranteed minimum in national health care, first promised by the Liberals in 1919, promised again by the same party in 1943, but always postponed or delayed either for cost or complexity-of-required-cooperation reasons. A national promise to subsidize hospitalization expenses was made and modified in 1957, but comprehensive medical insurance was still left to the provinces. Saskatchewan, the one province with a CCF government (since 1944), was the lone actor in the field—in 1962. Three others subsidized the premiums of "poor risks" with private companies. The rest left individuals to provide for themselves.

In 1961, Diefenbaker had appointed a Royal Commission on Health Services under Emmett Hall, Chief Justice of Saskatchewan. After an extensive study of the matter, the Hall Commission endorsed the Saskatchewan model in 1964 by proposing to make "all the fruits of the health sciences available to all our residents without hindrance of any kind." One year later, Pearson put the proposal before the premiers. Then, in July 1966, Allan MacEachen, Minister of Health and Welfare, introduced the legislation to Parliament.

In the development of the health insurance initiative, great care was taken to find an approach that was not simply one more monolithic shared-cost program. In the diplomacy of 1965, Pearson declared that the federal government had no intention of designing one specific scheme for each province to join or to ignore. The particulars (whether all doctors would be included, whether recipients would pay premiums or provinces would pay their share out of general revenues, schedules of fees to be paid to doctors, etc.) were to be determined by each province individually. But any provincial plan that conformed to certain broad criteria would be eligible for matching federal funds to a maximum of 50 percent of the cost of the program, estimated at $28 per person for 1967, the date set for the launch of the new initiative in federal-provincial cooperation. The criteria were indeed broad: any publicly-administered, comprehensive scheme, covering all residents for all services wherever they traveled in Canada, could be eligible for the grants.

Pearson and MacEachen hoped that the enabling legislation introduced in 1966 could be passed in time for a July 1 inauguration date the next year. Pearson liked the symbolism of completing the fundamentals of the social security state on the 100th anniversary of Confederation. The target date was missed, however, because Mitchell Sharp, the Minister of Finance, was convinced that medicare would be inflationary in 1967. For fiscal reasons, the inaugural day for the program was postponed 12 months, even though the legislation passed Parliament in December 1966. Thus, the provinces gained an additional year to devise qualifying plans; but even with the additional time, only two—Saskatchewan and British Columbia—had qualifying schemes on July 1, 1968. Five more followed in 1969. Prince Edward Island and Quebec inaugurated their plans in 1970. New Brunswick and the Territories followed in 1971-72.

Given the substance of the change, and the method of implementation, medicare did serve as a positive example of paying federalism in practice. The benefit was real. The federal commitment to pay 50 percent up to the specified maximum was certainly generous. And the criteria of qualification were broad enough to provide great flexibility for provincial tailoring to fit each plan to specific circumstances—or opt out completely if a province preferred to hold out on principle. The only criticisms that could be made against the scheme were either petty or separatist. A petty politician would say that a province had no choice but to act if the others moved. The separatist line would be that if the Government of Canada were out of the field of direct taxation altogether, a province such as Quebec would not need the $14-per-head subsidy. Of course the separatist argument would raise the issue of national identification. To the extent that Quebeckers did not identify with Canada as their national government, they would resent use of any Quebec-generated revenue for non-Quebec purposes. On that account, the symbolic issue became connected with the substantive questions of federal-provincial relations.

The key strategy to enhance Quebeckers' identification with Canada as a government of their own was to recruit high-profile French-Canadians for the government in Ottawa. In 1965, Maurice Lamontagne, perhaps the most prominent Quebecker already in the federal cabinet, agreed to attempt to recruit Jean Marchand, the head of the largest branch of the Quebec labour movement. Marchand accepted the invitation on the condition that it also be extended to two of his friends. One was Gérard Pelletier, a Quebec journalist. Like Marchand, Pelletier's career was deeply involved in the recent history of organized labour in Quebec. In Pelletier's case, revulsion at Duplessis had led to the founding of *Cité Libre*, a quarterly magazine of social criticism in which Pelletier and his fellows offered as much criticism of the reigning Liberals as of local villains.

A frequent contributor to *Cité Libre* was Marchand's second friend, Pierre Trudeau. Unlike Pelletier or Marchand, Trudeau had known the advantages of wealth and position all his life. He was educated at the best schools, well traveled, then—even in his mid-40s—Trudeau was (as Marchand politely put it) "under employed." He wrote a little, lectured in law at the University of Montreal, and still seemed to enjoy travel more than any other activity. In 1965, Trudeau was a wealthy dilettante who had won the respect of Pelletier and Marchand for his role in social criticism. But like the other writers for *Cité Libre*, Trudeau had not limited his scorn to local enemies. In 1963, for example, Trudeau had called Pearson a "Defrocked Priest of Peace" for his position on the nuclear armaments issue. On the more positive side (from the standpoint of Liberals in Ottawa), Trudeau had denounced the racist nationalism of Quebec (even after the Quiet Revolution), embracing federalism as the appropriate counterweight to such irrationalism, as had Pelletier. Such divided identity made both more acceptable to Pearson. It was the tie to Marchand, however, that was most important initially. To get the big fish, the Liberals had to take the lesser fry as well. Ironically, it was Trudeau—not Marchand or Pelletier—who subsequently had the greatest impact on national politics.

After successful election to the safe seats for which the "three wise men" were recruited, all were given important positions in the Government of Canada late in 1965. Trudeau became Minister of Justice early in 1967. Then, while Pearson and MacEachen finished making headlines with medicare, Trudeau's name went into bolder type for his promotion of reforms of Canada's divorce law and the criminal code (broadening the grounds for marriage dissolution, legalizing lotteries, accommodating therapeutic abortions, and sanctioning homosexuality between consenting adults).

In the circumstances of 1967, Canada's Centennial year, such activity merged nicely with commemoration and celebration, the remembering of things passed and celebrating the present, especially at the site of the showplace of Canada's year-long birthday party—Expo '67 in Montreal. Fifty million visitors toured the man-made island in the St. Lawrence River, marveling at the mood of the place and enjoying the good living in Canada's still-largest city, a quality of life that was not then apparent in Edmonton, Toronto, Halifax, St. John's, or other provincial capitals. More than a few of the visitors were Canadians who returned home saying, like one visitor from Toronto, "You have to give them credit. It's not just Expo; they're really living in Montreal. I wish I could find a job there."

Enjoyment of Expo and local Centennial celebrations brought about a momentary adulation of Canada as Canada. The flag nobody knew, the banner some critics dismissed as unfit to grace the label of a beer bottle when it was adopted in great Parliamentary rancour in 1964, suddenly became sentimentally Canada's own in 1967. More than one million of the red maple leaf symbols were sold or given away. They showed up everywhere, especially on the packsacks or jeans of young Canadians trooping across the country and Europe (anxious to distinguish themselves from Americans).

John Diefenbaker (and many others) had never reconciled themselves to the "Pearson Pennant" or the other dizziness of 1967. Increasingly, it became evident to Diefenbaker's party that "the Chief" was a liability as well as an embarrassment. By 1967, the Tories had fallen to 25 percent—behind even the NDP—in the Gallup polls. That was persuasive evidence to nearly everyone but the old leader that a change in direction was needed. A leadership convention followed in September. Still, Diefenbaker refused to resign gracefully, standing for re-election and finishing fifth on the first ballot. Ultimately, Robert Stanfield, the Premier of Nova Scotia, was elected. Diefenbaker congratulated the new leader, asked the delegates to unite behind Stanfield, then left the convention pouting about his party's ingratitude and subsequently ignored his own advice about unity. Diefenbaker's hurt pride notwithstanding, the change of leaders did prove immediately beneficial to the Tories whose popularity moved ahead of both the NDP and the Liberals in just two months. By December, Pearson knew that his time had come, announced his imminent retirement, and called for a leadership convention to take place the following April.

Since the Liberals observed an unofficial tradition of alternating between French-Canadian and non-French-origin leaders, Pearson's successor had to be a Quebecker. Pearson tried to convince Jean Marchand to accept the challenge, but Marchand thought that he lacked the administrative talent and an adequate command of English. Pearson then encouraged the Quebec Liberal who lacked Marchand's political skills but who was perfectly bilingual and had developed a remarkable media persona since his first appearance in Ottawa in 1965. Pierre Trudeau had also achieved a following by proclaiming himself a "new guy with new ideas." Commentators at the time, and historians since, have agreed that if Expo had been a person, that individual was Pierre Trudeau.

Even so, as much as he exemplified invigorated commitment to "new ideas" and unity, Trudeau represented old-style centralism and unprecedented toughness in its enforcement. He made his determination to be tough on "special status" and "separatist" demands plain in a televised federal-provincial conference on the constitution in mid-February 1968. More than for his flamboyance with law reform, Trudeau's stand against

Premier Johnson on the issue of federalism won him instant attention and approval, even in Quebec. Naturally, the Liberals elected him leader.

Three days after becoming Prime Minister, Trudeau plunged the country into a general election. Since it was called so suddenly, he was free to run against the record of his own party as well as his major opponent. And because Stanfield was relatively new to his job, Canada then faced the kind of contest that the Americans confront every four or eight years between two leaders unknown except by personality. In that respect, Stanfield was at a complete disadvantage. He wanted to tour the country making major policy addresses. He loathed the informality of reporters rushing up to politicians, shoving a "bunch of microphones in your face," and expecting profound and intelligent answers to complicated issues in 30-second recordings.

Neither the informality nor the minor bit parts seemed to bother Pierre Trudeau. He would plunge into a crowd on foot, utter a few compelling words about the "Just Society" he hoped to build, and warn that there would be no giveaways. "It is more important to have a sound dollar than to satisfy this or that particular interest," he said. Such boldness was provocation for heckling, of course. Then Trudeau's quick wit would turn criticism to his own advantage. Even sceptics warmed to his style. At the end, without having developed any particular point elaborately, Trudeau would simply dare people to vote for him: "If Canadians want to take a bit of a risk, if they want to take a chance on the future, then we're asking them to vote for us." Wherever he went—even in the West—Canadians seemed to respond positively to his style. Such enthusiasm had not been seen since Diefenbaker's 1958 vision speeches. The press called the new enthusiasm "Trudeau-mania." Richard Gwyn suggests that post-Expo "Canada-mania" sums up the reaction more accurately.

Stanfield complained that the Trudeau style was nothing but theatrics and, forgetting Diefenbaker, asserted that "for the first time in Canadian history a prime minister has asked the people for a blank cheque." Similarly, the leader of the NDP, T.C. Douglas, warned Canadians that beyond the image of the innovator was "the orthodoxy of the 1930s." Both attempted to call the electorate back to specific issues. Stanfield made promises "by the bucketful." He proposed innovations in public housing, agriculture, regional development—even a guaranteed annual income. Striking the same note, Douglas proposed a "Minimum Program for a New Canadian Society" that included schemes to deal with foreign ownership, inequities in tax law and corporate power, as well as social welfare. But in the end, on June 25, 45 percent of the voters gave their nod to Trudeau candidates. For the first time in a decade, Canadians elected a majority government.

— 2. Trudeau in Power —

Even as the 1968 election euphoria was at its height, some observers were predicting that the voters' enthusiasm for their new Prime Minister would be short-lived. Dalton Camp suggested that Trudeau's arousal of enthusiastic support from Canadians with "opposite views and conflicting interests" would lead to trouble as soon as it was discovered that they admired the same leader for contradictory reasons. For the moment, however, Pierre Trudeau said simply that he was the "new guy with new ideas" and everyone waited eagerly to see what he meant.

Trudeau did have intentions to pursue bold policies for promoting bilingualism, advancing French-Canadians in the public service, reducing regional disparities, and adjusting government priorities to reduce defence commitments so that greater resources would be freed for domestic programs. All were areas in which the government subsequently did move. Language legislation and a lavish regional development program were introduced in 1968. A 50-percent phased reduction of the NATO commitment was announced in 1969. Other dramatic initiatives were attempted in Indian affairs, tax reform, and augmented unemployment-insurance benefits. In 1970, the Government of Canada established diplomatic relations with China (the second country in the West to do so, following France). Finally, there was an effort to coordinate the activities of more than 100 provincial marketing boards in order to assure continuing prosperity for farmers whose collective position continued to improve despite falling world prices and transportation problems.

The Trudeau record between 1968 and 1972 was broad ranging. Even so, there was growing disillusionment. Like Diefenbaker, the disappointment in Trudeau was said to have arisen from a fatal flaw of character. Where Diefenbaker was criticized for his "indecision," Trudeau's weakness was called "arrogance." Observers seized upon the alleged characteristic because many thought that it described not only his own personality but also the leading quality of the administration he molded in Ottawa. Trudeau's personal staff was the largest ever—a "Supergroup," according to Walter Stewart, that seemed to matter more than the cabinet itself. Parliamentary power was said to have all but vanished, and the federal bureaucracy grew three times faster than the rate of population increase. Under Trudeau, the technocrats appeared to have taken charge completely. The alleged "arrogance" wa thus more than a personality foible of its leading personage; the criticism applied as well to the overbearing aloofness of an entire administration.

The mood of the civil service mandarins following the 1968 election was that the real work of making a Canadian nation was only then beginning. The Official Languages Act was perhaps the first indication that Trudeau thought himself a pioneer, like Sir John A. Macdonald, attempting to fashion a continent-wide country out of a geographically-fragmented federation. In the case of Macdonald's CPR, however, there was general agreement that the railway was needed, sooner or later. The consensus was less clear on Trudeau's proposed measure to break down cultural fragmentation by assuring more meaningful equality to the French and English languages in Canada. Introduced in October 1968, passed in July 1969, the Official Languages Act extended the minimal guarantees already in the BNA Act and asserted that Canada was one nation with two languages, rather than a country in two linguistic solitudes. A Gallup poll showed that Canadians as a whole supported the new language law in principle. But in the regional distribution of opinion, 70 percent of the West did not favour even the *idea* of two official languages. With one region so solidly opposed, it was suggested that the policy would promote division more than unity. Trudeau's reply was that he was providing insurance against separatism.

The cause of separatism was becoming more organized in Quebec. Lévesque's sovereignty association movement, formed in October 1967, had become a political party, the Parti québécois, just as Members of Parliament began to debate the Official Languages Act in 1968. The original *péquiste* support amounted to about ten percent but had grown to 23 percent by the time of the next provincial election in April 1970. Then, their one-quarter share of the vote translated into a mere seven percent of the seats. If some *péquistes* wondered whether their votes were always going to be wasted ballots, there were more radical *indépendantistes* to whom they might turn. The Front de Libération du Québec (FLQ), a radical group interested in independence before social revolution, was willing to take direct action regardless of elections. In recent years they had been bombing mailboxes. In 1970, their targets were human. On October 5, two men took the British Trade Commissioner, James Cross, from his Montreal home at gunpoint. On the way to their car idling at the curb, one of the kidnappers turned to a passer-by and announced, "We're the FLQ."

At first, the Cross kidnapping was treated as just another local police matter, but the ransom demanded was extraordinary. Among other things, the kidnappers wanted the release of 23 "political prisoners" (comrades convicted of spectacular deeds such as mailbox vandalism), $500 000 in gold, and safe conduct and transportation to Cuba or Algeria. When the government appeared unwilling to meet any of their demands, rather than kill Cross, another FLQ "cell" seized a second dignitary, the Quebec Minister of Labour, Pierre Laporte, on October 10. Local government then became frantic lest more kidnappings follow. Premier Bourassa moved into a guarded suite in downtown Montreal. Troops were posted outside the homes of federal cabinet ministers in Ottawa, and Prime Minister Trudeau began to talk about doing whatever was necessary to preserve public order.

"How far would you be willing to go?" a reporter asked on October 12. "Just watch me," Trudeau replied.

On October 16, the Government of Canada invoked the War Measures Act to give the police special powers to undertake "ceaseless pursuit" of the FLQ. Two days later, Laporte was strangled by his captors and Cross continued to be held by persons unknown. Eventually, the location of Cross and the murderers of Laporte were both uncovered by routine police work. The question arises: what had the government accomplished by declaring martial law?

Historians supporting the action, such as Robert Bothwell, claim that the jailing of everyone remotely sympathetic to the FLQ "made plain that those who played at parlour revolution faced real and immediate sanctions." Consequently, the "enthusiasm for a day at the barricades . . . noticeably diminished." Moreover, bold action was vindicated in the court of public opinion since 87 percent of the population—including that of Quebec—approved the government's course. On the other side, critics of the action assert that the use of a cannon to swat a fly did irreparable harm to the cause of civil liberties in Canada. They suggest that most of the 500 persons detained without charge did not have the remotest connection with terrorism. Not one instance of overlapping membership between the FLQ and the PQ was uncovered, even though most of those arrested were *péquistes*. The suspicion, then and later, was that there were in fact two targets in the round-up: the FLQ (for the reasons stated by the government), and the PQ (for general intimidation value admitted only in private). The public face of government was that the PQ had every right to pursue its separatist objective by democratic means, but the facts of the police action support the conclusion that no distinction was drawn between separatism and terrorism in law enforcement or surveillance.

Before and after the October crisis, the cabinet approved extraordinary measures to fight separatism. Under John Starnes, its Director-General of Security and Intelligence, the RCMP prepared a special memorandum in 1970 on groups "likely to promote violent confrontation with authority." At the head of the list was the Parti québécois. Despite the inclusion of the PQ on the Starnes subversives list, Trudeau praised the review as a "damn fine piece of work," gave the RCMP a long leash, and did not prevent the force from indulging in Gestapo-like activities to disrupt separatism. Here as well, the arrogance was not simply Trudeau's, but the smug assumption of the bureaucracy that the state they supported was so superior to any that might emerge from unfettered democracy that they were justified in defamation of character, invasion of privacy, or criminal acts (including theft and arson) if such tactics discouraged separatism.

So all-pervading was the arrogance of the Ottawa mandarins that even potentially useful programs of equalization and economic development became subtle—and not so subtle—devices for expanding federal power in areas hitherto exclusively reserved to the provinces. Thus "education" became "training"; "municipal affairs" became "problems of urban growth"; and "community development" emerged in the guise of the "fight against unemployment." Rather than follow the more cooperative approach pioneered by Pearson, the Department of Regional Economic Expansion (DREE) engaged in flag-raising contests with the provinces as it pursued projects of its own design for local impact.

By 1972, most of the electorate had decided that the "new guy with new ideas" was not offering a fresh approach to old problems so much as a new push of centralism upon a country that was not prepared to accept an expanded central power. Trudeau attempted to counter the criticism by telling Maritimers how much DREE was doing to correct their economic backwardness, Quebeckers that their status had been enhanced by their growing influence in Ottawa; and by warning the West and Ontario that Canada needed a strong leader to keep separatism under control.

Sixty-two percent of the voters were unconvinced that Trudeau was the right leader to continue in power. A significant number of voters shifted from the Liberals to the NDP, and the result was a Parliament of minorities: NDP 31, Liberals 109, and Conservatives 107. David Lewis (the successor to T.C. Douglas) was thus in roughly the same position in

1972 as J.S. Woodsworth in 1926, and Pierre Trudeau responded to Lewis in approximately the same way as King had dealt with Woodsworth. For 18 months, Trudeau was as progressive as he had claimed to be, more innovative than he had managed to be with his own majority.

The record of Trudeau's minority government was truly impressive. Acting finally on the Watkins Report on foreign ownership (submitted in 1968), a Foreign Investment Review Agency (FIRA) was created to monitor the growth of non-resident ownership of Canadian business. There were tax reforms including the indexing of income-tax rates to the rate of inflation; improvements in pension and family-allowance benefits; and the century-old Elections Act was reformed to require disclosure of the sources of large campaign contributions. A number of conferences and inquiries (such as the Western Economic Opportunities Conference and the Berger inquiry into the social and environmental impact of a petroleum pipeline down the Mackenzie Valley) showed a more consultative approach to development issues. And most importantly, a bold policy to cope with a sudden and unexpected rise in the price of oil was announced at the end of 1973.

A few months before the oil crisis, the energy minister, Donald Macdonald, forecast a price of five dollars per barrel for the year 2000. Then on October 6, war broke out in the Middle East, and unified Arab exporters in an embargo of shipments to supporters of Israel. Their action led to the first successful escalation of prices by the 13-year-old cartel, the Organization of Petroleum Exporting Countries (OPEC), and the oil that sold for three dollars per barrel before the war reached ten dollars by year's end.

The acute shortage and the dramatic rise in price caused Prime Minister Trudeau to announce a complex program for meeting the emergency before the onset of winter. The five eastern provinces dependent on imported oil were to receive a subsidy on imports derived from a tax on oil and gas still to be exported from the producing provinces in western Canada to the United States. In this way, a controlled single price was assured. To make the East less dependent on imports, pipelines were to be extended as quickly as possible; and to cope with the increased demands on domestic production, the government announced a new program of incentives to encourage exploration and development of hitherto unexploited deposits of heavy oil and tar sands. One of the vehicles for the new production was to be a national petroleum corporation—Petro Canada.

Largely due to the program announced in December, Canadians weathered the winter of 1973-74 oil shortages without the wild rise in prices that continued elsewhere. But an inflation scare soon replaced the oil concern. Robert Stanfield's Conservatives demanded wage-and-price controls. Trudeau refused. Instead, his finance minister introduced a budget loaded with tax concessions to corporations—bound to be intolerable to the NDP. In effect, the Liberals engineered defeat in the House of Commons at a time of their own choosing, and went to the people heaping abuse on Stanfield's proposed incomes policy. The Prime Minister called controls a "proven disaster looking for a new place to happen," and suggested that since Canada imported one third of what the country consumed, controlling prices was absurd. "The only thing controls will control with be your wages," he told the working people of Canada. With such effective condemnation of the Tories, and having shown, in Richard Gwyn's judgement, that he could be "the best Prime Minister around . . . when he wanted to be," the electorate restored Trudeau's majority on July 8, 1974. But having gone after controls "like a terrier after a rat," he left little room to maneuvre subsequently. By 1975, most Canadians wanted an incomes policy. By 1975, according to a Gallup poll, the leading difficulty was excessive wage demands extorted by overpowerful unions.

— 3. Organized Labour and the Economic Malaise —

"Big labour" had come relatively late to Canada, long after big business and big government. At the outbreak of the Second World War, the percentage of the non-agricultural workforce in unions was about the same as in 1914. But in the context of full employment for war production (and wartime wage controls), labour organizers made enormous gains. In 1943 and 1944, several provincial governments adopted labour laws that protected workers in their organizational drives and also required employers to negotiate with unions certified as the chosen agent of a majority of the employees. The Government of Canada followed in 1944 with a wartime regulation of its own that universalized such rights. Under the protection of an Order in Council (PC 1003), first agreements were negotiated by workers in hundreds of companies that had resisted unionization for decades. Such recognition did not usually take the form of the "closed shop"—employees were not required to join a union as a condition of employment. But to give labour organizations some measure of security once certified, Ontario endorsed a device known as the Rand Formula (after its author, Justice Ivan Rand), by which employees could join or refuse to join, but non-joiners would find the equivalent of union dues deducted from their wages. After the war, the Government of Canada grafted its wartime labour policies onto the old Industrial Disputes Investigation Act, renaming the amended law the Industrial Relations and Disputes Investigation Act. Since the IRDI Act was a regular statute (rather than a wartime order, such as PC 1003), its provisions applied only to workers under federal jurisdiction. Subsequently, however, the provinces that did not already have labour relations acts did adopt such laws, usually patterned after the IRDI Act. The result was that the wartime gains were not lost in the postwar period.

By the 1950s, organized labour had grown to nearly one million persons and included most of the workforce in major manufacturing, mining, and forest products. But small industry was still largely unorganized, and even those workers who were in unions were not part of a unified movement. One division was regional, since the unionized labour of Quebec tended to be organized in unions of the Canadian and Catholic Confederation of Labour (CCCL), separate from the rest of Canada and systematically intimidated by the government of Maurice Duplessis. Elsewhere, the situation was similarly weakened by division but of a different sort. The largest group of organized labour in English-speaking Canada consisted of 522 000 workers affiliated with the Trades and Labour Congress of Canada (TLC). Like the American Federation of Labor (AFL), TLC unions tended to be craft-oriented and limited their objectives to narrow wages and hours issues. Like the profit-maximizers who owned the means of production, their goal was simply "more and more."

A competing group sought industrial organization to promote broader issues of social change and consciously repudiated the "business unionism" of the conservative TLC. The Canadian Congress of Labour (CCL), like the Congress of Industrial Organizations (CIO) in the United States, was a breakaway group promoting more massive organization and broader political aims. But from its appearance in 1939, the Canadian Congress of Labour was as divided within its own ranks as from the TLC. In the 1940s, approximately one third of CCL leaders called themselves communists, the others supported the CCF. By 1950 (due to government repression and opposition from the rank and file), the once significant communist presence in the CCL had all but disappeared. In the same period, the CIO in the United States moved even further towards the right and converted to business unionism. When merger inevitably followed with the AFL in 1955, the CCL in Canada almost immediately united with the TLC, emerging as the Canadian Labour Congress (CLC).

The reason that the divisions and alliances between the AFL-CIO and TLC-CCL were parallel is that nearly 70 percent of the organized workers in English-speaking Canada were members of "international" (meaning *American*) unions. In this sense, the CLC was largely a northern echo of the AFL-CIO. But the Canadian group did harbour a stronger commitment to "political unionism," a fact that was particularly evident in 1961, when the New Democratic Party emerged from a convention of 710 delegates from the CCF, 613 delegates from unions, and 318 representatives of "New Party Clubs." Since the leaders of the CLC claimed to speak for all working people of Canada, there were great expectations that a Canadian Labour Party might be emerging. But less than one third of the non-agricultural workforce was unionized in 1961, and three quarters of the union members continued to vote for the Liberals or Conservatives.

Nothing developed between 1961 and 1974 to suggest that workers were finding a keener interest in political unionism, but there was a dramatic surge in the number of persons unionized after 1965. The year before, the Government of Quebec unveiled a new labour code that conceded collective bargaining rights to all public service employees except firefighters and police officers. Prior to Quebec's move to permit meaningful organization of civil servants, only Saskatchewan had given civil servants collective bargaining rights (in 1944 after the election of the CCF). In the Quebec code of 1964, there was a catch, however, in that a clause prevented any public employee from joining a union that endorsed a political party. Thus, the CLC was effectively barred from organizing the public service of Quebec because it still endorsed the NDP. The old confessional unions, secularized and renamed the Confederation of National Trade Unions (CNTU), thus had privileged access to the growth sector of the labour movement in French Canada. After the Government of Canada and the other provinces granted similar rights to their civil servants (the federal government leading the way in 1967), the CLC was also to take advantage of the boom in public service organization. By 1970, the public service unions emerged as rivals to all but the largest internationals and the portion of the non-agricultural work force that was unionized grew to 40 percent of the total.

By the 1970s, organized labour in Canada had thus reached its own centennial and could point with pride to many accomplishments—especially in the period since 1940. From a minority movement of less than ten percent of the work force, organized labour appeared to be edging towards majority status, with a membership of 2.2 million persons contributing $100 million in dues in 1970. Wages had quadrupled since the Second

World War, and workers' purchasing power had doubled. But organized labour was almost as divided as ever, with leaders of the CLC continuing to enter political debates as if they spoke for all when in fact they could barely unite conventions of 1 000 committed delegates. More importantly, most workers (organized or not) had begun to think that strikes were becoming too common and wages (except their own) were too high.

In 1974 and 1975, time lost in strikes, average wage settlements, and the rate of inflation reached unprecedented levels. Many commentators determined that the fault lay with the demands of organized labour, a conclusion that was seized upon in the summer of 1975 when the inside postal workers struck and won a 71-percent wage increase for a new 30-hour week. But overall, Canadian wage settlements were considerably behind those of West Germany and Japan, the two countries that were frequently mentioned as models of restraint in wage demands.

The more basic problem in Canada was the systematic relation between business' demands for high profits, workers' desire to keep up with rising prices, and the cost of government programs to support workers who were laid off as business exercised its only effective defence against profit squeezing—unemployment. In the years between 1971 and 1974, profits of the largest corporations increased rapidly, while wages, salaries, and the incomes of smaller businesses did not grow at nearly the same pace. When workers raced to catch up in 1974 and 1975, two record years of strikes resulted, and negotiated wage settlements averaged 17 percent. Facing recessionary prospects, large corporations imposed massive layoffs. Government programs automatically injected enormous amounts of public spending into the economy in the form of such payments as unemployment benefits. Public-sector deficits inevitably reached record levels in their turn. The result was stagnation with high inflation— "stagflation" in the jargon of the panic of 1975.

In the face of 14-percent inflation, rising unemployment, and a fiscal situation that seemed out of control, the government was forced to act. The Conservative opposition said that if their controls program had been implemented as they had demanded in 1974, no such crisis would be developing. The Minister of Finance, John Turner, still refused to implement mandatory controls. He appealed for voluntary restraint but as voluntarism was failing, Turner realized that the government's options were narrowing and requested a different cabinet portfolio. When Trudeau refused to consider Turner's release from his politically disastrous post, Turner resigned from politics altogether. After a cabinet shuffle that put the former energy minister, Donald Macdonald, in the position of Minister of Finance, a crash program of compulsory wage-and-price controls was designed for implementation in October.

On Thanksgiving Day, October 13, 1975, Prime Minister Trudeau appeared on television to announce that the country had to swallow "strong medicine." He announced that any private company with more than 500 employees, and every public service worker in the federal civil service would be subject to three years of wage-and-price controls effective immediately. The limit for the first year was ten percent, eight percent in year two, and six percent in the final 12 months of the program. All provinces agreed to cooperate with imposition of the same levels on provincial civil services—even Saskatchewan and Manitoba (their NDP premiers explaining that an "incomes policy" was a necessary feature of any truly planned economy). Equally interesting, a Gallup poll showed that 62 percent of the general population endorsed controls at the time of their inauguration; this endorsement did not recede dramatically in most provinces over the next 12 months. Business leaders also favoured at least the wage controls aspect of the scheme. But they did grow increasingly nervous about the economic planning that Premiers Blakeney and Shreyer had advocated, especially as Prime Minister Trudeau seemed determined to embark in the same direction.

At the end of 1975, Trudeau suggested that the controls program was no long-term solution to Canada's economic malaise, only a short breathing space. Looking to the post-controls period, he warned that if Canadians did not "change [their] social structure and values . . . then the same economic mainsprings will create inflation and unemployment all over again." Trudeau said that controls were only the beginning of a much vaster, overdue intervention by the government in the economy. The Prime Minister knew that the country faced real panic. He knew that his policy had been accepted despite the obligatory grumbling from the leaders of the unions. He also seemed to sense that basic structural changes in the Canadian economy might have been accepted during the inflation crisis, just as basic changes had been implemented at the time of the energy panic in 1973. But during the earlier emergency, he faced the daily possibility of defeat in the House of Commons. In 1975 his majority was restored. As was his custom in the comfort of power, Trudeau dithered and wandered in abstractions rather than taking effective action. In the end, the rhetoric of basic change proved to be nothing more than prime ministerial mutterings aloud.

The kinds of reforms that Trudeau had the opportunity to launch early in 1976 (but ultimately avoided) pertained to the fundamental underdevelopment of the Canadian economy. Two thirds of the country's exports continued to be resource products shipped out of the country in a raw or semi-finished form, while the value of manufactured goods imported exceeded those exported by about $10 billion. What was needed was an ambitious program to encourage import-replacing manufacturing to provide high productivity jobs for Canadians making, for example, the $6 billion worth of equipment imported for mining and agriculture. The time was right, in other words, for the government to implement an ambitious "industrial strategy." Instead, Trudeau and his ministers offered homilies about the need to change "attitudes" and hoped that a world recovery might promote another boom in Canada's raw materials in the near future. In the meantime, the government counted on the many divisions within organized labour and more generally within the Canadian working class to keep opposition to a minimum. But workers became less willing to forego increases once it became apparent that the main purpose of wage-and-price controls was to make them worried about their jobs, less prone to strike, and, therefore, tolerant of wage increases below the rate of inflation. The first such workers to mount an effective opposition on this account were those of Quebec, with the apparent triumph of separatism on November 15, 1976.

— 4. Rise of the Parti Québécois —

At its founding convention in the middle of October 1968, the Parti québécois promised a unilateral declaration of independence from Canada as soon as it attained majority status in the provincial assembly. Its first business would be the negotiation of a common market with the provinces left behind, then sweeping changes in the new nation. The proposed domestic reforms included establishment of French as the official language of the province, and regulations to control the export of profits by foreigners. As a palliative to the English-speaking minority, there was a promise to continue English-language schools, thus repeating the experiment in dualism first launched by Canada in 1867 but on a smaller scale and with the English rather than the French in the subordinate, at least minority, position.

Of course, the new party was not immediately popular. It has already been shown that the PQ's initial support of one in ten of the voters increased to merely one in four by the time of its first big electoral contest in April 1970. In the meantime, the two larger parties had adjusted their

313

images to distinguish themselves from one another as much as from the PQ. The Liberals backed away from anything resembling separatism or the special status option still sought by the UN. The Liberal alternative emphasized economic development to the near exclusion of any consideration of constitutional issues. On that stance, they received 42 percent of the vote and 72 of the 108 seats in the provincial legislature.

Lévesque had hoped that the UN would be more uniformly popular. But in the 1970 election, there were only pockets of UN support. The main show emerged as a contest between Liberals and *péquistes* with the PQ running as a significant, but distant, minority movement in almost every riding. They lost nearly every riding. Lévesque himself failed in the riding in which he had run successfully before as a Liberal. To some separatists, the irony of winning fewer seats than the UN, having polled more votes than the official opposition (23 *versus* 20 percent), was simply infuriating. They began to lose interest in the movement or became more radical in their outlook. It is doubtful if *péquistes* moved in any significant number to the FLQ; Lévesque called the radical *indépendantistes* "sewer rats" (and the feeling was probably mutual). His strategy after defeat was to emphasize the social reform intentions of the PQ over its separatist aspirations. As a result, the party developed as a Quebec social democratic movement, with separatism somewhat incidental to its larger program after 1970.

In the next provincial election, that of 1973, voters polarized more than in 1970—without the PQ having gained enough strength to offer a significant challenge to the Liberals. The PQ did increase in popularity to about 30 percent, but since the increase was so uniformly distributed and since the UN showing was even weaker than in 1970, the *péquistes* actually lost strength in the legislature. In 1973, 30 percent of the votes elected only six members. In the new National Assembly, the Liberals occupied nearly every seat.

Once again, Lévesque responded by downplaying the separatist aspect of his party. Independence—the PQ's ostensible reason for being—was shelved by a device that Wilfrid Laurier and Mackenzie King would have recognized as their own style of accommodation and evasion. Assisted by Claude Morin, the two leaders persuaded the party faithful that any newly-elected PQ government would hold a referendum on the question before establishing independence; it was the ideal way to disassociate the party from the separatist issue without seeming hypocritical or flaccid. What remained was the party's still strong advocacy of social democracy, likely to appeal to the increasingly militant Quebec labour movement. And working-class support was widely regarded as the PQ's essential ticket for crossing the magical 40 percent threshold of popularity to get a majority of seats in the National Assembly. To be sure, after election, there would have to be a referendum on separatism, but not necessarily independence.

In the meantime, the reigning Liberals moved from one crisis to another, exhibiting opportunism more than competence. In Quebec, as in the rest of the country, the most difficult problems were economic. Bourassa's Liberals appeared particularly inept in dealing with the most militant unions and in controlling expenditures for worthwhile projects such as a gigantic hydroelectric development on James Bay (see map 15.1), or frivolous but expensive undertakings such as the installations for the billion-dollar Olympic Games held in Montreal in 1976. Then, too, there was anger over language legislation that English-speaking Quebeckers regarded as discriminatory, Trudeau called "politically stupid," and the *péquistes* dismissed as too little too late. Additional disasters were a nine-day strike over the exclusive use of English between pilots and air traffic controllers in Quebec, and growing resentment over Ottawa's incomes policy. Everything was set for a strong protest vote once Bourassa called an election for late-autumn 1976.

Given the problems of the moment, and the PQ's almost complete disassociation from separatism, the PQ looked especially attractive to middle- and lower-class French-speaking Quebeckers. Lévesque's party promised to reform labour law, elaborate existing social programs, and stand against Ottawa. A slightly reinvigorated Union nationale, and a significantly less popular Liberal Party meant that the electoral system finally worked as Lévesque had hoped. On November 15, its evenly distributed 41 percent of the vote gave the Parti québécois almost three quarters of the seats in the legislature.

The rest of Canada was stunned by the victory that was the proudest day in Lévesque's life. Nearly everyone but Trudeau seemed to be thrown into a momentary panic. The Prime Minister went on television to congratulate the PQ on their spectacular success and promised the same cooperation with Lévesque's government as Canada extended to any other province, while stressing that the country did face a grave crisis. Trudeau seemed to have every confidence that appropriate constitutional reforms would demonstrate that it was "possible to be at one and the same time, a good Canadian and a good Quebecker." Should the process fail, however, Trudeau stressed that no military or police action would be used to keep Quebec within Canada. "Canada cannot, Canada must not, survive by force," he declared. The bond that would hold the country together had to

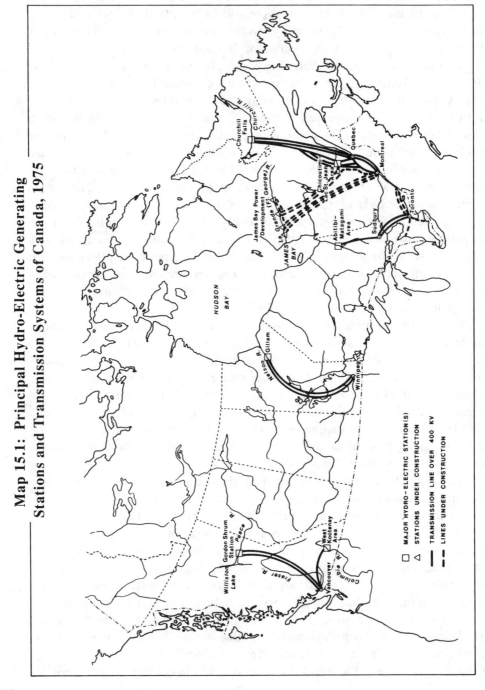

Map 15.1: Principal Hydro-Electric Generating Stations and Transmission Systems of Canada, 1975

be that of "fraternity, of hope and of charity in the scriptural sense, for if the Canadian nation is to survive, it will only survive in mutual respect and in love for one another."

Trudeau's message of November 24 seemed to close an era of confrontation with conciliation. More than a decade earlier, in January 1965, Daniel Johnson had said that if a government in Quebec were "to lay the ground for independence," the rest of the country would come round quickly "to grant equality for the French-Canadian nation in a truly bi-national Canada." In the spring of 1977, something of a spirit of accommodation seemed to develop as Canadians affirmed faith in their country from coast to coast. Even Lévesque began to talk about building "a true Confederation" instead of simply abandoning the old one. It appeared that Canada might yet resolve its constitutional difficulties, and then, having achieved a new accommodation in that area, make headway on the more serious economic problems.

Suggested Reading

The most comprehensive general history of the Trudeau-Lévesque period from 1968 through 1976 is Robert Bothwell, *et al., Canada since 1945: Power, Politics, and Provincialism* (1981). Unfortunately, Bothwell's work tends merely to chronicle events or to defend Trudeau's actions rather than to attempt a balanced critique. Much more satisfactory as an analysis of Trudeau in power is Richard Gwyn, *The Northern Magus: Pierre Trudeau and Canadians* (1980). Other provocative biographical accounts are Geoffrey Stevens, *Robert Stanfield* (1973), which offers an excellent account of Trudeau's language policy, and Walter Stewart, *Shrug: Trudeau in Power* (1971), too harshly critical in most respects but still useful in its analysis of the parliamentary and administrative changes that tended to concentrate power in the Prime Minister's Office.

The important development that Trudeau's meteoric rise obscured and upstaged was the advent of medicare between 1965 and 1968, described fully by Malcom G. Taylor, *Health Insurance and Canadian Public Policy: The Seven Decisions that Created the Canadian Health Insurance System* (1978), and C. David Naylor, *Private Practice, Public Payment: Canadian Medicine and the Politics of Health Insurance, 1911-1966* (1986).

The event that generated the greatest notoriety for Trudeau once in power was the October crisis, criticized from the standpoint of a civil libertarian, Denis Smith, in *Bleeding Hearts . . . Bleeding Country: Canada and the Quebec Crisis* (1971), and described from the inside by Gérard Pelletier in *The October Crisis* (1971).

The event that was most notable in Trudeau's second majority, wage-and-price controls, is unintelligible without background in labour history and labour economics. The background is provided by Desmond Morton and Terry Copp in *Working People: An Illustrated History of Canadian Labour (1980),* and Irving Abella, *Nationalism, Communism, and Canadian Labour* (1973). The book to read for labour economics is Cy Gonick, *Out of Work: Why There's So Much Unemployment and Why It's Getting Worse* (1978).

For understanding the capstone of the first Trudeau period, the development of separatism in Quebec, an autobiographical account by Lévesque himself and a chronicle of events by John Saywell are both useful. Lévesque's autobiography is entitled *Memoirs/René Lévesque* (1986). Saywell's narrative is *The Rise of the Parti Québécois* (1977).

**Pierre Trudeau (left) and Jean Chrétien (right)
during Constitutional Conference, Ottawa, 1981.**

SOURCE: ROBERT COOPER/NATIONAL ARCHIVES OF CANADA/PA-141504

*"Nine of the ten provinces . . . did
find acceptable wording for an
amending formula . . . ."*

CHAPTER 16
CONSTITUTIONAL DRAW,
1976-1982

— 1. Decline and Fall of the Liberal Party —

The election of the Parti québécois in November 1976 had a tonic effect on Prime Minister Trudeau's popularity. A majority of the country took his November 24 address promising constitutional reform seriously, and many thousands of Canadians appeared willing to accept bold innovation to hold the country together. The government did appoint a Task Force on Canadian Unity (headed by Jean Luc Pépin, former administrator of wage-and-price controls, and John Robarts, former Premier of Ontario). The Pépin-Robarts Commission toured the country gathering constitutional wisdom and there was no shortage of submissions to its proceedings. But to Trudeau's displeasure, most followed from the supposition that Canada was a federation of two—or more—national entities, rather than one people who happened to speak two languages. Trudeau warned against a hasty rush to the "panacea of decentralization." Curiously, however, his own proposals were not forthcoming, and did not appear until nearly two years after the election of the PQ.

In June 1978, Trudeau's package was anti-climatic to say the least. Despite the ironic title (*A Time for Action*) the opportunity to act was already lost. Moreover, the document offered far too little. The national acceptance of the need for constitutional reform had peaked the year before, between April and September. Had *A Time for Action* offered more, its tardy appearance might not have mattered except for the difficulty of getting the package through. But instead of presenting an imaginative approach to restructuring the Canadian federation, Trudeau's document, according to Robert Bothwell, was "a badly written and worse-conceived potpouri of Senate reform and Supreme Court fiddlings." Literally too little too late, the federal position "fell with a dull thud before an astonished and somewhat bemused populace."

By the early summer of 1978, the main preoccupation of Canadians was no longer unity, but the state of the economy. The dollar had begun a day-by-day slide, from parity with American currency at the first of the year, to 86 cents by May. Unemployment had risen to 8.6 percent. Inflation was still ten percent, and the federal budget deficit was approaching the record level of $12 billion (the equivalent of one quarter of Ottawa's total revenue, or five percent of the entire GNP). Many economists (and almost all Tories) claimed that the apparently uncontrolled spending was the leading factor in the entire malaise because it eroded business confidence and discouraged investment, which in turn led to unemployment.

After attending an economic conference with other government heads in July (and receiving public opinion data that showed an increasing number of voters were blaming expensive government for their woes), Trudeau and his advisors decided that the deficit was the top priority and aimed to trim it in the summer of 1978 in preparation for an election.

The problem of the federal deficit was too complicated, however, for the government to simply—and suddenly—decide to spend a great deal less. Some payments were fixed and uncontrollable except by the dismantling of existing programs such as unemployment insurance, pension benefits, or the oil-price subsidy for the eastern provinces. All expenditures associated with ongoing programs were determined by statute, and the amounts payable varied by the number of eligible applicants rather than by budget decisions. There was no way for the government to reduce expenditures on such fixed costs, except by changing the law establishing regional equality in oil prices, or lowering pension benefits, or turning its back on the unemployed. The only area in which the federal government could cut expenditures and hurt only itself, in a sense, was the $12.6 billion spent on maintaining the federal bureaucracy. Since Trudeau and his advisors were not about to reduce the Government of Canada to a cipher, and since they were equally loathe to reduce subsidies and grants that pinched individual taxpayers (also voters), the bold program announced in mid-August to "ensure our continued prosperity," in the end, was largely cosmetic, trimming no more than one fifth of the anticipated deficit.

More significant was the adoption of a new fiscal remedy advocated by an American economist, Milton Friedman. In Friedman's approach, the trend-setting central bank of a country was to increase its interest rates to unprecedented levels in the expectation that tighter credit would offset the inflationary impact of larger government deficits, thus reducing the rate of inflation generally. Higher returns to lenders would bring in a rush of foreign investment, thus increasing the value of the currency of the country with the highest interest rates. With falling inflation and a rising dollar, general investor confidence was also supposed to grow, ultimately affecting unemployment as general investment levels increased. The new orthodoxy (called *monetarism*) caused some excitement because it seemed to go beyond old-fashioned Keynesian economics. Moreover, advocates of monetarism claimed to be capable of achieving greater control by the vastly simpler manipulation of interest rates. To be sure, the potential for international "beggar thy neighbour" and internal suffering caused by increased bankruptcy and unemployment was much greater than the damage that might have followed from the 30-percent tax increase necessary to cover the deficit (or the suffering that would follow from cancelled subsidies and grants that would enable government the better to live within existing revenues). But in the summer of 1978, monetarism and neoconservative rhetoric about balancing the budget, "deregulation," and returning certain functions of government to the private sector seemed more politically opportune than tax increases or intervention to restructure Canada's truncated industrial sector.

Unfortunately for Trudeau, his modest budget cuts and rising interest rates were denounced by the left as "fighting inflation on the backs of the poor," and from the right as trivial "tinkering" that left the budget and the civil service still "out of control."

A series of by-elections in the autumn of 1978 underscored the depth of Canadians' dissatisfaction, and foretold defeat for the Liberals in a general election that would have to occur in the summer of 1979 at the latest. Trudeau responded by attempting to divert attention from economic problems to the unity issue—by suggesting that the country needed a Prime Minister who was a strong leader and not afraid to stand up to the premiers. "Who shall speak for Canada?" he asked late in 1978. He warned that the business cycle would rise and fall, but if the central government did not look to the long term and insist upon the welfare of the country as a constitutional entity, "we'll have a piece of geography with ten . . . semi-sovereign states, and a federal government that can't do anything."

The leaders of the opposition parties (Joe Clark of the Conservatives and Ed Broadbent of the NDP) answered that the unity problem was largely of Trudeau's own making. Both agreed that Trudeau seemed to prefer confrontation to negotiation, and Joe Clark asserted that Trudeau's concept of Canada was unrealistic. Clark suggested that the federal government had to recognize that the Canadian state was "a community of communities." Insistence upon centralism would only lead to further trouble. He called for greater flexibility to put a "fresh face on federalism."

Dismissing Clark as a "puppet of the Premiers," Trudeau called the election for May 22. Then, shoulders back, head held high, he strode directly into disaster, asserting, like a warrior in single-champion combat, that the issue was leadership. But the opposition parties—and most of the electorate—placed economic concerns at the forefront. The NDP went after "cut backs" and made its alliance with the Canadian Labour Congress more explicit than ever in the hope of rallying workers in the industrial heartland of Ontario. The Conservatives, aiming to rally the middle class, promised a balanced budget and interest-rate relief to homebuyers.

The Liberal Party was defeated, of course; but the curious aspect of the election of 1979 is that the Liberals went down to defeat even though they won more seats than in 1972 (114 to 109), and they won four percentage points more of the votes than did the Conservatives. But in 1979, the NDP fared less well against the Tories, who did especially well in the West, where the Liberals were defeated almost totally. Trudeau's inability to win seats in the West was especially disastrous because the region had undergone a quiet revolution of its own in the 1970s, a progression of changes that the Government of Canada at first ignored and then opposed. In this way, the already complex constitutional problems with Quebec were further complicated by the dissatisfaction of another region that was more important than Quebec by the number-of-seats-in-Parliament criterion. In 1979, Quebec returned 75 representatives to the House of Commons; the provinces west of Ontario elected 77. In 1979, only three western Members of Parliament were Liberals.

— 2. Quiet Revolutions in Alberta and Saskatchewan —

The western provinces, like Quebec, complained of a long history of colonial domination. In the case of the prairie provinces, however, colonialism in the sense of political and financial hegemony was constitutionally sanctioned by Section 109 of the BNA Act, a clause that conspicuously excluded them from provincial control of their natural resources. It was not until 1930 that the law was amended to provide official equality. But, it was not until the post-Second World War period that substantial benefits began to be realized from provincial resources in the form of royalties. Manitoba gained from mining, hydroelectric development, and the exploitation of forest products. Alberta and Saskatchewan had oil. Saskatchewan also began to exploit uranium and especially its potash, a mineral fertilizer occurring more abundantly west of Regina than anywhere else on earth. But not all prairie provinces prospered equally from the resource boom of the 1950s and 1960s, and (as another indicator of the effects of long-standing colonialism) all tended to trade low "rents" for rapid development. In short, the terms of resource exploitation were more advantageous to investors (normally foreign corporations) than to the resident population.

Beginning in the 1970s, however, a remarkable trend towards reversing what John Richards and Larry Pratt have called "the inglorious rentier traditions" became especially clear in the cases of Alberta and Saskatchewan. Of particular interest is the fact that the governments of both provinces adopted bold strategies in the 1970s for promoting local entrepreneurship in the resource sector—but from remarkably different ideological perspectives. The agency of change in Saskatchewan was a bureaucratic elite wedded to socialist approaches to economic development. In Alberta, by contrast, the leading members of the bureaucracy had their origins in business, and retained those connections to use the power of the state for promoting more aggressive local capitalism.

The leading figure in the quiet revolution in Alberta was Peter Lougheed, grandson of James A. Lougheed (one of Alberta's pioneers and perhaps the greatest land speculator in the history of the province). Lougheed was thus a part of Alberta's established society. He was also an important figure in the business community by his association with the Loram Company, a huge Calgary-based construction and engineering conglomerate. In 1962, Lougheed added a political career to his interest in business. Three years later he accepted the leadership of Alberta's Conservatives when they were just "one step from outright decrepitude."

The reigning party of Alberta was Social Credit, of course, still as fundamentalist as when it came to power in the mid-1930s under "Bible Bill" Aberhart. His successor and protégé, Ernest Manning, was himself a radio preacher. Lougheed, schooled in the new North American traditions of image politics, thus found it easy to depict Manning and his party as "reactionary." While Manning continued to broadcast calls for Christian regeneration on his weekly "Back to the Bible Hour," Lougheed studied *The Making of the President 1960,* and refined his television image as a young, dynamic scion of one of Alberta's best families.

To Alberta's growing urban middle class, the product of the oil boom, Social Credit had been tolerable because it was dependably friendly to business. But "socred" was still something of an embarrassment because Manning and his Protestant fundamentalism were almost totally lacking in swank. Lougheed was ostentatiously smart and urbane. Moreover, he offered a plausible critique of Manning that was still safely right of centre. Lougheed claimed that the province was too dependent on oil and gas extraction and the old staples of agriculture. He warned that the oil was running out; so too would Alberta's prosperity. Assuming that there was considerable unrealized potential for manufacturing in the West, Lougheed criticized Manning for "coasting" and for failing to realize sufficient "capital revenues" from oil to promote such development. Lougheed suggested that the outside forces that would strive to keep manufacturing in central Canada needed to be neutralized; on the anti-Ottawa ground, the Manning regime was also found wanting, because Lougheed claimed that Social Credit had been consistently "out-negotiated by the Federal government."

Lougheed's critique of the Manning government appealed to Alberta's urban voters, the dominant part of the electorate by 1970. As a result, they ended the 45-year dynasty of Social Credit in August 1971 and elected 49 Tories to the 75-member legislature. The new government provided substantial change as well as the image of dynamism.

The first evident change was a growing competence and expertise in the government bureaucracy, which was enlarged and upgraded to foster a provincial economic nationalism over the "Toronto-Montreal establishment" and "its" federal government. Ironically, foreign capital was perceived as a powerful ally. The result was a perpetuation of foreign influences, but also what Richards and Pratt have called a "break with marginality," meaning a "new consciousness" and "growing restlessness with the West's hinterland status."

After OPEC dramatically increased the price of oil at the end of 1973 and the Government of Canada imposed price controls, along with the export tax and subsidy regime discussed in the previous chapter, Alberta interpreted such protection of Canadian consumers by Ottawa as simply the latest instance of central Canadian arrogance. One of the more printable Alberta rejoinders to the national oil pollicy was an offer to trade its oil at fixed prices if Ottawa would compel Ontario to sell the produce of its gold mines at the 1972 price—half of the world price in 1974. Angered by the forced sale of a non-renewable resource at artificially low prices, the Government of Alberta doubled the *rate* of its own royalty between 1973 and 1975 because the price of Canadian-produced oil was held by the federal government to about half of its current market value. Then, in 1976, the Government of Alberta created a Heritage Savings Trust Fund with an initial balance of $1.5 billion and the statutory assurance that one third of the royalties from all non-renewable resources would be added to the fund in the future. Eighty-five percent of the huge and growing savings account was meant to provide development capital for infrastructure or outright loans to local investors; only 15 percent was available to borrowers outside Alberta.

An activism similar to Alberta's blossomed in Saskatchewan, except that the boom staple was potash as well as oil, and the development strategy was socialism as well as corporatism on the Alberta model. The leading proponent of the alternative approach was Allan Blakeney, a Nova-Scotia-born Rhodes scholar and former civil servant, who entered politics in 1958 on the side of the CCF. Blakeney's philosophy was that the state should own the most important industries, especially in the resource sector.

Although active in politics for over a decade, most of Blakeney's career prior to 1971 was in opposition because the CCF had been defeated by the Liberals in 1964. Notorious for his denunciations of CCF experiments in public ownership, the Liberal Premier, Ross Thatcher, asserted that the CCF's usual practice was to put "some teacher or preacher or someone who knows nothing about business . . . in charge of an enterprise," the result being failure even where success was certain, because, according to Thatcher, "the CCF can't sell nuts to chimps." Thus, one problem for Blakeney, stepping into the leadership of the NDP and easily winning the election of 1971, was to change the image of incompetent management in public enterprise.

Blakeney's other problem was to mediate a deep split within his own party. A troublesome group known as the "Waffle" faction had emerged in 1969, to head the local and national NDP into a more frankly socialist direction. Having been badly beaten at the national level in 1971 (and after facing outright expulsion from the British Columbia and Ontario provincial parties), the Waffle still maintained some degree of influence in Saskatchewan. The question after Blakeney's electoral success in 1971 was whether he would prove more accommodating than NDP leaders elsewhere. Blakeney did move accommodatingly, but so cautiously that he exhausted the patience of the radicals, who withdrew voluntarily from the Saskatchewan NDP in 1973 (ironically, just as the events that led to a new Alberta began to have even more radical consequences for Saskatchewan).

Following Lougheed, Blakeney dramatically increased royalties on oil—and potash. Unlike the resource industries of Alberta, however, those that faced similar increases in Saskatchewan staged a dramatic rebellion in 1974. The potash industry led by a series of legal actions challenging the authority of Saskatchewan to impose such taxation. Blakeney went to the electorate for a renewal of his mandate and confronted the companies with the nationalization of the industry in 1975. In the meantime, the oil companies mounted their own legal battle with Saskatchewan.

In the important case of CIGOL versus the Government of Saskatchewan, the plaintiff (Canadian Industrial Gas and Oil Limited) claimed that the new levy was not a royalty at all, but a tax, and since it imposed costs that were passed on to the consumer, the form of taxation was indirect, and therefore, not within the power of a provincial government. On the face of the issues at stake, it appeared that the dispute involved just one company and the province. But because the case had implications for the federal government's ability to tax resources or the royalties that other provinces might levy, a long line of interveners fell in behind CIGOL and Saskatchewan. Most conspicuously, the Government of Canada intervened on the side of CIGOL, and Alberta sided with Saskatchewan. Finally, in 1977, the Supreme Court of Canada supported the companies and the Government of Canada by declaring that the Saskatchewan royalty scheme was unconstitutional because it amounted to indirect taxation. Clearly, the CIGOL case posed an equal threat to Alberta's ability to extract higher rents from its resources.

By the end of 1977, it had become clear that the provinces that retained ownership of their natural resources and developed them through Crown corporations were likely to enjoy the more secure return, for two reasons. Firstly, public ownership bypassed the royalty versus tax and direct versus indirect taxation issues. Secondly, a provincial Crown corporation was exempt from taxation by the federal government. Both points were not lost on Alberta, where dedication to private enterprise had become a secular religion. One result was a position paper on the constitution issued in 1978, Harmony in Diversity, in which the government of Alberta demanded broader powers of taxation and clarification of provincial paramountcy in resource development.

The events of the 1970s thus led to the discovery of new justifications for public ownership in the case of Saskatchewan, and a new stridency for constitutional special status—this time from Alberta. Like the government of Quebec, that of Alberta sought a new division of power, but just the reverse of what Quebec demanded: Alberta's ideal was for ten economic sovereignties in one political association rather than ten political sovereignties in the economic union sought by Lévesque.

The Government of Canada's intervention in the constitutional cases on control of resources showed a resistance to the Western autonomy demand that was as strong as its opposition to Quebec separatism. But Trudeau's constant striving to preserve and protect the French fact in a wider context meant that he had been able to resist the autonomy aspirations of Quebec without seeming anti-French. No such positive counterweight balanced Trudeau's dismissal of the Westerners' position on resources, or the Maritimers' desire to control the development of their offshore oil potential or inshore fisheries. Since the West was completely united on the resource question—and since western Canada returned more members to Parliament than Quebec—the Liberals were defeated in 1979 by the quiet revolutions they had ignored as much as they had been saved earlier by the original revolution in which Pierre Trudeau had taken part.

— 3. Resurrection and Referendum —

Some observers imagined that new leadership might put new life into federalism. Pierre Trudeau had developed a deep personal antipathy to René Lévesque, in particular, and Westerners in general. It seemed that Trudeau had become a cause as much as a master of Canada's national unity problems. The new government of Joe Clark, having denounced the "confrontation" tactics exhibited by Canada in recent years, began to deliver on its promise of "flexibility" with Quebec, concession of offshore resources to Newfoundland, and negotiation of resource issues with the West.

The old Prime Minister was discouraged by the apparent popularity of what he continued to call the "panacea of decentralization." Moreover, because he had always in power (one way or another) after his entry onto the federal political stage in 1965, functioning in opposition was a role he did not know or wish to learn. On November 21, roughly six months after his electoral defeat, he resigned. "It's all over," he told the Liberal caucus. Then the news of the end of an era was bestowed on the nation. Naturally, the newspapers were filled with assessments of Trudeau's career. Most were critical, agreeing with Geoffrey Stevens of the *Globe and Mail:* "He controlled the political system absolutely but he could not make it work." Most also agreed that the country was worse off in 1979 than in 1968, and that much of Canada's constitutional "disarray" was of Trudeau's own making. Would the Tories do better?

The leaderless status of the Liberal Party seemed to give Joe Clark's minority government a free rein. It was certainly unthinkable that the Liberals, being unprepared to enter an election, would unite with the rest of the opposition to defeat the plurality Tories. It seemed safe, in other words, for the Conservatives to act as if they had a majority and to pursue domestic economic policies that were known to be unpopular but nevertheless correct from the standpoint of monetarist theory and the instincts of the Minister of Finance, John Crosbie. On December 11, he imposed a budget of "short term pains for long term gains." The specific feature of the Crosbie budget that was especially unpopular was a four-cent-per-litre tax on gasoline, denounced by all opposition parties because it bore proportionately more heavily on low-income Canadians. On December 12, Trudeau told reporters that the Liberals would vote against the budget, and the next day the unthinkable did happen: the leaderless Liberals joined the rest of the opposition to show non-confidence in the Conservatives.

As the country prepared for a general election in February, the Liberals resurrected their old leader. Polls showed that they were 20 percentage points ahead of the Tories. The same surveys also confirmed that Trudeau was the most electable leader. Would he return? Nearly one full week passed before the announcement came. On December 18, Trudeau declared: "It is my duty to accept the draft of the party." Then, as if making his first election promise, he affirmed that the February 1980 campaign would be his last.

Other promises addressed what Trudeau denounced as Tory softness with the oil-producing western provinces. He promised the country cheaper gasoline by imposing a "blended price" on the Canadian petroleum industry. In other words, he promised to continue the policy first inaugurated in 1973. When Premier Lougheed replied that such a continued imposition on Alberta was intolerable, the impression that was left in the minds of eastern voters was that the anti-separatist Prime Minister was the man to subdue the West as well as Quebec. French-speaking Quebeckers continued to believe that Trudeau was their champion as much as their opponent; the unity stance produced continued good feeling there. On February 18, the Liberals won every seat but one in Trudeau's home province. In the West, by contrast, they lost every seat but two. Still, Quebec and Ontario support were enough to prevent disaster, indeed, were sufficient for a Parliamentary majority.

Within days of the reappearance of Pierre Trudeau in the prime ministerial office, René Lévesque indicated that the time had come to hold the referendum promised by his party since 1973. The question began with a declaration:

> The Government of Québec has made public its proposal to negotiate a new agreement with the rest of Canada, based on the equality of nations; this agreement would enable Québec to acquire exclusive power to make its laws, levy its taxes and establish relations abroad—in other words, sovereignty—and at the same time, to maintain with Canada an economic association including a common currency; no change in political status resulting from these negotiations will be effected without approval from the people through another referendum; on these terms, do you give the Government of Québec the mandate to negotiate the proposed agreement between Québec and Canada? (Quoted in R. Bothwell, et al., Canada since 1945 [1981], p. 403.)

The "public proposal" cited in the first clause of the rambling question was a White Paper issued the previous November to elaborate the association that the PQ sought to obtain from Canada. Four links were proposed: the first, a kind of Parliament in which the two countries would share "fundamental legal equality"; the second was a standing commission of inquiry to provide a steady flow of advice on economic development; the third would be a supreme court; and the last was a monetary authority analogous to the Bank of Canada. In this way, Quebec was supposed to obtain full political sovereignty while developing a new association based on mutual economic interest.

The provincial opposition led by Claude Ryan (former editor of *Le Devoir*) had responded with proposals of its own in January. Ryan's "beige paper" was a complex package advocating the kind of decentralization

331

Trudeau had been denouncing since the mid-1970s but falling considerably short of Lévesque's "sovereignty association." Consequently, Lévesque was able to campaign for a YES answer without organized or coherent opposition. Moreover, the question itself seemed to have little more effect than to underscore the power the PQ already enjoyed as the legitimate government of Quebec.

All circumstances—and the question itself—seemed set for an easy YES victory. Early in the spring of 1980, Lévesque announced that the vote would take place on May 20, and he began a tour of the province to tell Quebeckers they were witnessing the first stages of the birth of a nation. It was "a question of honour," he said. A resounding YES vote would not lead to independence immediately, but it would say "this is the direction we want to go in."

Gradually, however, it became clear that much of the equality Lévesque demanded had, in fact, already been achieved. A significant ommission from the referendum campaign was the assertion that Quebec had to separate from the rest of Canada to preserve its own language and culture. The Government of Quebec had already asserted its cultural sovereignty without truculance from the rest of the country. After the 1976 election, the first bill the new government introduced (in April 1977) affirmed the full and unequivocally French character of Quebec. Bill 101 banned English from most governmental and legal proceedings, and from businesses of 50 or more employees; and all children except Anglo-Quebeckers were henceforth to enrol in French-language schools. The one and only official language of Quebec was French. The rest of the country was stunned. But the most vocal critics of Bill 101 outside Quebec were the stalwart admirers of Trudeau's one-people-two-languages vision of Canada, or archmonarchists who still gloated over the conquest of Quebec in 1759 and questioned whether French should have any standing anywhere in the British Kingdom of Canada. Those in between considered the measure narrow and chauvinistic; perhaps because moderates were accustomed to similar discouragement of French by local English majorities, they did not demand remedial action by the federal government, and Ottawa was ill-disposed to act on its own. The result for the referendum campaign in 1980 was that Lévesque's claim that a YES would begin a process of "clearing away" (*déblocage*) did not ring true. The process seemed already too well advanced to appear frustrated.

Near the end, both leaders of the major national parties made excursions to Quebec. Joe Clark, on behalf of the Tories, asserted that "The Canada that Mr. Lévesque wants to separate from no longer exists," and

Trudeau sounded the same note with a "solemn declaration" that a NO vote would not be taken as an endorsement of the status quo. He promised a process of substantial constitutional change after the referendum. Such an affirmation may have convinced many Quebeckers that they could vote "no thanks" with dignity. When the votes were counted on May 20, 60 percent of the electorate did vote NO. Then, as emotional as he had been on November 15 four years before, Lévesque appeared on television to hold Trudeau to his pledge, saying that the ball was back in the federal court.

— 4. Patriation Versus Reform —

Prime Minister Trudeau oversaw discussions of the constitution immediately, saying, "Everything is negotiable." His assertion was consistent with other affirmations of goodwill that followed the referendum, but even the most optimistic observers qualified their hopes with memories that the federal government and the provinces had conceded little on constitutional issues in the past. Basically, there were two sets of constitutional questions confronting Canadians in 1980. One problem had been on the agenda since 1926; another, far more important set of issues had arisen only since the 1960s.

The long-standing, relatively unimportant matter was "patriation." Since Canada's constitution was a statute of Great Britain, each amendment had to be enacted by the Parliament of that country. Once Canada had been declared equal and in no way subordinate to the United Kingdom, continuing to call upon the British for amendments was anomalous, to say the least. But before the constitution could be patriated to Canada (thus relieving the British of their ratification role), an alternative procedure had to be invented. Past practice was too diverse to offer easy guidance for the future. Occasionally the federal government acted unilaterally (as in the case of the BNA Act of 1871, for example), but usually the Government of Canada obtained unanimous consent from the provinces before passing a joint resolution of the two houses of the Canadian Parliament asking Britain for an amendment. The subtle variety of approaches in between meant that the federal government and the provinces could never agree on one set procedure to be observed for every instance in the future. As a result, it had been more convenient to leave the BNA Act in British custody and to expend governmental energy on the more important problems of the day.

In the 1960s, however, constitutional questions surfaced in a new, more urgent form. When Quebec attempted to exercise its full powers under the BNA Act, it found them wanting because so much of the control it sought over taxation and social policy had developed as shared areas of jurisdiction. By the mid-1960s, it seemed that the country had outgrown the latest form of federalism that had emerged under the general umbrella of the BNA Act. The first form of federalism, lasting from 1867 to about 1885, was hardly federal at all since the central government attempted to rule the constituent parts as subordinate jurisdictions. But after the rebellion of Ontario and court decisions in favour of that province in the 1880s, a more classical form of federalism did emerge by the end of the century; it was recognized that each level of government had exclusive powers that had to be respected. Consequently, Canada developed between 1885 and 1914 more as an association of provinces than the unitary state Macdonald had wanted. But with the coming of the Great War, and the passage of the War Measures Act, closer union developed in the guise of emergency federalism. In the new formula, the federal government could trespass upon provincial powers whenever emergency dictated. The constitutional problem of the 1920s and 1930s was in defining *peacetime* emergencies. With the obvious emergency of the Second World War, the Government of Canada reinstated the War Measures Act and consolidated power more completely. The benefits of such consolidation seemed so manifestly clear to most Canadians in 1945 that they did not want the powers abandoned after the war. Consequently, emergency federalism was redefined as cooperative federalism. In the new formula, provinces were nominally still powerful in the area of social policy and direct taxation, but by "renting" their power of direct taxation to the federal government, Ottawa was given the means to rule the country by way of shared-cost programs. After 1960, the nub of the problem with Quebec was its demand for the restoration of the old powers by explicit revision of the BNA Act, defining more clearly the areas in which a province was paramount.

Having yielded about one third of the field of direct taxation, and admitted broad areas of "concurrent" power in the field of social legislation, the Government of Canada believed that Ottawa's ability to behave as a "national" government would dangerously diminish if the federal level were no longer able to speak for Canada in foreign affairs, work to maintain a national minimum in social welfare, or play a role in lessening regional disparities by raising a revenue for equalization payments to the poorer provinces. Quebec, however, refused to consider concurrent power in the field of social legislation and called equalization a sham. According to Claude Morin, the so-called have-not provinces (Quebec included) gained no more from federal expenditures than the taxation contributed. Eventually, Westerners joined in the same denunciation. George Wood-cock (a Manitoban transplanted to British Columbia by way of Great Britain), called equalization a "charity system" imposed by the federal government's "right hand giving crusts from the loaves which the left hand still takes away by sustaining an economy that continues to benefit the central provinces." In time, Westerners and Quebeckers would agree (more or less) with Woodcock's observation that what was needed was "a genuine confederation in which no region profits to the detriment of the rest, and in which every region has an equal political voice," a regime, according to Morin, that "lets Quebec function as a true government" rather than as "a mere regional administration bereft of meaningful prerogative." The four western provinces, Newfoundland, and Quebec eventually agreed that any meaningful discussion of the constitution must include a clarification of the distribution of powers. The federal politicians—supported by the mandarins anxious to defend their bureaucratic empires—insisted that any further devolution would either weaken the country beyond repair, or jeopardize flexible responses to unanticipated problems by imposing a constitutional straitjacket upon future generations. In this way, the two orders of government appeared anxious to resolve the constitutional malaise, but they approached the problem from irreconcilable positions. Ottawa consistently sought to preserve powers recently won *de facto*. The provinces increasingly wanted a clarification of the distribution of powers in order to undo the centralization that had arisen from the first vaguely written BNA Act.

Initially, Quebec was the most outspoken in demanding a new definition of provincial powers, and Ottawa used Quebec's isolation effectively to defeat the province's demand for "special status." The federal position was further enhanced by the election of an outspokenly federalist government in Quebec in April 1970, when Robert Bourassa came to power promising to ease federal-provincial tensions by emphasizing economic issues rather than constitutional matters. Almost immediately after his election, the Government of Canada brought a constitutional proposal to Quebec City, a package that contained an amending formula (giving Quebec and Ontario veto powers), entrenchment of certain civil rights, and some tinkering with concurrent powers in taxation and social policy. When Bourassa did not reject outright the federal initiative, it was presented individually to the other provinces with the assertion that "substantial agreement" had already been secured with Quebec. Then all governments agreed to consider the matter at a meeting to be held in Victoria in June 1971.

By the time arrangements for the Victoria conference had been made, the new government of Quebec was informed that Bourassa had endorsed a constitutional position that two preceding governments had already rejected. Moreover, Bourassa was convinced that he had blundered. Consequently, just before the Victoria meeting, the government of Quebec informed the other premiers and the Government of Canada that provincial paramountcy in social policy would have to be included in any package acceptable to Quebec. The federal government responded with advice to the premiers of the poorer provinces that such a change might lead to wholesale opting-out from existing national programs so that the federal government would no longer have any reason to participate with the rest; the success of Quebec's position would thus lead to a costly transfer of responsibilities. Predictably, Quebec lost practically all support from the others to establish provincial paramountcy in social policy.

The Victoria conference unfolded then as a closed-door marathon concerned with patriation, an amending formula, and Quebec's peculiar concern with social development issues. Despite the full agenda, "tentative" agreement was established on a package that included the federal government's conceding clarification of the sections of the BNA Act pertaining to social policy. Then Trudeau announced that the provinces had ten days to accept or reject the tentative agreement finally. "If there isn't agreement, then that is the end of the matter for now . . . . "

On his return to Quebec, Bourassa came under heavy pressure to withhold agreement until the final wording had been achieved. Consequently, he announced on June 23 his government's concern for "agreement . . . on clear and precise constitutional texts." Although Quebec's announcement left the way open for further discussion, Prime Minister Trudeau, true to his word, decided that Quebec's second thoughts were final, and the failure to conclude agreement on a take-it-or-leave-it basis ended the matter for nearly a decade.

Many observers (from fellow Liberals such as Claude Ryan to academic commentators such as Dale Posgate and Kenneth McRoberts) argued subsequently that Trudeau's "intransigence" in refusing to continue negotiations not only blocked the development of a new constitutional accommodation, but by seeming to prove that French Canada could never speak to Ottawa as an "equal," gave active encouragement to separatism as well. For that reason, when Lévesque announced that the ball was back in the federal court in May 1980, Trudeau's assertion that everything was negotiable seemed to have special significance indeed.

— 5. Patriation —

In the summer of 1980, Jean Chrétien, the Minister of Justice, functioned as Trudeau's ambassador to the provinces, preparing the way for a constitutional conference in the early autumn. Unlike preparations for the Victoria meeting ten years earlier, there was, however, more than one wild card in the deck. Newfoundland and the four western provinces sought clarification of their powers in resource development just as Quebec had insisted upon its superiority in the field of social development earlier. Consequently, Chrétien found his summer perambulations disappointing. He discovered that all provinces were willing to listen to a federal proposal on patriation, an amending formula, and a Charter of Canadian Rights and Freedoms, but for their concession of exclusive jurisdiction over civil rights, they wanted something in return. Various provinces mentioned different resources, or family law, or communications, or other aspects of social and economic development. Chrétien complained that it was "depressing bargaining rights against administrative advantages for the provinces." In fact, the federal government was as anxious about the distribution of powers as were the provinces. The difference was that Chrétien sought to defend a balance that already favoured his side.

It was not surprising that the summer's meetings proved inconclusive and that vast differences appeared once the two orders of government met in full conference in September. Prime Minister Trudeau continued to insist upon what Murray Beck called his "splendid, if idealistic and impracticable, concept of . . . an open society, all of whose citizens would be protected by an entrenched bill of rights guaranteeing, among other things, their linguistic rights . . . ." He viewed Canada as "an association of people," while nearly all of the premiers contended that the country was an "association of provinces." In their view, it did not matter a great deal that a Canadian might migrate from one province to another and discover that the migrant had moved to a remarkably different society and economy, with different social policies and a new language. Naturally, between such divergent concepts of Canada, no agreement was easy. The conference ended in failure.

Less than one month after the "First Ministers" failed to agree on a constitutional package, Prime Minister Trudeau added fuel to an already inflamed situation by announcing on October 2 that he intended to patriate the BNA Act unilaterally—and with a charter of rights. He said that the amending formula and rights charter were interim arrangements subject to revision at conferences to take place later. Then, if agreement still proved

337

impossible, what was meant to be temporary would become permanent. Charles Lynch, the senior journalist in Ottawa, declared that the "method is shocking" but having reported on so many previous failures, Lynch agreed that there was "no other way" to break the impasse.

Conspicuously absent in the Trudeau patriation scheme was any clarification of provincial power in social policy or resource ownership. Here the second shock was a federal announcement on October 28 that a National Energy Policy (NEP) would come into effect immediately, to use the power of the central government to effect 50-percent Canadian ownership and self-sufficiency in the petroleum industry by 1990. To that end, Ottawa was expanding its "rent" on oil and gas from ten to 23 percent, reducing the return to the producing provinces by two percentage points, and to the companies by nearly one fifth. Premier Lougheed denounced the scheme as "an outright attempt to take over the resources" of the provinces, and warned that Alberta would reduce production by 180 000 barrels per day (in three steps, at three-month intervals after the first of the coming year) unless the Government of Canada backed down from its bold assertion of concurrent power in the resource sector.

In the meantime, Trudeau's patriation scheme was referred by Parliament to a joint Senate-Commons committee to hear submissions from the general public; and, in Britain, a similar committee headed by Sir Anthony Kershaw considered the legality of unilateralism. In Canada, civil libertarians generally agreed that the list of rights and liberties to be safeguarded was not sufficiently lengthy and the safeguards were not appropriately stringent. In Britain, the Kershaw committee concluded that the British Parliament would not have to accept the package unless a substantial number of provinces concurred with the action. Trudeau hinted that Britain's refusal to do Canada's bidding would provoke a grave crisis: "If they're wise they'll get through it quickly and hold their nose while they're doing it . . . ." Chrétien predicted that the whole business would be finished by Easter 1981.

In the end, the package was delayed by one full year; the scheme that finally passed bore little resemblance to Trudeau's original proposal because of decisive intervention by the Canadian courts. Early in 1981, the provinces of Manitoba, Quebec, and Newfoundland challenged the constitutionality of Trudeau's unilateral action, and five other dissenting premiers immediately joined as interveners. The "gang of eight" lost their appeals in Manitoba and Quebec; but at the end of March, the Supreme Court of Newfoundland ruled unanimously that unilateralism was illegal. Then the federal Tories launched a filibuster in the House of Commons demanding postponement of further proceedings until the Supreme Court of Canada could rule on the decision of the Newfoundland court. Imagining that such a concession could only cost time, Trudeau agreed to wait for the last judgment.

In September, the Supreme Court rendered a surprise decision. A majority (seven to two, led by Chief Justice Bora Laskin), ruled that the proposed unilateral patriation process did not contravene any law the courts of Canada had the power to enforce. They said that unilateralism was legal, but only in a narrow, technical sense. Even so, a second majority (six to three) declared that such a course would be most unwise, because it would violate a century-old convention that required the consent of the provinces before requesting any changes that affected their rights.

What followed was a flurry of informal negotiation in October, culminating in an agreement to convene the premiers in Ottawa for one last attempt in November. There, nine of the ten provinces and the federal government did find acceptable wording for an amending formula and also a charter of rights. The amending formula allowed ratification of changes approved by any combination of at least seven provinces containing at least 50 percent of the national population, even if the approving seven did not include Quebec or Ontario. Up to three provinces could dissent, and enjoy exemption from the provisions ratified by the others, until choosing to opt-in; but once the change was accepted, such late-comers would be bound forever. Previously, Trudeau had criticized the opt-out provision as "incremental separatism . . . a Confederation of 500 shopping centres." Accepting the proviso was, therefore, a massive concession on his part. The premiers showed flexibility by accepting an entrenched bill of rights, palatable in November 1981 because an override clause permitted provincial legislatures to breach civil rights (the charter "notwithstanding"). In this respect, the new charter was no more binding than the old Diefenbaker bill of rights had been on the Parliament of Canada. In the new charter, however, certain rights such as the equality of the sexes and the two official languages were deeply entrenched in the sense that neither could be overridden by the "notwithstanding clause."

Given that the rights of English- and French-speaking minorities ("where numbers warrant") were among the more deeply-entrenched freedoms, the government of Quebec withheld its consent and claimed the patriation scheme was illegal because it violated the "fundamental duality" of Canada by ignoring Quebec's veto. On the last day of the conference, perhaps because he was anticipating future challenges to his

Bill 101, Premier Lévesque growled prophetically that the proceedings would have "incalculable consequences."

Subsequently, the patriation scheme passed by the Canadian Parliament in the first week of December was approved by the British early in 1982. Both issues of the amending formula and the charter of rights seemed at last settled. But the manner of the settlement invited future difficulty by what was accomplished as well as by what was ignored. At best, the new Canada Act (see text in Appendix B) was only peripheral to the major questions raised in the previous decade. The settlement inflamed and isolated Quebec, and no clarification of the distribution of powers for dealing with the economy was obtained. The struggle ended as no one's victory. The constitutional tug-of-war concluded in celebrated stalemate.

Suggested Reading

Trudeau's decline and resurrection are described by Robert Bothwell, *et al., Canada since 1945: Power, Politics, and Provincialism* (1981); analysis of developments is offered by Richard Gwyn in *The Northern Magus: Pierre Trudeau and Canadians* (1980). The same contrast applies to Trudeau's role in the constitutional initiatives of the period: the Bothwell volume is hardly more than a chronicle; Gwyn (despite his proximity to the events as both observer and actor) offers an analysis that is singular for both its depth and balance.

Since the subjects treated in this chapter are still of quite recent development, specialized history remains to be written. Still, a surprising number of works of considerable use and interest have appeared. On the subject of the development of the new West, for example, rather antiseptic treatments of the themes of urbanization, urban politics, and the decline of the Liberal party are available. Roger Gibbins, *Prairie Politics and Society: Regionalism in Decline* (1980), contends that the West's politics have become progressively more like those of the East, a contention that contrasts considerably with another recent work on Prairie politics by David Smith, *The Regional Decline of a National Party: Liberals on the Prairies* (1981).

By far the most interesting works on the new West, however, are those that focus on its struggle for decolonization. David Jay Bercuson, ed., *Canada and the Burden of Unity* (1977), and Martin Robins' two-volume work on British Columbia, *The Company Province* (1972-73), provide background for understanding what John Richards and Larry Pratt call the "rentier tradition." The work of Richards and Pratt, *Prairie Capitalism: Power and Influence in the New West* (1979), is a brilliant analysis of the developments in the 1970s that have promoted decolonization in Saskatchewan and Alberta. Richards and Pratt also offer a useful discussion of the constitutional position of the West in the same work.

A more strident, yet interesting, tract for the times is George Woodcock's, *Confederation Betrayed!: The Case Against Trudeau's Canada* (1981). More sober views than Woodcock's are found in R.B. Byers and R.W. Reford, *Canada Challenged: The Viability of Confederation* (1979). Here, the essay by J. Murray Beck, "Overlapping and Divided Jurisdictions: "The Nub of the Debate," is particularly helpful to readers seeking a brief summary of complex issues. More technical is Edward McWhinney, *Canada and the Constitution, 1979-1982* (1982).

Meech Lake official announcement.

*"Mulroney was centre-stage, seeming
almost frantic in his quest for effective reconciliation."*

CHAPTER 17

SECLECTIVE
RECONCILIATION,
1983-1990

— 1. Trudeau's Final Exit —

The proclamation of Canada's altered constitution on July 1, 1982 ended the confrontation between Trudeau and his principal adversaries—but more by mutual exhaustion than by settlement of the issues. The Charter of Rights and amending formula were dramatically less than the Prime Minister had hoped for; the energy-producing provinces did not see federal paramountcy diminished in resource development; and Quebec nationalists claimed that the rights of their province were disregarded. Still, more than five years of constitutional wrangling were over, and the termination of the dispute was an armistice more than anyone's instrument of surrender.

Like Robert Borden seeking escape from the agenda of more mundane domestic concerns after the end of the Great War, Pierre Trudeau began to pursue lofty international questions in the twilight of his political career. For the next two years he moved from conference to conference promoting

"North-South dialogue" between wealthy industrial nations and poor un-
derdeveloped countries. He visited leaders East and West to promote
Canada's rhetorical commitment to arms reduction and world peace. At
the same time, however, Trudeau's government avoided initiatives to
diminish domestic poverty or internal colonialism, and permitted the
Americans to refine the guidance system of their latest nuclear weapon,
the Cruise missile, by testing the device in the Siberia-like conditions of
Canada's north. Inflation and unemployment remained close to ten percent
and federal deficits were still staggering.

In the context of such discouraging domestic developments, Trudeau
and his party plummetted in popularity. By January 1983, the Conservatives held a comfortable lead in public-opinion polls. But a growing
number of Tories were becoming increasingly dissatisfied with their lack-
lustre leader, Joe Clark. He chose to settle the issue through a leadership
convention in June and lost to a Quebec businessman, more conservative
and polished than himself but a neophyte in electoral experience. Brian
Mulroney had never held elective office before. In 1983, he was president
of Iron Ore Company of Canada. Conservative insiders knew him better
than the public did—as a veteran of 25 years of PC organizational
proceedings. Ironically, one of Mulroney's first declared purposes after
becoming Tory leader was to make Canadian politics less subject to
manipulation by the "back room boys."

The new Conservative leader's first attempt at elective office came in
the autumn of 1983 in a Nova Scotia by-election that made him the
Member of Parliament for Central Nova. Over the winter of 1983-84,
Canadians discovered that the new Leader of the Opposition had a genuine
talent for effective confrontation with the old Prime Minister. As the
Liberals sank further behind the Tories in popularity, Trudeau announced
in February 1984 that he intended to retire as soon as the party named his
successor.

At the leadership convention in June, the Liberals appeared to have
found a Mulroney of their own: a good-looking lawyer with ties to business, and no recent electoral experience. Their new leader was John
Turner, the Minister of Finance who had resigned from Cabinet over
wage-and-price controls in 1975, and left politics altogether six months
later. For almost a decade, Turner was a politically unknown commodity.
In that capacity, he led his party into a general election within days of
becoming leader at the end of June. In the context of the disorganized
campaign, John Turner appeared but a wooden replica of the real Mulroney, and the Liberal Party suffered its greatest defeat in Canadian

history. The September election returned only 40 Liberals to Parliament. Broadbent's NDP came through with 30. The other 211 members of the House of Commons were Progressive Conservatives—a majority larger than Diefenbaker's in 1958.

As earlier, the huge majority fumbled and faltered, reeling from one scandal to another. But despite the stellar incompetence and corruption of those around him, Mulroney seemed determined to win a place in history as the great conciliator. Emotional social issues (such as bilingualism, capital punishment, and abortion), complex matters in federal-provincial relations (energy policy and Quebec's position in the new federalism), and sensitive aspects of Canadian-American relations (in trade and defence), all made constant headlines. In each instance, Mulroney was centre-stage, seeming almost frantic in his quest for effective reconciliation. And yet, there were clear limits to the scope of the intended consensus. The government reached further for constitutional concessions to calm provincial premiers than for means to accommodate native leaders or women's groups; Mulroney found it easier to negotiate economic terms favourable to the United States than to seek a compromise with the demands of organized labour. The one set of responses is seen in the government's dealings with constitutional loose ends inherited from Trudeau. The other is found in Mulroney's own initiative in trade policy.

— 2. Constitutional Accord and Discord —

The Trudeau legacy of unfinished constitutional business pertained most directly to the rights of three collectivities: women, native people, and Quebec. Significant numbers of each group had hoped for a constitutional liberation from traditional practices that restricted their freedom in four essential ways. Historically, they had been integrated into a dominant society on subordinate terms; they had found obstacles to passage into the society of the dominant group because of discrimination on the basis of "race" or gender; and their aspirations for autonomy had been continually frustrated by devices of indirect rule (conceding some of the form of authority to leaders of the subordinate group while keeping ultimate control in the hands of the dominant society).

In the case of women, the unfinished business was bringing provincial and federal laws into accord with the equality provisions of the Charter of Rights (Sections 15 and 28) that were to come into effect three years after proclamation of the Constitution Act in 1982. Much was to be done. In fact, the "emancipation" of women had hardly begun. Inclusion in the franchise (for the nefarious reasons discussed earlier in connection with the Great War) had little impact on women's participation in the political process except to include them in the ranks of docile supporters of the male-dominated parties. Women remained legal non-persons with respect, for example, to eligibility to sit in the Canadian Senate until 1929, and remained non-persons with respect to control of their reproductive systems for most of the rest of the century. During the Second World War, women's participation in industrial employment doubled; but work was largely de-skilled for female employees and there were no training programs that envisioned long-term positions in traditionally male-dominated trades. Moreover, in the immediate postwar period, affirmative action programs for male veterans and tax disincentives for married females soon displaced most women from the positions they had taken for the duration of the wartime emergency. Ruth Pierson has shown that the result was deliberate, "the aim was to return to a pre-war social reality."

By the 1960s, however, principles for gender equalization had gained currency. In 1966, women formed the Fédération des femmes du Québec demanding attention to questions of gender inequality in the context of the general decolonization demand in their province; women elsewhere associated for the same purpose, calling themselves the Committee for the Equality of Women in Canada. The Pearson government responded in 1967 with a Royal Commission on the Status of Women chaired by Florence Bird, a public broadcaster better known by her performance name, Anne Francis.

While the commission toured the country amassing evidence of the reality of the issue, women's liberation groups organized in every major city and prepared to act on the commission's report. In the meantime, the federal government took its first halting steps towards conceding women's control of reproduction. In 1969, advocacy or advertisement of birth control ceased to be an obscenity "tending to corrupt morals" under the Criminal Code. At the same time, abortion under certain narrowly-defined conditions ceased to be a criminal offence. But access was so restrictive, legal abortions remained virtually unavailable to women in most provinces. Consequently, nothing that any government had enacted since the period of the Great War had considerably diminished the relevance of the many recommendations of the Bird Commission when its report appeared in 1970. Women had still not attained: equality of access to employment; equal responsibility with men for child-care; social compensation for the biological overtime contributed in the task of human reproduction; and affirmative action by government to eradicate the consequences of deeply entrenched discrimination on the basis of sex.

To realize the agenda of the 167 recommendations of the Bird Commission, the Committee for the Equality of Women in Canada became the National Ad Hoc Committee in 1971, and a more permanent National Action Committee on the Status of Women (NAC) in 1972. But little concrete action followed. In fact, the first head of the NAC, Laura Sabia, declared that her day of liberation came when she resigned the "albatross" of ineffective leadership. "From 'Royal Commission' to 'Councils,'" she wrote in 1976, "we have been kept busy pushing paper. 'Do advise us,' say the astute politicians . . . . And we fell for it, God help us, hook, line, and sinker."

The reality was that those in control of the dominant group were neither prepared nor willing to share their power. By 1982, more than 80 percent of those polled by Gallup still believed that a woman's place was in the home, especially homes with children, even though employment data showed that two thirds of all married women under 45 were part of the paid labour force, probably for the same reasons as their predecessors in early industrial Canada: one income was simply not adequate to support a family in the comfort most Canadians demanded. Moreover, a woman was more likely than a man to find her out-of-home employment in low-skilled, low-paid work. Almost half of the women in the paid labour force were hired for just seven occupational classes: secretary-clerk, salesperson, bank teller, waitress, janitor, or the two "women's professions," nursing and teaching.

Responding to the equality requirement of the Charter of Rights, the Mulroney government removed what Alison Prentice has termed some of the more "egregiously sexist items of law and public policy." One dramatic change that occurred in 1985 was partial removal of the bar against women from combat roles in the armed forces; another in the same year was a revision of the Indian Act (Section 12 1.b) that prohibited Indian women from marrying non-Indians on the penalty of losing Indian status (Indian men who married non-Indian women suffered no such sanction). Still, there were no positive initiatives in accord with the broader agenda of the NAC. In January 1988, women did gain freedom of reproductive choice, but not because the Mulroney government had agreed to revise the remaining anti-abortion provision of the Criminal Code. Rather, the change followed from the Supreme Court of Canada's discovery that the law was in conflict with the Charter of Rights—because it violated the right to "life, liberty and security of the person" defined in

Section 7. The anti-choice lobby immediately demanded re-enactment of an even more stringent abortion section of the Criminal Code that would have required Parliament to invoke the override clause in Section 33. The Mulroney government hesitated, perhaps hoping for some basis of reconciling discordant opinion on the question.

A similar mix of timid action, delay, and inconclusive reconciliation characterizes the Mulroney government's dealing with Native Peoples, another group whose first effective organized demands for decolonization dated from the 1960s, in their case, in response to a bold attempt by the Trudeau government to scrap Canada's century-old Indian policy. In March 1969, the Minister of Indian Affairs, Jean Chrétien, made public a White Paper revealing the government's intent to repeal the Indian Act, dissolve the Department of Indian Affairs, and distribute its responsibilities to the other federal departments or provincial ministries. From the government's point of view, Native Peoples would cease to be wards of the state—in one easy stroke.

Everyone could agree that the old Indian Act did represent a "vicious mechanism of social control," designed for the declared purpose of "civilizing savages" in the mid-1870s and 1880s, that was only marginally softened in its intended cultural genocide in two subsequent overhauls: one in the late 1920s, the other in the early 1950s. Native Peoples still could not control their education, land, or local government. They had no authority in defining who their own people were. They could not even vote until 1960. All such matters and a host of others were despicable aspects of the law from the group's perspective. But in one aspect, the old law was positive: it defined a special status for "Indians" relative to the rest of Canada. No Indian Act, no special status was the fear of many. The basic complaint against intended repeal was that the move represented a desperate push by the government toward complete assimilation.

The fear was not without foundation. Of the 300 000 Native Peoples that the Government of Canada accepted as "status Indians" within the terms of the Indian Act, approximately 120 000 were descended from forebears who had never negotiated a treaty with the Crown. The first seven treaties negotiated by Canada between 1871 and 1877 had been supplemented by only four, according to Brian Titley, as "potential profits to be gleaned from land that was hitherto regarded as worthless precipitated moves to extinguish the title of the native occupiers." Still, vast tracts remained "unsurrendered" after 1921, the date of the last treaty. And even where treaties existed, or the status of non-treaty Indians and

Inuit was not denied, another group of perhaps 700 000 aboriginal people were not Indians within the meaning of the Indian Act. Such non-recognition was significant because it excluded non-status Indians and Métis from certain benefits with respect to health care, access to education, and exemption from taxation. The two categories of "status Indians" (treaty and non-treaty) and the much larger population whose aboriginal standing was ignored by Canada (non-status Indians and Métis) feared that because the government had become increasingly reluctant to recognize "aboriginal rights" in principle (refusing, for example, to negotiate any new treaties since 1921), repeal of the Indian Act had to be opposed until the government proved willing to recognize the existence of aboriginal peoples by other means. Since the Trudeau government despised the "special status" concept in any guise, no such alternative was forthcoming, and the policy intention opposed so vociferously in 1969 was merely "retracted" with nothing to replace it in 1971.

Native Peoples were not prepared to accept such a negative outcome. The momentum of opposing the policy trial balloon carried over to more direct opposition in the next several years. British Columbia Indians initiated court action, and won recognition by the Supreme Court of Canada in 1973 as a group whose aboriginal title had not been extinguished by treaty. When the Yukon Indians subsequently proceeded to court in Yellowknife, the Government of Canada created an Office of Native Claims (ONC) in 1974 to consider *comprehensive* claims dealing with Native Peoples without treaties, and *specific* claims arising from unkept treaty promises. For a brief two-year period at the end of the decade, the government even considered claims of the Métis and non-status Indians.

In the early 1980s, a time of intensified constitutional discussion, and the negotiation of the Charter of Rights in particular, it might have seemed logical for the government to have recognized the "existing rights" of aboriginal peoples—Indians, Inuit, and the Métis. But just as the government found it easier to create the Office of Native Claims in 1974 than to honour the many hundreds of claims approved by that office by 1984, so too was it simpler to recognize "aboriginal rights" in principle than in practice. The constitutional loose end in native rights inherited by the Mulroney government was the necessity required by Section 37 to convene conferences to define "existing" rights, *i.e.* to distinguish between the past and the present, to separate rights that were current from those that were spent. The process was inconclusive. By the time of the failure of the fourth such meeting early in 1985, only the Supreme Court was acting decisively on native rights. In the Musqueam case, the Court declared that the government had a lawful obligation to compensate Native Peoples for reserve lands mismanaged by officials acting on the group's behalf. As with women and the abortion question, the Court was bolder than government, and Mulroney's quest for reconciliation failed.

Perhaps Mulroney's failures on women's and native rights questions made him all the more determined to establish a basis of reconciliation with the third collectivity interested in decolonization. The government of Quebec had refused to endorse the constitution of 1982 for two principal reasons: the amending formula that denied the province its traditional veto, and the Charter of Rights that brought a cloud over Quebec's recent language legislation. By 1985, however, Canada had a Prime Minister who was declaring that he "wouldn't have signed that kind of constitutional deal" either. Moreover, René Lévesque was moving into retirement, and the PQ was declining in popularity. Lévesque left politics in June, and his party was defeated in December 1985.

Early in 1986, the new Liberal government led by a recycled Robert Bourassa made it plain that if Canada and the provinces could accept five modifications of the arrangement Lévesque had rejected, Bourassa would sign. Secret negotiations began, and Bourassa reached a point of agreement in principle with Canada and the other premiers in a closed-door meeting at Mulroney's Meech Lake retreat near Ottawa in April 1987. Quebec was to gain constitutional recognition as a "distinct society," and because its most unique feature was its language, the province, unlike the rest, would appear to have gained the promise of enhanced power to preserve, promote, and protect that difference. At the same time, Quebec was promised a constitutional guarantee of a one-third share of the Supreme Court judges, greater control of immigration, financial compensation for non-participation in future shared-cost programs, and a veto power over a broadened spectrum of future amendments to the constitution. Given that the other premiers gained the same advantages with respect to shared-cost programs and future amendments, as well as guaranteed annual conferences on Senate reform and control of east- and west-coast fisheries, constitutional experts such as Brian Schwartz refused to herald the "Meech Lake Accord" as a great work of national reconciliation. According to Schwartz, the meeting was merely a "federal potlatch for the premiers." It remained to be seen if all ten provincial legislatures and the Parliament of Canada would endorse after public discussion that which Mulroney had negotiated in secret.

— 3. The Free-Trade Debate —

The problem of ratifying the result of an agreement negotiated in secret arose again over the Mulroney government's achievement in Canadian-American relations. Since assuming power, Mulroney had lamented the cool state of relations with the United States. He claimed that Canada was shirking an important partnership responsibility by failing to maintain a full share of the defence commitment to NATO, and impeding economic growth by such economic-nationalist discouragements as the Foreign Investment Review Agency (FIRA) and the National Energy Program (NEP). Mulroney promised to enlarge and modernize the military and to convince American investors that Canada was "open for business again."

After launching a multi-billion-dollar reequipment program for the forces, dismantling the NEP, and beginning to run FIRA in reverse as a foreign capital recruitment agency called Investment Canada, the government embarked on the boldest foreign trade initiative since the Liberals' abortive free-trade discussions of 1948. The main purpose was to seek some exemption from the hundreds of protectionist proposals that were beginning to appear before the American Congress in the face of record trade deficits in the United States. Canada stood to lose in any general restriction on imports because every third Canadian was employed in a job directly tied to the American market. One estimate suggested that for every percentage-point increase in US duties on Canadian exports, there would be a one-percent increase in the overall unemployment rate in Canada. It seemed to follow that a general exemption from growing American protectionism would save jobs. The Americans agreed to discuss such favoured treatment in return for reciprocal consideration that would extend beyond tariff barriers and would include exemption of US companies from any future government's resurrection of FIRA or reenactment of programs such as the NEP.

Face-to-face discussions between the American negotiator, Peter Murphy, and the Canadian representative, Simon Reisman, ran from April 1986 through the summer of 1987 and concluded with an "integrated model agreement" in September. Through the autumn, the rough outline of principles became "elements of agreement" released to the public early in October, and finally a "legal text" signed by the President and Prime Minister on January 2, 1988. After passage by Congress and Parliament, the terms of the agreement were to come into effect by stages over a ten year period beginning in January 1989.

The major terms of the agreement covered tariffs, of course, and also the questions of foreign ownership, supplies of strategic commodities, the use of social policies as subsidies to special industries, and cross-border employment. The tariff aspect was meant to abolish all remaining import duties imposed on US-origin commodities entering Canada, and vice versa. To Canadian consumers familiar with the exercise of mentally guessing the after-tax cost of goods from American mail-order companies, the proposed innovation would be less stunning than the parity implication of "free trade." A bit of hardware that had cost $10 US and about $16 Canadian to land in Canada (not counting shipping costs), prior to the implementation of free trade would fall in price by two dollars, merely, because in the years since the 1930s, most of the tax on imports had been reclassified. Customs officers in the 1980s were still collecting a hefty duty on goods but with less called "tariff" and more designated "excise." The proposed trade agreement was about tariffs, not federal sales taxes. Tariffs were scheduled to disappear, sales taxes would be unaffected if applied to Canadian as well as American suppliers.

The concept of "national" (rather than "discriminatory") treatment was the key to the other cardinal aspects of the 3 000-page legal text of the agreement. More elaborately stated, national treatment would permit either government to follow any policy it chose as long as the divergent course did not discriminate solely on the basis of nationality. On the question of foreign ownership, neither government would devise regulations for non-resident companies that did not apply with equal force to domestic firms, nor would they permit transformation of foreign-owned companies into publicly-owned corporations without "reasonable rules of procedure." Similarly, social policies would have to pass the "national treatment" rule to eliminate unfair subsidies in disguise. If self-employed producers were generally excluded from unemployment insurance, for example, Canada could not distribute unemployment benefits to select categories of the self-employed such as farmers and fishermen on the grounds that they were seasonally unemployed and deserved compensation. Such social policies would be subsidies in breach of the national treatment rule. On the other hand, Canada could legislate a minimum national income policy that would benefit poor labourers as well as certain farmers and fishermen, even though such a policy (along with Medicare) would be at complete variance with American practice.

In its application to strategic, continental resources, the national treatment rule had a different effect. In the energy field, national treatment meant guaranteed supply of Canadian natural gas, oil, and electricity to the American market. The agreement would confirm by treaty what the Mulroney government had accomplished in policy: no export controls, or minimum export prices, and no export taxes. Most importantly, in the event of diminishing Canadian production, the fall in supply would be shared in proportion to the existing ratios of distribution regardless of national distinctions.

Predictably, such a sweeping agreement with so many far-reaching economic and political implications was controversial. Supporters of the proposal stressed its supposed economic benefits: "free trade" would save Canada from US protectionism and provide easier access to the market that already absorbed 80 percent of Canadian exports. Expanding trade would create new employment (300 000 new jobs according to the Economic Council of Canada). Opponents suggested that any new employment would be offset by jobs lost with closure of American branch-plants. But defenders of the agreement, such as the economist A.E. Safarian, suggested that parent companies would be more likely to follow the example of the auto industry under the Auto-Pact and rationalize operations continentally rather than retreat to main-plant capacity. And where a firm did sell off its Canadian subsidiary, another would be likely to buy the factory for a different use. Safarian predicted "increased foreign direct investment and technology contacts in both directions." As for the dislocation of workers (the stated reason for organized labour's outright rejection of the proposition), other analysts suggested that there was no novelty to such mobility in Canada. According to another economist, Ronald Wonnacott, one in four Canadians changed jobs every year already. The question was not whether workers would have the same job from one year to the next, but whether overall employment opportunities would expand or diminish. All supporters of the free-trade agreement argued that from the employment standpoint, the proposal was worthwhile if only for the security it provided against US protectionism, on the one hand, and encouragement to more investment by Americans, on the other.

The increased integration of the two economies that was admitted by the agreement's principal defenders was the critics' most effective argument against "free trade." Thirty percent of the entire Canadian GNP and 80 percent of all exports were already tied to the American economy. With Canada's entire defence posture determined by the American-dominated NATO and NORAD structures, critics argued that Canada was uniquely vulnerable to even minor adjustments of American policy in present circumstances. Nationalists of the left and right united in opposing any deliberate increase in Canadian dependency. If opposition to the bilateral agreement was foolish because of the existing level of dependence, they argued that acquiescence in the scheme was worse because there would be even less room for independent action once the two economies became even more "interconnected."

Unfortunately, the free-trade debate that ended in the dissolution of Parliament on October 1, 1988, tended to remain on the level of nationalistic slogan-shouting, partly because the Liberals had no other means to object to the proposal. Mulroney's Tories were merely concluding what King's Liberals had begun. King's own agreement of 1948 was dropped more for fear of controversy than for the discomfort he felt with the continentalism that he had promoted during the war. The trend continued under Diefenbaker, Pearson, and most of the Trudeau era. The policy brought to culmination by Mulroney was the dominant tradition of all major parties since 1940. Still, as opposition leader, Turner had to oppose the traditional position of his party espoused in 1988 by the Tories. He wrapped himself in the flag, and told Parliament and the people that he was the one true defender of Canadian history and pride.

More was possible with the opposition potential of the NDP. The Tories kept telling Canadians, still shaky in the piecemeal recovery from recession, that Canada's enduring prosperity depended upon a bold defence from American protectionism. Free trade was the best salvation for jobs, they declared. It would boost the value of the dollar and provide insurance against runaway inflation and skyrocketing interest rates. What was the democratic-socialist defence against US protectionism? Neither the leader of the NDP nor his party offered such an alternative in the two-month campaign before the election of November 21.

The NDP's unwillingness to move the free-trade debate from the categories claimed by Turner arose from the same dynamic that inhibited the CCF in its opposition to King in 1945. In both elections, public-opinion polls put Canada's orthodox leftwing in first-place position before the campaign began. And on both occasions, party strategists moderated their stance in the hope that such was the key to consolidating success. Moreover, because Turner was a survivor of internal party discord more than the true leader of effective opposition, NDP strategists were convinced that they were on the right track to replay the old drama in the new circumstances. If they minimized the party's socialist origins, appeared more fiscally responsible than the Liberals or the Tories, and opposed free trade on the basis that it jeopardized long-established social programs designed to guarantee "fairness for ordinary families," Ed Broadbent was certain to gain at least the second-place position.

For nearly the first half of the campaign the strategy seemed at least plausible. But since Turner and Broadbent were both assuming merely oppositional stances, and the Liberals were traditionally the stronger party, Turner became the more effective Jeremiah. In one particularly dramatic 30 seconds of televised debate with the other leaders at the end of October, he gained the attention of most persons opposing free trade and kept it through November. Still, that constituency was not as large as the portion of the electorate persuaded by Mulroney. Three days before the election, public-opinion polls showed that roughly half of the voters in every region believed that if they defeated free trade, they would pay with rising unemployment, a falling dollar, and higher interest rates. Perhaps for those reasons, Canadians re-elected a Mulroney majority on November 21, not by the same margin as in 1984, of course, but still comfortably ahead of the defeated opposition (43 percent *versus* 32 percent Liberal, 20 percent NDP, and five percent other).

— 4.   Dangerous Cynicism —

After the election, the new Parliament convened in a short December session to ratify the free-trade agreement so that the first phase of implementation could begin on schedule, January 1, 1989. Near the end of the year, however, 80 percent of those questioned in a CBC-*Globe and Mail* public-opinion poll reported that the beginnings of implementation had made no apparent difference to their individual well-being. Perhaps respondents were registering dissatisfaction with the persistence of all that free-trade—even in its first phase—was supposed to prevent: rising unemployment, escalating interest rates, and new initiatives in US protectionism aimed, in 1989, at Canadian pork and fish products. Moreover, punitively high duties on Canadian softwood lumber continued at tradewar levels. Predictably, support for the expected long-term effects of the agreement diminished; the public became increasingly cynical about the government's still-inflated claims for the benefits of free trade in the future. Even greater cynicism developed over renewed crisis in the state of federal-provincial relations.

Anticipating diminishing federal revenue with the gradual removal of the 15 percent (on average) tariff component of "customs and excise taxes" on US imports, and worried about the disadvantage to Canadian manufacturers having to pay a 13.5 percent "federal sales tax" imposed at the factory door, the Minister of Finance, Michael Wilson, proposed removal of the levy on manufacturers and imposition of a new nine percent goods and services tax (GST) at the point of distribution to consumers. In effect, the collection of the tariff on US imports was to be moved from the border to the retail cash register; but since the GST would apply to other imports as well as American, and goods of Canadian—as well as foreign—origin, the tax would not violate the "national treatment" rule under the free-trade agreement. Manufacturers would still gain a competitive advantage for the international market, and the federal government would realize substantial net revenue since the GST would apply to services as well as goods. Which services? Which goods? And how were the collectors of the tax to be compensated for time spent in the accounting nightmare of the new collection above and beyond all other taxes, federal and provincial?

Wilson offered a rough outline in the course of budget disclosures in April, 1989; but because implementation was left for 1991, that allowed almost two years for fine tuning the proposal and neutralizing the opposition. Clearly, one sales tax apportioned between two levels of government would be less complicated to collect, and potentially less burdensome to consumers. But such a scheme required agreement with premiers who were no more willing to relinquish control of provincial systems of sales taxes than were their predecessors to yield the personal income-tax collection to the federal government. And even if the provinces had been willing to co-operate, the public was worried about increasing the level of such regressive taxation because the government had already treated corporations to tax concessions that many Canadians considered too generous. In 1956, taxes on corporations accounted for one-fifth of the national revenue. Over the next 20 years, the figure had shrunk to 11 percent, and had dropped to nine percent of the total by 1989. But Michael Wilson insisted that continued easing of the corporate burden would result in Canada becoming more competitive internationally, and hence a brighter future for all, including the working poor, whose tax burden had increased 44 percent since 1984. Business lobby groups such as the Business Council on National Issues (representing the interests of Canada's largest corporations) were nearly alone in their support for the GST. Even so, the CBC-*Globe and Mail* poll in late October revealed that while 80 percent of respondents opposed the tax at nine percent, 54 percent said that they could accept a GST of seven percent. After nearly a year of insisting that the original figure was an absolute minimum, Michael Wilson announced just before Christmas 1989, that the tax would be implemented at the lower rate in 1991. Although the premiers still opposed the GST in principle, the possibility of a revolt of the public was at least blunted for the moment.

At the end of 1989, there was greater reason for concern over another contentious issue in federal-provincial relations. Three premiers stalled ratification of the Meech Lake constitutional compromise after all parties in the House of Commons, the Senate, and eight provincial governments endorsed the agreement in 1987 and 1988. None of the three "spoiler" premiers (Gary Filmon of Manitoba, Frank McKenna of New Brunswick, and Clyde Wells of Newfoundland) was involved in the negotiation of the accord. Each was convinced that his predecessor had struck a bad bargain; but Filmon alone had no choice in the matter. He faced political defeat if he moved to ratify the accord (McKenna's party controlled every seat in the New Brunswick legislature, and Wells had to mobilize his majority to rescind what the previous government had already signed and ratified). Filmon's situation was that of a Tory premier opposing Mulroney, and the only premier leading a minority in his own legislature—opposed by Liberals and New Democrats dedicated to defeating him at the first vote on the question. By force of circumstances, Filmon had to play a clever game.

First he delayed. Then, at the moment of an expected crisis over French-language legislation in Quebec, Filmon introduced a resolution proposing Manitoba's ratification of the accord and spoke in support of the motion on December 15, 1988. Simultaneously, the Supreme Court of Canada handed down its decision upholding those of the Quebec Superior Court (1984) and the Quebec Court of Appeal (1986) to overturn a clause in Quebec's Bill 101 that required all signs, posters, and commercial advertising in the province to be French only. The Supreme Court declared that the provision violated the freedom of expression sections in the Quebec and Canadian charters of rights; but a revised law could require "the predominant display of the French language, even its marked predominance" without posing any conflict with the qualification of the freedom of expression to be found in Section 1 of the Canadian charter, and the obligation to promote a *visage linguistique* for French contained in Section 9.1 of the Quebec charter. In effect, the Court told the plaintiff, stationer Allan Singer, that his individual right to freedom of expression did not extend to hanging a sign in English only in front of his shop. At the same time, the Supreme Court told the government of Quebec that its responsibility for safeguarding francophones' collective right to French did not extend to banning the less visible display of English or any other language. The Court proposed a remedy for the inconsistency between Quebec's language legislation and the province's charter of rights, while simultaneously asserting that the Canadian charter applied to Quebec as well as the rest of the country.

Predictably, *sovereigntistes* took note mainly of the secondary pronouncement and acted as René Lévesque had prophesied in 1982. Bourassa had to act boldly, moreso (he felt) than by enacting the made-in-Ottawa compromise proposed by the Supreme Court. On December 18, he announced that he was invoking the "notwithstanding" clauses of both charters to reassert the offending provision of Bill 101.

On December 19, the Manitoba premier withdrew his resolution in support of the Meech Lake accord. Filmon indicated that Quebec had to present statutory assurance that it would not use the "distinct society" clause to "trample on linguistic minorities" before he would resume his support of the agreement. At the same time, Filmon struck an all-party committee of the Manitoba legislature to seek other flaws in the existing text of the Meech Lake compromise and promised to wait for public hearings and the committee report before proceeding further—even if Quebec surrendered unconditionally in the interim.

Bourassa's reply to Filmon was that Quebec has "no lesson to receive from Manitoba on how to treat its linguistic minorities." The Meech Lake accord was not open for renegotiation. Given that the document required unanimous approval before June 23, 1990, commentators observing the Bourassa-Filmon standoff shifted their attention from the "promise of reconciliation" perceived in 1987-88, to the probable consequences of defeat of the ratification process in 1989-90, especially as other premiers sided with Filmon, and support for ratification evaporated in public opinion, falling to less than 20 percent outside Quebec by October, 1989.

By the time the chorus of denunciation had become an irresistible voice of opposition outside Quebec, the ground of criticism shifted from Filmon's expressed resentment over French domination, to the loftier plane of defeating the accord allegedly to preserve Canada. Well-educated opponents with children enrolled in French immersion programs stressed that the accord's alteration of the constitutional amending formula to require unanimity for Senate reform, admission of new provinces, and alteration of the federal spending power to give any province the right to opt out of national shared cost programs if the program happened to be in an area of exclusive provincial jurisdiction (and if the province intended to provide a similar or equivalent program of its own), would frustrate any future federal initiatives in social programs. Ignoring the history of the enactment of medicare (a program created under such conditions of universal opt-out), pointing instead to the dilapidated state of Newfoundland's confessional school system, Clyde Wells said, "We have already got complete jurisdiction in education and we cannot provide adequate schools for our children now." Still, his criticisms of the alterations of the federal spending power and the amending formula were never as heated as his denunciation of the "special status" implication of the "distinct society" clause. Wells said he was quite willing to say that Quebec is "indeed a society that it distinctly different." His and others' passions were aroused "when you go out and say the Constitution must be interpreted in such a way as to acknowledge . . . that the government and legislature of Quebec has a role and responsibility to protect and promote that character." According to Wells, "It is a situation that will wreck this country in the long term."

The tragedy of the Meech Lake constitutional compromise was that there was growing evidence that the reverse was also true: denying Quebec power and responsibility to protect its distinctiveness would encourage separatism. At the end of 1989, pollsters began to discover the scope of such resentment with more than half of the Quebeckers polled stating that they would prefer the Meech Lake compromise to separatism, but political sovereignty in economic association (Lévesque's option for Quebec) to continuation of the *status quo*. The disturbing cynicism developing in the rest of Canada (especially the deep West) was to reply, "bon voyage."

As Canada approached the last decade before the third millennium, the old conflicts appeared to have lost most of their poignancy. The crisis was as severe as any previous dispute in French-English relations; the novelty was the apparent lack of enthusiasm to act on extreme opinions. Such passivity suggested growing cynicism. At the same time, Quebeckers and the rest of the electorate may simply have registered their indifference for politics of the old agenda, suspending their political energy for new associations and leaders concerned in the 1990s with matters of more global significance, such as catastrophic change in the natural environment. In 1988—for the first time in a national election—candidates for Parliament had to offer at least verbal notification that they were concerned with environmental issues. None of the three parties proposed any profound solutions. But in this area, more than with the free-trade debate, the Meech Lake accord, the proposed goods and services tax, or even the arms race, Canada stood at a crossroads in 1990—and not alone.

—————————————————————————————— **Suggested Reading**

General history of the late 1980s has not appeared. David Bercuson, *et al.,* *Sacred Trust? Brian Mulroney and the Conservative Party in Power* (1986), chronicles the scandals. Work on the other questions in relation to the larger agenda is not available.

A bibliography of scholarly work on women's history since the 1960s would fill several pages. Veronica Strong-Boag, *The New Day Recalled: Lives of Girls and Women in English Canada, 1919-1939* (1988), and Ruth Pierson, *"They're Still Women After All: The Second World War and Canadian Womanhood* (1986), cover the disappointing years after women's enfranchisement. Alison Prentice, *et al., Canadian Women: A History* (1988), attempts a general synthesis. Veronica Strong-Boag and Anita Clair Fellman, eds., *Rethinking Canada: The Promise of Women's History* (1986), presents thoughtful essays. Also useful are the *Report of the Royal Commission on the Status of Women* (1970), and the sequel by the Canadian Advisory Council on the Status of Women, *Ten Years Later* (1980).

The appropriate background to the story of the political mobilization of Indians is E. Brian Titley, *A Narrow Vision: Duncan Campbell Scott and the Administration of Indian Affairs in Canada* (1986). Sally M. Weaver, *Making Canadian Indian Policy: The Hidden Agenda, 1968-1970* (1981), gives the history of the White Paper withdrawn in 1971; J. Rick Ponting, ed., *Arduous Journey: Canadian Indians and Decolonization* (1986), presents essays by 13 scholars concerned with contemporary native policy.

The literature of the everlasting constitutional question tends to lapse with the pause in developments in 1982. To date, only one thoughtful book-length account of the Mulroney accord has appeared from the work of a constitutional lawyer. Brian Schwartz, *Fathoming Meech Lake* (1987), denounces the arrangement.

Most of the writing pertaining to Mulroney's relations with the United States is equally critical. Stephen Clarkson, *Canada and the Reagan Challenge*, 2nd ed. (1985), continues Clarkson's lifelong plea for an independent Canada. James Laxer, *Leap of Faith: Free Trade and the Future of Canada* (1986), challenges the trade arrangement in particular. John Crispo, ed., *Free Trade: The Real Story* (1988), presents the case in favour of the agreement.

CONCLUSION

THE LIMITS AND RELEVANCE
OF CANADIAN HISTORY

While Canadian history continues toward unforeseeable outcomes, conclusions are still possible concerning the apparent structure of responses to recurring problems. The pattern of recurrence suggests certain *limits* of Canadian history.

1) *Canada has shown remarkable tolerance for energetic government.* Following French and British imperial traditions, Canadians have displayed a persistent willingness to regard the state as a positive, creative force. The internal improvement schemes of the nineteenth century and the public utility crown corporations and social security programs of the twentieth century are some of the more conspicuous results of permitting relatively unfettered government. The doctrine of legislative supremacy has had more appeal than the American view that a parliament is not to be trusted unless there are checks on its power by independent executive and judicial branches.

2) *Canada has shown a marked aversion to confessional politics.* The trust in powerful government has had, as a corollary aspect, the expectation that those vested with the public power will reward their friends and fulfill tangible projects for the benefit of the public. In Canadian history,

the politician who simply denounces patronage, stresses principles over practice, and sincerity over results, rarely gains widespread popularity. Canadians elected Alexander Mackenzie's party in a rare burst of moral indignation in 1874, and threw the "reformers" out of office four years later. Borden's reform government came to power in 1911 and passed into disrepute in 1920. Diefenbaker was the last and most popular of this type of politician, yet he fell furthest from grace and in less time than did Mackenzie. The more enduring movements of protest and dissent, such as the CCF-NDP third party phenomenon nationally, have not been merely oppositional but positive proponents of schemes of their own; the more popular aspects of their programs have been implemented by the major parties whenever necessary to avoid or recover from situations of minority government.

3) *Canada has regarded competing levels of jurisdiction as the best check against abuse of power.* Perhaps Canadians have not been more responsive to the call for moral aggression in national politics because they have been so consistently skillful at using the concrete purposes of one level of government against another. Prior to Confederation, the appeal against a provincial government went to the Colonial Office. After 1867, the play was between the provinces and Ottawa. Consequently, there have been long dynasties of Tories and Liberals in the national government and usually their opposites, Liberals and Tories, locally.

4) *Canada has shown extraordinary confidence in protection by external authority.* The power of Great Britain in North America did not end with Confederation. The British continued to command Canada's defence establishment in some ways into the 1940s, and provided Canada's last court of judicial appeal until 1949. Progressively from the 1850s, the United States assumed more importance, first in trade, then for investment capital, ultimately in defence.

5) *The external powers guaranteeing Canada's military security have served, also, as the principal markets for Canadian exports.* Collaboration with foreign powers for the purpose of military security is supposed to have conveyed an enhanced "sense of power" and greater prosperity through privileged access to imperial markets. On the identity theme, Canadians of British orientation enjoyed a sense of cosmopolitanism that was called "pride of empire" in the nineteenth century; more recently those with an "Atlantic community" or "continentalist" outlook regard positively their country's "responsible partnership in the Western Alliance." Such good feeling links with economic expectations in that

Canadians have imagined that the pace and scale of resource development have been directly aided by such fortuitous imperial connections.

6) *Canada's resource-base role in the world economy has been perceived as part of a natural order of justice.* Canadians have been reluctant to undo the colonialism in their imperial connections. On the one hand, they imagine that they are surviving tolerably well in a harsh climate by heroic struggle to exploit natural resources that do not yield their bounty easily. On the other, they imagine that those countries less inclined to dependency on exports of raw materials, or more oriented to export manufacturing, are simply more fortunate. Canada's continuing underdevelopment is not generally regarded as proof of betrayal by policies of governments (past and present). The have-not status of certain regions and individuals so frequently denounced in the rhetoric of opposition leaders and premiers opposing Ottawa is usually not a priority of politicians once they are in positions of power.

7) *Canada has cultivated economic nationalism as the one certain unifier and legitimate projection of the country into the future.* Sir John A. Macdonald's "National Policy," one of the first articulations of national purpose after Confederation, has been the most enduring. The rhetoric of protectionism fits the image of building a nation, even though the NP has afforded little protection from imports used in manufacturing. Indeed, the tariff was designed specifically to encourage branch-plant assembly operations. Still, protectionist affirmations have remained critically important for electoral purposes, as discovered by every politician from Laurier to Mulroney.

8) *Canadians have tended to regard the French-English duality as a continuing threat to national unity, therefore, a perennial weakness.* The principal reason for cultivating Canadian nationalism in rhetorical economic terms was that Canada has always been too divided by language and religion to pursue the more common variants of nineteenth-century ideological nationalism. As Canada divides along lines of its "primary antithesis," the grave misgivings about national unity erupt, periodically, in anti-French "equal rights for all, special privileges for none" sentiment. In such crises, the fundamental duality of the country is only too apparent and ordinarily perceived as a flaw that is potentially fatal.

Here, then, are a number of fundamentals of political practice in Canada that are likely to determine the limits of future possibility: statism, anti-confessionalism, federalism, imperialism, colonialism, staple economics, economic nationalism, ethnic diversity and conflict. One need not have the gift of prophecy to make such a prediction—only familiarity with the drift of Canadian history over the last several centuries. Another kind of observation that follows from the same knowledge concerns the relevance of Canadian history to world history because the study of national experience offers comparative insight. What can Canadian history show outside observers that may not be points of pride to Canadians but certainly matters of interest from a more global perspective?

One point would concern the contribution that Canada has made in the area of human rights. Whether they like it or not, Canadians are at the international forefront of the development of a jurisprudence of individual and collective rights. Most legal systems tend to be biased almost entirely one way or the other. But, in Canada, persons have individual rights as defined by the majority; and through the democratic process, majorities have conceded certain rights to minorities as collectivities. In the area of individual rights, the promise of privacy, freedom of speech, and access to government and justice are accorded to all because these are to be exercised and enforced on an individual basis. But some individuals are members of labour unions or Indian communities, speak a minority language, or are residents of a have-not province entitled to equalization payments. They have additional protection as members of such minorities because in Canada, the law recognizes the context of human rights. It is theoretically possible to deny an individual right and harm only one person. But the denial of a collective right harms an entire minority. The marvel of Canadian law is the richness of the developing safeguards on both aspects of human rights.

Of course, many Canadians would prefer to see the more simplistic individualist democracy of the United States prevail in their country. Americans have no constitutional guarantee that the poor states will be subsidized by the national government to guarantee a minimum level of social services. Minority languages such as Spanish have no protection in American law. Americans have a concept of one ideal way of life that is supposed to be served best by majority rule, unfettered by minority rights. The only collectivity to be recognized in law is the total population. "Equal rights for all, special privileges for none" is a fundamental in the American creed, but political bigotry in Canada. Consequently, a second aspect of Canadian history with relevance for world history is the country's failure to replace minority language and culture with one true Canadian tongue and creed. In this respect, Canadians probably enjoy more freedom than their southern neighbours because they are more alone to define themselves personally. Nobody knows a "100 percent Canadian."

Even so, a third likely impression of Canada by outside observers is how little the freedom inherent in the human rights and cultural diversity aspects has compelled independent action on the international stage, especially in the post-1945 period. In a world threatened by two military superpowers, Canada is unique for sharing boundaries with both—ideally situated by geography to play the Soviet Union and the United States against one another and assume a role of positive leadership among the non-aligned countries of the world. Instead, Canadians continue to seek security in the American alliance. Such dependency is not explicable by proximity: in geographical terms, the Canadian Arctic is as close to the Soviet Union as Windsor is to Detroit. And the explanation does not seem inherent in the similarity of the two economic systems. The Finns are nearly as "socialist" as the Russians, but Finland is no Warsaw pact "partner" of the USSR. Canada seeks "partnership" with the United States for reasons found in the previously mentioned limits of Canadian history. Whether these limits are immutable, the future will tell.

General Bibliographical Note

No form of historical literature becomes obsolete more rapidly than lists or essays covering "recent" publications. Such material is necessarily serialized. On a quarterly basis, *The Canadian Historical Review (CHR)* and *The Journal of Canadian Studies (JCS)* both publish extensive reviews of new books, and cumulative lists of materials not reviewed. Less current, but more comprehensive, are the essays in *A Reader's Guide to Canadian History*, 2 vols. (1982). The first volume, D.A. Muise, ed., covers *Beginnings to Confederation*. The second volume, G.L. Granatstein and Paul Stevens, eds., covers *Confederation to the Present*. But neither is well indexed and both are becoming rapidly out of date. The guide that fills the need of quarterly updating the reader while providing more than a mere listing of recent works is *America: History and Life*. Subjects in Canadian history are covered almost as thoroughly as the *CHR's* "Recent Publications Relating to Canada," and items are well indexed.

APPENDIX I: Statistical Tables

TABLE 1 Population of Canada, by province, census dates, 1851 to 1981

Year	Canada	Newfoundland	Prince Edward Island	Nova Scotia	New Brunswick	Quebec	Ontario	Manitoba	Saskatchewan	Alberta	British Columbia	Yukon	Northwest Territories
1981	24 498 900	570 500	123 000	850 000	698 600	6 455 700	8 664 700	1 029 900	977 400	2 287 400	2 771 300	23 800	46 500
1971	21 731 000	528 000	112 000	793 000	640 000	6 047 000	7 777 000	989 000	919 000	1 644 000	2 227 000	19 000	36 000
1961	18 238 247	457 853	104 629	737 007	597 936	5 259 211	6 236 092	921 686	925 181	1 331 944	1 629 082	14 628	22 998
1956	16 080 791	415 074	99 285	694 717	554 616	4 628 378	5 404 933	850 040	880 665	1 123 116	1 398 464	12 190	19 313
1951	14 009 429	361 416	98 429	642 584	515 697	4 055 681	4 597 542	776 541	831 728	939 501	1 165 210	9 096	16 004
1941	11 506 655	—	95 047	577 962	457 401	3 331 882	3 787 655	729 744	895 992	796 169	817 861	4 914	12 028
1931	10 376 786	—	88 038	512 846	408 219	2 874 662	3 431 683	700 139	921 785	731 605	694 263	4 230	9 316
1921	8 787 949	—	88 615	523 837	387 876	2 360 510	2 933 662	610 118	757 510	588 454	524 582	4 157	8 143
1911	7 206 643	—	93 728	492 338	351 889	2 005 776	2 527 292	461 394	492 432	374 295	392 480	8 512	6 507
1901	5 371 315	—	103 259	459 574	331 120	1 648 898	2 182 947	255 211	91 279	73 022	178 657	27 219	20 129
1891	4 833 239	—	109 078	450 396	321 263	1 488 535	2 114 321	152 506	—	—	98 173	—	98 967
1881	4 324 810	—	108 891	440 572	321 233	1 359 027	1 926 922	62 260	—	—	49 459	—	56 446
1871	3 689 257	—	94 021	387 800	285 594	1 191 516	1 620 851	25 228	—	—	36 247	—	48 000
1861	3 229 633	—	80 857	330 857	252 047	1 111 566	1 396 091	—	—	—	51 524	—	6 691[3]
1851	2 436 297	—	62 678	276 854	193 800	890 261	952 004	—	—	—	55 000	—	5 700[3]

SOURCES: M. C. Urquhart and K. A. H. Buckley, eds., *Historical Statistics of Canada* (Toronto, 1965), p. 14, and, *Canadian Statistical Review*, 1971, 1982.

TABLE 2   Urban Population of Canada, 1871 to 1971

Year	*100 000 persons and over*	*30 000–99 999 persons*	*5 000–29 999 persons*	*1 000–4 999 persons*	*Urban Total*
1971	5 767 205	3 045 306	3 314 026	1 536 623	13 663 160
1961	4 154 341	2 206 106	2 898 528	1 372 666	10 631 641
1951	3 260 939	1 147 888	1 947 128	1 155 584	7 511 539
1941	2 645 133	928 367	1 370 375	909 728	5 853 603
1931	2 328 175	696 680	1 305 304	830 742	5 160 901
1921	1 658 697	495 566	1 057 965	764 836	3 977 064
1911	1 080 960	488 748	782 771	655 097	3 007 576
1901	475 770	343 266	503 187	545 037	1 867 260
1891	397 865	224 760	390 670	427 310	1 440 605
1881	140 747	220 922	298 371	316 000	976 040
1871	107 225	115 791	228 354	196 000	647 370

SOURCE: Urquhart and Buckley, *Historical Statistics*, p. 15; ibid., 2nd ed. (Ottawa, 1983), series A67–69.

TABLE 3   Immigrant arrivals in Canada, 1852 to 1977

Year	Numbers	Year	Numbers	Year	Numbers	Year	Numbers
—	—	1945	22 722	1910	286 839	1875	27 382
—	—	1944	12 801	1909	173 694	1874	39 373
—	—	1943	8 504	1908	143 326	1873	50 050
1977	114 914	1942	7 576	1907	272 409	1872	36 578
1976	149 429	1941	9 329	1906	211 653	1871	27 773
1975	187 881	1940	11 324	1905	141 465	1870	24 706
1974	218 465	1939	16 994	1904	131 252	1869	18 630
1973	184 200	1938	17 244	1903	138 660	1868	12 765
1972	122 006	1937	15 101	1902	89 102	1867	10 666
1971	121 900	1936	11 643	1901	55 747	1866	11 427
1970	147 713	1935	11 277	1900	41 681	1865	18 958
1969	161 531	1934	12 476	1899	44 543	1864	24 779
1968	183 974	1933	14 382	1898	31 900	1863	21 000
1967	222 876	1932	20 591	1897	21 716	1862	18 294
1966	194 743	1931	27 530	1896	16 835	1861	13 589
1965	146 758	1930	104 806	1895	18 790	1860	6 276
1964	112 606	1929	164 993	1894	20 829	1859	6 300
1963	93 151	1928	166 783	1893	29 633	1858	12 339
1962	74 586	1927	158 886	1892	30 996	1857	33 854
1961	71 689	1926	135 982	1891	82 165	1856	22 544
1960	104 111	1925	84 907	1890	75 067	1855	25 296
1959	106 928	1924	124 164	1889	91 600	1854	37 263
1958	124 851	1923	133 729	1888	88 766	1853	29 464
1957	282 164	1922	64 224	1887	84 526	1852	29 307
1956	164 857	1921	91 728	1886	69 152	—	—
1955	109 946	1920	138 824	1885	79 169	—	—
1954	154 227	1919	107 698	1884	103 824	—	—
1953	168 868	1918	41 845	1883	133 624	—	—
1952	164 498	1917	72 910	1882	112 458	—	—
1951	194 391	1916	55 914	1881	47 991	—	—
1950	73 912	1915	36 665	1880	38 505	—	—
1949	95 217	1914	150 484	1879	40 492	—	—
1948	125 414	1913	400 870	1878	29 807	—	—
1947	64 127	1912	357 756	1877	27 082	—	—
1946	71 719	1911	331 288	1876	25 633	—	—

SOURCE: Urquhart and Buckley, *Historical Statistics*, p. 23; ibid, 2nd ed., series A350.

TABLE 4 Estimates of changes in the population ten years and over through natural increase and migration, 1881 to 1976 (thousands)

Appendix I

Interval	Population and changes	Canada[1]	Prince Edward Island	Nova Scotia	New Brunswick	Quebec	Ontario	Manitoba	Saskatchewan	Alberta	British Columbia	Yukon	Northwest Territories	Newfoundland[2]
1971–76	Natural increase	931	5	32	33	226	326	45	38	96	83	—	—	42
	Net migration	+493	+2	+7	+10	-19	+236	-12	-43	+114	+199	—	—	-6
1966–71	Natural increase	1 089	5	37	35	289	373	49	51	105	88	—	—	49
	Net migration	+464	-2	-4	-17	-42	+369	-24	-80	+59	+222	—	—	-20
1961–66	Natural increase	1 518	9	60	53	458	488	70	76	135	104	—	—	60
	Net migration	+259	-5	-40	-34	+64	+237	-29	-46	-33	+140	—	—	-24
1956–61	Natural increase	1 675	9	65	60	522	523	76	86	144	126	—	—	59
	Net migration	+482	-3	-23	-16	+109	+308	-4	-42	+65	+105	—	—	-16
1951–56	Natural increase	1 473	9	63	60	477	430	74	86	121	98	—	—	52
	Net migration	+598	-8	-11	-21	+96	+377	—	-37	+63	+135	—	—	+2
1941–51	Natural increase	1 972	—	—	—	—	—	—	—	—	—	—	—	—
	Net migration	+169	—	—	—	—	—	—	—	—	—	—	—	—
1931–41	Natural increase	1 352	9	60	62	495	322	89	156	109	48	—	2	—
	Net migration	-112	-2	+2	-13	-32	+75	-41	-138	-35	+72	—	—	—
1921–31	Natural increase	1 389	9	69	61	443	338	116	173	116	62	—	2	—
	Net migration	+103	-9	-70	-43	-10	+129	-10	-5	+22	+101	-4	-1	—
1911–21	Natural increase	1 036	9	62	52	378	259	82	93	64	36	—	1	—
	Net migration	+113	-14	-37	-25	-99	+46	+24	+78	+85	+58	-4	—	—
1901–11	Natural increase	711	12	52	44	284	218	48	18	15	16	-1	4	—
	Net migration	+715	-17	-28	-30	-29	+74	+111	+283	+218	+164	-17	-14	—
1891–1901	Natural increase	654	14	50	43	249	245	30	—	—	8	—	17	—
	Net migration	-181	-17	-40	-32	-121	-144	+48	—	—	+58	—	+68	—
1881–91	Natural increase	669	16	60	48	235	282	13	—	—	5	—	13	—
	Net migration	-205	-14	-43	-44	-132	-84	+52	—	—	+37	—	+21	—

SOURCE: Urquhart and Buckley, *Historical Statistics*, p. 22, ibid., 2nd ed., series A339–350.
[1]Includes the Yukon and Northwest Territories after 1941.
[2]Newfoundland included only for period after entry to Confederation.

**TABLE 5   Population and Economic Development,
US and Canada, 1870-1955**

Year	Population in millions		Gross national product in billions of 1929 dollars	
	Can.	U.S.	Can.	U.S.
1870	3.63	39.91	.88	9.40
1880	4.26	50.26	1.13	17.45
1890	4.78	63.06	1.57	26.20
1900	5.30	76.09	2.16	38.20
1910	6.99	92.41	3.55	56.50
1915	7.98	100.55	4.15	60.42
1916	8.00	101.97	4.32	68.87
1917	8.06	103.27	4.40	67.26
1918	8.15	103.20	4.45	73.36
1919	8.31	104.51	4.55	74.16
1920	8.56	106.47	4.42	73.31
1921	8.79	108.54	4.03	71.58
1922	8.92	110.06	4.35	75.79
1923	9.01	111.95	4.51	85.82
1924	9.14	114.11	4.51	88.36
1925	9.29	115.83	4.82	90.53
1926	9.45	117.4	5.13	96.4
1927	9.64	119.0	5.60	97.3
1928	9.84	120.5	6.12	98.5
1929	10.03	121.8	6.13	104.4
1930	10.21	123.1	5.88	95.1
1931	10.38	124.0	5.12	89.5
1932	10.51	124.8	4.60	76.4
1933	10.63	125.6	4.31	74.2
1934	10.74	126.4	4.83	80.8
1935	10.85	127.3	5.20	91.4
1936	10.95	128.1	5.43	100.9
1937	11.05	128.8	5.97	109.1
1938	11.15	129.8	6.01	103.2
1939	11.27	130.9	6.46	111.0
1940	11.38	132.0	7.39	121.0
1941	11.51	133.1	8.45	138.7
1942	11.65	133.9	10.36	154.7
1943	11.80	134.2	10.44	170.2
1944	11.95	132.9	10.8	183.6
1945	12.07	132.5	10.5	180.9
1946	12.29	140.1	10.3	165.6
1947	12.55	143.4	10.5	164.1
1948	12.82	146.1	10.7	173.0
1949	13.45	148.7	11.1	170.6
1950	13.71	151.2	11.8	187.4
1951	14.01	153.4	12.6	199.4
1952	14.46	155.8	13.6	205.8
1953	14.85	158.3	14.1	214.0
1954	15.29	161.2	13.7	208.6
1955	15.70	164.3	14.8	225.6

SOURCE: J. H. Dales, *The Protective Tariff in Canada's Development*
(Toronto: University of Toronto Press), pp. 136-137.

TABLE 6   Canadian Export Trade, selective years, 1869-1959 (thousands of dollars)

Year	A. Exports to United Kingdom	A/D (%)	B. Exports to United States	B/D (%)	C. Exports to Other Countries	D. Value of Total Exports
1869	20 486	39.1	26 718	51.0	5 197	52 401
1874	35 769	46.6	33 196	43.3	7 777	76 742
1879	29 393	47.1	25 491	40.8	7 546	62 431
1884	37 411	46.9	34 333	43.0	8 090	79 833
1889	33 504	41.7	39 520	49.2	7 248	80 272
1894	60 878	58.6	32 563	31.4	10 411	103 852
1899	85 114	62.0	39 327	29.0	12 921	137 361
1904	110 121	55.5	66 857	33.7	21 437	198 414
1909	126 385	52.1	85 335	35.2	30 884	242 604
1914	215 254	49.9	163 373	37.9	52 962	431 588
1919	540 751	44.5	454 873	37.4	220 820	1 216 444
1924	360 057	34.4	430 707	41.2	254 585	1 045 351
1929	429 730	31.4	504 161	36.8	434 367	1 368 259
1934	288 582	43.3	220 072	33.0	157 298	665 954
1939	325 465	36.0	375 939	39.9	225 557	926 962
1944	1 235 030	35.9	1 301 322	37.8	903 601	3 439 953
1949	709 261	23.5	1 524 024	50.4	789 168	3 022 453
1954	658 315	16.7	2 367 439	60.0	921 163	3 946 917
1959	797 098	15.4	3 206 543	62.0	1 175 737	5 179 378

SOURCE: C. P. Stacey, *Canada and the Age of Conflict*, Vol. I (Toronto: Macmillan, 1977), p. 356-357, Vol. II (Toronto: University of Toronto Press, 1981), p. 434-435; and Urquhart and Buckley, *Historical Statistics*, p. 183.

TABLE 7   Canadian Import Trade, selected years, 1869-1959 (thousands of dollars)

Year	A. *Imports from* *United Kingdom*	A/D *(%)*	B. *Imports from* *United States*	B/D *(%)*	C. *Imports from* *Other Countries*	D. *Value of* *Total Imports*
1869	35 497	56.2	21 497	34.0	6 161	63 155
1874	61 424	49.9	51 707	42.0	10 050	123 181
1879	30 968	39.3	42 170	53.6	5 564	78 703
1884	41 925	39.6	49 786	47.0	14 262	105 973
1889	42 251	38.7	50 029	46.0	16 818	109 098
1894	37 036	34.0	50 746	46.5	21 289	109 071
1899	36 967	24.7	88 507	59.2	23 949	149 422
1904	61 725	25.3	143 330	58.7	38 855	243 909
1909	70 683	24.5	170 432	59.0	47 479	288 594
1914	132 070.	21.4	396 302	64.0	90 821	619 194
1919	73 035	8.0	750 203	81.6	96 474	919 712
1924	153 586	17.2	601 256	67.3	138 523	893 366
1929	194 041	15.3	868 012	68.6	203 625	1 265 679
1934	105 100	24.2	238 187	54.9	90 510	433 789
1939	115 636	17.6	412 476	62.7	130 115	658 228
1944	110 599	6.3	1 447 226	82.3	201 073	1 758 898
1949	307 450	11.1	1 951 860	70.7	501 897	2 761 207
1954	392 472	9.6	2 961 380	72.3	739 344	4 093 196
1959	596 562	10.6	3 829 438	67.7	1 228 423	5 654 423

SOURCE: C. P. Stacey, *Canada and the Age of Conflict,* Vol. I (Toronto: Macmillan, 1977), p. 356-357, Vol. II (Toronto: University of Toronto Press, 1981), p. 434-435; and Urquhart and Buckley, *Historical Statistics,* p. 183.

TABLE 8 Tax Revenues of the Federal Government, 1867 to 1960 (millions of dollars)

| | Direct taxes | | | | | | Indirect taxes | | | | | | |
Year[1]	Income tax Corporation	Income tax Individual	Non-resident	Estate tax[2]	Excess profits tax	Total direct taxes	Net sales tax	Other excise taxes	Excise duties	Customs import duties	Miscellaneous indirect taxes	Total indirect taxes	Total tax revenue
1960	1 276.6	1 711.2	88.2	84.9	—	3 160.9	720.6	290.7	344.9	498.7	—	1 854.9	5 015.8
1959	1 142.9	1 566.6	73.3	88.4	—	2 871.2	732.7	286.6	335.2	525.7	.9	1 881.1	4 752.3
1958	1 020.6	1 353.5	61.2	72.6	—	2 507.9	694.5	240.6	316.7	486.5	1.2	1 739.5	4 247.4
1957	1 234.8	1 499.8	64.3	71.6	—	2 870.5	703.2	249.4	300.1	498.1	1.5	1 752.3	4 622.8
1956	1 268.3	1 400.5	76.4	79.7	—	2 824.9	717.1	267.1	271.4	549.1	18.3	1 823.0	4 647.9
1955	1 027.7	1 185.6	66.2	66.6	—	2 346.1	641.5	260.7	240.4	481.2	16.8	1 640.6	3 995.7
1954	1 020.6	1 183.4	61.3	44.8	—	2 310.1	572.2	252.0	226.5	397.2	15.5	1 463.4	3 773.5
1953	1 191.2	1 187.7	53.8	39.1	—	2 471.8	587.3	296.0	226.7	407.3	14.5	1 531.8	4 003.6
1952	1 240.1	1 180.0	53.7	38.1	—	2 511.9	566.2	275.7	241.4	389.4	13.0	1 485.7	3 997.6
1951	1 130.7	975.7	55.0	38.2	2.3	2 201.9	573.5	312.4	217.0	346.4	5.7	1 455.9	3 657.8
1950	799.2	652.3	61.6	33.6	10.1	1 556.8	460.1	226.7	241.1	295.7	4.9	1 228.5	2 785.3
1949	603.2	622.0	47.5	29.9	-1.8	1 300.8	403.4	168.0	220.6	225.9	4.4	1 022.3	2 323.1
1948	492.0	762.6	43.4	25.5	44.8	1 368.3	377.3	258.8	204.6	223.0	4.1	1 067.8	2 436.1
1947	364.2	659.8	35.9	30.8	227.0	1 317.7	372.3	268.5	196.8	293.0	3.8	1 134.4	2 452.1
1946	238.8	670.5	30.1	23.6	442.5	1 405.5	298.2	280.8	196.0	237.4	9.7	1 022.1	2 427.6
1945	217.8	686.6	28.3	21.5	426.7	1 380.9	212.2	284.7	186.7	128.9	9.0	821.5	2 202.4
1944	276.4	672.8	28.5	17.3	341.3	1 336.3	209.4	333.7	151.9	115.1	8.2	818.3	2 154.6
1943	311.4	698.4	26.9	15.1	428.7	1 480.5	304.9	333.8	142.1	167.8	7.7	956.3	2 436.8
1942	348.0	484.2	28.0	13.3	434.6	1 308.1	232.9	255.8	138.7	119.0	12.2	758.6	2 066.7
1941	185.8	296.2	28.2	7.0	135.2	652.4	236.2	217.2	110.1	142.4	2.6	708.5	1 360.9
1940	131.6	103.5	13.0	—	24.0	272.1	179.7	104.4	88.6	130.8	2.5	506.0	778.1
1939	77.9	45.4	11.1	—	.	134.4	137.4	28.6	61.1	104.3	2.4	333.8	468.2
1938	85.2	46.9	9.9	—	—	142.0	122.1	39.6	51.3	78.8	2.4	294.2	436.2
1937	69.8	40.4	10.2	—	—	120.4	138.0	42.8	52.0	93.5	2.5	328.8	449.2
1936	58.0	35.5	8.9	—	—	102.4	112.8	39.7	45.9	83.8	2.4	284.6	387.0
1935	42.5	33.0	7.2	—	—	82.7	77.6	35.1	44.4	74.0	3.8	234.9	317.6
1934	35.8	25.2	5.8	—	—	66.8	72.4	39.8	43.2	76.6	6.1	238.1	304.9
1933	27.4	29.2	4.8	—	—	61.4	61.4	45.2	35.5	66.3	2.3	210.7	272.1
1932	36.0	26.0	—	—	—	62.0	56.8	25.4	37.8	70.1	2.4	192.5	254.5

TABLE 8 Tax Revenues of the Federal Government, 1867 to 1960 (millions of dollars) (continuation)

Year[1]	Direct taxes						Indirect taxes						Total tax revenue
	Income tax		Non-resident	Estate tax[2]	Excess profits tax	Total direct taxes	Net sales tax	Other excise taxes	Excise duties	Customs import duties	Miscellaneous indirect taxes	Total indirect taxes	
	Corporation	Individual											
1931	36.5	24.8	—	—	—	61.3	41.7	17.9	48.7	104.1	1.7	214.1	275.4
1930	44.4	26.6	—	—	—	71.0	20.2	14.5	57.7	131.2	2.1	225.7	296.7
1929	41.8	27.2	—	—	.2	69.2	44.1	19.3	65.0	179.4	1.8	309.6	378.8
1928	34.6	24.8	—	—	.5	59.9	62.6	20.4	63.7	187.2	2.4	336.3	396.2
1927	33.4	23.2	—	—	.9	57.5	70.6	19.6	57.4	157.0	2.9	307.5	365.0
1926	29.3	18.1	—	—	.7	48.1	81.2	24.4	48.5	141.9	2.9	298.9	347.0
1925	31.7	23.9	—	—	1.2	56.8	72.9	25.2	42.9	127.3	2.8	271.1	327.9
1924	31.0	25.2	—	—	2.7	58.9	63.2	22.6	38.6	108.1	2.5	235.0	293.0
1923	28.5	25.7	—	—	4.7	58.9	98.0	22.7	38.2	121.5	2.4	282.8	341.7
1922	28.0	31.7	—	—	13.0	72.7	89.8	16.7	35.8	118.0	2.4	262.7	335.4
1921	38.9	39.8	—	—	22.8	101.5	61.3	12.4	36.7	105.7	2.3	218.4	319.9
1920	13.9	32.5	—	—	40.8	87.2	37.6	41.2	37.1	163.3	2.4	281.6	368.8
1919	7.1	13.2	—	—	44.1	64.4	—	15.6	42.7	168.8	2.1	229.2	293.6
1918	1.4	8.0	—	—	32.9	42.3	—	11.8	30.3	147.1	2.2	191.4	233.7
1917	—	—	—	—	21.2	21.2	—	2.2	27.2	144.2	1.9	175.5	196.7
1916	—	—	—	—	12.5	12.5	—	2.1	24.4	134.1	1.7	162.3	174.8
1915	—	—	—	—	—	—	—	1.6	22.4	98.6	2.1	124.7	124.7
1914	—	—	—	—	—	—	—	.1	21.5	75.9	—	97.5	97.5
1913	—	—	—	—	—	—	—	—	21.4	104.7	—	126.1	126.1
1912	—	—	—	—	—	—	—	—	21.4	111.8	—	133.2	133.2
1911	—	—	—	—	—	—	—	—	19.3	85.0	—	104.3	104.3
1910	—	—	—	—	—	—	—	—	16.9	71.8	—	88.7	88.7
1909	—	—	—	—	—	—	—	—	15.2	59.8	—	75.0	75.0
1908	—	—	—	—	—	—	—	—	14.9	47.1	—	62.0	62.0
1907	—	—	—	—	—	—	—	—	15.8	57.2	—	73.0	73.0
1906	—	—	—	—	—	—	—	—	11.8	39.7	—	51.5	51.5
1905	—	—	—	—	—	—	—	—	14.0	46.1	—	60.1	60.1
1904	—	—	—	—	—	—	—	—	12.6	41.5	—	54.1	54.1
1903	—	—	—	—	—	—	—	—	12.9	40.5	—	53.4	53.4
1902	—	—	—	—	—	—	—	—	12.0	36.7	—	48.7	48.7
1901	—	—	—	—	—	—	—	—	11.2	31.9	—	43.1	43.1
1900	—	—	—	—	—	—	—	—	10.3	28.3	—	38.6	38.6
1899	—	—	—	—	—	—	—	—	9.9	28.2	—	38.1	38.1
1898	—	—	—	—	—	—	—	—	9.6	25.2	—	34.8	34.8
1897	—	—	—	—	—	—	—	—	7.9	21.6	—	29.5	29.5
1896	—	—	—	—	—	—	—	—	9.2	19.4	—	28.6	28.6

Year					
1895	27.7	27.7	—	19.8	7.9
1894	25.4	25.4	—	17.6	7.8
1893	27.5	27.5	—	19.1	8.4
1892	29.3	29.3	—	20.9	8.4
1891	28.4	28.4	—	20.5	7.9
1890	30.3	30.3	—	23.4	6.9
1889	31.5	31.5	—	23.9	7.6
1888	30.6	30.6	—	23.7	6.9
1887	28.2	28.2	—	22.1	6.1
1886	28.7	28.7	—	22.4	6.3
1885	25.2	25.2	—	19.4	5.8
1884	25.4	25.4	—	18.9	6.5
1883	25.5	25.5	—	20.0	5.5
1882	29.3	29.3	—	23.0	6.3
1881	27.5	27.5	—	21.6	5.9
1880	23.7	23.7	—	18.4	5.3
1879	18.3	18.3	—	14.1	4.2
1878	18.3	18.3	—	12.9	5.4
1877	17.6	17.6	—	12.8	4.8
1876	17.5	17.5	—	12.6	4.9
1875	18.4	18.4	—	12.8	5.6
1874	20.4	20.4	—	15.3	5.1
1873	19.9	19.9	—	14.3	5.6
1872	17.4	17.4	—	12.9	4.5
1871	17.5	17.5	—	12.8	4.7
1870	16.1	16.1	—	11.8	4.3
1869	12.9	12.9	—	9.3	3.6
1868	11.1	11.1	—	8.4	2.7
1867	11.6	11.6	—	8.6	3.0

SOURCE: Urquhart and Buckley, *Historical Statistics,* pp. 197-198.

379

TABLE 9   Expenditures of the Federal Government, 1867 to 1960 (millions of dollars)

Year	Defence and mutual aid	Health	Family allowances	Unemployment assistance and relief projects	Old age assistance, blind and disabled persons allowances	Public debt charges	General government	Payments to provincial and municipal governments	budgetary expenditure
1960	1 537.9	269.8	506.2	51.5	51.3	797.6	386.9	563.4	5 958.1
1959	1 536.8	227.2	491.2	40.2	50.6	783.5	368.0	542.5	5 702.9
1958	1 442.4	132.1	474.8	23.9	49.7	648.0	378.4	490.0	5 364.0
1957	1 687.4	64.6	437.9	8.2	39.8	567.4	405.8	401.2	5 087.4
1956	1 783.8	62.0	397.5	7.9	30.5	534.1	410.6	405.7	4 849.0
1955	1 768.6	56.4	382.5	—	29.5	514.3	291.9	358.5	4 433.1
1954	1 687.9	53.1	366.5	—	24.3	502.3	286.5	362.6	4 275.3
1953	1 857.8	49.5	350.1	—	23.2	495.7	279.4	344.6	4 350.5
1952	1 972.9	44.9	334.2	—	22.1	464.9	236.9	341.7	4 337.3
1951	1 446.5	41.0	320.5	—	83.2	531.0	299.6	129.5	3 732.9
1950	787.3	33.1	309.5	2.9	103.2	439.0	221.8	125.5	2 901.2
1949	387.2	29.5	297.5	3.6	93.2	450.8	170.0	104.6	2 448.6
1948	268.8	19.1	270.9	—	66.8	475.2	150.3	101.7	2 175.9
1947	196.0	8.4	263.2	—	59.1	466.7	156.4	155.9	2 195.6
1946	387.6	6.0	245.1	—	45.4	477.2	165.1	108.8	2 634.2
1945	2 942.1	2.3	172.6	—	42.8	437.6	129.9	112.7	5 136.2
1944	3 999.9	1.1	—	—	41.0	339.8	138.6	108.2	5 245.6
1943	4 241.6	.7	—	—	33.5	262.1	66.7	109.8	5 322.2
1942	2 563.3	1.1	—	—	31.0	202.5	69.5	109.1	4 387.1
1941	1 267.7	1.1	—	2.0	29.6	171.6	90.0	35.5	1 885.0
1940	730.1	1.0	—	19.7	29.9	145.7	66.7	19.4	1 249.6
1939	125.7	.9	—	39.7	30.0	134.6	38.3	19.4	680.8
1938	34.8	.9	—	42.8	29.1	133.1	45.1	21.4	553.1
1937	32.7	.1	—	68.5	28.7	132.1	41.7	21.3	534.4
1936	22.9	.1	—	78.0	21.1	137.4	37.3	16.9	532.0
1935	17.2	.6	—	79.4	16.7	134.5	36.5	17.8	532.6
1934	13.9	.5	—	61.0	14.9	138.5	26.0	15.4	478.1
1933	13.2	.5	—	36.0	12.3	139.7	30.4	15.3	458.2
1932	13.5	.6	—	36.7	11.5	135.0	33.1	15.3	532.4
1931	17.9	.9	—	38.3	10.1	121.1	33.5	14.0	448.7
1930	23.4	.9	—	4.4	5.6	121.3	29.3	19.2	441.6
1929	21.8	1.0	—	—	1.5	121.6	28.9	14.4	405.3
1928	19.6	.9	—	—	.8	125.0	28.4	14.2	394.1
1927	17.6	.8	—	2.0	.2	128.9	22.7	14.4	379.8
1926	14.8	.7	—	—	.1	129.7	20.7	12.7	359.2

Year									
1925	355.6	12.7	19.5	130.7	—	—	—	.6	14.1
1924	352.2	12.6	16.6	134.8	—	—	—	.6	13.2
1923	371.8	12.7	18.8	136.2	—	—	—	.6	13.4
1922	441.2	12.2	19.5	137.9	—	.9	—	.7	14.2
1921	476.3	12.2	23.4	135.2	—	.5	—	.7	17.5
1920	528.9	11.5	20.2	139.5	—	—	—	.7	30.2
1919	740.1	11.5	23.2	125.4	—	1.5	—	.5	346.6
1918	695.6	11.3	8.0	77.4	—	—	—	.4	438.7
1917	573.5	11.3	16.3	47.8	—	—	—	.4	343.8
1916	496.7	11.5	14.4	35.8	—	—	—	.4	312.0
1915	337.9	11.5	9.5	21.4	—	—	—	.3	172.5
1914	246.4	11.5	13.2	15.7	—	—	—	.4	72.4
1913	184.9	11.4	14.6	12.9	—	—	—	.2	13.5
1912	143.1	13.2	9.8	12.6	—	—	—	.1	11.4
1911	136.0	10.3	7.5	12.3	—	—	—	.1	9.7
1910	121.6	9.1	8.2	12.5	—	—	—	.1	9.2
1909	113.9	9.4	8.1	13.1	—	—	—	—	6.1
1908	131.5	9.1	7.1	11.6	—	—	—	—	6.5
1907	110.3	9.1	6.0	11.0	—	—	—	—	6.9
1906[1]	64.6	9.7	4.1	6.7	—	—	—	—	4.4
1905	81.0	6.7	5.3	10.8	—	—	—	—	5.7
1904	76.5	4.5	5.6	10.6	—	—	—	—	4.2
1903	69.9	9.8	5.1	11.1	—	—	—	—	3.7
1902	59.1	4.4	4.3	11.1	—	—	—	—	2.6
1901	61.4	4.4	4.2	11.0	—	—	—	—	2.8
1900	55.5	4.3	4.1	10.8	—	—	—	—	3.2
1899	50.2	4.3	4.2	10.7	—	—	—	—	3.6
1898	49.0	4.2	4.1	10.8	—	—	—	—	2.6
1897	43.0	4.2	4.2	10.5	—	—	—	—	1.8
1896	40.9	4.2	4.3	10.6	—	—	—	—	2.6
1895	42.0	4.2	4.4	10.5	—	—	—	—	2.2
1894	40.9	4.2	4.5	10.5	—	—	—	—	1.7
1893	40.9	4.2	4.1	10.2	—	—	—	—	1.4
1892	38.7	3.9	4.0	9.8	—	—	—	—	1.5
1891	40.2	3.9	3.9	9.8	—	—	—	—	1.4
1890	38.9	3.9	3.9	9.6	—	—	—	—	1.4
1889	39.9	3.9	3.5	9.7	—	—	—	—	1.4
1888	41.8	4.1	3.7	10.1	—	—	—	—	1.4
1887	43.1	4.2	3.5	9.8	—	—	—	—	1.9
1886	39.9	4.2	2.3	9.7	—	—	—	—	1.6
1885	60.2	4.2	4.4	10.1	—	—	—	—	4.5
1884	47.6	4.0	2.8	9.4	—	—	—	—	2.8
1883	56.5	3.6	3.0	7.7	—	—	—	—	1.1
1882	41.6	3.6	2.8	7.7	—	—	—	—	.8
1881	33.4	3.5	2.6	7.7	—	—	—	—	.9

TABLE 9 Expenditures of the Federal Government, 1867 to 1960 (millions of dollars) (continuation)

Year	Defence and mutual aid	Health	Family allowances	Unemployment assistance and relief projects	Old age assistance, blind and disabled persons allowances	Public debt charges	General government	Payments to provincial and municipal governments	budgetary expenditure
1880	.8	—	—	—	—	7.6	2.6	3.5	32.6
1879	.8	—	—	—	—	7.8	2.3	3.4	32.8
1878	.8	—	—	—	—	7.2	2.4	3.4	29.6
1877	.6	—	—	—	—	7.0	2.5	3.5	29.5
1876	.6	—	—	—	—	6.8	2.3	3.6	31.6
1875	1.1	—	—	—	—	6.4	2.4	3.7	31.1
1874	1.1	—	—	—	—	6.6	2.5	3.8	32.3
1873	1.3	—	—	—	—	5.7	2.5	3.8	33.0
1872	1.3	—	—	—	—	5.2	2.6	2.9	38.6
1871	1.7	—	—	—	—	5.2	1.6	2.9	25.2
1870	.9	—	—	—	—	5.1	1.4	2.6	18.9
1869	1.2	—	—	—	—	5.0	1.4	2.6	17.9
1868	.9	—	—	—	—	4.9	1.6	2.6	14.5
1867	.8	—	—	—	—	4.1	1.5	2.6	13.7

SOURCE: Urquhart and Buckley, *Historical Statistics*, pp. 200-203.

TABLE 10 Revenues of the Provinces, selected years, 1933-1960 (millions of dollars)

| Year[1] | Taxes — Income tax | | | General sales | Motor fuel | Total taxes | Liquor control | Privileges, licences and permits | | | | Government enterprises | Other revenue | Sub-total | Transfers from other governments | | | | Total net revenues |
	Corporate	Individual	Total					Motor vehicles	Natural resources	Other	Total				Federal-provincial tax sharing	Federal-provincial tax rentals	Subsidies etc.	Sub-total	
1960[2]	269	61	330	212	402	1 246	47	172	277	28	524	191	53	2 014	480	—	58	538	2 552
1959	249	54	303	209	382	1 168	45	164	303	27	539	186	52	1 945	460	—	58	518	2 463
1958	226	48	274	187	364	1 010	38	146	259	23	466	180	53	1 709	398	—	69	467	2 176
1957	214	41	255	183	347	955	40	140	278	20	478	167	40	1 640	353	—	29	382	2 022
1956	62	36	98	178	300	732	33	128	288	20	469	157	37	1 395	—	366	29	395	1 790
1955	54	30	84	149	269	664	33	114	257	18	422	141	32	1 259	—	320	32	352	1 611
1954	49	25	74	129	240	566	31	94	185	17	327	130	30	1 053	—	327	32	359	1 412
1953	49	—	49	108	224	506	32	88	195	16	331	128	28	993	—	309	32	341	1 334
1952	65	—	65	101	200	487	31	81	—[2]	170	282	130	25	924	—	303	31	334	1 258
1951	163	—	163	91	182	566	28	73	—[2]	139	240	118	25	949	—	96	31	127	1 076
1950	127	—	127	76	157	478	27	67	99	14	207	115	28	828	93	—	30	123	951
1949	106	—	106	62	139	418	26	58	82	12	178	111	26	733	80	—	28	108	841
1948	88	—	88	48	125	363	25	50	59	11	145	107	27	642	84	—	19	103	745
1947	62	—	62	31	112	287	24	46	42	11	123	103	27	540	131	—	19	150	690
1946	1	—	1	25	74	165	21	38	42	10	111	104	21	401	84	—	17	101	502
1945	—	—	—	21	59	131	20	32	—[2]	47	99	80	12	322	88	—	19	107	429
1943	—	1	1	18	46	108	—[3]	30	33	10	—	—[3]	70	251	93	—	17	110	361
1941	31	11	42	16	60	178	—[3]	32	34	9	—	—[3]	49	302	20	—	17	37	339
1939	11	12	23	3	53	139	—[3]	28	24	9	—	—[3]	36	236	—	—	22	22	258
1937	9	12	21	2	39	129	—[3]	26	25	9	—	—[3]	32	221	—	—	24	24	245
1933	3	5	8	—	26	73	—[3]	20	13	8	—	—[3]	19	133	—	—	19	19	152

[1] Figures are for fiscal year ending nearest 31 December of year named.
[2] Included in 'other privileges, licences and permits'.
[3] Included in 'other revenue'.

SOURCE: Urquhart and Buckley, *Historical Statistics*, pp. 200-209.

TABLE 11   Expenditures of the Provinces, selected years, 1933–1960 (millions of dollars)

Year[1]	Health	Social welfare	Education	Transportation and communication	Natural resources and primary industries	Debt charges	General	Protection of persons and property	Other	Sub-total	Subsidies to municipalities	Total net expenditure
1960	508	257	698	713	201	67	125	136	93	2 798	70	2 868
1959	436	206	602	680	174	57	110	126	86	2 477	66	2 543
1958	330	191	521	622	158	55	95	116	76	2 164	61	2 225
1957	301	168	452	587	147	55	83	108	78	1 979	54	2 033
1956	261	143	362	561	132	55	70	92	54	1 730	41	1 771
1955	246	134	333	447	122	55	65	82	53	1 537	36	1 573
1954	234	124	274	371	107	57	55	78	47	1 347	37	1 384
1953	209	103	234	353	102	53	52	77	44	1 227	30	1 257
1952	192	95	221	367	94	57	48	67	39	1 180	27	1 207
1951	174	92	196	299	85	57	45	61	41	1 050	23	1 073
1950	158	87	183	250	72	52	37	51	35	925	16	941
1949	143	80	160	254	60	53	33	46	33	862	14	876
1948	102	62	142	255	75	52	34	35	28	785	13	798
1947	78	54	124	207	60	49	28	29	19	648	8	656
1946	57	44	88	135	46	51	21	24	12	478	9	487
1945	42	41	70	78	37	56	22	21	9	376	9	385
1943	35	33	50	55	30	60	—[2]	—[2]	38	301	3	304
1941	30	34	43	71	32	63	—[2]	—[2]	38	311	3	314
1939	30	68	38	89	30	61	—[2]	—[2]	39	355	5	360
1937	26	82	33	101	29	54	—[2]	—[2]	35	360	3	363
1933	19	46	28	34	17	50	—[2]	—[2]	25	219	—	219

1 Figures are for fiscal year ending nearest to 31 December of year named.
2 Included in 'other expenditure'.
SOURCE: Urquhart and Buckley, *Historical Statistics*, p. 209.

TABLE 12   Canadian Ministries, 1867–1988

Year	Number	Prime Minister	Dates of Ministry	Party
1984–	24	Rt. Hon. Martin Brian Mulroney	17 September 1984	Cons.
1984	23	Rt. Hon. John Napier Turner	30 June 1984– 17 September 1984	Lib.
1980–1984	22	Rt. Hon. Pierre Elliott Trudeau	3 March 1980– 30 June 1984	Lib.
1979-1980	21	Rt. Hon. Charles Joseph Clark	4 June 1979- 3 March 1980	Cons.
1968-1979	20	Rt. Hon. Pierre Elliott Trudeau	20 April 1968- 4 June 1979	Lib.
1963-1968	19	Rt. Hon. Lester Bowles Pearson	22 April 1963- 20 April 1968	Lib.
1957-1963	18	Rt. Hon. John George Diefenbaker	21 June 1957- 22 April 1963	Cons.
1948-1957	17	Rt. Hon. Louis Stephen St. Laurent	15 November 1948- 21 June 1957	Lib.
1935-1948	16	Rt. Hon. William Lyon Mackenzie King	23 October 1935- 15 November 1948	Lib.
1930-1935	15	Rt. Hon. Richard Bedford Bennett	7 August 1930- 23 October 1935	Cons.
1926-1930	14	Rt. Hon. William Lyon Mackenzie King	25 September 1926- 6 August 1930	Lib.
1926	13	Rt. Hon. Arthur Meighen	29 June 1926- 25 September 1926	Cons.
1921-1926	12	Rt. Hon. William Lyon Mackenzie King	29 December 1921- 28 June 1926	Lib.
1920-1921	11	Rt. Hon. Arthur Meighen	10 July 1920- 29 December 1921	Unionist
1917-1920	10	Rt. Hon. Sir Robert Laird Borden	12 October 1917- 10 July 1920	Unionist
1911-1917	9	Rt. Hon. Sir Robert Laird Borden	10 October 1911- 12 October 1917	Cons.
1896-1911	8	Rt. Hon. Sir Wilfrid Laurier	11 July 1896- 6 October 1911	Lib.
1896	7	Hon. Sir Charles Tupper	1 May 1896- 8 July 1896	Cons.
1894-1896	6	Hon. Sir. Mackenzie Bowell	21 December 1894- 27 April 1896	Cons.
1892-1894	5	Rt. Hon. Sir John Sparrow David Thompson	5 December 1892- 12 December 1894	Cons.
1891-1892	4	Hon. Sir John Joseph Caldwell Abbott	16 June 1891- 24 November 1892	Cons.
1878-1891	3	Rt. Hon. Sir John Alexander Macdonald	17 October 1878- 6 June 1891	Cons.
1873-1878	2	Hon. Alexander Mackenzie	7 November 1873- 9 October 1878	Lib.
1867-1873	1	Rt. Hon. Sir John Alexander Macdonald	1 July 1867- 5 November 1873	Cons.

SOURCE: Urquhart and Buckley, *Historical Statistics*, p. 613; and *Canadian Parliamentary Guide,* 1987.

TABLE 13   Votes Polled in Federal General Elections, 1867–1988

21 November 1988

Province	Progressive Conservative	Liberal	New Democratic Party			Other
Newfoundland	108 349	115 588	31 769	—	—	1 025
Nova Scotia	196 390	223 175	54 515	—	—	5 761
New Brunswick	155 056	173 967	35 790	—	—	18 758
Prince Edward Island	31 372	37 761	5 661	—	—	850
Quebec	1 844 279	1 058 952	488 633	—	—	109 239
Ontario	1 787 291	1 819 095	939 928	—	—	133 716
Manitoba	200 100	198 408	115 638	—	—	28 795
Saskatchewan	190 597	95 295	231 358	—	—	6 503
Alberta	602 848	159 807	202 847	—	—	199 452
British Columbia	541 172	312 803	566 582	—	—	112 469
Yukon and NWT	10 109	10 221	12 587	—	—	1 088
Totals for Canada	5 667 563	4 205 072	2 685 308	—	—	617 656

4 September 1984

Province	Progressive Conservative	Liberal	New Democratic Party	Social Credit	Ralliement de Créditistes de Québec	Others
Newfoundland	138 867	87 778	13 993	—	—	521
Nova Scotia	233 713	154 954	70 190	—	—	1 561
New Brunswick	202 144	120 326	53 332	102	—	1 446
Prince Edward Island	38 160	30 075	4 737	—	—	119
Quebec	1 728 196	1 219 124	301 928	—	6 633	180 430
Ontario	2 113 187	1 323 835	921 504	865	—	34 791
Manitoba	221 947	112 123	139 999	—	—	39 765
Saskatchewan	218 000	95 143	200 918	—	—	8 739
Alberta	701 344	129 945	143 588	5 965	—	36 552
British Columbia	668 432	235 394	502 331	3 094	—	23 544
Yukon and NWT	14 707	7 789	7 395	—	—	686
Totals for Canada	6 278 697	3 516 486	2 359 915	16 659	6 633	328 154

TABLE 13   Votes Polled in Federal General Elections (continuation)

18 February 1980

Province	Progressive Conservative	Liberal	New Democratic Party	Social Credit	Ralliement des Créditistes de Québec	Others
Newfoundland	72 999	95 354	33 943	—	—	749
Nova Scotia	163 459	168 304	88 052	—	—	2 427
New Brunswick	109 056	168 316	54 517	—	—	3 841
Prince Edward Island	30 653	31 005	4 339	—	—	208
Quebec	373 317	2 017 156	268 409	—	174 583	123 577
Ontario	1 420 436	1 675 519	874 229	804	—	29 853
Manitoba	179 607	133 253	159 434	—	—	3 610
Saskatchewan	177 376	110 517	165 308	178	—	2 395
Alberta	516 079	176 601	81 755	8 158	—	12 852
British Columbia	502 088	268 262	426 858	1 763	—	10 841
Yukon and NWT	7 924	9 627	8 143	—	—	180
Totals for Canada	3 552 994	4 853 914	2 164 987	10 903	174 583	190 533

22 May 1979

Province	Progressive Conservative	Liberal	New Democratic Party	Social Credit	Ralliement des Créditistes de Québec	Others
Newfoundland	59 893	81 861	59 978	—	—	—
Nova Scotia	193 099	151 078	76 603	—	—	1 829
New Brunswick	134 998	150 634	51 642	—	—	258
Prince Edward Island	34 147	26 231	4 181	—	512 995	54
Quebec	432 199	1 975 526	163 492	—	—	119 817
Ontario	1 732 717	1 509 926	873 182	1 002	—	26 168
Manitoba	222 787	120 493	167 850	1 044	—	1 599
Saskatchewan	201 803	106 550	175 011	2 514	—	3 526
Alberta	559 588	188 295	84 236	8 164	—	12 894
British Columbia	530 678	274 946	381 678	1 885	—	6 923
Yukon and NWT	9 948	8 779	7 926	—	—	273
Totals for Canada	4 111 559	4 594 319	2 048 779	14 609	512 995	173 341

TABLE 13   Votes Polled in Federal General Elections (continuation)

8 July 1974

Province	Progressive Conservative	Liberal	New Democratic Party	Social Credit	Ralliement des Créditistes de Québec	Others
Newfoundland	75 816	81 299	16 445	143	—	242
Nova Scotia	183 897	157 582	43 470	1 457	—	458
New Brunswick	94 934	135 723	24 869	—	8 407	23 417
Prince Edward Island	28 578	26 932	2 666	—	—	77
Quebec	520 632	1 330 337	162 080	—	420 018	25 608
Ontario	1 252 082	1 609 786	680 113	6 575	—	16 981
Manitoba	212 990	122 470	104 829	4 750	—	1 692
Saskatchewan	150 846	127 282	130 391	4 539	—	876
Alberta	417 422	168 973	63 310	22 909	—	9 955
British Columbia	423 954	336 435	232 547	12 453	—	5 512
Yukon and NWT	8 184	5 957	7 028	—	—	—
Totals for Canada	3 369 335	4 102 776	1 467 748	52 806	428 425	84 818

30 October 1972

Province	Progressive Conservative	Liberal	New Democratic Party	Social Credit	Ralliement des Créditistes de Québec	Others
Newfoundland	85 857	78 505	8 165	266	—	2 253
Nova Scotia	204 460	129 738	47 072	1 316	—	501
New Brunswick	131 455	125 935	16 703	—	16 450	1 948
Prince Edward Island	29 419	22 950	4 229	55	—	—
Quebec	457 418	1 289 139	168 910	—	639 207	70 362
Ontario	1 399 148	1 366 922	768 076	12 937	—	30 969
Manitoba	184 363	136 906	116 474	3 228	—	2 183
Saskatchewan	159 629	109 342	155 195	7 717	—	621
Alberta	409 857	177 599	89 811	31 689	—	1 996
British Columbia	313 253	274 468	332 345	25 107	—	3 116
Yukon and NWT	8 671	6 754	6 548	—	—	—
Totals for Canada	3 383 530	3 718 258	1 713 528	82 315	655 657	114 201

TABLE 13   Votes Polled in Federal General Elections (continuation)

25 June 1968

Province	Progressive Conservative	Liberal	New Democratic Party	Social Credit	Ralliement des Créditistes de Québec	Others
Newfoundland	84 521	68 492	7 035	126	—	—
Nova Scotia	186 071	127 920	22 683	—	—	294
New Brunswick	125 263	111 847	12 262	—	1 769	821
Prince Edward Island	26 283	22 786	1 639	—	—	—
Quebec	466 259	1 170 610	164 363	—	358 116	24 574
Ontario	942 755	1 372 612	607 019	889	—	24 715
Manitoba	125 713	166 022	99 974	5 969	—	2 708
Saskatchewan	153 228	112 333	147 950	—	—	919
Alberta	283 997	201 015	52 688	10 940	—	15 139
British Columbia	155 350	334 171	261 253	46 105	—	2 725
Yukon and NWT	5 325	9 067	1 523	—	—	—
Totals for Canada	2 554 765	3 696 875	1 378 389	64 029	359 885	71 895

8 November 1965

Province	Progressive Conservative	Liberal	New Democratic Party	Social Credit	Ralliement des Créditistes de Québec	Others
Newfoundland	47 638	94 291	1 742	2 352	—	1 022
Nova Scotia	203 123	175 415	38 043	—	—	1 249
New Brunswick	102 714	114 781	22 759	352	1 081	—
Prince Edward Island	38 566	31 532	1 463	—	—	—
Quebec	432 901	928 530	244 339	—	357 153	74 389
Ontario	933 753	1 196 308	594 112	9 791	1 204	8 615
Manitoba	154 253	117 442	91 193	16 315	—	237
Saskatchewan	193 254	96 740	104 626	7 526	—	179
Alberta	247 734	119 014	43 818	119 586	—	1 275
British Columbia	139 226	217 726	239 132	126 532	—	3 368
Yukon and NWT	6 751	7 740	431	—	—	—
Totals for Canada	2 499 913	3 099 519	1 381 658	282 454	359 438	90 334

TABLE 13   Votes Polled in Federal General Elections (continuation)

Province	Progressive Conservative	Liberal	18 June 1962 New Democratic Party	Social Credit	Others
Newfoundland	55 396	90 896	7 590	158	—
Nova Scotia	198 902	178 520	39 689	3 764	—
New Brunswick	115 973	110 850	13 220	9 016	441
Prince Edward Island	37 388	31 603	3 802	153	—
Quebec	617 762	818 760	91 795	542 433	19 173
Ontario	1 056 095	1 122 222	456 459	49 734	3 135
Manitoba	161 824	121 041	76 514	26 662	3 297
Saskatchewan	213 385	96 676	93 444	19 648	317
Alberta	214 699	97 322	42 305	146 662	997
British Columbia	187 389	187 438	212 035	97 396	1 931
Yukon and NWT	6 769	6 506	—	948	—
Totals for Canada	2 865 582	2 861 834	1 036 853	896 574	29 291

TABLE 13   Votes Polled in Federal General Elections (continuation)

Province	31 March 1958						10 June 1957					
	Progressive Conservative	Liberal	Cooperative Commonwealth Federation	Social Credit	Labour Progressive Party	Others	Liberal	Progressive Conservative	Cooperative Commonwealth Federation	Social Credit[3]	Labour Progressive Party	Others
Newfoundland	72 282	86 960	240	—	—	263	56 993	34 795	321	—	—	—
Prince Edward Island	42 911	25 847	215	—	—	—	31 162	34 965	680	473	—	—
Nova Scotia	237 422	160 026	18 911	—	—	—	176 891	197 676	17 117	—	—	—
New Brunswick	133 935	107 297	4 541	1 711	—	—	112 518	114 060	2 001	2 420	—	3 159
Quebec	1 005 120	935 881	45 594	12 858	1 162	23 634	1 116 028	562 133	31 780	3 877	2 377	73 865
Ontario	1 413 730	815 524	262 120	8 386	3 035	1 718	845 308	1 104 366	274 069	38 418	1 432	978
Manitoba	216 948	82 450	74 906	6 753	1 503	—	93 258	124 867	82 398	45 803	1 579	205
Saskatchewan	204 442	78 121	112 800	1 745	458	146	118 282	90 359	140 293	40 830	212	122
Alberta	269 942	61 583	19 666	97 502	1 196	—	119 190	118 225	27 127	162 083	815	212
British Columbia	308 971	100 889	153 405	59 762	2 515	—	121 301	192 988	131 873	143 145	1 345	887
Yukon	3 069	2 340	—	—	—	—	2 422	2 358	—	—	—	—
Mackenzie River	2 080	2 782	—	—	—	—	2 686	1 253	—	—	—	—
Totals for Canada	3 910 852	2 459 700	692 398	188 717	9 869	25 761	2 796 039	2 578 045	707 659	437 049	7 760	79 428

TABLE 13   Votes Polled in Federal General Elections (continuation)

10 August 1953

Province	Liberal	Progressive Conservative	Cooperative Commonwealth Federation	Social Credit	Labour Progressive Party	Others
Newfoundland	74 357	31 060	707	—	—	4 459
Prince Edward Island	33 874	31 836	552	—	—	—
Nova Scotia	176 554	133 498	22 357	—	794	—
New Brunswick	121 936	93 450	6 769	931	—	—
Quebec	1 001 655	455 688	23 833	—	10 819	54 778
Ontario	898 692	772 691	212 224	5 427	18 414	7 972
Manitoba	110 843	73 644	64 402	17 260	6 194	434
Saskatchewan	133 493	41 538	156 406	18 810	3 906	—
Alberta	118 941	49 450	23 573	138 847	9 155	275
British Columbia	145 570	66 426	125 487	123 700	10 340	—
Yukon	2 176	590	—	998	—	—
Mackenzie River	1 722	1 344	—	—	—	421
Totals for Canada	2 819 813	1 751 215	636 310	305 973	59 622	68 339

27 June 1949

Province	Liberal	Progressive Conservative	Cooperative Commonwealth Federation	Social Credit[3]	Union des Electeurs	Labour Progressive Party	Others
Newfoundland	75 235	29 203	197	—	—	—	—
Prince Edward Island	33 480	32 989	1 626	—	—	—	—
Nova Scotia	177 680	126 365	33 333	—	—	—	533
New Brunswick	123 453	88 049	9 450	—	2 172	—	—
Quebec	984 131	397 803	17 767	—	80 990	4 868	107 741
Ontario	930 719	757 987	306 551	3 225	2 036	13 613	8 043
Manitoba	153 857	70 689	83 176	—	—	6 523	6 666
Saskatchewan	161 887	53 624	152 399	3 474	—	1 531	—
Alberta	116 647	56 947	31 329	131 007	—	2 201	11 992
British Columbia	169 018	128 620	145 442	2 109	—	3 887	2 283
Yukon	3 284	—	1 140	—	—	—	—
Mackenzie River	—	—	—	—	—	—	—
Totals for Canada	2 929 391	1 742 276	782 410	139 815	85 198	32 623	137 258

TABLE 13   Votes Polled in Federal General Elections (continuation)

Province	11 June 1945							26 March 1940				
	Liberal	Progressive Conservative	Cooperative Commonwealth Federation	Social Credit	Bloc Populaire	Labour Progressive Party	Others	Liberal	Conservative	Cooperative Commonwealth Federation	New Democrat	Others
Prince Edward Island	30 696	30 025	2 685	—	—	—	—	34 664	28 028	—	—	—
Nova Scotia	141 911	114 214	51 892	—	—	1 800	850	151 731	112 206	17 715	—	—
New Brunswick	100 939	77 225	14 999	2 300	—	—	6 423	97 062	74 970	761	—	—
Quebec	722 707	138 344	33 729	63 310	168 389	14 641	273 049	868 663	231 851	7 610	11 191	52 182
Ontario	745 571	757 057	260 502	3 906	5 038	36 333	6 560	834 166	687 816	61 166	786	25 480
Manitoba	111 863	80 303	101 892	10 322	—	15 984	2 451	151 480	82 240	61 448	5 831	15 884
Saskatchewan	124 191	70 830	167 233	11 449	—	3 183	—	159 530	52 496	106 267	12 106	40 735
Alberta	67 662	58 077	57 077	113 821	—	14 136	—	102 060	35 116	35 082	93 023	4 062
British Columbia	125 085	128 529	132 068	9 890	—	25 128	7 741	136 065	110 619	103 181	506	12 773
Yukon	—	849	584	—	—	687	—	793	915	—	—	—
Totals for Canada	2 170 625	1 455 453	822 661	214 998	173 427	111 892	297 074	2 536 514	1 416 257	393 230	123 443	151 116

TABLE 13   Votes Polled in Federal General Elections (continuation)

14 October 1935

Province	Liberal	Conservative	Re-construction	Cooperative Common-wealth Federation	Social Credit	Independent Liberal	Communist	Others	Rejected Ballots
Prince Edward Island	35 757	23 602	2 089	—	—	—	—	—	193
Nova Scotia	142 334	87 893	38 175	—	—	—	5 365	—	1 756
New Brunswick	100 537	56 145	18 408	—	—	672	—	—	1 723
Quebec	623 579	323 177	103 857	7 326	—	70 504	3 385	14 693	16 341
Ontario	675 803	562 513	181 981	129 457	—	14 459	8 945	21 089	13 997
Manitoba	100 535	75 574	16 439	54 491	5 751	18 973	9 229	—	3 597
Saskatchewan	134 914	71 285	2 273	73 505	63 593	—	—	—	1 966
Alberta	50 539	40 236	1 785	29 066	111 627	—	2 672	2 588	2 594
British Columbia	91 729	71 034	19 208	97 015	1 796	—	1 555	6 446	3 640
Yukon	—	—	—	—	—	555	—	696	14
Totals for Canada	1 955 727	1 311 459	384 215	390 860	182 767	105 163	31 151	45 512	45 821

28 July 1930

Province	Conservative	Liberal	Progressive	Labour Progressive	Labour	Independent	United Farmers of Alberta	Farmer	Communist
Prince Edward Island	29 692	29 698	—	—	—	—	—	—	—
Nova Scotia	140 513	127 189	—	—	—	—	—	—	—
New Brunswick	109 839	75 221	—	—	—	—	—	—	—
Quebec	456 037	542 135	—	—	—	21 776	—	—	313
Ontario	745 414	590 071	12 815	—	992	8 785	—	—	1 499
Manitoba	111 312	37 234	—	59 155	19 809	2 018	—	—	3 873
Saskatchewan	129 420	153 673	18 178	—	—	6 155	—	22 766	—
Alberta	67 808	60 148	—	—	8 769	2 727	60 924	—	—
British Columbia	119 074	98 933	—	—	15 732	7 894	—	—	—
Yukon	846	558	—	—	—	—	—	—	—
Totals for Canada	1 909 955	1 714 860	30 993	59 155	45 302	49 355	60 924	22 766	5 685

TABLE 13 Votes Polled in Federal General Elections (continuation)

Province	14 September 1926								29 October 1925				
	Conservative	Liberal	Progressive	Labour Progressive	Labour	Independent	United Farmers of Alberta	Rejected Ballots	Liberal	Conservative	Progressive	Labour	Independent
Prince Edward Island	26 217	29 222	—	—	—	—	—	130	25 681	23 799	—	—	—
Nova Scotia	122 965	99 581	—	—	6 412	—	—	888	92 525	124 545	—	3 617	—
New Brunswick	87 080	74 465	—	—	—	—	—	1 232	61 161	90 405	—	—	84
Quebec	266 824	507 775	—	—	—	8 787	—	5 909	469 475	273 818	—	1 685	58 588
Ontario	680 742	441 254	50 360	38 112	6 282	5 356	—	4 161	392 039	691 365	108 051	9 552	19 104
Manitoba	83 100	36 242	22 092	38 379	17 194	—	—	1 021	34 538	70 264	45 859	18 335	—
Saskatchewan	67 524	125 849	38 324	13 413	—	—	—	1 350	82 810	51 512	62 268	—	1 914
Alberta	49 514	38 451	—	—	8 148	163	60 740	977	44 291	51 114	50 592	8 572	6 040
British Columbia	100 066	68 317	—	—	11 757	4 330	—	875	63 506	90 032	15 829	11 463	888
Yukon	823	648	—	—	—	—	—	11	508	742	—	—	—
Totals for Canada	1 504 855	1 421 804	110 776	89 904	49 793	18 636	60 740	16 554	1 266 534	1 467 596	282 599	53 224	87 618

TABLE 13 Votes Polled in Federal General Elections (continuation)

Province	6 December 1921				17 December 1917				21 September 1911		
					Unionist		Laurier-Liberals				
	Liberal	Conservative	Progressive	Independent	Civilian	Soldiers	Civilian	Soldiers	Conservative	Liberal	Other
Prince Edward Island	23 950	19 504	8 990	—	10 450	2 775	12 224	434	14 638	13 998	—
Nova Scotia	136 064	87 988	35 741	—	40 985	10 699	49 831	1 474	55 209	57 462	351
New Brunswick	76 653	61 172	17 447	—	35 871	9 934	32 397	919	38 880	40 192	—
Quebec	558 056	163 743	31 790	39 477	61 808	14 206	240 504	2 927	159 299	164 281	459
Ontario	351 717	445 150	329 502	9 003	419 928	95 212	263 300	5 793	269 930	207 078	3 564
Manitoba	29 525	46 486	83 350	13 361	83 469	23 698	26 073	1 157	40 356	34 781	2 559
Saskatchewan	46 447	37 345	136 486	3 610	68 424	12 996	30 829	2 672	34 700	52 924	1 419
Alberta	27 404	35 181	104 295	6 024	60 399	19 575	48 865	1 055	29 675	37 208	2 892
British Columbia	46 249	74 226	21 786	12 739	59 944	26 461	40 050	2 059	25 622	16 350	1 587
Yukon	658	707	—	18	666	293	776	32	1 285	829	—
Totals for Canada	1 296 723	971 502	769 387	84 232	841 944	215 849	744 849	18 522	669 594	625 103	12 831

TABLE 13 Votes Polled in Federal General Elections (continuation)

Province	| 26 October 1908 Liberal	Conservative	Other	| 3 November 1904 Liberal	Conservative	Other	| 7 November 1900 Liberal	Conservative	Other	| 23 June 1896 Liberal	Conservative	Other
Prince Edward Island	14 496	14 286	—	14 441	14 986	—	10 887	10 139	—	9 515	9 157	—
Nova Scotia	56 638	54 500	—	56 526	46 131	994	54 384	50 810	—	49 176	50 772	737
New Brunswick	40 716	34 935	—	37 158	35 503	138	35 401	32 638	228	28 383	31 399	4 318
Quebec	162 176	115 579	5 377	144 992	111 550	522	133 566	103 253	501	120 321	102 884	1 485
Ontario	217 963	237 548	6 769	219 871	223 627	759	212 595	212 413	2 165	169 480	189 927	62 668
Manitoba	30 892	35 078	2 077	26 713	20 119	1 290	21 597	20 177	—	11 519	15 459	5 906
Saskatchewan	33 885	22 007	3 976									
Alberta	23 100	20 433	2 439	27 173	19 367	136	13 012	10 606	—	8 191	7 811	1 786
British Columbia	13 412	17 503	6 453	12 458	9 781	2 945	12 985	10 814	2 652	8 921	9 231	—
Yukon	992	265	1 208	1 495	2 113	—	—	—	—	—	—	—
Totals for Canada	594 270	552 134	28 299	540 827	483 177	6 784	494 427	450 790	5 546	405 506	416 640	76 900

SOURCE: Urquhart and Buckley, *Historical Statistics*, p. 615.

TABLE 13   Votes Polled in Federal General Elections (continuation)

Province	Conservative	Liberal	Other
	5 March 1891		
Nova Scotia	46 934	40 155	1 223
New Brunswick	34 730	24 939	2 377
Prince Edward Island	17 892	18 966	—
Quebec	94 837	88 711	3 097
Ontario	183 208	182 213	5 658
Manitoba	9 369	8 281	—
British Columbia	4 009	1 592	—
NWT	6 752	1 960	1 619
Totals for Canada	397 731	366 817	13 974
	22 February 1887		
Nova Scotia	41 411	39 255	2 584
New Brunswick	28 884	28 994	277
Prince Edward Island	17 145	19 733	—
Quebec	79 155	78 098	2 383
Ontario	181 537	176 001	455
Manitoba	7 712	7 280	—
British Columbia	2 571	603	1 424
NWT	4 217	2 220	783
Totals for Canada	362 632	352 184	7 906
	20 June 1882		
Nova Scotia	28 967	25 345	2 058
New Brunswick	18 848	17 625	2 298
Prince Edward Island	15 188	15 270	—
Quebec	55 476	44 801	5 790
Ontario	137 947	134 204	1 628
Manitoba	3 305	3 855	73
British Columbia	1 562	300	964
Totals for Canada	261 293	241 400	12 811
	17 September 1878		
Nova Scotia	33 226	28 880	2 054
New Brunswick	17 964	20 148	1 768
Prince Edward Island	13 978	10 621	—
Quebec	78 719	61 523	877
Ontario	133 633	125 316	815
Manitoba	546	555	—
British Columbia	2 158	—	1 160
Totals for Canada	280 224	247 043	6 674

TABLE 13   Votes Polled in Federal General Elections (continuation)

	22 January 1874		
Province	*Conservative*	*Liberal*	*Other*
Nova Scotia	16 466	23 377	—
New Brunswick	10 367	13 872	30
Prince Edward Island	2 502	7 226	—
Quebec	31 449	34 328	576
Ontario	83 556	94 736	1 088
Manitoba	861	938	264
British Columbia	1 264	—	719
Totals for Canada	146 465	173 477	2 677

	20 July 1872-12 October 1872		
Province	*Conservative*	*Liberal*	*Other*
Nova Scotia	19 939	19 974	—
New Brunswick	11 590	12 705	684
Quebec	45 092	41 957	1 578
Ontario	80 896	81 146	520
Manitoba	646	583	76
British Columbia	843	—	113
Totals for Canada	159 006	156 365	2 971

	7 August 1867-20 September 1867		
Province	*Government*	*Opposition*	*Others*
Nova Scotia	14 862	21 139	362
New Brunswick	9 137	9 939	505
Quebec	38 796	32 654	962
Ontario	71 474	67 632	755
Totals for Canada	134 269	131 364	2 584

SOURCES: Murray Beck, *Pendulum of Power: Canada's Federal Elections*, (Scarborough, Ontario: Prentice-Hall of Canada, 1968); Urquhart and Buckley, *Historical Statistics*, pp. 616–618; Report of the Chief Electoral Officer, 1972, 1974, 1979, 1980, 1984, and 1988.

399

TABLE 14 Members Elected to the House of Commons, 1867–1988

Year	Party	Totals for Canada	Newfoundland	Prince Edward Island	Nova Scotia	New Brunswick	Quebec	Ontario	Manitoba	Saskatchewan	Alberta	British Columbia	Yukon and Northwest Territories
1988	Progressive Conservative	169	2	—	5	5	63	46	7	4	25	12	—
	Liberal	83	5	4	6	5	12	43	5	10	1	1	2
	New Democratic Party	43	—	—	—	—	—	10	2	10	1	19	1
1984	Liberal	40	3	1	2	1	17	14	1	—	—	1	—
	Progressive Conservative	211	4	3	9	9	58	67	9	9	21	19	3
	New Democratic Party	30	—	—	—	—	—	13	4	5	—	8	—
1980	Liberal	147	5	2	5	7	74	52	2	—	—	—	—
	Progressive Conservative	103	2	2	6	3	1	38	5	7	21	16	2
	New Democratic Party	32	—	—	—	—	—	5	7	7	—	12	1
1979	Progressive Conservative	136	2	4	8	4	2	57	7	10	21	19	2
	Liberal	114	4	—	2	6	67	32	2	—	—	1	—
	New Democratic Party	26	1	—	1	—	—	6	5	4	—	8	1
	Créditiste	6	—	—	—	—	6	—	—	—	—	—	—
1974	Liberal	141	4	1	2	6	60	55	2	3	—	8	—
	Progressive Conservative	95	3	3	8	3	3	25	9	8	19	13	1
	New Democratic Party	16	—	—	1	—	—	8	2	2	—	2	1
	Créditiste	11	—	—	—	—	11	—	—	—	—	—	—
	Independent	1	—	—	—	1	—	—	—	—	—	—	—
1972	Liberal	109	3	1	1	5	56	36	2	1	—	4	—
	Progressive Conservative	107	4	3	10	5	2	40	8	7	19	8	1
	New Democratic Party	31	—	—	—	—	—	11	3	5	—	11	1
	Créditiste	15	—	—	—	—	15	—	—	—	—	—	—
	Independent	2	—	—	—	—	1	1	—	—	—	—	—
1968	Liberal	155	1	—	1	5	56	64	5	2	4	16	1
	Progressive Conservative	72	6	4	10	5	4	17	5	5	15	—	1
	New Democratic Party	22	—	—	—	—	—	6	3	6	—	7	—
	Créditiste	14	—	—	—	—	14	—	—	—	—	—	—
	Independent	1	—	—	—	—	—	1	—	—	—	—	—
1965	Liberal	131	7	—	2	6	56	51	1	—	—	7	1
	Progressive Conservative	97	—	4	10	4	8	25	10	17	15	3	1
	New Democratic Party	21	—	—	—	—	—	9	3	—	—	9	—
	Créditiste	9	—	—	—	—	9	—	—	—	—	—	—
	Social Credit	5	—	—	—	—	—	—	—	—	2	3	—
	Independent	2	—	—	—	—	2	—	—	—	—	—	—

Appendix I

Year	Party	Total											
1963	Liberal	129	7	2	5	6	47	52	2	—	1	7	—
	Progressive Conservative	95	—	2	7	4	8	27	10	17	14	4	2
	Social Credit	24	—	—	—	—	20	—	—	—	2	2	—
	New Democratic Party	17	—	—	—	—	—	6	2	—	—	9	—
1962	Progressive Conservative	116	1	4	9	4	14	35	11	16	15	6	1
	Liberal	100	6	—	2	6	35	43	1	1	—	4	2
	Social Credit	30	—	—	—	—	26	—	—	—	2	2	—
	New Democratic Party	19	—	—	1	—	—	6	2	1	—	10	—
	Independent	1	—	—	—	—	—	1	—	—	—	—	—
1958	Progressive Conservative	208	2	4	12	7	50	67	14	16	17	18	1
	Liberal	48	5	—	—	3	25	14	—	—	—	—	1
	Cooperative Commonwealth Federation	8	—	—	—	—	—	3	—	1	—	4	—
	Liberal Labour	1	—	—	—	—	—	1	—	—	—	—	—
1957	Progressive Conservative	112	2	4	10	5	9	61	8	3	3	7	*
	Liberal	105	5	*	2	5	63	20	1	4	1	2	2
	Independent Liberal	1	*	*	*	*	1	*	*	*	*	*	*
	Cooperative Commonwealth Federation	25	*	*	*	*	*	3	5	10	*	7	*
	Social Credit	19	*	*	*	*	*	*	*	*	13	6	*
	Liberal Labour	1	*	*	*	*	*	1	*	*	*	*	*
	Independent	2	*	*	*	*	2	*	*	*	*	*	*
1953	Liberal	170	7	3	10	7	66	50	8	5	4	8	2
	Independent Liberal	2	*	*	*	*	2	*	*	*	*	*	*
	Progressive Conservative	51	*	1	1	3	4	33	3	1	2	3	*
	Cooperative Commonwealth Federation	23	*	*	1	*	*	1	3	11	*	7	*
	Social Credit	15	*	*	*	*	*	*	*	*	11	4	*
	Independent	3	*	*	*	*	3	*	*	*	*	*	*
	Liberal Labour	1	*	*	*	*	*	1	*	*	*	*	*
1949	Liberal	190	5	3	10	7	66	56	12	14	5	11	1
	Independent Liberal	3	*	*	*	1	1	1	*	*	*	*	*
	Progressive Conservative	41	2	1	2	2	2	25	1	1	2	3	*
	Cooperative Commonwealth Federation	13	*	*	1	*	*	1	3	5	*	3	*
	Social Credit	10	*	*	*	*	1	*	*	*	10	*	*
	Independent	5	*	*	*	*	4	1	*	*	*	1	*

TABLE 14 Members Elected to the House of Commons (continuation)

Year	Party	Totals for Canada	New-foundland	Prince Edward Island	Nova Scotia	New Brunswick	Quebec	Ontario	Manitoba	Saskat-chewan	Alberta	British Columbia	Yukon and Northwest Territories
1945	Liberal	125	—	3	8	7	54	34	10	2	2	5	*
	Independent Liberal	2	—	*	*	*	2	*	*	*	*	*	*
	Progressive Conservative	67	—	1	3	3	1	48	2	1	2	5	1
	Independent Conservative	1	—	*	*	*	1	*	*	*	*	*	*
	Cooperative Commonwealth Federation	28	—	*	1	*	*	*	5	18	*	4	*
	Independent Cooperative Commonwealth Federation	1	—	*	*	1	*	*	*	*	*	*	*
	Social Credit	13	—	*	*	*	*	*	*	*	13	1	*
	Independent	5	—	*	*	*	4	*	*	*	*	1	*
	Bloc Populaire	2	—	*	*	*	2	*	*	*	*	*	*
	Labour Progressive Party	1	—	*	*	*	1	*	*	*	*	*	*
1940	Liberal	178	—	4	10	5	61	55	14	12	7	10	*
	Independent Liberal	3	—	*	*	*	3	*	*	*	*	*	*
	Conservative	39	—	*	1	5	*	25	1	2	*	4	1
	Independent Conservative	1	—	*	*	*	1	*	*	*	*	*	*
	Social Credit	10	—	*	*	*	*	*	*	*	10	*	*
	Cooperative Commonwealth Federation	8	—	*	1	*	*	*	1	5	*	1	*
	Liberal Progressive	3	—	*	*	*	*	2	1	*	*	1	*
	Independent	1	—	*	*	*	*	*	*	*	*	*	*
	Unity	2	—	*	*	*	*	*	*	2	*	*	*
1935	Liberal	171	—	4	12	9	55	56	12	16	1	6	*
	Independent Liberal	5	—	*	*	*	5	*	*	*	*	*	*
	Conservative	39	—	*	1	1	5	25	1	1	1	5	1
	Independent Conservative	1	—	*	*	*	*	*	*	*	*	*	1
	Social Credit	17	—	*	*	*	*	*	*	2	15	*	*
	Cooperative Commonwealth Federation	7	—	*	*	*	*	*	2	2	*	3	*
	Liberal Progressive	2	—	*	*	*	*	*	2	*	*	*	*
	Reconstruction	1	—	*	*	*	*	*	*	*	*	1	*
	Independent	1	—	*	*	*	*	*	*	*	*	1	*
	United Farmers of Ontario — Labour	1	—	*	*	*	*	1	*	*	*	*	*

Appendix I

Year	Party	Total	P.E.I.	N.S.	N.B.	Que.	Ont.	Man.	Sask.	Alta.	B.C.	Terr./Yukon
1930	Conservative	137	3	10	10	24	59	11	8	4	7	1
	Liberal	88	1	4	1	40	22	1	11	3	5	*
	United Farmers	10	*	*	*	*	1	*	*	9	*	*
	Progressive	2	*	*	*	*	*	*	2	*	*	*
	Liberal Progressive	3	*	*	*	*	*	3	*	*	*	*
	Labour	2	*	*	*	*	*	2	*	*	*	*
	Independent Labour	1	*	*	*	*	*	*	*	*	1	*
	Independent	2	*	*	*	1	*	*	*	*	1	*
1926	Liberal	116	3	2	4	60	23	4	16	3	1	*
	Conservative	91	1	12	7	4	53	○	○	1	12	1
	United Farmers of Alberta	11	*	*	*	*	*	*	*	11	*	*
	Progressive	13	○	○	○	○	4	4	5	○	○	*
	Liberal Progressive	9	○	○	○	○	2	7	○	○	○	*
	Labour	3	*	*	*	*	*	2	*	1	*	*
	Independent	2	*	*	*	1	*	*	*	*	1	*
1925	Liberal	101	2	3	1	60	12	1	15	4	3	*
	Conservative	116	2	11	10	4	68	7	○	3	10	1
	Progressive	24	○	○	○	○	2	7	6	9	○	*
	Labour	2	*	*	*	*	*	2	*	*	*	*
	Independent	2	*	*	*	1	*	*	*	*	1	*
1921	Liberal	117	4	16	5	65	21	2	1	○	3	*
	Conservative	50	○	○	5	○	37	○	○	○	7	1
	Progressive	64	○	○	1	○	24	12	15	10	2	*
	Labour	3	*	*	*	*	*	1	*	2	*	*
	Independent	1	*	*	*	*	*	*	*	*	1	*
1917	Unionist	153	2	12	7	3	74	14	16	11	13	1
	Liberal	82	2	4	4	62	8	1	○	1	○	○
1911	Conservative	133	2	9	5	27	72	8	1	1	7	1
	Liberal	86	2	9	8	37	13	2	9	6	○	○
	Independent	2	*	*	*	1	1	*	*	*	*	*
1908	Liberal	133	3	12	11	53	36	2	9	4	2	1
	Conservative	85	1	6	2	11	48	8	1	3	5	○
	Independent	3	*	*	*	1	2	*	*	*	*	*
1904	Liberal	139	1	18	7	54	38	7	—	—	7	7
	Conservative	75	3	○	6	11	48	3	—	—	○	4
1900	Liberal	128	3	15	9	56	35	2	—	—	3	5
	Conservative	78	2	5	5	7	54	3	—	—	3	○
	Other (no details)	8	—	—	—	—	—	—	—	—	—	—

TABLE 14   Members Elected to the House of Commons (continuation)

Year	Party	Totals for Canada	New- foundland	Prince Edward Island	Nova Scotia	New Brunswick	Quebec	Ontario	Manitoba	Saskat- chewan	Alberta	British Columbia	Yukon and Northwest Territories
1896	Liberal	117	—	2	10	5	49	43	2	—	—	4	2
	Conservative	89	—	3	10	9	16	44	4	—	—	2	1
	Independent	7	—	*	*	*	*	5	1	—	—	*	1
1891	Conservative	123	—	2	16	13	30	48	4	—	—	6	4
	Liberal	92	—	4	5	3	35	44	1	—	—	O	O
1887	Conservative	123	—	O	14	10	33	52	4	—	—	6	4
	Liberal	92	—	6	7	6	32	40	1	—	—	O	O
1882	Conservative	139	—	4	15	10	48	54	2	—	—	6	—
	Liberal	71	—	2	6	6	17	37	3	—	—	O	—
1878	Conservative	137	—	5	14	5	45	59	3	—	—	6	—
	Liberal	69	—	1	7	11	20	29	1	—	—	O	—
1874	Liberal	133	—	6	17	11	33	64	2	—	—	6	—
	Conservative	73	—	O	4	5	32	24	2	—	—	6	—
1872	Conservative	103	—	—	11	7	38	38	3	—	—	6	—
	Liberal	97	—	—	10	9	27	50	1	—	—	O	—
1867	Conservative	101	—	—	3	7	45	46	—	—	—	—	—
	Liberal	80	—	—	16	8	20	36	—	—	—	—	—

SOURCES: Urquhart and Buckley, *Historical Statistics*, pp. 619—620, *Canadian Parliamentary Guide*, 1984; and Report of the Chief Electoral Officer of Canada, 1988.

O   An open circle indicates that before 1930, as far as the records show, a party ran candidates without success.

*   An asterisk indicates that no candidates were entered in the election.

APPENDIX II PART A: The British North America Act (with amendments to 1975)

The text that follows is the BNA Act (1867) with subsequent amendments to 1975 prepared by Elmes A. Driedger and published by the Canadian Department of Justice as *A Consolidation of the British North America Acts*, 1867 to 1975 (Ottawa: Canadian Government Publishing Centre, 1976). The schedules (covering electoral districts of Ontario and Quebec, public works and assets, and oaths of allegiance and qualification) are not reproduced.

THE BRITISH NORTH AMERICA ACT, 1867

30 & 31 Victoria, c. 3.

(Consolidated with amendments)

An Act for the Union of Canada, Nova Scotia, and New Brunswick, and the Government thereof; and for Purposes connected therewith.

(29th March, 1867.)

WHEREAS the Provinces of Canada, Nova Scotia and New Brunswick have expressed their Desire to be federally united into One Dominion under the Crown of the United Kingdom of Great Britain and Ireland, with a Constitution similar in Principle to that of the United Kingdom:

And whereas such a Union would conduce to the Welfare of the Provinces and promote the Interests of the British Empire:

And whereas on the Establishment of the Union by Authority of Parliament it is expedient, not only that the Constitution of the Legislative Authority in the Dominion be provided for, but also that the Nature of the Executive Government therein be declared:

And whereas it is expedient that Provision be made for the eventual Admission into the Union of other Parts of British North America: (1)

I.—PRELIMINARY.

1. This Act may be cited as The British North America Act, 1867. Short title.

2. Repealed. (2)

---

(1) The enacting clause was repealed by the *Statute Law Revision Act. 1893*, 56-57 Vict., c 14 (U.K). It read as follows:

> Be it therefore enacted and declared by the Queen's Most Excellent Majesty, by and with the Advice and Consent of the Lords Spiritual and Temporal, and Commons, in this present Parliament assembled, and by the Authority of the same, as follows:

(2) Section 2, repealed by the *Statute Law Revision Act, 1893*, 56-57 Vict., c. 14 (U.K.), read as follows:

> **2.** The Provisions of this Act referring to Her Majesty the Queen extend also to the Heirs and Successors of Her Mamesty, Kings and Queens of the United Kingdom of Great Britain and Ireland.

II.—UNION.

Declaration of Union.

3. It shall be lawful for the Queen, by and with the Advice of Her Majesty's Most Honourable Privy Council, to declare by Proclamation that, on and after a Day therein appointed, not being more than Six Months after the passing of this Act, the Provinces of Canada, Nova Scotia, and New Brunswick shall form and be One Dominion under the Name of Canada; and on and after that Day those Three Provinces shall form and be One Dominion under that Name accordingly. (3)

Construction of subsequent Provisions of Act.

4. Unless it is otherwise expressed or implied, the Name Canada shall be taken to mean Canada as constituted under this Act. (4)

Four Provinces.

5. Canada shall be divided into Four Provinces, named Ontario, Quebec, Nova Scotia, and New Brunswick. (5)

---

(3) The first day of July, 1867, was fixed by proclamation dated May 22, 1867.

(4) Partially repealed by the *Statute Law Revision Act, 1893*, 56-57 Vict., c. 14 (U.K.). As originally enacted the section read as follows:

> **4.** The subsequent Provisions of this Act, shall, unless it is otherwise expressed or implied, commence and have effect on and after the Union, that is to say, on and after the Day appointed for the Union taking effect in the Queen's Proclamation; and in the same Provisions, unless it is otherwise expressed or implied, the Name Canada shall be taken to mean Canada as constituted under this Act.

(5) Canada now consists of ten provinces (Ontario, Quebec, Nova Scotia, New Brunswick, Manitoba, British Columbia, Prince Edward Island, Alberta, Saskatchewan and Newfoundland) and two territories (the Yukon Territory and the Northwest Territories).

The first territories added to the Union were Rupert's Land and the North-Western Territory, (subsequently designated the Northwest Territories), which were admitted pursuant to section 146 of the *British North America Act, 1867* and the *Rupert's Land Act, 1868*, 31-32 Vict., c. 105 (U.K.), by Order in Council of June 23, 1870, effective July 15, 1870. Prior to the admission of these territories the Parliament of Canada enacted the *Act for the temporary Government of Rupert's Land and the North-Western Territory when united with Canada* (32-33 Vict., c. 3), and the *Manitoba Act* (33 Vict., c. 3), which provided for the formation of the Province of Manitoba.

British Columbia was admitted into the Union pursuant to section 146 of the *British North America Act, 1867*, by Order in Council of May 16, 1871, effective July 20, 1871.

Prince Edward Island was admitted pursuant to section 146 of the *British North America Act, 1867*, by Order in Council of June 26, 1873, effective July 1, 1873.

On June 29, 1871, the United Kingdom Parliament enacted the *British North America Act, 1871* (34-35 Vict., c. 28) authorizing the creation of additional provinces out of territories not included in any province. Pursuant to this statute, the Parliament of Canada enacted *The Alberta Act*, (July 20, 1905, 4-5 Edw. VII, c. 3) and *The Saskatchewan Act*, (July 20, 1905, 4-5 Edw. VII, c. 42), providing for the creation of the provinces of Alberta and Saskatchewan respectively. Both these Acts came into force on Sept. 1, 1905.

Meanwhile, all remaining British possessions and territories in North America and the islands adjacent thereto, except the colony of Newfoundland and its dependencies, were admitted into the Canadian Confederation by Order in Council dated July 31, 1880.

The Parliament of Canada added portions of the Northwest Territories to the adjoining provinces in 1912 by *The Ontario Boundaries Extension Act*, 2 Geo. V, c. 40, *The Quebec Boundaries Extension Act, 1912*, 2 Geo. V, c. 45 and *The Manitoba Boundaries Extension Act, 1912*, 2 Geo. V, c. 32, and further additions were made to Manitoba by *The Manitoba Boundaries Extension Act, 1930*, 20-21 Geo. V, c. 28.

The Yukon Territory was created out of the Northwest Territories in 1898 by *The Yukon Territory Act*, 61 Vict., c. 6, (Canada).

Newfoundland was added on March 31, 1949, by the *British North America Act, 1949*, (U.K.), 12-13 Geo. VI, c. 22, which ratified the Terms of Union between Canada and Newfoundland.

6. The Parts of the Province of Canada (as it exists at the passing of this Act) which formerly constituted respectively the Provinces of Upper Canada and Lower Canada shall be deemed to be severed, and shall form Two separate Provinces. The Part which formerly constituted the Province of Upper Canada shall constitute the Province of Ontario; and the Part which formerly constituted the Province of Lower Canada shall constitute the Province of Quebec. *Provinces of Ontario and Quebec.*

7. The Provinces of Nova Scotia and New Brunswick shall have the same Limits as at the passing of this Act. *Provinces of Nova Scotia and New Brunswick.*

8. In the general Census of the Population of Canada which is hereby required to be taken in the Year One thousand eight hundred and seventy-one, and in every Tenth Year thereafter, the respective Populations of the Four Provinces shall be distinguished. *Decennial Census.*

III.—EXECUTIVE POWER.

9. The Executive Government and Authority of and over Canada is hereby declared to continue and be vested in the Queen. *Declaration of Executive Power in the Queen.*

10. The Provisions of this Act referring to the Governor General extend and apply to the Governor General for the Time being of Canada, or other the Chief Executive Officer or Administrator for the Time being carrying on the Government of Canada on behalf and in the Name of the Queen, by whatever Title he is designated. *Application of Provisions referring to Governor General.*

11. There shall be a Council to aid and advise in the Government of Canada, to be styled the Queen's Privy Council for Canada; and the Persons who are to be Members of that Council shall be from Time to Time chosen and summoned by the Governor General and sworn in as Privy Councillors, and Members thereof may be from Time to Time removed by the Governor General. *Constitution of Privy Council for Canada.*

12. All Powers, Authorities, and Functions which under any Act of the Parliament of Great Britain, or of the Parliament of the United Kingdom of Great Britain and Ireland, or of the Legislature of Upper Canada, Lower Canada, Canada, Nova Scotia, or New Brunswick, are at the Union vested in or exerciseable by the respective Governors or Lieutenant Governors of those Provinces, with the Advice, or with the Advice and Consent, of the respective Executive Councils thereof, or in conjunction with those Councils, or with any Number of Members thereof, or by those Governors or Lieutenant Governors individually, shall, as far as the same continue in existence and capable of being exercised after the Union in relation to the Government of Canada, be vested in and exerciseable by the Governor General, with the Advice or with the Advice and Consent of or in conjunction with the *All Powers under Acts to be exercised by Governor General with Advice of Privy Council, or alone.*

Queen's Privy Council for Canada, or any Member thereof, or by the Governor General individually, as the Case requires, subject nevertheless (except with respect to such as exist under Acts of the Parliament of Great Britain or of the Parliament of the United Kingdom of Great Britain and Ireland) to be abolished or altered by the Parliament of Canada. (6)

Application of Provisions referring to Governor General in Council.

13. The Provisions of this Act referring to the Governor General in Council shall be construed as referring to the Governor General acting by and with the Advice of the Queen's Privy Council for Canada.

Power to Her Majesty to authorize Governor General to appoint Deputies.

14. It shall be lawful for the Queen, if Her Majesty thinks fit, to authorize the Governor General from Time to Time to appoint any Person or any Persons jointly or severally to be his Deputy or Deputies within any Part or Parts of Canada, and in that Capacity to exercise during the Pleasure of the Governor General such of the Powers, Authorities, and Functions of the Governor General as the Governor General deems it necessary or expedient to assign to him or them, subject to any Limitations or Directions expressed or given by the Queen; but the Appointment of such a Deputy or Deputies shall not affect the Exercise by the Governor General himself of any Power, Authority or Function.

Command of armed Forces to continue to be vested in the Queen.

15. The Command-in-Chief of the Land and Naval Militia, and of all Naval and Military Forces, of and in Canada, is hereby declared to continue and be vested in the Queen.

Seat of Government of Canada.

16. Until the Queen otherwise directs, the Seat of Government of Canada shall be Ottawa.

IV.—LEGISLATIVE POWER.

Constitution of Parliament of Canada.

17. There shall be One Parliament for Canada, consisting of the Queen, an Upper House styled the Senate, and the House of Commons:

Privileges, etc., of Houses.

18. The privileges, immunities, and powers to be held, enjoyed, and exercised by the Senate and by the House of Commons, and by the Members thereof respectively, shall be such as are from time to time defined by Act of the Parliament of Canada, but so that any Act of the Parliament of Canada defining such privileges, immunities, and powers shall not confer any privileges, immunities, or powers exceeding those at the passing of such Act held, enjoyed, and exercised by the Commons House of Parliament of the

---

(6) See the notes to section 129, *infra.*

United Kingdom of Great Britain and Ireland, and by the Members thereof. (7)

19. The Parliament of Canada shall be called together not later than Six Months after the Union. (8) First Session of the Parliament of Canada.

20. There shall be a Session of the Parliament of Canada once at least in every Year, so that Twelve Months shall not intervene between the last Sitting of the Parliament in one Session and its first Sitting in the next Session. (9) Yearly Session of the Parliament of Canada.

The Senate.

21. The Senate shall, subject to the Provisions of this Act, consist of One Hundred and four Members, who shall be styled Senators. (10) Number of Senators.

22. In relation to the Constitution of the Senate Canada shall be deemed to consist of Four Divisions:— Representation of Provinces in Senate.

1. Ontario;
2. Quebec;
3. The Maritime Provinces, Nova Scotia and New Brunswick, and Prince Edward Island;
4. The Western Provinces of Manitoba, British Columbia, Saskatchewan, and Alberta;

which Four Divisions shall (subject to the Provisions of this Act) be equally represented in the Senate as follows: Ontario by twenty-four senators; Quebec by twenty-four senators; the Maritime Provinces and Prince Edward Island by twenty-four senators, ten thereof representing Nova Scotia, ten thereof representing New Brunswick, and four thereof representing Prince Edward Island; the Western Provinces by

---

(7) Repealed and re-enacted by the *Parliament of Canada Act, 1875,* 38-39 Vict., c. 38 (U.K.). The original section read as follows:

> **18.** The Privileges Immunities, and Powers to be held, enjoyed, and exercised by the Senate and by the House of Commons and by the Members thereof respectively shall be such as are from Time to Time defined by Act of the Parliament of Canada, but so that the same shall never exceed those at the passing of this Act held, enjoyed, and exercised by the Commons House of Parliament of the United Kingdom of Great Britain and Ireland and by the Members thereof.

(8) Spent. The first session of the first Parliament began on November 6, 1867.

(9) The term of the twelfth Parliament was extended by the *British North America Act, 1916,* 6-7 Geo. V, c. 19 (U.K.), which Act was repealed by the *Statute Law Revision Act, 1927,* 17-18 Geo. V, c. 42 (U.K.).

(10) As amended by the *British North America Act, 1915,* 5-6 Geo. V, c. 45 (U.K.), and modified by the *British North America Act, 1949,* 12-13 Geo. VI, c. 22 (U.K.), and the *British North America Act, (No. 2) 1975,* S.C. 1974-75-76, c. 53.

The original section read as follows:

> **21.** The Senate shall, subject to the Provisions of this Act, consist of Seventy-two Members, who shall be styled Senators.

The *Manitoba Act* added two for Manitoba; the Order in Council admitting British Columbia added three; upon admission of Prince Edward Island four more were provided by section 147 of the *British North America Act, 1867*; *The Alberta Act* and *The Saskatchewan Act* each added four. The Senate was reconstituted at 96 by the *British North America Act, 1915*, six more Senators were added upon union with Newfoundland, and one Senator each was added for the Yukon Territory and the Northwest Territories by the *British North America Act, (No. 2) 1975.*

twenty-four senators, six thereof representing Manitoba, six thereof representing British Columbia, six thereof representing Saskatchewan, and six thereof representing Alberta; Newfoundland shall be entitled to be represented in the Senate by six members; the Yukon Territory and the Northwest Territories shall be entitled to be represented in the Senate by one member each.

In the Case of Quebec each of the Twenty-four Senators representing that Province shall be appointed for One of the Twenty-four Electoral Divisions of Lower Canada specified in Schedule A. to Chapter One of the Consolidated statutes of Canada. (11)

Qualifications of Senator.

23. The Qualification of a Senator shall be as follows:

(1) He shall be of the full age of Thirty Years:

(2) He shall be either a natural-born Subject of the Queen, or a Subject of the Queen naturalized by an Act of the Parliament of Great Britain, or of the Parliament of the United Kingdom of Great Britain and Ireland, or of the Legislature of One of the Provinces of Upper Canada, Lower Canada, Canada, Nova Scotia, or New Brunswick, before the Union, or of the Parliament of Canada, after the Union:

(3) He shall be legally or equitably seised as of Freehold for his own Use and Benefit of Lands or Tenements held in Free and Common Socage, or seised or possessed for his own Use and Benefit of Lands or Tenements held in Franc-alleu or in Roture, within the Province for which he is appointed, of the Value of Four thousand Dollars, over and above all Rents, Dues, Debts, Charges, Mortgages, and Incumbrances due or payable out of or charged on or affecting the same:

(4) His Real and Personal Property shall be together worth Four thousand Dollars over and above his Debts and Liabilities:

(11) As amended by the *British North America Act, 1915*, the *British North America Act, 1949*, 12-13 Geo. VI, c. 22 (U.K.), and the *British North America Act, (No. 2) 1975*, S.C. 1974-75-76, c. 53. The original section read as follows:

> **22.** In relation to the Constitution of the Senate, Canada shall be deemed to consist of Three Divisions:
>
> 1. Ontario;
>
> 2. Quebec;
>
> 3. The Maritime Provinces, Nova Scotia and New Brunswick;
> which Three Divisions shall (subject to the Provisions of this Act) be equally represented in the Senate as follows: Ontario by Twenty-four Senators; Quebec by Twenty-four Senators; and the Maritime Provinces by Twenty-four Senators, Twelve thereof representing Nova Scotia, and Twelve thereof representing New Brunswick.
>
> In the case of Quebec each of the Twenty-four Senators representing that Province shall be appointed for One of the Twenty-four Electoral Divisions of Lower Canada specified in Schedule A. to Chapter One of the Consolidated Statutes of Canada.

(5) He shall be resident in the Province for which he is appointed:

(6) In the Case of Quebec he shall have his Real Property Qualification in the Electoral Division for which he is appointed, or shall be resident in that Division. (11A)

24. The Governor General shall from Time to Time, in the Queen's Name, by Instrument under the Great Seal of Canada, summon qualified Persons to the Senate; and, subject to the Provisions of this Act, every Person so summoned shall become and be a Member of the Senate and a Senator.

Summons of Senator.

25. Repealed. (12)

26. If at any Time on the Recommendation of the Governor General the Queen thinks fit to direct that Four or Eight Members be added to the Senate, the Governor General may by Summons to Four or Eight qualified Persons (as the Case may be), representing equally the Four Divisions of Canada, add to the Senate accordingly. (13)

Addition of Senators in certain cases.

27. In case of such Addition being at any Time made, the Governor General shall not summon any Person to the Senate, except upon a further like Direction by the Queen on the like Recommendation, to represent one of the Four Divisions until such Division is represented by Twenty-four Senators and no more. (14)

Reduction of Senate to normal Number.

(11A) Section 2 of the *British North America Act, (No. 2) 1975,* S.C. 1974-75-76, c. 53 provided that for the purposes of that Act (which added one Senator each for the Yukon Territory and the Northwest Territories) the term "Province" in section 23 of the *British North America Act, 1867,* has the same meaning as is assigned to the term "province" by section 28 of the *Interpretation Act,* R.S.C. 1970, c. I-23, which provides that the term "province" means "a province of Canada, and includes the Yukon Territory and the Northwest Territories."

(12) Repealed by the *Statute Law Revision Act, 1893,* 56-57 Vict., 14 (U.K.). The section read as follows:

> **25.** Such Persons shall be first summoned to the Senate as the Queen by Warrant under Her Majesty's Royal Sign Manual thinks fit to approve, and their Names shall be inserted in the Queen's Proclamation of Union.

(13) As amended by the *British North America Act, 1915,* 5-6 Geo. V, c. 45 (U.K.). The original section read as follows:

> **26.** If at any Time on the Recommendation of the Governor General the Queen thinks fit to direct that Three or Six Members be added to the Senate, the Governor General may by Summons to Three or Six qualified Persons (as the Case may be), representing equally the Three Divisions of Canada, add to the Senate accordingly.

(14) As amended by the *British North America Act, 1915,* 5-6 Geo. V, c. 45 (U.K.). The original section read as follows:

> **27.** In case of such Addition being at any Time made the Governor General shall not summon any Person to the Senate, except on a further like Direction by the Queen on the like Recommendation, until each of the Three Divisions of Canada is represented by Twenty-four Senators and no more.

Maximum Number of Senators.

28. The Number of Senators shall not at any Time exceed One Hundred and twelve. (15)

Tenure of Place in Senate.

29. (1) Subject to subsection (2), a Senator shall, subject to the provisions of this Act, hold his place in the Senate for life.

Retirement upon attaining age of seventy-five years.

(2) A Senator who is summoned to the Senate after the coming into force of this subsection shall, subject to this Act, hold his place in the Senate until he attains the age of seventy-five years. (15A)

Resignation of Place in Senate.

30. A Senator may by Writing under his Hand addressed to the Governor General resign his Place in the Senate, and thereupon the same shall be vacant.

Disqualification of Senators.

31. The Place of a Senator shall become vacant in any of the following Cases:

(1) If for Two consecutive Sessions of the Parliament he fails to give his Attendance in the Senate:

(2) If he takes an Oath or makes a Declaration or Acknowledgment of Allegiance, Obedience, or Adherence to a Foreign Power, or does an Act whereby he becomes a Subject or Citizen, or entitled to the Rights or Privileges of a Subject or Citizen, of a Foreign Power:

(3) If he is adjudged Bankrupt or Insolvent, or applies for the Benefit of any Law relating to Insolvent Debtors, or becomes a public Defaulter:

(4) If he is attainted of Treason or convicted of Felony or of any infamous Crime:

(5) If he ceases to be qualified in respect of Property or of Residence; provided, that a Senator shall not be deemed to have ceased to be qualified in respect of Residence by reason only of his residing at the Seat of the Government of Canada while holding an Office under that Government requiring his Presence there.

Summons on Vacancy in Senate.

32. When a Vacancy happens in the Senate by Resignation, Death, or otherwise, the Governor General shall by Summons to a fit and qualified Person fill the Vacancy.

---

(15) As amended by the *British North America Act, 1915*, 5-6 Geo. V, c. 45 (U.K.), and the *British North America Act, (No. 2) 1975*, S.C. 1974-75-76, c. 53. The original section read as follows:

28. The Number of Senators shall not at any Time exceed Seventy-eight.

(15A) As enacted by the *British North America Act, 1965*, Statutes of Canada, 1965, c. 4 which came into force on the 1st of June 1965. The original section read as follows:

29. A Senator shall, subject to the Provisions of this Act, hold his Place in the Senate for Life.

33. If any Question arises respecting the Qualification of a Senator or a Vacancy in the Senate the same shall be heard and determined by the Senate. Questions as to Qualifications and Vacancies in Senate.

34. The Governor General may from Time to Time, by Instrument under the Great Seal of Canada, appoint a Senator to be Speaker of the Senate, and may remove him and appoint another in his Stead. (16) Appointment of Speaker of Senate.

35. Until the Parliament of Canada otherwise provides, the Presence of at least Fifteen Senators, including the Speaker, shall be necessary to constitute a Meeting of the Senate for the Exercise of its Powers. Quorum of Senate.

36. Questions arising in the Senate shall be decided by a Majority of Voices, and the Speaker shall in all Cases have a Vote, and when the Voices are equal the Decision shall be deemed to be in the Negative. Voting in Senate.

The House of Commons.

37. The House of Commons shall, subject to the Provisions of this Act, consist of two hundred and eighty-two members of whom ninety-five shall be elected for Ontario, seventy-five for Quebec, eleven for Nova Scotia, ten for New Brunswick, fourteen for Manitoba, twenty-eight for British Columbia, four for Prince Edward Island, twenty-one for Alberta, fourteen for Saskatchewan, seven for Newfoundland, one for the Yukon Territory and two for the Northwest Territories. (17) Constitution of House of Commons in Canada.

38. The Governor General shall from Time to Time, in the Queen's Name, by Instrument under the Great Seal of Canada, summon and call together the House of Commons. Summoning of House of Commons.

39. A Senator shall not be capable of being elected or of sitting or voting as a Member of the House of Commons. Senators not to sit in House of Commons.

---

(16) Provision for exercising the functions of Speaker during his absence is made by the *Speaker of the Senate Act*, R.S.C. 1970, c. S-14. Doubts as to the power of Parliament to enact such an Act were removed by the *Canadian Speaker (Appointment of Deputy) Act, 1895*, 59 Vict., c. 3, (U.K.).

(17) The figures given here would result from the application of section 51, as enacted by the *British North America Act, 1974*, S.C. 1974-75-76, c. 13 and amended by the *British North America Act, 1975*, S.C. 1974-75-76, c. 28. At press time effect had not yet been given to this readjustment as contemplated by the *Electoral Boundaries Readjustment Act*, R.S.C. 1970, c. E-2. Section 6 of the *Representation Act, 1974* provides that the number of members of the House of Commons and the representation of the provinces therein on the thirtieth day of December, 1974, remain unchanged until adjusted pursuant to section 51(1). As of that date the number of members was 264, as follows: 88 for Ontario, 74 for Quebec, 11 for Nova Scotia, 10 for New Brunswick, 13 for Manitoba, 23 for British Columbia, 4 for Prince Edward Island, 19 for Alberta, 13 for Saskatchewan, 7 for Newfoundland, 1 for the Yukon Territory, and 1 for the Northwest Territories. The original section (which was altered from time to time as the result of the addition of new provinces and changes in population) read as follows:

> **37.** The House of Commons shall, subject to the Provisions of this Act, consist of one hundred and eighty-one members, of whom Eighty-two shall be elected for Ontario, Sixty-five for Quebec, Nineteen for Nova Scotia, and Fifteen for New Brunswick.

40. Until the Parliament of Canada otherwise provides, Ontario, Quebec, Nova Scotia, and New Brunswick shall, for the Purposes of the Election of Members to serve in the House of Commons, be divided into Electoral Districts as follows:

Electoral districts of the Four Provinces.

1.—ONTARIO.

Ontario shall be divided into the Counties, Ridings of Counties, Cities, Parts of Cities, and Towns enumerated in the First Schedule to this Act, each whereof shall be an Electoral District, each such District as numbered in that Schedule being entitled to return One Member.

2.—QUEBEC.

Quebec shall be divided into Sixty-five Electoral Districts, composed of the Sixty-five Electoral Divisions into which Lower Canada is at the passing of this Act divided under Chapter Two of the Consolidated Statutes of Canada, Chapter Seventy-five of the Consolidated Statutes for Lower Canada, and the Act of the Province of Canada of the Twenty-third Year of the Queen, Chapter One, or any other Act amending the same in force at the Union, so that each such Electoral Division shall be for the Purposes of this Act an Electoral District entitled to return One Member.

3.—NOVA SCOTIA.

Each of the Eighteen Counties of Nova Scotia shall be an Electoral District. The County of Halifax shall be entitled to return Two Members, and each of the other Counties One Member.

4.—NEW BRUNSWICK.

Each of the Fourteen Counties into which New Brunswick is divided, including the City and County of St. John, shall be an Electoral District. The City of St. John shall also be a separate Electoral District. Each of those Fifteen Electoral Districts shall be entitled to return One Member. (18)

Continuance of existing Election Laws until Parliament of Canada otherwise provides.

41. Until the Parliament of Canada otherwise provides, all Laws in force in the several Provinces at the Union relative to the following Matters or any of them, namely,— the Qualifications and Disqualifications of Persons to be elected or to sit or vote as Members of the House of Assembly or Legislative Assembly in the several Provinces, the Voters at Elections of such Members, the Oaths to be taken by Voters, the Returning Officers, their Powers and Duties, the Proceedings at Elections, the Periods during

---

(18) Spent. The electoral districts are now established by Proclamations issued from time to time under the *Electoral Boundaries Readjustment Act,* R.S.C., c. 1970, E-2, as amended for particular districts by Acts of Parliament, for which see the most recent Table of Public Statutes.

which Elections may be continued, the Trial of controverted Elections, and Proceedings incident thereto, the vacating of Seats of Members, and the Execution of new Writs in case of Seats vacated otherwise than by Dissolution,—shall respectively apply to Elections of Members to serve in the House of Commons for the same several Provinces.

Provided that, until the Parliament of Canada otherwise provides, at any Election for a Member of the House of Commons for the District of Algoma, in addition to Persons qualified by the Law of the Province of Canada to vote, every Male British Subject, aged Twenty-one Years or upwards, being a Householder, shall have a Vote.(19)

42. Repealed. (20)

43. Repealed. (21)

44. The House of Commons on its first assembling after a General Election shall proceed with all practicable Speed to elect One of its Members to be Speaker.

As to Election of Speaker of House of Commons.

45. In case of a Vacancy happening in the Office of Speaker by Death, Resignation, or otherwise, the House of Commons shall with all practicable Speed proceed to elect another of its Members to be Speaker.

As to filling up Vacancy in Office of Speaker.

46. The Speaker shall preside at all Meetings of the House of Commons.

Speaker to preside.

47. Until the Parliament of Canada otherwise provides, in case of the Absence for any Reason of the Speaker from the Chair of the House of Commons for a Period of Forty-eight

Provision in case of Absence of Speaker.

---

(19) Spent. Elections are now provided for by the *Canada Elections Act*, R.S.C. 1970 (1st Supp.), c. 14; controverted elections by the *Dominion Controverted Elections Act*, R.S.C. 1970, c. C-28; qualifications and disqualifications of members by the *House of Commons Act*, R.S.C. 1970, c. H-9 and the *Senate and House of Commons Act*, R.S.C. 1970, c. S-8.

(20) Repealed by the *Statute Law Revision Act, 1893*, 56-57 Vict., c. 14 (U.K.). The section read as follows:

> **42.** For the First Election of Members to serve in the House of Commons the Governor General shall cause Writs to be issued by such Person, in such Form, and addressed to such Returning Officers as he thinks fit.
>
> The Person issuing Writs under this Section shall have the like Powers as are possessed at the Union by the Officers charged with the issuing of Writs for the Election of Members to serve in the respective House of Assembly or Legislative Assembly of the Province of Canada, Nova Scotia, or New Brunswick; and the Returning Officers to whom Writs are directed under this Section shall have the like Powers as are possessed at the Union by the Officers charged with the returning of Writs for the Election of Members to serve in the same respective House of Assembly or Legislative Assembly.

(21) Repealed by the *Statute Law Revision Act, 1893*, 56-57 Vict., c. 14 (U.K.) The section read as follows:

> **43.** In case a Vacancy in the Representation in the House of Commons of any Electoral District happens before the Meeting of the Parliament, or after the Meeting of the Parliament before Provision is made by the Parliament in this Behalf, the Provisions of the last foregoing Section of this Act shall extend and apply to the issuing and returning of a Writ in respect of such vacant District.

consecutive Hours, the House may elect another of its Members to act as Speaker, and the Member so elected shall during the Continuance of such Absence of the Speaker have and execute all the Powers, Privileges, and Duties of Speaker. (22)

Quorum of House of Commons.

48. The Presence of at least Twenty Members of the House of Commons shall be necessary to constitute a Meeting of the House for the Exercise of its Powers, and for that Purpose the Speaker shall be reckoned as a Member.

Voting in House of Commons.

49. Questions arising in the House of Commons shall be decided by a Majority of Voices other than that of the Speaker, and when the Voices are equal, but not otherwise, the Speaker shall have a Vote.

Duration of House of Commons.

50. Every House of Commons shall continue for Five Years from the Day of the Return of the Writs for choosing the House (subject to be sooner dissolved by the Governor General), and no longer.

Readjustment of representation in Commons.

51. (1) The number of members of the House of Commons and the representation of the provinces therein shall upon the coming into force of this subsection and thereafter on the completion of each decennial census be readjusted by such authority, in such manner, and from such time as the Parliament of Canada from time to time provides, subject and according to the following Rules:

Rules.

1. There shall be assigned to Quebec seventy-five members in the readjustment following the completion of the decennial census taken in the year 1971, and thereafter four additional members in each subsequent readjustment.

2. Subject to Rules 5(2) and (3), there shall be assigned to a large province a number of members equal to the number obtained by dividing the population of the large province by the electoral quotient of Quebec.

3. Subject to Rules 5(2) and (3), there shall be assigned to a small province a number of members equal to the number obtained by dividing

(*a*) the sum of the populations, determined according to the results of the penultimate decennial census, of the provinces (other than Quebec) having populations of less than one and a half million, determined according to the results of that census, by the sum of the numbers of members assigned to those provinces in the readjustment following the completion of that census; and

---

(22) Provision for exercising the functions of Speaker during his absence is now made by the *Speaker of the House of Commons Act*, R.S.C. 1970, c. S-13.

(*b*) the population of the small province by the quotient obtained under paragraph (*a*).

4. Subject to Rules 5(1)(*a*), (2) and (3), there shall be assigned to an intermediate province a number of members equal to the number obtained

(*a*) by dividing the sum of the populations of the provinces (other than Quebec) having populations of less than one and a half million by the sum of the number of members assigned to those provinces under any of Rules 3, 5(1)*b*), (2) and (3);

(*b*) by dividing the population of the intermediate province by the quotient obtained under paragraph (*a*); and

(*c*) by adding to the number of members assigned to the intermediate province in the readjustment following the completion of the penultimate decennial census one-half of the difference resulting from the subtraction of that number from the quotient obtained under paragraph (*b*).

5. (1) On any readjustment,

(*a*) if no province (other than Quebec) has a population of less than one and a half million, Rule 4 shall not be applied and, subject to Rules 5(2) and (3), there shall be assigned to an intermediate province a number of members equal to the number obtained by dividing

(i) the sum of the populations, determined according to the results of the penultimate decennial census, of the provinces (other than Quebec) having populations of not less than one and a half million and not more than two and a half million, determined according to the results of that census, by the sum of the numbers of members assigned to those provinces in the readjustment following the completion of that census, and

(ii) the population of the intermediate province by the quotient obtained under subparagraph (i);

(*b*) if a province (other than Quebec) having a population of

(i) less than one and a half million, or

(ii) not less than one and a half million and not more than two and a half million

does not have a population greater than its population determined according to the results of the penultimate decennial census, it shall, subject to Rules 5(2) and (3), be assigned the number of members assigned to it in the readjustment following the completion of that census.

(2) On any readjustment,

(*a*) if, under any of Rules 2 to 5(1), the number of members to be assigned to a province (in this paragraph referred to as "the first province") is smaller than the number of members to be assigned to any other province not having a population greater than that of the first province, those Rules shall not be applied to the first province and it shall be assigned a number of members equal to the largest number of members to be assigned to any other province not having a population greater than that of the first province;

(*b*) if, under any of Rules 2 to 5(1)(*a*), the number of members to be assigned to a province is smaller than the number of members assigned to it in the readjustment following the completion of the penultimate decennial census, those Rules shall not be applied to it and it shall be assigned the latter number of members;

(*c*) if both paragraphs (*a*) and (*b*) apply to a province, it shall be assigned a number of members equal to the greater of the numbers produced under those paragraphs.

(3) On any readjustment,

(*a*) if the electoral quotient of a province (in this paragraph referred to as "the first province") obtained by dividing its population by the number of members to be assigned to it under any of Rules 2 to 5(2) is greater than the electoral quotient of Quebec, those Rules shall not be applied to the first province and it shall be assigned a number of members equal to the number obtained by dividing its population by the electoral quotient of Quebec;

(*b*) if, as a result of the application of Rule 6(2)(*a*), the number of members assigned to a province under paragraph (*a*) equals the number of members to be assigned to it under any of Rules 2 to 5(2), it shall be assigned that number of members and paragraph (*a*) shall cease to apply to that province.

6. (1) In these Rules,

"electoral quotient" means, in respect of a province, the quotient obtained by dividing its population, determined according to the results of the then most recent decennial census, by the number of members to be assigned to it under any of Rules 1 to 5(3) in the readjustment following the completion of that census;

"intermediate province" means a province (other than Quebec) having a population greater than its population determined according to the results of the penultimate decennial census but not more than two and a half million and not less than one and a half million;

"large province" means a province (other than Quebec) having a population greater than two and a half million;

"penultimate decennial census" means the decennial census that preceded the then most recent decennial census;

"population" means, except where otherwise specified, the population determined according to the results of the then most recent decennial census;

"small province" means a province (other than Quebec) having a population greater than its population determined according to the results of the penultimate decennial census and less than one and a half million.

(2) For the purposes of these Rules,

(*a*) if any fraction less than one remains upon completion of the final calculation that produces the number of members to be assigned to a province, that number of members shall equal the number so produced disregarding the fraction;

(*b*) if more than one readjustment follows the completion of a decennial census, the most recent of those readjustments shall, upon taking effect, be deemed to be the only readjustment following the completion of that census;

(*c*) a readjustment shall not take effect until the termination of the then existing Parliament. (23)

---

(23) As enacted by the *British North America Act 1974*, S.C. 1974-75-76, c. 13, which came into force on December 31, 1974. The section, as originally enacted, read as follows:

51. On the Completion of the Census in the Year One Thousand eight hundred and seventy-one, and of each subsequent decennial Census, the Representation of the Four Provinces shall be readjusted by such Authority, in such Manner, and from such Time, as the Parliament of Canada from Time to Time provides, subject and according to the following Rules:

(1) Quebec shall have the fixed Number of Sixty-five Members:

(2) There shall be assigned to each of the other Provinces such a Number of Members as will bear the same Proportion to the Number of its Population (ascertained at such Census) as the Number Sixty-five bears to the Number of the Population of Quebec (so ascertained):

(3) In the Computation of the Number of Members for a Province a fractional Part not exceeding One Half of the whole Number requisite for entitling the Province to a Member shall be disregarded; but a fractional Part exceeding One Half of that Number shall be equivalent to the whole Number:

(4) On any such Re-adjustment the Number of Members for a Province shall not be reduced unless the Proportion which the Number of the Population of the Province bore to the Number of the aggregate Population of Canada at the then last preceding Re-adjustment of the Number of Members for the Province is ascertained at the then latest Census to be diminished by One Twentieth Part or upwards:

(5) Such Re-adjustment shall not take effect until the Termination of the then existing Parliament.

The section was amended by the *Statute Law Revision Act, 1893*, 56-57 Vict., c. 14 (U.K.) by repealing the words from "of the census" to "seventy-one and" and the word "subsequent".

By the *British North America Act, 1943*, 6-7 Geo VI, c. 30 (U.K.) redistribution of seats following the 1941 census was postponed until the first session of Parliament after the war. The section was re-enacted by the *British North America Act, 1946*, 9-10 Geo. VI, c. 63 (U.K.) to read as follows:

51. (1) The number of members of the House of Commons shall be two hundred and fifty-five and the representation of the provinces therein shall forthwith upon the coming into force of this section and thereafter on the completion of each decennial census be readjusted by such authority, in such manner, and from such time as the Parliament of Canada from time to time provides, subject and according to the following rules:—

(1) Subject as hereinafter provided, there shall be assigned to each of the provinces a number of members computed by dividing the total population of the provinces by two hundred and fifty-four and by dividing the population of each province by the quotient so obtained, disregarding, except as hereinafter in this section provided, the remainder, if any, after the said process of division.

(2) If the total number of members assigned to all the provinces pursuant to rule one is less than two hundred and fifty-four, additional members shall be assigned to the provinces (one to a province) having remainders in the computation under rule one commencing with the province having the largest remainder and continuing with the other provinces in the order of the magnitude of their respective remainders until the total number of members assigned is two hundred and fifty-four.

(3) Notwithstanding anything in this section, if upon completion of a computation under rules one and two, the number of members to be assigned to a province is less than the number of senators representing the said province, rules one and two shall cease to apply in respect of the said province, and there shall be assigned to the said province a number of members equal to the said number of senators.

(4) In the event that rules one and two cease to apply in respect of a province then, for the purpose of computing the number of members to be assigned to the provinces in respect of which rules one and two continue to apply, the total population of the provinces shall be reduced by the number of the population of the province in respect of which rules one and two have ceased to apply and the number two hundred and fifty-four shall be reduced by the number of members assigned to such province pursuant to rule three.

(5) Such readjustment shall not take effect until the termination of the then existing Parliament.

(2) The Yukon Territory as constituted by Chapter forty-one of the Statutes of Canada, 1901, together with any Part of Canada not comprised within a province which may from time to time be included therein by the Parliament of Canada for the purposes of representation in Parliament, shall be entitled to one member.

The section was re-enacted by the *British North America Act, 1952,* S.C. 1952, c. 15 as follows:

51. (1) Subject as hereinafter provided, the number of members of the House of Commons shall be two hundred and sixty-three and the representation of the provinces therein shall forthwith upon the coming into force of this section and thereafter on the completion of each decennial census be readjusted by such authority, in such manner, and from such time as the Parliament of Canada from time to time provides, subject and according to the following rules:

1. There shall be assigned to each of the provinces a number of members computed by dividing the total population of the provinces by two hundred and sixty-one and by dividing the population of each province by the quotient so obtained, disregarding, except as hereinafter in this section provided, the remainder, if any, after the said process of division.

2. If the total number of members assigned to all the provinces pursuant to rule one is less than two hundred and sixty-one, additional members shall be assigned to the provinces (one to a province) having remainders in the computation under rule one commencing with the province having the largest remainder and continuing with the other provinces in the order of the magnitude of their respective remainders until the total number of members assigned is two hundred and sixty-one.

3. Notwithstanding anything in this section, if upon completion of a computation under rules one and two the number of members to be assigned to a province is less than the number of senators representing the said province, rules one and two shall cease to apply in respect of the said province, and there shall be assigned to the said province a number of members equal to the said number of senators.

4. In the event that rules one and two cease to apply in respect of a province then, for the purposes of computing the number of members to be assigned to the provinces in respect of which rules one and two continue to apply, the total population of the provinces shall be reduced by the number of the population of the province in respect of which rules one and two have ceased to apply and the number two hundred and sixty-one shall be reduced by the number of members assigned to such province pursuant to rule three.

5. On any such readjustment the number of members for any province shall not be reduced by more than fifteen per cent below the representation to which such province was entitled under rules one to four of this subsection at the last preceding readjustment of the representation of that province, and

(2) The Yukon Territory as bounded and described in the schedule to chapter Y-2 of the Revised Statutes of Canada, 1970, shall be entitled to one member, and the Northwest Territories as bounded and described in section 2 of chapter N-22 of the Revised Statutes of Canada, 1970, shall be entitled to two members. (24)

Yukon Territory and Northwest Territories.

51A. Notwithstanding anything in this Act a province shall always be entitled to a number of members in the House of Commons not less than the number of senators representing such province. (25)

Constitution of House of Commons.

52. The Number of Members of the House of Commons may be from Time to Time increased by the Parliament of Canada, provided the proportionate Representation of the Provinces prescribed by this Act is not thereby disturbed.

Increase of Number of House of Commons.

Money Votes; Royal Assent.

53. Bills for appropriating any Part of the Public Revenue, or for imposing any Tax or Impost, shall originate in the House of Commons.

Appropriation and Tax Bills.

54. It shall not be lawful for the House of Commons to adopt or pass any Vote, Resolution, Address, or Bill for the Appropriation of any Part of the Public Revenue, or of any Tax or Impost, to any Purpose that has not been first recommended to that House by Message of the Governor General in the Session in which such Vote, Resolution, Address, or Bill is proposed.

Recommendation of Money Votes.

55. Where a Bill passed by the Houses of the Parliament is presented to the Governor General for the Queen's Assent, he shall declare, according to his Discretion, but subject to the Provisions of this Act and to Her Majesty's Instructions, either that he assents thereto in the Queen's Name, or that he withholds the Queen's Assent, or that he reserves the Bill for the Signification of the Queen's Pleasure.

Royal Assent to Bills, etc.

---

there shall be no reduction in the representation of any province as a result of which that province would have a smaller number of members than any other province that according to the results of the then last decennial census did not have a larger population; but for the purposes of any subsequent readjustment of representation under this section any increase in the number of members of the House of Commons resulting from the application of this rule shall not be included in the divisor mentioned in rules one to four of this subsection.

6. Such readjustment shall not take effect until the termination of the then existing Parliament.

(2) The Yukon Territory as constituted by chapter forty-one of the statutes of Canada, 1901, shall be entitled to one member, and such other part of Canada not comprised within a province as may from time to time be defined by the Parliament of Canada shall be entitled to one member.

(24) As enacted by the *British North America Act, 1975*, S.C. 1974-75-76, c. 28.

(25) As enacted by the *British North America Act, 1915*, 5-6 Geo. V, c. 45 (U.K.).

56. Where the Governor General assents to a Bill in the Queen's Name, he shall by the first convenient Opportunity send an authentic Copy of the Act to one of Her Majesty's Principal Secretaries of State, and if the Queen in Council within Two Years after Receipt thereof by the Secretary of State thinks fit to disallow the Act, such Disallowance (with a Certificate of the Secretary of State of the Day on which the Act was received by him) being signified by the Governor General, by Speech or Message to each of the Houses of the Parliament or by Proclamation, shall annul the Act from and after the Day of such Signification.

Disallowance by Order in Council of Act assented to by Governor General.

57. A Bill reserved for the Signification of the Queen's Pleasure shall not have any Force unless and until, within Two Years from the Day on which it was presented to the Governor General for the Queen's Assent, the Governor General signifies, by Speech or Message to each of the Houses of the Parliament or by Proclamation, that it has received the Assent of the Queen in Council.

Signification of Queen's Pleasure on Bill reserved.

An Entry of every such Speech, Message, or Proclamation shall be made in the Journal of each House, and a Duplicate thereof duly attested shall be delivered to the proper Officer to be kept among the Records of Canada.

V.—PROVINCIAL CONSTITUTIONS.

Executive Power.

58. For each Province there shall be an Officer, styled the Lieutenant Governor, appointed by the Governor General in Council by Instrument under the Great Seal of Canada.

Appointment of Lieutenant Governors of Provinces.

59. A Lieutenant Governor shall hold Office during the Pleasure of the Governor General; but any Lieutenant Governor appointed after the Commencement of the First Session of the Parliament of Canada shall not be removeable within Five Years from his Appointment, except for Cause assigned, which shall be communicated to him in Writing within One Month after the Order for his Removal is made, and shall be communicated by Message to the Senate and to the House of Commons within One Week thereafter if the Parliament is then sitting, and if not then within One Week after the Commencement of the next Session of the Parliament.

Tenure of Office of Lieutenant Governor.

60. The Salaries of the Lieutenant Governors shall be fixed and provided by the Parliament of Canada. (26)

Salaries of Lieutenant Governors.

61. Every Lieutenant Governor shall, before assuming the Duties of his Office, make and subscribe before the Governor

Oaths, etc., of Lieutenant Governor.

(26) Provided for by the *Salaries Act*, R.S.C. 1970, c. S-2.

General or some Person authorized by him Oaths of Allegiance and Office similar to those taken by the Governor General.

62. The Provisions of this Act referring to the Lieutenant Governor extend and apply to the Lieutenant Governor for the Time being of each Province, or other the Chief Executive Officer or Administrator for the Time being carrying on the Government of the Province, by whatever Title he is designated.

Application of provisions referring to Lieutenant Governor.

63. The Executive Council of Ontario and of Quebec shall be composed of such Persons as the Lieutenant Governor from Time to Time thinks fit, and in the first instance of the following Officers, namely,—the Attorney General, the Secretary and Registrar of the Province, the Treasurer of the Province, the Commissioner of Crown Lands, and the Commissioner of Agriculture and Public Works, with in Quebec the Speaker of the Legislative Council and the Solicitor General. (27)

Appointment of Executive Officers for Ontario and Quebec.

64. The Constitution of the Executive Authority in each of the Provinces of Nova Scotia and New Brunswick shall, subject to the Provisions of this Act, continue as it exists at the Union until altered under the Authority of this Act. (28)

Executive Government of Nova Scotia and New Brunswick.

65. All Powers, Authorities, and Functions which under any Act of the Parliament of Great Britain, or of the Parliament of the United Kingdom of Great Britain and Ireland, or of the Legislature of Upper Canada, Lower Canada, or Canada, were or are before or at the Union vested in or exerciseable by the respective Governors or Lieutenant Governors of those Provinces, with the Advice or with the Advice and Consent of the respective Executive Councils thereof, or in conjunction with those Councils, or with any Number of Members thereof, or by those Governors or Lieutenant Governors individually, shall, as far as the same are capable of being exercised after the Union in relation to the Government of Ontario and Quebec respectively, be vested in and shall or may be exercised by the Lieutenant Governor of Ontario and Quebec respectively, with the Advice or with the Advice and Consent of or in conjunction with the respective Executive Councils, or any Members thereof, or by the Lieutenant Governor individually, as the Case requires, subject nevertheless (except with respect to such as exist under Acts of the Parliament of Great Britain, or of the Parliament of the

Powers to be exercised by Lieutenant Governor of Ontario or Quebec with Advice, or alone.

---

(27) Now provided for in Ontario by the *Executive Council Act,* R.S.O. 1970, c. 153, and in Quebec by the *Executive Power Act,* R.S.Q. 1964, c. 9.

(28) A similar provision was included in each of the instruments admitting British Columbia, Prince Edward Island, and Newfoundland. The Executive Authorities for Manitoba, Alberta and Saskatchewan were established by the statutes creating those provinces. See the footnotes to section 5, *supra.*

United Kingdom of Great Britain and Ireland,) to be abolished or altered by the respective Legislatures of Ontario and Quebec. (29)

Application of Provisions referring to Lieutenant Governor in Council.

66. The Provisions of this Act referring to the Lieutenant Governor in Council shall be construed as referring to the Lieutenant Governor of the Province acting by and with the Advice of the Executive Council thereof.

Administration in Absence, etc., of Lieutenant Governor.

67. The Governor General in Council may from Time to Time appoint an Administrator to execute the Office and Functions of Lieutenant Governor during his Absence, Illness, or other Inability.

Seats of Provincial Governments.

68. Unless and until the Executive Government of any Province otherwise directs with respect to that Province, the Seats of Government of the Provinces shall be as follows, namely,—of Ontario, the City of Toronto; of Quebec, the City of Quebec; of Nova Scotia, the City of Halifax; and of New Brunswick, the City of Fredericton.

Legislative Power.

1.—ONTARIO.

Legislature for Ontario.

69. There shall be a Legislature for Ontario consisting of the Lieutenant Governor and of One House, styled the Legislative Assembly of Ontario.

Electoral districts.

70. The Legislative Assembly of Ontario shall be composed of Eighty-two Members, to be elected to represent the Eighty-two Electoral Districts set forth in the First Schedule to this Act. (30)

2.—QUEBEC.

Legislature for Quebec.

71. There shall be a Legislature for Quebec consisting of the Lieutenant Governor and of Two Houses, styled the Legislative Council of Quebec and the Legislative Assembly of Quebec. (31)

Constitution of Legislative Council.

72. The Legislative Council of Quebec shall be composed of Twenty-four Members, to be appointed by the Lieutenant Governor, in the Queen's Name, by Instrument under the Great Seal of Quebec, One being appointed to represent each of the Twenty-four Electoral Divisions of Lower Canada in this Act referred to, and each holding Office for the Term of his Life, unless the Legislature of Quebec otherwise provides under the Provisions of this Act.

---

(29) See the notes to section 129, *infra*.

(30) Spent. Now covered by the *Representation Act*, R.S.O. 1970, c. 413.

(31) The Act respecting the Legislative Council of Quebec, S.Q. 1968, c. 9, provided that the Legislature for Quebec shall consist of the Lieutenant Governor and the National Assembly of Quebec, and repealed the provisions of the *Legislature Act*, R.S.Q. 1964, c. 6, relating to the Legislative Council of Quebec. Sections 72 to 79 following are therefore completely spent.

73. The Qualifications of the Legislative Councillors of Quebec shall be the same as those of the Senators for Quebec. Qualification of Legislative Councillors.

74. The Place of a Legislative Councillor of Quebec shall become vacant in the Cases, *mutatis mutandis*, in which the Place of Senator becomes vacant. Resignation, Disqualification, etc.

75. When a Vacancy happens in the Legislative Council of Quebec by Resignation, Death, or otherwise, the Lieutenant Governor, in the Queen's Name, by Instrument under the Great Seal of Quebec, shall appoint a fit and qualified Person to fill the Vacancy. Vacancies.

76. If any Question arises respecting the Qualification of a Legislative Councillor of Quebec, or a Vacancy in the Legislative Council of Quebec, the same shall be heard and determined by the Legislative Council. Questions as to Vacancies, etc.

77. The Lieutenant Governor may from Time to Time, by Instrument under the Great Seal of Quebec, appoint a Member of the Legislative Council of Quebec to be Speaker thereof, and may remove him and appoint another in his Stead. Speaker of Legislative Council.

78. Until the Legislature of Quebec otherwise provides, the Presence of at least Ten Members of the Legislative Council, including the Speaker, shall be necessary to constitute a Meeting for the Exercise of its Powers. Quorum of Legislative Council.

79. Questions arising in the Legislative Council of Quebec shall be decided by a Majority of Voices, and the Speaker shall in all Cases have a Vote, and when the Voices are equal the Decision shall be deemed to be in the Negative. Voting in Legislative Council.

80. The Legislative Assembly of Quebec shall be composed of Sixty-five Members, to be elected to represent the Sixty-five Electoral Divisions or Districts of Lower Canada in this Act referred to, subject to Alteration thereof by the Legislature of Quebec: Provided that it shall not be lawful to present to the Lieutenant Governor of Quebec for Assent any Bill for altering the Limits of any of the Electoral Divisions or Districts mentioned in the Second Schedule to this Act, unless the Second and Third Readings of such Bill have been passed in the Legislative Assembly with the Concurrence of the Majority of the Members representing all those Electoral Divisions or Districts, and the Assent shall not be given to such Bill unless an Address has been presented by the Legislative Assembly to the Lieutenant Governor stating that it has been so passed. (32) Constitution of Legislative Assembly of Quebec.

---

(32) The Act respecting electoral districts, S.Q. 1970, c. 7, s. 1, provides that this section no longer has effect.

3.—ONTARIO AND QUEBEC.

81. Repealed. (33)

Summoning of Legislative Assemblies.

82. The Lieutenant Governor of Ontario and of Quebec shall from Time to Time, in the Queen's Name, by Instrument under the Great Seal of the Province, summon and call together the Legislative Assembly of the Province.

Restriction on election of Holders of offices.

83. Until the Legislature of Ontario or of Quebec otherwise provides, a Person accepting or holding in Ontario or in Quebec any Office, Commission, or Employment, permanent or temporary, at the Nomination of the Lieutenant Governor, to which an annual Salary, or any Fee, Allowance, Emolument, or Profit of any Kind or Amount whatever from the Province is attached, shall not be eligible as a Member of the Legislative Assembly of the respective Province, nor shall he sit or vote as such; but nothing in this Section shall make ineligible any Person being a Member of the Executive Council of the respective Province, or holding any of the following Offices, that is to say, the Offices of Attorney General, Secretary and Registrar of the Province, Treasurer of the Province, Commissioner of Crown Lands, and Commissioner of Agriculture and Public Works, and in Quebec Solicitor General, or shall disqualify him to sit or vote in the House for which he is elected, provided he is elected while holding such Office. (34)

Continuance of existing Election Laws.

84. Until the Legislatures of Ontario and Quebec respectively otherwise provide, all Laws which at the Union are in force in those Provinces respectively, relative to the following Matters, or any of them, namely,—the Qualifications and Disqualifications of Persons to be elected or to sit or vote as Members of the Assembly of Canada, the Qualifications or Disqualifications of Voters, the Oaths to be taken by Voters, the Returning Officers, their Powers and Duties, the Proceedings at Elections, the Periods during which such Elections may be continued, and the Trial of controverted Elections and the Proceedings incident thereto, the vacating of the Seats of Members and the issuing and execution of new Writs in case of Seats vacated otherwise than by Dissolution,—shall respectively apply to Elections of Members to serve in the respective Legislative Assemblies of Ontario and Quebec.

Provided that, until the Legislature of Ontario otherwise provides, at any Election for a Member of the Legislative Assembly of Ontario for the District of Algoma, in addition

---

(33) Repealed by the *Statute Law Revision Act, 1893,* 56-57 Vict., c. 14 (U.K.). The section read as follows:

> **81.** The Legislatures of Ontario and Quebec respectively shall be called together not later than Six Months after the Union.

(34) Probably spent. The subject-matter of this section is now covered in Ontario by the *Legislative Assembly Act,* R.S.O. 1970, c. 240, and in Quebec by the *Legislature Act,* R.S.Q. 1964, c. 6.

to Persons qualified by the Law of the Province of Canada to vote, every male British Subject, aged Twenty-one Years or upwards, being a Householder, shall have a vote. (35)

85. Every Legislative Assembly of Ontario and every Legislative Assembly of Quebec shall continue for Four Years from the Day of the Return of the Writs for choosing the same (subject nevertheless to either the Legislative Assembly of Ontario or the Legislative Assembly of Quebec being sooner dissolved by the Lieutenant Governor of the Province), and no longer. (36)

Duration of Legislative Assemblies.

86. There shall be a Session of the Legislature of Ontario and of that of Quebec once at least in every Year, so that Twelve Months shall not intervene between the last Sitting of the Legislature in each Province in one Session and its first Sitting in the next Session.

Yearly Session of Legislature.

87. The following Provisions of this Act respecting the House of Commons of Canada shall extend and apply to the Legislative Assemblies of Ontario and Quebec, that is to say,—the Provisions relating to the Election of a Speaker originally and on Vacancies, the Duties of the Speaker, the Absence of the Speaker, the Quorum, and the Mode of voting, as if those Provisions were here re-enacted and made applicable in Terms to each such Legislative Assembly.

Speaker, Quorum, etc.

4.—NOVA SCOTIA AND NEW BRUNSWICK.

88. The Constitution of the Legislature of each of the Provinces of Nova Scotia and New Brunswick shall, subject to the Provisions of this Act, continue as it exists at the Union until altered under the Authority of this Act. (37)

Constitutions of Legislatures of Nova Scotia and New Brunswick.

---

(35) Probably spent. The subject-matter of this section is now covered in Ontario by the *Election Act*, R.S.O. 1970, c. 142, the *Controverted Elections Act*, R.S.O. 1970, c. 84 and the *Legislative Assembly Act*, R.S.O. 1970, c. 240, in Quebec by the *Elections Act*, R.S.Q. 1964, c. 7, the *Provincial Controverted Elections Act*, R.S.Q. 1964, c. 8 and the *Legislature Act*, R.S.Q. 1964, c. 6.

(36) The maximum duration of the Legislative Assembly for Ontario and Quebec has been changed to five years by the *Legislative Assembly Act*, R.S.O. 1970, c. 240, and the *Legislature Act*, R.S.Q. 1964, c. 6 respectively.

(37) Partially repealed by the *Statute Law Revision Act, 1893*, 56-57 Vict., c. 14 (U.K.) which deleted the following concluding words of the original enactment:

> and the House of Assembly of New Brunswick existing at the passing of this Act shall, unless sooner dissolved, continue for the Period for which it was elected.

A similar provision was included in each of the instruments admitting British Columbia, Prince Edward Island, and Newfoundland. The Legislatures of Manitoba, Alberta and Saskatchewan were established by the statutes creating those provinces. See the footnotes to section 5, *supra*.

89. Repealed. (38)

6.—THE FOUR PROVINCES.

Application to
Legislatures of
Provisions
respecting
Money Votes,
etc.

90. The following Provisions of this Act respecting the Parliament of Canada, namely,—the Provisions relating to Appropriation and Tax Bills, the Recommendation of Money Votes, the Assent to Bills, the Disallowance of Acts, and the Signification of Pleasure on Bills reserved,—shall extend and apply to the Legislatures of the several Provinces as if those Provisions were here re-enacted and made applicable in Terms to the respective Provinces and the Legislatures thereof, with the Substitution of the Lieutenant Governor of the Province for the Governor General, of the Governor General for the Queen and for a Secretary of State, of One Year for Two Years, and of the Province for Canada.

VI.—DISTRIBUTION OF LEGISLATIVE POWERS.

Powers of the Parliament.

Legislative
Authority of
Parliament of
Canada.

91. It shall be lawful for the Queen, by and with the Advice and Consent of the Senate and House of Commons, to make Laws for the Peace, Order, and good Government of Canada, in relation to all Matters not coming within the Classes of Subjects by this Act assigned exclusively to the Legislatures of the Provinces; and for greater Certainty, but not so as to restrict the Generality of the foregoing Terms of this Section, it is hereby declared that (notwithstanding anything in this Act) the exclusive Legislative Authority of the Parliament of Canada extends to all Matters coming within the Classes of Subjects next herein-after enumerated; that is to say,—

1. The amendment from time to time of the Constitution of Canada, except as regards matters coming within the classes of subjects by this Act assigned exclusively to the Legislatures of the provinces, or as regards rights or privileges by this or any other Constitutional Act granted or secured to the Legislature or the Government of a province, or to any class of persons with respect to

---

(38) Repealed by the *Statute Law Revision Act, 1893,* 56-57 Vict., c. 14 (U.K.). The section read as follows:

5.—ONTARIO, QUEBEC, AND NOVA SCOTIA.

89. Each of the Lieutenant Governors of Ontario, Quebec and Nova Scotia shall cause Writs to be issued for the First Election of Members of the Legislative Assembly thereof in such Form and by such Person as he thinks fit, and at such Time and addressed to such Returning Officer as the Governor General directs, and so that the First Election of Member of Assembly for any Electoral District or any Subdivision thereof shall be held at the same Time and at the same Places as the Election for a Member to serve in the House of Commons of Canada for the Electoral District.

schools or as regards the use of the English or the French language or as regards the requirements that there shall be a session of the Parliament of Canada at least once each year, and that no House of Commons shall continue for more than five years from the day of the return of the Writs for choosing the House: provided, however, that a House of Commons may in time of real or apprehended war, invasion or insurrection be continued by the Parliament of Canada if such continuation is not opposed by the votes of more than one-third of the members of such House. (39)

1A. The Public Debt and Property. (40)
  2. The Regulation of Trade and Commerce.
2A. Unemployment insurance. (41)
  3. The raising of Money by any Mode or System of Taxation.
  4. The borrowing of Money on the Public Credit.
  5. Postal Service.
  6. The Census and Statistics.
  7. Militia, Military and Naval Service, and Defence.
  8. The fixing of and providing for the Salaries and Allowances of Civil and other Officers of the Government of Canada.
  9. Beacons, Buoys. Lighthouses, and Sable Island.
10. Navigation and Shipping.
11. Quarantine and the Establishment and Maintenance of Marine Hospitals.
12. Sea Coast and Inland Fisheries.
13. Ferries between a Province and any British or Foreign Country or between Two Provinces.
14. Currency and Coinage.
15. Banking, Incorporation of Banks, and the Issue of Paper Money.
16. Savings Banks.
17. Weights and Measures.
18. Bills of Exchange and Promissory Notes.
19. Interest.
20. Legal Tender.
21. Bankruptcy and Insolvency.
22. Patents of Invention and Discovery.
23. Copyrights.
24. Indians, and Lands reserved for the Indians.
25. Naturalization and Aliens.
26. Marriage and Divorce.

---

(39) Added by the *British North America (No. 2) Act, 1949*, 13 Geo. VI, c. 81 (U.K.).

(40) Re-numbered by the *British North America (No. 2) Act, 1949*.

(41) Added by the *British North America Act, 1940*, 3-4 Geo. VI, c. 36 (U.K.).

27. The Criminal Law, except the Constitution of Courts of Criminal Jurisdiction, but including the Procedure in Criminal Matters.

28. The Establishment, Maintenance, and Management of Penitentiaries.

29. Such Classes of Subjects as are expressly excepted in the Enumeration of the Classes of Subjects by this Act assigned exclusively to the Legislatures of the Provinces.

And any Matter coming within any of the Classes of Subjects enumerated in this Section shall not be deemed to come within the Class of Matters of a local or private Nature comprised in the Enumeration of the Classes of Subjects by this Act assigned exclusively to the Legislatures of the Provinces. (42)

---

(42) Legislative authority has been conferred on Parliament by other Acts as follows:

1. The *British North America Act, 1871,* 34-35 Vict., c. 28 (U.K.).

2. The Parliament of Canada, may from time to time establish new Provinces in any territories forming for the time being part of the Dominion of Canada, but not included in any Province thereof, and may, at the time of such establishment, make provision for the constitution and administration of any such Province, and for the passing of laws for the peace, order, and good government of such Province, and for its representation in the said Parliament.

3. The Parliament of Canada may from time to time, with the consent of the Legislature of any Province of the said Dominion, increase, diminish, or otherwise alter the limits of such Province, upon such terms and conditions as may be agreed to by the said Legislature, and may, with the like consent, make provision respecting the effect and operation of any such increase or diminution or alteration of territory in relation to any Province affected thereby.

4. The Parliament of Canada may from time to time make provision for the administration peace, order, and good government of any territory not for the time being included in any Province.

5. The following Acts passed by the said Parliament of Canada, and intituled respectively,—"An Act for the temporary government of Rupert's Land and the North Western Territory when united with Canada"; and "An Act to amend and continue the Act thirty-two and thirty-three Victoria, chapter three, and to establish and provide for the government of "the Province of Manitoba," shall be and be deemed to have been valid and effectual for all purposes whatsoever from the date at which they respectively received the assent, in the Queen's name, of the Governor General of the said Dominion of Canada.

6. Except as provided by the third section of this Act, it shall not be competent for the Parliament of Canada to alter the provisions of the last-mentioned Act of the said Parliament in so far as it relates to the Province of Manitoba, or of any other Act hereafter establishing new Provinces in the said Dominion, subject always to the right of the Legislature of the Province of Manitoba to alter from time to time the provisions of any law respecting the qualification of electors and members of the Legislative Assembly, and to make laws respecting elections in the said Province.

The *Rupert's Land Act 1868*, 31-32 Vict., c. 105 (U.K.) (repealed by the *Statute Law Revision Act, 1893*, 56-57 Vict., c. 14 (U.K.)) had previously conferred similar authority in relation to Rupert's Land and the North-Western Territory upon admission of those areas.

2. The *British North America Act, 1886*, 49-50 Vict., c. 35, (U.K.).

1. The Parliament of Canada may from time to time make provision for the representation in the Senate and House of Commons of Canada, or in either of them, of any territories which for the time being form part of the Dominion of Canada, but are not included in any province thereof.

3. The *Statute of Westminster, 1931*, 22 Geo. V, c. 4, (U.K.).

3. It is hereby declared and enacted that the Parliament of a Dominion has full power to make laws having extra-territorial operation.

Exclusive Powers of Provincial Legislatures.

92. In each Province the Legislature may exclusively make Laws in relation to Matters coming within the Classes of Subject next herein-after enumerated; that is to say,—

1. The Amendment from Time to Time, notwithstanding anything in this Act, of the Constitution of the Province, except as regards the Office of Lieutenant Governor.

2. Direct Taxation within the Province in order to the raising of a Revenue for Provincial Purposes.

3. The borrowing of Money on the sole Credit of the Province.

4. The Establishment and Tenure of Provincial Offices and the Appointment and Payment of Provincial Officers.

5. The Management and Sale of the Public Lands belonging to the Province and of the Timber and Wood thereon.

6. The Establishment, Maintenance, and Management of Public and Reformatory Prisons in and for the Province.

7. The Establishment, Maintenance, and Management of Hospitals, Asylums, Charities, and Eleemosynary Institutions in and for the Province, other than Marine Hospitals.

8. Municipal Institutions in the Province.

9. Shop, Saloon, Tavern, Auctioneer, and other Licences in order to the raising of a Revenue for Provincial, Local, or Municipal Purposes.

10. Local Works and Undertakings other than such as are of the following Classes:—

    (*a*) Lines of Steam or other Ships, Railways, Canals, Telegraphs, and other Works and Undertakings connecting the Province with any other or others of the Provinces, or extending beyond the Limits of the Province;

    (*b*) Lines of Steam Ships between the Province and any British or Foreign Country;

    (*c*) Such Works as, although wholly situate within the Province, are before or after their Execution declared by the Parliament of Canada to be for the general Advantage of Canada or for the Advantage of Two or more of the Provinces.

11. The Incorporation of Companies with Provincial Objects.

12. The Solemnization of Marriage in the Province.

13. Property and Civil Rights in the Province.

14. The Administration of Justice in the Province, including the Constitution, Maintenance, and Organization of Provincial Courts, both of Civil and of Criminal Jurisdiction, and including Procedure in Civil Matters in those Courts.

15. The Imposition of Punishment by Fine, Penalty, or Imprisonment for enforcing any Law of the Province made in relation to any Matter coming within any of the Classes of Subjects enumerated in this Section.

16. Generally all Matters of a merely local or private Nature in the Province.

Education.

Legislation respecting Education.

93. In and for each Province the Legislature may exclusively make Laws in relation to Education, subject and according to the following Provisions:—

(1) Nothing in any such Law shall prejudicially affect any Right or Privilege with respect to Denominational Schools which any Class of Persons have by Law in the Province at the Union:

(2) All the Powers, Privileges, and Duties at the Union by Law conferred and imposed in Upper Canada on the Separate Schools and School Trustees of the Queen's Roman Catholic Subjects shall be and the same are hereby extended to the Dissentient Schools of the Queen's Protestant and Roman Catholic Subjects in Quebec:

(3) Where in any Province a System of Separate or Dissentient Schools exists by Law at the Union or is thereafter established by the Legislature of the Province, an Appeal shall lie to the Governor General in Council from any Act or Decision of any Provincial Authority affecting any Right or Privilege of the Protestant or Roman Catholic Minority of the Queen's Subjects in relation to Education:

(4) In case any such Provincial Law as from Time to Time seems to the Governor General in Council requisite for the due Execution of the Provisions of this Section is not made, or in case any Decision of the Governor General in Council on any Appeal under this Section is not duly executed by the proper Provincial Authority in that Behalf, then and in every such Case, and as far only as the Circumstances of each Case require, the Parliament of Canada may make remedial Laws for the due Execution of the

Provisions of this Section and of any Decision of the
Governor General in Council under this Section. (43)

*Uniformity of Laws in Ontario, Nova Scotia and New
Brunswick.*

94. Notwithstanding anything in this Act, the Parliament
of Canada may make Provision for the Uniformity of all or

Legislation for
Uniformity of
Laws in Three
Provinces.

---

(43) Altered for Manitoba by section 22 of the *Manitoba Act*, 33 Vict., c. 3 (Canada),
(confirmed by the *British North America Act, 1871*), which reads as follows:

> **22.** In and for the Province, the said Legislature may exclusively make Laws in
> relation to Education, subject and according to the following provisions:—
>
> (1) Nothing in any such Law shall prejudicially affect any right or privilege with
> respect to Denominational Schools which any class of persons have by Law or
> practice in the Province at the Union:
>
> (2) An appeal shall lie to the Governor General in Council from any Act or
> decision of the Legislature of the Province, or of any Provincial Authority, affecting
> any right or privilege, of the Protestant or Roman Catholic minority of the Queen's
> subjects in relation to Education:
>
> (3) In case any such Provincial Law, as from time to time seems to the Governor
> General in Council requisite for the due execution of the provisions of this section, is
> not made, or in case any decision of the Governor General in Council on any appeal
> under this section is not duly executed by the proper Provincial Authority in that
> behalf, then, and in every such case, and as far only as the circumstances of each
> case require, the Parliament of Canada may make remedial Laws for the due
> execution of the provisions of this section, and of any decision of the Governor
> General in Council under this section.

Altered for Alberta by section 17 of *The Alberta Act*, 4-5 Edw. VII, c. 3 which reads as follows:

> **17.** Section 93 of The British North America Act, 1867, shall apply to the said
> province, with the substitution for paragraph (1) of the said section 93 of the
> following paragraph:—
>
> (1) Nothing in any such law shall prejudicially affect any right or privilege with
> respect to separate schools which any class of persons have at the date of the passing
> of this Act, under the terms of chapters 29 and 30 of the Ordinances of the
> Northwest Territories, passed in the year 1901, or with respect to religious instruc-
> tion in any public or separate school as provided for in the said ordinances.
>
> **2.** In the appropriation by the Legislature or distribution by the Government of
> the province of any moneys for the support of schools organized and carried on in
> accordance with the said chapter 29 or any Act passed in amendment thereof, or in
> substitution therefor, there shall be no discrimination against schools of any class
> described in the said chapter 29.
>
> **3.** Where the expression "by law" is employed in paragraph 3 of the said section
> 93, it shall be held to mean the law as set out in the said chapters 29 and 30, and
> where the expression "at the Union" is employed, in the said paragraph 3, it shall be
> held to mean the date at which this Act comes into force.

Altered for Saskatchewan by section 17 of *The Saskatchewan* Act, 4-5 Edw. VII, c. 42, which
reads as follows:

> **17.** Section 93 of the British North America Act, 1867, shall apply to the said
> province, with the substitution for paragraph (1) of the said section 93, of the
> following paragraph:—
>
> (1) Nothing in any such law shall prejudicially affect any right or privilege with
> respect to separate schools which any class of persons have at the date of the passing
> of this Act, under the terms of chapters 29 and 30 of the Ordinances of the
> Northwest Territories, passed in the year 1901, or with respect to religious instruc-
> tion in any public or separate school as provided for in the said ordinances.
>
> **2.** In the appropriation by the Legislature or distribution by the Government of
> the province of any moneys for the support of schools organized and carried on in
> accordance with the said chapter 29, or any Act passed in amendment thereof or in
> substitution therefor, there shall be no discrimination against schools of any class
> described in the said chapter 29.
>
> **3.** Where the expression "by law" is employed in paragraph (3) of the said
> section 93, it shall be held to mean the law as set out in the said chapters 29 and 30;
> and where the expression "at the Union" is employed in the said paragraph (3), it
> shall be held to mean the date at which this Act comes into force.

any of the Laws relative to Property and Civil Rights in Ontario, Nova Scotia, and New Brunswick, and of the Procedure of all or any of the Courts in Those Three Provinces, and from and after the passing of any Act in that Behalf the Power of the Parliament of Canada to make Laws in relation to any Matter comprised in any such Act shall, notwithstanding anything in this Act, be unrestricted; but any Act of the Parliament of Canada making Provision for such Uniformity shall not have effect in any Province unless and until it is adopted and enacted as Law by the Legislature thereof.

Old Age Pensions.

Legislation respecting old age pensions and supplementary benefits.

94A. The Parliament of Canada may make laws in relation to old age pensions and supplementary benefits, including survivors' and disability benefits irrespective of age, but no such law shall affect the operation of any law present or future of a provincial legislature in relation to any such matter. (44)

Agriculture and Immigration.

Concurrent Powers of Legislation respecting Agriculture, etc.

95. In each Province the Legislature may make Laws in relation to Agriculture in the Province, and to Immigration into the Province; and it is hereby declared that the Parliament of Canada may from Time to Time make Laws in relation to Agriculture in all or any of the Provinces, and to Immigration into all or any of the Provinces; and any Law of the Legislature of a Province relative to Agriculture or to Immigration shall have effect in and for the Province as long and as far only as it is not repugnant to any Act of the Parliament of Canada.

Altered by Term 17 of the Terms of Union of Newfoundland with Canada (confirmed by the *British North America Act, 1949*, 12-13 Geo. VI, c. 22 (UK.)), which reads as follows:

17. In lieu of section ninety-three of the British North America Act, 1867, the following term shall apply in respect of the Province of Newfoundland:

In and for the Province of Newfoundland the Legislature shall have exclusive authority to make laws in relation to education, but the Legislature will not have authority to make laws prejudicially affecting any right or privilege with respect to denominational schools, common (amalgamated) schools, or denominational colleges, that any class or classes of persons have by law in Newfoundland at the date of Union, and out of public funds of the Province of Newfoundland, provided for education,

(a) all such schools shall receive their share of such funds in accordance with scales determined on a non-discriminatory basis from time to time by the Legislature for all schools then being conducted under authority of the Legislature; and

(b) all such colleges shall receive their share of any grant from time to time voted for all colleges then being conducted under authority of the Legislature, such grant being distributed on a non-discriminatory basis.

(44) Added by the *British North America Act, 1964*, 12-13, Eliz. II, c. 73 (U.K.). Originally enacted by the *British North America Act, 1951*, 14-15 Geo. VI, c. 32 (U.K.), as follows:

94A. It is hereby declared that the Parliament of Canada may from time to time make laws in relation to old age pensions in Canada, but no law made by the Parliament of Canada in relation to old age pensions shall affect the operation of any law present or future of a Provincial Legislature in relation to old age pensions.

VII.—JUDICATURE.

96. The Governor General shall appoint the Judges of the Superior, District, and County Courts in each Province, except those of the Courts of Probate in Nova Scotia and New Brunswick.

Appointment of Judges.

97. Until the laws relative to Property and Civil Rights in Ontario, Nova Scotia, and New Brunswick, and the Procedure of the Courts in those Provinces, are made uniform, the Judges of the Courts of those Provinces appointed by the Governor General shall be selected from the respective Bars of those Provinces.

Selection of Judges in Ontario, etc.

98. The Judges of the Courts of Quebec shall be selected from the Bar of that Province.

Selection of Judges in Quebec.

99. (1) Subject to subsection two of this section, the Judges of the Superior Courts shall hold office during good behaviour, but shall be removable by the Governor General on Address of the Senate and House of Commons.

Tenure of office of Judges.

(2) A Judge of a Superior Court, whether appointed before or after the coming into force of this section, shall cease to hold office upon attaining the age of seventy-five years, or upon the coming into force of this section if at that time he has already attained that age. (44A)

Termination at age 75.

100. The Salaries, Allowances, and Pensions of the Judges of the Superior, District, and County Courts (except the Courts of Probate in Nova Scotia and New Brunswick), and of the Admiralty Courts in Cases where the Judges thereof are for the Time being paid by Salary, shall be fixed and provided by the Parliament of Canada. (45)

Salaries etc., of Judges.

101. The Parliament of Canada may, notwithstanding anything in this Act, from Time to Time provide for the Constitution, Maintenance, and Organization of a General Court of Appeal for Canada, and for the Establishment of any additional Courts for the better Administration of the Laws of Canada. (46)

General Court of Appeal, etc.

VIII.—REVENUES; DEBTS; ASSETS; TAXATION

102. All Duties and Revenues over which the respective Legislatures of Canada, Nova Scotia, and New Brunswick before and at the Union had and have Power of Appropria-

Creation of Consolidated Revenue Fund.

(44A) Repealed and re-enacted by the *British North America Act, 1960,* 9 Eliz. II, c. 2 (U.K.), which came into force on the 1st day of March, 1961. The original section read as follows:

> **99.** The Judges of the Superior Courts shall hold Office during good Behaviour, but shall be removable by the Governor General on Address of the Senate and House of Commons.

(45) Now provided for in the *Judges Act,* R.S.C. 1970, c. J-1.

(46) See the *Supreme Court Act,* R.S.C. 1970, c. S-19, and the *Federal Court Act,* R.S.C. 1970, (2nd Supp.) c. 10.

tion, except such Portions thereof as are by this Act reserved to the respective Legislatures of the Provinces, or are raised by them in accordance with the special Powers conferred on them by this Act, shall form One Consolidated Revenue Fund, to be appropriated for the Public Service of Canada in the Manner and subject to the Charges in this Act provided.

Expenses of Collection, etc. **103.** The Consolidated Revenue Fund of Canada shall be permanently charged with the Costs, Charges, and Expenses incident to the Collection, Management, and Receipt thereof, and the same shall form the First Charge thereon, subject to be reviewed and audited in such Manner as shall be ordered by the Governor General in Council until the Parliament otherwise provides.

Interest of Provincial Public Debts. **104.** The annual Interest of the Public Debts of the several Provinces of Canada, Nova Scotia, and New Brunswick at the Union shall form the Second Charge on the Consolidated Revenue Fund of Canada.

Salary of Governor General. **105.** Unless altered by the Parliament of Canada, the Salary of the Governor General shall be Ten thousand Pounds Sterling Money of the United Kingdom of Great Britain and Ireland, payable out of the Consolidated Revenue Fund of Canada, and the same shall form the Third Charge thereon. (47)

Appropriation from Time to Time. **106.** Subject to the several Payments by this Act charged on the Consolidated Revenue Fund of Canada, the same shall be appropriated by the Parliament of Canada for the Public Service.

Transfer of Stocks, etc. **107.** All Stocks, Cash, Banker's Balances, and Securities for Money belonging to each Province at the Time of the Union, except as in this Act mentioned, shall be the Property of Canada, and shall be taken in Reduction of the Amount of the respective Debts of the Provinces at the Union.

Transfer of Property in Schedule. **108.** The Public Works and Property of each Province, enumerated in the Third Schedule to this Act, shall be the Property of Canada.

Property in Lands, Mines, etc. **109.** All Lands, Mines, Minerals, and Royalties belonging to the several Provinces of Canada, Nova Scotia, and New Brunswick at the Union, and all Sums then due or payable for such Lands, Mines, Minerals, or Royalties, shall belong to the several Provinces of Ontario, Quebec, Nova Scotia, and New Brunswick in which the same are situate or arise, subject to any Trusts existing in respect thereof, and to any Interest other than that of the Province in the same. (48)

(47) Now covered by the *Governor General's Act,* R.S.C. 1970, c. G-14.

(48) The four western provinces were placed in the same position as the original provinces by the *British North America Act, 1930,* 21 Geo. V, c. 26 (U.K.).

110. All Assets connected with such Portions of the Public Debt of each Province as are assumed by that Province shall belong to that Province.

111. Canada shall be liable for the Debts and Liabilities of each Province existing at the Union.

112. Ontario and Quebec conjointly shall be liable to Canada for the Amount (if any) by which the Debt of the Province of Canada exceeds at the Union Sixty-two million five hundred thousand Dollars, and shall be charged with Interest at the Rate of Five per Centum per Annum thereon.

113. The Assets enumerated in the Fourth Schedule to this Act belonging at the Union to the Province of Canada shall be the Property of Ontario and Quebec conjointly.

114. Nova Scotia shall be liable to Canada for the Amount (if any) by which its Public Debt exceeds at the Union Eight million Dollars, and shall be charged with Interest at the Rate of Five per Centum per Annum thereon. (49)

115. New Brunswick shall be liable to Canada for the Amount (if any) by which its Public Debt exceeds at the Union Seven million Dollars, and shall be charged with Interest at the Rate of Five per Centum per Annum thereon.

116. In case the Public Debts of Nova Scotia and New Brunswick do not at the Union amount to Eight million and Seven million Dollars respectively, they shall respectively receive by half-yearly Payments in advance from the Government of Canada Interest at Five per Centum per Annum on the Difference between the actual Amounts of their respective Debts and such stipulated Amounts.

117. The several Provinces shall retain all their respective Public Property not otherwise disposed of in this Act, subject to the Right of Canada to assume any Lands or Public Property required for Fortifications or for the Defence of the Country.

118. Repealed. (50)

---

(49) The obligations imposed by this section, sections 115 and 116, and similar obligations under the instruments creating or admitting other provinces, have been carried into legislation of the Parliament of Canada and are now to be found in the *Provincial Subsidies Act*, R.S.C. 1970, c. P-26.

(50) Repealed by the *Statute Law Revision Act, 1950*, 14 Geo. VI, c. 6 (U.K.). As originally enacted the section read as follows:

118. The following Sums shall be paid yearly by Canada to the several Provinces for the Support of their Governments and Legislatures:

	Dollars
Ontario	Eighty thousand.
Quebec	Seventy thousand.
Nova Scotia	Sixty thousand.
New Brunswick	Fifty thousand.

Two hundred and sixty thousand; and an annual Grant in aid of each Province shall be made, equal to Eighty Cents per Head of the Population as ascertained by the Census of One thousand eight hundred and sixty-one, and in the Case of Nova Scotia and New Brunswick, by each subsequent Decennial Census until the Population of each of those two Provinces amounts to Four hundred thousand Souls, at which Rate such Grant shall thereafter remain. Such Grants shall be in full Settlement of all future Demands on Canada, and shall be paid half-yearly in advance to each Province; but the Government of Canada shall deduct from such Grants, as against any Province, all Sums chargeable as Interest on the Public Debt of that Province in excess of the several Amounts stipulated in this Act.

The section was made obsolete by the *British North America Act, 1907*, 7 Edw. VII, c. 11 (U.K.) which provided:

1. (1) The following grants shall be made yearly by Canada to every province, which at the commencement of this Act is a province of the Dominion, for its local purposes and the support of its Government and Legislature:—

(*a*) A fixed grant—
where the population of the province is under one hundred and fifty thousand, of one hundred thousand dollars;
where the population of the province is one hundred and fifty thousand, but does not exceed two hundred thousand, of one hundred and fifty thousand dollars;
where the population of the province is two hundred thousand, but does not exceed four hundred thousand, of one hundred and eighty thousand dollars;
where the population of the province is four hundred thousand, but does not exceed eight hundred thousand, of one hundred and ninety thousand dollars;
where the population of the province is eight hundred thousand, but does not exceed one million five hundred thousand, of two hundred and twenty thousand dollars;
where the population of the province exceeds one million five hundred thousand, of two hundred and forty thousand dollars; and

(*b*) Subject to the special provisions of this Act as to the provinces of British Columbia and Prince Edward Island, a grant at the rate of eighty cents per head of the population of the province up to the number of two million five hundred thousand, and at the rate of sixty cents per head of so much of the population as exceeds that number.

(2) An additional grant of one hundred thousand dollars shall be made yearly to the province of British Columbia for a period of ten years from the commencement of this Act.

(3) The population of a province shall be ascertained from time to time in the case of the provinces of Manitoba, Saskatchewan, and Alberta respectively by the last quinquennial census or statutory estimate of population made under the Acts establishing those provinces or any other Act of the Parliament of Canada making provision for the purpose, and in the case of any other province by the last decennial census for the time being.

(4) The grants payable under this Act shall be paid half-yearly in advance to each province.

(5) The grants payable under this Act shall be substituted for the grants or subsidies (in this Act referred to as existing grants) payable for the like purposes at the commencement of this Act to the several provinces of the Dominion under the provisions of section one hundred and eighteen of the British North America Act 1867, or of any Order in Council establishing a province, or of any Act of the Parliament of Canada containing directions for the payment of any such grant or subsidy, and those provisions shall cease to have effect.

(6) The Government of Canada shall have the same power of deducting sums charged against a province on account of the interest on public debt in the case of the grant payable under this Act to the province as they have in the case of the existing grant.

(7) Nothing in this Act shall affect the obligation of the Government of Canada to pay to any province any grant which is payable to that province, other than the existing grant for which the grant under this Act is substituted.

(8) In the case of the provinces of British Columbia and Prince Edward Island, the amount paid on account of the grant payable per head of the population to the provinces under this Act shall not at any time be less than the amount of the corresponding grant payable at the commencement of this Act, and if it is found on any decennial census that the population of the province has decreased since the last decennial census, the amount paid on account of the grant shall not be decreased below the amount then payable, notwithstanding the decrease of the population.

See the *Provincial Subsidies Act*, R.S.C. 1970, c. P-26, *The Maritime Provinces Additional Subsidies Act*, 1942-43, c. 14, and the Terms of Union of Newfoundland with Canada, appended to the *British North America Act, 1949*, and also to *An Act to approve the Terms of Union of Newfoundland with Canada*, chapter 1 of the statutes of Canada, 1949.

119. New Brunswick shall receive by half-yearly Payments in advance from Canada for the Period of Ten Years from the Union an additional Allowance of Sixty-three thousand Dollars per Annum; but as long as the Public Debt of that Province remains under Seven million Dollars, a Deduction equal to the Interest at Five per Centum per Annum on such Deficiency shall be made from that Allowance of Sixty-three thousand Dollars. (51)

<small>Further Grant to New Brunswick.</small>

120. All Payments to be made under this Act, or in discharge of Liabilities created under any Act of the Provinces of Canada, Nova Scotia, and New Brunswick respectively, and assumed by Canada, shall, until the Parliament of Canada otherwise directs, be made in such Form and Manner as may from Time to Time be ordered by the Governor General in Council.

<small>Form of Payments.</small>

121. All Articles of the Growth, Produce, or Manufacture of any one of the Provinces shall, from and after the Union, be admitted free into each of the other Provinces.

<small>Canadian Manufactures, etc.</small>

122. The Customs and Excise Laws of each Province shall, subject to the Provisions of this Act, continue in force until altered by the Parliament of Canada. (52)

<small>Continuance of Customs and Excise Laws.</small>

123. Where Customs Duties are, at the Union, leviable on any Goods, Wares, or Merchandises in any Two Provinces, those Goods, Wares, and Merchandises may, from and after the Union, be imported from one of those Provinces into the other of them on Proof of Payment of the Customs Duty leviable thereon in the Province of Exportation, and on Payment of such further Amount (if any) of Customs Duty as is leviable thereon in the Province of Importation. (53)

<small>Exportation and Importation as between Two Provinces.</small>

124. Nothing in this Act shall affect the Right of New Brunswick to levy the Lumber Dues provided in Chapter Fifteen of Title Three of the Revised Statutes of New Brunswick, or in any Act amending that Act before or after the Union, and not increasing the Amount of such Dues; but the Lumber of any of the Provinces other than New Brunswick shall not be subject to such Dues. (54)

<small>Lumber Dues in New Brunswick.</small>

125. No Lands or Property belonging to Canada or any Province shall be liable to Taxation.

<small>Exemption of Public Lands, etc.</small>

---

(51) Spent.

(52) Spent. Now covered by the *Customs Act*, R.S.C. 1970, c. C-40, the *Customs Tariff*, R.S.C. 1970, c. C-41, the *Excise Act*, R.S.C. 1970, c. E-12 and the *Excise Tax Act*, R.S.C. 1970, c. E-13.

(53) Spent.

(54) These dues were repealed in 1873 by 36 Vict., c. 16 (N.B.). And see *An Act respecting the Export Duties imposed on Lumber*, etc., (1873) 36 Vict., c. 41 (Canada), and section 2 of the *Provincial Subsidies Act*, R.S.C. 1970, c. P-26.

Provincial
Consolidated
Revenue Fund.

126. Such Portions of the Duties and Revenues over which the respective Legislatures of Canada, Nova Scotia, and New Brunswick had before the Union Power of Appropriation as are by this Act reserved to the respective Governments or Legislatures of the Provinces, and all Duties and Revenues raised by them in accordance with the special Powers conferred upon them by this Act, shall in each Province form One Consolidated Revenue Fund to be appropriated for the Public Service of the Province.

IX.—MISCELLANEOUS PROVISIONS.

General.

127. Repealed. (55)

Oath of
Allegiance, etc.

128. Every Member of the Senate or House of Commons of Canada shall before taking his Seat therein take and subscribe before the Governor General or some Person authorized by him, and every Member of a Legislative Council or Legislative Assembly of any Province shall before taking his Seat therein take and subscribe before the Lieutenant Governor of the Province or some Person authorized by him, the Oath of Allegiance contained in the Fifth Schedule to this Act; and every Member of the Senate of Canada and every Member of the Legislative Council of Quebec shall also, before taking his Seat therein, take and subscribe before the Governor General, or some Person authorized by him, the Declaration of Qualification contained in the same Schedule.

Continuance of
existing Laws,
Courts,
Officers, etc.

129. Except as otherwise provided by this Act, all Laws in force in Canada, Nova Scotia, or New Brunswick at the Union, and all Courts of Civil and Criminal Jurisdiction, and all legal Commissions, Powers, and Authorities, and all Officers, Judicial, Administrative, and Ministerial, existing therein at the Union, shall continue in Ontario, Quebec, Nova Scotia, and New Brunswick respectively, as if the Union had not been made; subject nevertheless (except with respect to such as are enacted by or exist under Acts of the Parliament of Great Britain or of the Parliament of the United Kingdom of Great Britain and Ireland,) to be repealed, abolished, or altered by the Parliament of Canada, or by the Legislature of

---

(55) Repealed by the *Statute Law Revision Act, 1893*, 56-57 Vict., c. 14 (U.K.). The section read as follows:

127. If any Person being at the passing of this Act a Member of the Legislative Council of Canada, Nova Scotia, or New Brunswick to whom a Place in the Senate is offered, does not within Thirty Days thereafter, by Writing under his Hand addressed to the Governor General of the Province of Canada or to the Lieutenant Governor of Nova Scotia or New Brunswick (as the Case may be), accept the same, he shall be deemed to have declined the same; and any Person who, being at the passing of this Act a Member of the Legislative Council of Nova Scotia or New Brunswick, accepts a Place in the Senate, shall thereby vacate his Seat in such Legislative Council.

the respective Province, according to the Authority of the Parliament or of that Legislature under this Act. (56)

130. Until the Parliament of Canada otherwise provides, all Officers of the several Provinces having Duties to discharge in relation to Matters other than those coming within the Classes of Subjects by this Act assigned exclusively to the Legislatures of the Provinces shall be Officers of Canada, and shall continue to discharge the Duties of their respective Offices under the same Liabilities, Responsibilities, and Penalties as if the Union had not been made. (57)

Transfer of Officers to Canada.

131. Until the Parliament of Canada otherwise provides, the Governor General in Council may from Time to Time appoint such Officers as the Governor General in Council deems necessary or proper for the effectual Execution of this Act.

Appointment of new Officers.

132. The Parliament and Government of Canada shall have all Powers necessary or proper for performing the Obligations of Canada or of any Province thereof, as Part of the British Empire, towards Foreign Countries, arising under Treaties between the Empire and such Foreign Countries.

Treaty Obligations.

133. Either the English or the French Language may be used by any Person in the Debates of the Houses of the Parliament of Canada and of the Houses of the Legislature of Quebec; and both those Languages shall be used in the respective Records and Journals of those Houses; and either of those Languages may be used by any Person or in any Pleading or Process in or issuing from any Court of Canada established under this Act, and in or from all or any of the Courts of Quebec.

Use of English and French Languages.

The Acts of the Parliament of Canada and of the Legislature of Quebec shall be printed and published in both those Languages.

Ontario and Quebec.

134. Until the Legislature of Ontario or of Quebec otherwise provides, the Lieutenant Governors of Ontario and Quebec may each appoint under the Great Seal of the Province the following Officers, to hold Office during Pleasure, that is to say,—the Attorney General, the Secretary and Registrar of the Province, the Treasurer of the Province, the Commissioner of Crown Lands, and the Commissioner of Agriculture and Public Works, and in the Case of Quebec the

Appointment of Executive Officers for Ontario and Quebec.

---

(56) The restriction against altering or repealing laws enacted by or existing under statutes of the United Kingdom was removed by the *Statute of Westminster, 1931*, 22 Geo. V, c. 4 (U.K.).

(57) Spent.

Solicitor General, and may, by Order of the Lieutenant Governor in Council, from Time to Time prescribe the Duties of those Officers, and of the several Departments over which they shall preside or to which they shall belong, and of the Officers and Clerks thereof, and may also appoint other and additional Officers to hold Office during Pleasure, and may from Time to Time prescribe the Duties of those Officers, and of the several Departments over which they shall preside or to which they shall belong, and of the Officers and Clerks thereof. (58)

Powers, Duties, etc. of Executive Officers.

135. Until the Legislature of Ontario or Quebec otherwise provides, all Rights, Powers, Duties, Functions, Responsibilities, or Authorities at the passing of this Act vested in or imposed on the Attorney General, Solicitor General, Secretary and Registrar of the Province of Canada, Minister of Finance, Commissioner of Crown Lands, Commissioner of Public Works, and Minister of Agriculture and Receiver General, by any Law, Statute, or Ordinance of Upper Canada, Lower Canada, or Canada, and not repugnant to this Act, shall be vested in or imposed on any Officer to be appointed by the Lieutenant Governor for the Discharge of the same or any of them; and the Commissioner of Agriculture and Public Works shall perform the Duties and Functions of the Office of Minister of Agriculture at the passing of this Act imposed by the Law of the Province of Canada, as well as those of the Commissioner of Public Works. (59)

Great Seals.

136. Until altered by the Lieutenant Governor in Council, the Great Seals of Ontario and Quebec respectively shall be the same, or of the same Design, as those used in the Provinces of Upper Canada and Lower Canada respectively before their Union as the Province of Canada.

Construction of temporary Acts.

137. The words "and from thence to the End of the then next ensuing Session of the Legislature," or Words to the same Effect, used in any temporary Act of the Province of Canada not expired before the Union, shall be construed to extend and apply to the next Session of the Parliament of Canada if the Subject Matter of the Act is within the Powers of the same as defined by this Act, or to the next Sessions of the Legislatures of Ontario and Quebec respectively if the Subject Matter of the Act is within the Powers of the same as defined by this Act.

As to Errors in Names.

138. From and after the Union the Use of the Words "Upper Canada" instead of "Ontario," or "Lower Canada" instead of "Quebec," in any Deed, Writ, Process, Pleading, Document, Matter. or Thing. shall not invalidate the same.

---

(58) Spent. Now covered in Ontario by the *Executive Council Act*, R.S.O. 1970, c. 153 and in Quebec by the *Executive Power Act*, R.S.Q. 1964, c. 9.

(59) Probably spent.

139. Any Proclamation under the Great Seal of the Province of Canada issued before the Union to take effect at a Time which is subsequent to the Union, whether relating to that Province, or to Upper Canada, or to Lower Canada, and the several Matters and Things therein proclaimed, shall be and continue of like Force and Effect as if the Union had not been made. (60)

As to issue of Proclamations before Union, to commence after Union.

140. Any Proclamation which is authorized by any Act of the Legislature of the Province of Canada to be issued under the Great Seal of the Province of Canada, whether relating to that Province, or to Upper Canada, or to Lower Canada, and which is not issued before the Union, may be issued by the Lieutenant Governor of Ontario or of Quebec, as its Subject Matter requires, under the Great Seal thereof; and from and after the Issue of such Proclamation the same and the several Matters and Things therein proclaimed shall be and continue of the like Force and Effect in Ontario or Quebec as if the Union had not been made. (61)

As to issue of Proclamations after Union.

141. The Penitentiary of the Province of Canada shall, until the Parliament of Canada otherwise provides, be and continue the Penitentiary of Ontario and of Quebec. (62)

Peniteniary.

142. The Division and Adjustment of the Debts, Credits, Liabilities, Properties, and Assets of Upper Canada and Lower Canada shall be referred to the Arbitrament of Three Arbitrators, One chosen by the Government of Ontario, One by the Government of Quebec, and One by the Government of Canada; and the Selection of the Arbitrators shall not be made until the Parliament of Canada and the Legislatures of Ontario and Quebec have met; and the Arbitrator chosen by the Government of Canada shall not be a Resident either in Ontario or in Quebec. (63)

Arbitration respecting Debts, etc.

143. The Governor General in Council may from Time to Time order that such and so many of the Records, Books, and Documents of the Province of Canada as he thinks fit shall be appropriated and delivered either to Ontario or to Quebec, and the same shall thenceforth be the Property of that Province; and any Copy thereof or Extract therefrom, duly certified by the Officer having charge of the Original thereof, shall be admitted as Evidence. (64)

Division of Records.

---

(60) Probably spent.

(61) Probably spent.

(62) Spent. Penitentiaries are now provided for by the *Penitentiary Act*, R.S.C. 1970, c. P-6.

(63) Spent. See pages (xi) and (xii) of the Public Accounts, 1902-03.

(64) Probably spent. Two orders were made under this section on the 24th of January, 1868.

Constitution of Townships in Quebec.

144. The Lieutenant Governor of Quebec may from Time of Time, by Proclamation under the Great Seal of the Province, to take effect from a Day to be appointed therein, constitute Townships in those Parts of the Province of Quebec in which Townships are not then already constituted, and fix the Metes and Bounds thereof.

145. Repealed. (65)

XI.—ADMISSION OF OTHER COLONIES

Power to admit Newfoundland, etc., into the Union.

146. It shall be lawful for the Queen, by and with the Advice of Her Majesty's Most Honourable Privy Council, on Addresses from the Houses of the Parliament of Canada, and from the Houses of the respective Legislatures of the Colonies or Provinces of Newfoundland, Prince Edward Island, and British Columbia, to admit those Colonies or Provinces, or any of them, into the Union, and on Address from the Houses of the Parliament of Canada to admit Rupert's Land and the North-western Territory, or either of them, into the Union, on such Terms and Conditions in each Case as are in the Addresses expressed and as the Queen thinks fit to approve, subject to the Provisions of this Act; and the Provisions of any Order in Council in that Behalf shall have effect as if they had been enacted by the Parliament of the United Kingdom of Great Britain and Ireland. (66)

As to Representation of Newfoundland and Prince Edward Island in Senate.

147. In case of the Admission of Newfoundland and Prince Edward Island, or either of them, each shall be entitled to a Representation in the Senate of Canada of Four Members, and (notwithstanding anything in this Act) in case of the Admission of Newfoundland the normal Number of Senators shall be Seventy-six and their maximum Number shall be Eighty-two; but Prince Edward Island when admitted

---

(65) Repealed by the *Statute Law Revision Act, 1893*, 56-57 Vict., c. 14, (U.K.). The section reads as follows:

X.—INTERCOLONIAL RAILWAY.

145. Inasmuch as the Provinces of Canada, Nova Scotia, and New Brunswick have joined in a Declaration that the Construction of the Intercolonial Railway is essential to the Consolidation of the Union of British North America, and to the Assent thereto of Nova Scotia and New Brunswick, and have consequently agreed that Provision should be made for its immediate Construction by the Government of Canada: Therefore, in order to give effect to that Agreement, it shall be the Duty of the Government and Parliament of Canada to provide for the Commencement, within Six Months after the Union, of a Railway connecting the River St. Lawrence with the City of Halifax in Nova Scotia, and for the Construction thereof without Intermission, and the Completion thereof with all practicable Speed.

(66) All territories mentioned in this section are now part of Canada. See the notes to section 5, *supra.*

shall be deemed to be comprised in the Third of Three Divisions into which Canada is, in relation to the Constitution of the Senate, divided by this Act, and accordingly, after the Admission of Prince Edward Island, whether Newfoundland is admitted or not, the Representation of Nova Scotia and New Brunswick in the Senate shall, as Vacancies occur, be reduced from Twelve to Ten Members respectively, and the Representation of each of those Provinces shall not be increased at any Time beyond Ten, except under the Provisions of this Act for the Appointment of Three or Six additional Senators under the Direction of the Queen. (67)

---

(67) Spent. See the notes to sections 21, 22, 26, 27 and 28, *supra.*

APPENDIX II PART B: The Constitution Act, 1982

The text that follows reproduces the statute as published by Supply and Services Canada, *The Constitution Act, 1982* (Ottawa: Canadian Government Publishing Centre, 1982) omitting only the French translation.

CONSTITUTION ACT, 1982

PART I

CANADIAN CHARTER OF RIGHTS AND FREEDOMS

Whereas Canada is founded upon principles that recognize the supremacy of God and the rule of law:

Guarantee of Rights and Freedoms

Rights and freedoms in Canada

1. The *Canadian Charter of Rights and Freedoms* guarantees the rights and freedoms set out in it subject only to such reasonable limits prescribed by law as can be demonstrably justified in a free and democratic society.

Fundamental Freedoms

Fundamental freedoms

2. Everyone has the following fundamental freedoms:

(*a*) freedom of conscience and religion;

(*b*) freedom of thought, belief, opinion and expression, including freedom of the press and other media of communication;

(*c*) freedom of peaceful assembly; and

(*d*) freedom of association.

Democratic Rights

Democratic rights of citizens

3. Every citizen of Canada has the right to vote in an election of members of the House of Commons or of a legislative assembly and to be qualified for membership therein.

Maximum duration of legislative bodies

4. (1) No House of Commons and no legislative assembly shall continue for longer than five years from the date fixed for the return of the writs at a general election of its members.

Continuation in special circumstances

(2) In time of real or apprehended war, invasion or insurrection, a House of Commons may be continued by Parliament and a legislative assembly may be continued by the legislature beyond five years if such continuation is not opposed by the votes of more than one-third of the members of the House of Commons or the legislative assembly, as the case may be.

Annual sitting of legislative bodies

5. There shall be a sitting of Parliament and of each legislature at least once every twelve months.

Mobility Rights

Mobility of citizens

6. (1) Every citizen of Canada has the right to enter, remain in and leave Canada.

Rights to move and gain livelihood

(2) Every citizen of Canada and every person who has the status of a permanent resident of Canada has the right

(*a*) to move to and take up residence in any province; and

(*b*) to pursue the gaining of a livelihood in any province.

Limitation

(3) The rights specified in subsection (2) are subject to

(*a*) any laws or practices of general application in force in a province other than those that discriminate among persons primarily on the basis of province of present or previous residence; and

(*b*) any laws providing for reasonable residency requirements as a qualification for the receipt of publicly provided social services.

Affirmative action programs

(4) Subsections (2) and (3) do not preclude any law, program or activity that has as its object the amelioration in a province of conditions of individuals in that province who are socially or economically disadvantaged if the rate of employment in that province is below the rate of employment in Canada.

Legal Rights

Life, liberty and security of person

7. Everyone has the right to life, liberty and security of the person and the right not to be deprived thereof except in accordance with the principles of fundamental justice.

Search or seizure

8. Everyone has the right to be secure against unreasonable search or seizure.

Detention or imprisonment

9. Everyone has the right not to be arbitrarily detained or imprisoned.

Arrest or detention

10. Everyone has the right on arrest or detention

(*a*) to be informed promptly of the reasons therefor;

(*b*) to retain and instruct counsel without delay and to be informed of that right; and

(*c*) to have the validity of the detention determined by way of *habeas corpus* and to be released if the detention is not lawful.

Proceedings in criminal and penal matters

11. Any person charged with an offence has the right

(*a*) to be informed without unreasonable delay of the specific offence;

(*b*) to be tried within a reasonable time;

(*c*) not to be compelled to be a witness in proceedings against that person in respect of the offence;

(*d*) to be presumed innocent until proven guilty according to law in a fair and public hearing by an independent and impartial tribunal;

(*e*) not to be denied reasonable bail without just cause;

(*f*) except in the case of an offence under military law tried before a military tribunal, to the benefit of trial by jury where the maximum punishment for the offence is imprisonment for five years or a more severe punishment;

(*g*) not to be found guilty on account of any act or omission unless, at the time of the act or omission, it constituted an offence under Canadian or international law or was criminal according to the general principles of law recognized by the community of nations;

(*h*) if finally acquitted of the offence, not to be tried for it again and, if finally found guilty and punished for the offence, not to be tried or punished for it again; and

(*i*) if found guilty of the offence and if the punishment for the offence has been varied between the time of commission and the time of sentencing, to the benefit of the lesser punishment.

Treatment or punishment

12. Everyone has the right not to be subjected to any cruel and unusual treatment or punishment.

Self-crimination

13. A witness who testifies in any proceedings has the right not to have any incriminating evidence so given used to incriminate that witness in any other proceedings, except in a prosecution for perjury or for the giving of contradictory evidence.

Interpreter

14. A party or witness in any proceedings who does not understand or speak the language in which the proceedings are conducted or who is deaf has the right to the assistance of an interpreter.

Equality Rights

Equality before and under law and equal protection and benefit of law

15. (1) Every individual is equal before and under the law and has the right to the equal protection and equal benefit of the law without discrimination and, in particular, without discrimination based on race, national or ethnic origin, colour, religion, sex, age or mental or physical disability.

Affirmative action programs

(2) Subsection (1) does not preclude any law, program or activity that has as its object the amelioration of conditions of disadvantaged individuals or groups including those that are disadvantaged because of

race, national or ethnic origin, colour, religion, sex, age or mental or physical disability.

Official Languages of Canada

Official languages of Canada

16. (1) English and French are the official languages of Canada and have equality of status and equal rights and privileges as to their use in all institutions of the Parliament and government of Canada.

Official languages of New Brunswick

(2) English and French are the official languages of New Brunswick and have equality of status and equal rights and privileges as to their use in all institutions of the legislature and government of New Brunswick.

Advancement of status and use

(3) Nothing in this Charter limits the authority of Parliament or a legislature to advance the equality of status or use of English and French.

Proceedings of Parliament

17. (1) Everyone has the right to use English or French in any debates and other proceedings of Parliament.

Proceedings of New Brunswick legislature

(2) Everyone has the right to use English or French in any debates and other proceedings of the legislature of New Brunswick.

Parliamentary statutes and records

18. (1) The statutes, records and journals of Parliament shall be printed and published in English and French and both language versions are equally authoritative.

New Brunswick statutes and records

(2) The statutes, records and journals of the legislature of New Brunswick shall be printed and published in English and French and both language versions are equally authoritative.

Proceedings in courts established by Parliament

19. (1) Either English or French may be used by any person in, or in any pleading in or process issuing from, any court established by Parliament.

(2) Either English or French may be used by any person in, or in any pleading in or process issuing from, any court of New Brunswick.

Proceedings in New Brunswick courts

20. (1) Any member of the public in Canada has the right to communicate with, and to receive available services from, any head or central office of an institution of the Parliament or government of Canada in English or French, and has the same right with respect to any other office of any such institution where

(*a*) there is a significant demand for communications with and services from that office in such language; or

(*b*) due to the nature of the office, it is reasonable that communications with and services from that office be available in both English and French.

Communications by public with federal institutions

(2) Any member of the public in New Brunswick has the right to communicate with, and to receive available services from, any office of an institution of the legislature or government of New Brunswick in English or French.

Communications by public with New Brunswick institutions

21. Nothing in sections 16 to 20 abrogates or derogates from any right, privilege or obligation with respect to the English and French languages, or either of them, that exists or is continued by virtue of any other provision of the Constitution of Canada.

Continuation of existing constitutional provisions

22. Nothing in sections 16 to 20 abrogates or derogates from any legal or customary right or privilege acquired or enjoyed either before or after the coming into force of this Charter with respect to any language that is not English or French.

Rights and privileges preserved

Minority Language Educational Rights

23. (1) Citizens of Canada

(*a*) whose first language learned and still understood is that of the English or French linguistic

Language of instruction

minority population of the province in which they reside, or

(*b*) who have received their primary school instruction in Canada in English or French and reside in a province where the language in which they received that instruction is the language of the English or French linguistic minority population of the province,

have the right to have their children receive primary and secondary school instruction in that language in that province.

Continuity of language instruction

(2) Citizens of Canada of whom any child has received or is receiving primary or secondary school instruction in English or French in Canada, have the right to have all their children receive primary and secondary school instruction in the same language.

Application where numbers warrant

(3) The right of citizens of Canada under subsections (1) and (2) to have their children receive primary and secondary school instruction in the language of the English or French linguistic minority population of a province

(*a*) applies wherever in the province the number of children of citizens who have such a right is sufficient to warrant the provision to them out of public funds of minority language instruction; and

(*b*) includes, where the number of those children so warrants, the right to have them receive that instruction in minority language educational facilities provided out of public funds.

Enforcement

Enforcement of guaranteed rights and freedoms

24. (1) Anyone whose rights or freedoms, as guaranteed by this Charter, have been infringed or denied may apply to a court of competent jurisdiction to obtain such remedy as the court considers appropriate and just in the circumstances.

Exclusion of evidence bringing administration of justice into disrepute

(2) Where, in proceedings under subsection (1), a court concludes that evidence was obtained in a manner that infringed or denied any rights or freedoms guaranteed by this Charter, the evidence shall be excluded if it is established that, having regard to all the circumstances, the admission of it in the proceedings would bring the administration of justice into disrepute.

General

25. The guarantee in this Charter of certain rights and freedoms shall not be construed so as to abrogate or derogate from any aboriginal, treaty or other rights or freedoms that pertain to the aboriginal peoples of Canada including

Aboriginal rights and freedoms not affected by Charter

(*a*) any rights or freedoms that have been recognized by the Royal Proclamation of October 7, 1763; and

(*b*) any rights or freedoms that may be acquired by the aboriginal peoples of Canada by way of land claims settlement.

26. The guarantee in this Charter of certain rights and freedoms shall not be construed as denying the existence of any other rights or freedoms that exist in Canada.

Other rights and freedoms not affected by Charter

27. This Charter shall be interpreted in a manner consistent with the preservation and enhancement of the multicultural heritage of Canadians.

Multicultural heritage

28. Notwithstanding anything in this Charter, the rights and freedoms referred to in it are guaranteed equally to male and female persons.

Rights guaranteed equally to both sexes

29. Nothing in this Charter abrogates or derogates from any rights or privileges guaranteed by or under the Constitution of Canada in respect of denominational, separate or dissentient schools.

Rights respecting certain schools preserved

30. A reference in this Charter to a province or to the legislative assembly or legislature of a province shall be deemed to include a reference to the Yukon Territory and the Northwest Territories, or to the appropriate legislative authority thereof, as the case may be.

Application to territories and territorial authorities

Legislative powers not extended

31. Nothing in this Charter extends the legislative powers of any body or authority.

Application of Charter

Application of Charter

32. (1) This Charter applies

(*a*) to the Parliament and government of Canada in respect of all matters within the authority of Parliament including all matters relating to the Yukon Territory and Northwest Territories; and

(*b*) to the legislature and government of each province in respect of all matters within the authority of the legislature of each province.

Exception

(2) Notwithstanding subsection (1), section 15 shall not have effect until three years after this section comes into force.

Exception where express declaration

33. (1) Parliament or the legislature of a province may expressly declare in an Act of Parliament or of the legislature, as the case may be, that the Act or a provision thereof shall operate notwithstanding a provision included in section 2 or sections 7 to 15 of this Charter.

Operation of exception

(2) An Act or a provision of an Act in respect of which a declaration made under this section is in effect shall have such operation as it would have but for the provision of this Charter referred to in the declaration.

Five year limitation

(3) A declaration made under subsection (1) shall cease to have effect five years after it comes into force or on such earlier date as may be specified in the declaration.

Re-enactment

(4) Parliament or the legislature of a province may re-enact a declaration made under subsection (1).

Five year limitation

(5) Subsection (3) applies in respect of a re-enactment made under subsection (4).

Citation

Citation

34. This Part may be cited as the *Canadian Charter of Rights and Freedoms*.

PART II

RIGHTS OF THE ABORIGINAL PEOPLES OF CANADA

Recognition of existing aboriginal and treaty rights

35. (1) The existing aboriginal and treaty rights of the aboriginal peoples of Canada are hereby recognized and affirmed.

Definition of "aboriginal peoples of Canada"

(2) In this Act, "aboriginal peoples of Canada" includes the Indian, Inuit and Métis peoples of Canada.

PART III

EQUALIZATION AND REGIONAL DISPARITIES

Commitment to promote equal opportunities

36. (1) Without altering the legislative authority of Parliament or of the provincial legislatures, or the rights of any of them with respect to the exercise of their legislative authority, Parliament and the legislatures, together with the government of Canada and the provincial governments, are committed to

(*a*) promoting equal opportunities for the well-being of Canadians;

(*b*) furthering economic development to reduce disparity in opportunities; and

(*c*) providing essential public services of reasonable quality to all Canadians.

Commitment respecting public services

(2) Parliament and the government of Canada are committed to the principle of making equalization payments to ensure that provincial governments have sufficient revenues to provide reasonably comparable levels of public services at reasonably comparable levels of taxation.

PART IV

CONSTITUTIONAL CONFERENCE

Constitutional conference

37. (1) A constitutional conference composed of the Prime Minister of Canada and the first ministers of the provinces shall be convened by the Prime Minister of Canada within one year after this Part comes into force.

Participation of aboriginal peoples

(2) The conference convened under subsection (1) shall have included in its agenda an item respecting constitutional matters that directly affect the aboriginal peoples of Canada, including the identification and definition of the rights of those peoples to be included in the Constitution of Canada, and the Prime Minister of Canada shall invite representatives of those peoples to participate in the discussions on that item.

Participation of territories

(3) The Prime Minister of Canada shall invite elected representatives of the governments of the Yukon Territory and the Northwest Territories to participate in the discussions on any item on the agenda of the conference convened under subsection (1) that, in the opinion of the Prime Minister, directly affects the Yukon Territory and the Northwest Territories.

PART V

PROCEDURE FOR AMENDING CONSTITUTION OF CANADA

General procedure for amending Constitution of Canada

38. (1) An amendment to the Constitution of Canada may be made by proclamation issued by the Governor General under the Great Seal of Canada where so authorized by

(*a*) resolutions of the Senate and House of Commons; and

(*b*) resolutions of the legislative assemblies of at least two-thirds of the provinces that have, in the aggregate, according to the then latest general census, at least fifty per cent of the population of all the provinces.

Majority of members

(2) An amendment made under subsection (1) that derogates from the legislative powers, the proprietary rights or any other rights or privileges of the legislature or government of a province shall require a resolution supported by a majority of the members of each of the Senate, the House of Commons and the legislative assemblies required under subsection (1).

Expression of dissent

(3) An amendment referred to in subsection (2) shall not have effect in a province the legislative assembly of which has expressed its dissent thereto by resolution supported by a majority of its members prior to the issue of the proclamation to which the amendment relates unless that legislative assembly, subsequently, by resolution supported by a majority of its members, revokes its dissent and authorizes the amendment.

Revocation of dissent

(4) A resolution of dissent made for the purposes of subsection (3) may be revoked at any time before or after the issue of the proclamation to which it relates.

Restriction on proclamation

39. (1) A proclamation shall not be issued under subsection 38(1) before the expiration of one year from the adoption of the resolution initiating the amendment procedure thereunder, unless the legislative assembly of each province has previously adopted a resolution of assent or dissent.

Idem

(2) A proclamation shall not be issued under subsection 38(1) after the expiration of three years from the adoption of the resolution initiating the amendment procedure thereunder.

Compensation

40. Where an amendment is made under subsection 38(1) that transfers provincial legislative powers relating to education or other cultural matters from provincial legislatures to Parliament, Canada shall provide reasonable compensation to any province to which the amendment does not apply.

Amendment by unanimous consent

41. An amendment to the Constitution of Canada in relation to the following matters may be made by proclamation issued by the Governor General under the Great Seal of

Canada only where authorized by resolutions of the Senate and House of Commons and of the legislative assembly of each province:

(*a*) the office of the Queen, the Governor General and the Lieutenant Governor of a province;

(*b*) the right of a province to a number of members in the House of Commons not less than the number of Senators by which the province is entitled to be represented at the time this Part comes into force;

(*c*) subject to section 43, the use of the English or the French language;

(*d*) the composition of the Supreme Court of Canada; and

(*e*) an amendment to this Part.

Amendment by general procedure

42. (1) An amendment to the Constitution of Canada in relation to the following matters may be made only in accordance with subsection 38(1):

(*a*) the principle of proportionate representation of the provinces in the House of Commons prescribed by the Constitution of Canada;

(*b*) the powers of the Senate and the method of selecting Senators;

(*c*) the number of members by which a province is entitled to be represented in the Senate and the residence qualifications of Senators;

(*d*) subject to paragraph 41(*d*), the Supreme Court of Canada;

(*e*) the extension of existing provinces into the territories; and

(*f*) notwithstanding any other law or practice, the establishment of new provinces.

Exception

(2) Subsections 38(2) to (4) do not apply in respect of amendments in relation to matters referred to in subsection (1).

Amendment of provisions relating to some but not all provinces

43. An amendment to the Constitution of Canada in relation to any provision that applies to one or more, but not all, provinces, including

(*a*) any alteration to boundaries between provinces, and

(*b*) any amendment to any provision that relates to the use of the English or the French language within a province,

may be made by proclamation issued by the Governor General under the Great Seal of Canada only where so authorized by resolutions of the Senate and House of Commons and of the legislative assembly of each province to which the amendment applies.

Amendments by Parliament

44. Subject to sections 41 and 42, Parliament may exclusively make laws amending the Constitution of Canada in relation to the executive government of Canada or the Senate and House of Commons.

Amendments by provincial legislatures

45. Subject to section 41, the legislature of each province may exclusively make laws amending the constitution of the province.

Initiation of amendment procedures

46. (1) The procedures for amendment under sections 38, 41, 42 and 43 may be initiated either by the Senate or the House of Commons or by the legislative assembly of a province.

Revocation of authorization

(2) A resolution of assent made for the purposes of this Part may be revoked at any time before the issue of a proclamation authorized by it.

Amendments without Senate resolution

47. (1) An amendment to the Constitution of Canada made by proclamation under section 38, 41, 42 or 43 may be made without a resolution of the Senate authorizing the issue of the proclamation if, within one hundred and eighty days after the adoption by the House of Commons of a resolution authorizing its issue, the Senate has not adopted such a resolution and if, at any time after the expiration of that period, the House of Commons again adopts the resolution.

Computation of period

(2) Any period when Parliament is prorogued or dissolved shall not be counted in computing the one hundred and eighty day period referred to in subsection (1).

Advice to issue proclamation

48. The Queen's Privy Council for Canada shall advise the Governor General to issue a proclamation under this Part forthwith on the adoption of the resolutions required for an amendment made by proclamation under this Part.

Constitutional conference

49. A constitutional conference composed of the Prime Minister of Canada and the first ministers of the provinces shall be convened by the Prime Minister of Canada within fifteen years after this Part comes into force to review the provisions of this Part.

PART VI

AMENDMENT TO THE CONSTITUTION ACT, 1867

Amendment to *Constitution Act, 1867*

50. The *Constitution Act, 1867* (formerly named the *British North America Act, 1867*) is amended by adding thereto, immediately after section 92 thereof, the following heading and section:

"Non-Renewable Natural Resources, Forestry Resources and Electrical Energy

Laws respecting non-renewable natural resources, forestry resources and electrical energy

92A. (1) In each province, the legislature may exclusively make laws in relation to

(*a*) exploration for non-renewable natural resources in the province;

(*b*) development, conservation and management of non-renewable natural resources and forestry resources in the province, including laws in relation to the rate of primary production therefrom; and

(*c*) development, conservation and management of sites and facilities in the province for the generation and production of electrical energy.

Export from provinces of resources

(2) In each province, the legislature may make laws in relation to the export from the province to another part of Canada of the primary production from non-renewable natural resources and forestry

resources in the province and the production from facilities in the province for the generation of electrical energy, but such laws may not authorize or provide for discrimination in prices or in supplies exported to another part of Canada.

Authority of Parliament

(3) Nothing in subsection (2) derogates from the authority of Parliament to enact laws in relation to the matters referred to in that subsection and, where such a law of Parliament and a law of a province conflict, the law of Parliament prevails to the extent of the conflict.

Taxation of resources

(4) In each province, the legislature may make laws in relation to the raising of money by any mode or system of taxation in respect of

(*a*) non-renewable natural resources and forestry resources in the province and the primary production therefrom, and

(*b*) sites and facilities in the province for the generation of electrical energy and the production therefrom,

whether or not such production is exported in whole or in part from the province, but such laws may not authorize or provide for taxation that differentiates between production exported to another part of Canada and production not exported from the province.

"Primary production"

(5) The expression "primary production" has the meaning assigned by the Sixth Schedule.

Existing powers or rights

(6) Nothing in subsections (1) to (5) derogates from any powers or rights that a legislature or government of a province had immediately before the coming into force of this section."

Idem **51.** The said Act is further amended by adding thereto the following Schedule:

"THE SIXTH SCHEDULE

Primary Production from Non-Renewable Natural Resources and Forestry Resources

1. For the purposes of section 92A of this Act,

(*a*) production from a non-renewable natural resource is primary production therefrom if

(i) it is in the form in which it exists upon its recovery or severance from its natural state, or

(ii) it is a product resulting from processing or refining the resource, and is not a manufactured product or a product resulting from refining crude oil, refining upgraded heavy crude oil, refining gases or liquids derived from coal or refining a synthetic equivalent of crude oil; and

(*b*) production from a forestry resource is primary production therefrom if it consists of sawlogs, poles, lumber, wood chips, sawdust or any other primary wood product, or wood pulp, and is not a product manufactured from wood."

PART VII

GENERAL

Primacy of Constitution of Canada **52.** (1) The Constitution of Canada is the supreme law of Canada, and any law that is inconsistent with the provisions of the Constitution is, to the extent of the inconsistency, of no force or effect.

Constitution of Canada (2) The Constitution of Canada includes

(*a*) the *Canada Act 1982*, including this Act;

(*b*) the Acts and orders referred to in the schedule; and

(*c*) any amendment to any Act or order referred to in paragraph (*a*) or (*b*).

Amendments to Constitution of Canada (3) Amendments to the Constitution of Canada shall be made only in accordance with the authority contained in the Constitution of Canada.

Repeals and new names **53.** (1) The enactments referred to in Column I of the schedule are hereby repealed or amended to the extent indicated in Column II thereof and, unless repealed, shall continue as law in Canada under the names set out in Column III thereof.

Consequential amendments (2) Every enactment, except the *Canada Act 1982*, that refers to an enactment referred to in the schedule by the name in Column I thereof is hereby amended by substituting for that name the corresponding name in Column III thereof, and any British North America Act not referred to in the schedule may be cited as the *Constitution Act* followed by the year and number, if any, of its enactment.

Repeal and consequential amendments **54.** Part IV is repealed on the day that is one year after this Part comes into force and this section may be repealed and this Act renumbered, consequentially upon the repeal of Part IV and this section, by proclamation issued by the Governor General under the Great Seal of Canada.

French version of Constitution of Canada **55.** A French version of the portions of the Constitution of Canada referred to in the schedule shall be prepared by the Minister of Justice of Canada as expeditiously as possible and, when any portion thereof sufficient to warrant action being taken has been so prepared, it shall be put forward for enactment by proclamation issued by the Governor General under the Great Seal of Canada pursuant to the procedure then applicable to an amendment of the same provisions of the Constitution of Canada.

English and French versions of certain constitutional texts

56. Where any portion of the Constitution of Canada has been or is enacted in English and French or where a French version of any portion of the Constitution is enacted pursuant to section 55, the English and French versions of that portion of the Constitution are equally authoritative.

English and French versions of this Act

57. The English and French versions of this Act are equally authoritative.

Commencement

58. Subject to section 59, this Act shall come into force on a day to be fixed by proclamation issued by the Queen or the Governor General under the Great Seal of Canada.

Commencement of paragraph 23(1)(a) in respect of Quebec

59. (1) Paragraph 23(1)(*a*) shall come into force in respect of Quebec on a day to be fixed by proclamation issued by the Queen or the Governor General under the Great Seal of Canada.

(2) A proclamation under subsection (1) shall be issued only where authorized by the legislative assembly or government of Quebec. **Authorization of Quebec**

(3) This section may be repealed on the day paragraph 23(1)(*a*) comes into force in respect of Quebec and this Act amended and renumbered, consequentially upon the repeal of this section, by proclamation issued by the Queen or the Governor General under the Great Seal of Canada. **Repeal of this section**

60. This Act may be cited as the *Constitution Act, 1982*, and the Constitution Acts 1867 to 1975 (No. 2) and this Act may be cited together as the *Constitution Acts, 1867 to 1982*. **Short title and citations**

SCHEDULE

to the

CONSTITUTION ACT, 1982

MODERNIZATION OF THE CONSTITUTION

Item	Column I Act Affected	Column II Amendment	Column III New Name
1.	British North America Act, 1867, 30-31 Vict., c. 3 (U.K.)	(1) Section 1 is repealed and the following substituted therefor: "1. This Act may be cited as the *Constitution Act, 1867.*" (2) Section 20 is repealed. (3) Class 1 of section 91 is repealed. (4) Class 1 of section 92 is repealed.	Constitution Act, 1867
2.	An Act to amend and continue the Act 32-33 Victoria chapter 3; and to establish and provide for the Government of the Province of Manitoba, 1870, 33 Vict., c. 3 (Can.)	(1) The long title is repealed and the following substituted therefor: "*Manitoba Act, 1870.*" (2) Section 20 is repealed.	Manitoba Act, 1870
3.	Order of Her Majesty in Council admitting Rupert's Land and the North-Western Territory into the union, dated the 23rd day of June, 1870		Rupert's Land and North-Western Territory Order
4.	Order of Her Majesty in Council admitting British Columbia into the Union, dated the 16th day of May, 1871		British Columbia Terms of Union
5.	British North America Act, 1871, 34-35 Vict., c. 28 (U.K.)	Section 1 is repealed and the following substituted therefor: "1. This Act may be cited as the *Constitution Act, 1871.*"	Constitution Act, 1871
6.	Order of Her Majesty in Council admitting Prince Edward Island into the Union, dated the 26th day of June, 1873		Prince Edward Island Terms of Union
7.	Parliament of Canada Act, 1875, 38-39 Vict., c. 38 (U.K.)		Parliament of Canada Act, 1875
8.	Order of Her Majesty in Council admitting all British possessions and Territories in North America and islands adjacent thereto into the Union, dated the 31st day of July, 1880		Adjacent Territories Order

SCHEDULE

to the

CONSTITUTION ACT, 1982—*Continued*

Item	Column I Act Affected	Column II Amendment	Column III New Name
9.	British North America Act, 1886, 49-50 Vict., c. 35 (U.K.)	Section 3 is repealed and the following substituted therefor: "3. This Act may be cited as the *Constitution Act, 1886.*"	Constitution Act, 1886
10.	Canada (Ontario Boundary) Act, 1889, 52-53 Vict., c. 28 (U.K.)		Canada (Ontario Boundary) Act, 1889
11.	Canadian Speaker (Appointment of Deputy) Act, 1895, 2nd Sess., 59 Vict., c. 3 (U.K.)	The Act is repealed.	
12.	The Alberta Act, 1905, 4-5 Edw. VII, c. 3 (Can.)		Alberta Act
13.	The Saskatchewan Act, 1905, 4-5 Edw. VII, c. 42 (Can.)		Saskatchewan Act
14.	British North America Act, 1907, 7 Edw. VII, c. 11 (U.K.)	Section 2 is repealed and the following substituted therefor: "2. This Act may be cited as the *Constitution Act, 1907.*"	Constitution Act, 1907
15.	British North America Act, 1915, 5-6 Geo. V, c. 45 (U.K.)	Section 3 is repealed and the following substituted therefor: "3. This Act may be cited as the *Constitution Act, 1915.*"	Constitution Act, 1915
16.	British North America Act, 1930, 20-21 Geo. V, c. 26 (U.K.)	Section 3 is repealed and the following substituted therefor: "3. This Act may be cited as the *Constitution Act, 1930.*"	Constitution Act, 1930
17.	Statute of Westminster, 1931, 22 Geo. V, c. 4 (U.K.)	In so far as they apply to Canada, (*a*) section 4 is repealed; and (*b*) subsection 7(1) is repealed.	Statute of Westminster, 1931

SCHEDULE

to the

CONSTITUTION ACT, 1982—*Continued*

Item	Column I Act Affected	Column II Amendment	Column III New Name
18.	British North America Act, 1940, 3-4 Geo. VI, c. 36 (U.K.)	Section 2 is repealed and the following substituted therefor: "2. This Act may be cited as the *Constitution Act, 1940.*"	Constitution Act, 1940
19.	British North America Act, 1943, 6-7 Geo. VI, c. 30 (U.K.)	The Act is repealed.	
20.	British North America Act, 1946, 9-10 Geo. VI, c. 63 (U.K.)	The Act is repealed.	
21.	British North America Act, 1949, 12-13 Geo. VI, c. 22 (U.K.)	Section 3 is repealed and the following substituted therefor: "3. This Act may be cited as the *Newfoundland Act.*"	Newfoundland Act
22.	British North America (No. 2) Act, 1949, 13 Geo. VI, c. 81 (U.K.)	The Act is repealed.	
23.	British North America Act, 1951, 14-15 Geo. VI, c. 32 (U.K.)	The Act is repealed.	
24.	British North America Act, 1952, 1 Eliz. II, c. 15 (Can.)	The Act is repealed.	
25.	British North America Act, 1960, 9 Eliz. II, c. 2 (U.K.)	Section 2 is repealed and the following substituted therefor: "2. This Act may be cited as the *Constitution Act, 1960.*"	Constitution Act, 1960
26.	British North America Act, 1964, 12-13 Eliz. II, c. 73 (U.K.)	Section 2 is repealed and the following substituted therefor: "2. This Act may be cited as the *Constitution Act, 1964.*"	Constitution Act, 1964

SCHEDULE

to the

CONSTITUTION ACT, 1982—*Concluded*

Item	Column I Act Affected	Column II Amendment	Column III New Name
27.	British North America Act, 1965, 14 Eliz. II, c. 4, Part I (Can.)	Section 2 is repealed and the following substituted therefor: "2. This Part may be cited as the *Constitution Act, 1965.*"	Constitution Act, 1965
28.	British North America Act, 1974, 23 Eliz. II, c. 13, Part I (Can.)	Section 3, as amended by 25-26 Eliz. II, c. 28, s. 38(1) (Can.), is repealed and the following substituted therefor: "3. This Part may be cited as the *Constitution Act, 1974.*"	Constitution Act, 1974
29.	British North America Act, 1975, 23-24 Eliz. II, c. 28, Part I (Can.)	Section 3, as amended by 25-26 Eliz. II, c. 28, s. 31 (Can.), is repealed and the following substituted therefor: "3. This Part may be cited as the *Constitution Act (No. 1), 1975.*"	Constitution Act (No. 1), 1975
30.	British North America Act (No. 2), 1975, 23-24 Eliz. II, c. 53 (Can.)	Section 3 is repealed and the following substituted therefor: "3. This Act may be cited as the *Constitution Act (No. 2), 1975.*"	Constitution Act (No. 2), 1975

Index

Reader Response Questionnaire
(see over)

Fold here

To the User of this Book

We would like to know what you think of D.N. Sprague's *Post-Confederation Canada: The Structure of Canadian History Since 1867.*
Your comments will help us improve the book for future editions.

1. What type of course did you use this book for?
    _____ college
    _____ university
    _____ continuing education
    _____ other (please specify)

2. What is your major area of study?

Fold here

_____

3. Which chapters, if any, were not used in your course?

4. What single change would most improve the book?